DATE DUE

SEP 1 3 2007	
JUL 1 7 2008	

Allegorical Readers
and Cultural Revision
in Ancient Alexandria

Allegorical Readers
and Cultural Revision
in Ancient Alexandria

David Dawson

UNIVERSITY OF CALIFORNIA PRESS
Berkeley   Los Angeles   Oxford

University of California Press
Berkeley and Los Angeles, California
University of California Press, Ltd.
Oxford, England
© 1992 by
The Regents of the University of California

Library of Congress Cataloging-in-Publication Data
Dawson, David, 1957–
   Allegorical readers and cultural revision in ancient Alexandria.
   p.   cm.
   Includes bibliographical references and index.
   ISBN 0-520-07102-6 (alk. paper)
   1. Allegory.   2. Bible—Criticism, interpretation, etc.—History.
3. Bible.   O.T.—Criticism, interpretation, etc., Jewish.   4. Bible—
Criticism, interpretation, etc.—History—Early church, ca.
30–600.   5. Philo, of Alexandria.   6. Valentinus, 2nd cent.
7. Clement, of Alexandria, Saint, ca. 150–ca. 215.   8. Alexandria
(Egypt)—Religion.   9. Gnosticism.
BS500.D36   1992
121′.68′0932—dc20   91-2851
                                                        CIP

Printed in the United States of America
9   8   7   6   5   4   3   2   1

The paper used in this publication meets the minimum requirements of
American National Standard for Information Sciences—Permanence of Paper
for Printed Library Materials, ANSI Z39.48-1984. ⊗

To My Parents, John and Norma Dawson

CONTENTS

vii

ACKNOWLEDGMENTS

This book began as my doctoral dissertation (Yale University, 1988), and I am deeply grateful to my adviser, Bentley Layton, for his generous and vigorous critical responses to early drafts, as well as for his ongoing friendship and professional support. Among the many other persons who helped in some way in the early stages of the project, I must single out Susan Garrett, Dale Martin, Wayne Meeks, Alan Scott, and Kathryn Tanner. Each responded helpfully to various drafts and ideas and provided much needed encouragement. I completed the initial version of the manuscript while a Fellow at the Whitney Humanities Center at Yale; I would like to thank the former Director of the Center, Peter Brooks, along with the rest of the Fellows, for their interdisciplinary stimulation and warm collegiality.

Further research and writing took place at Haverford College, another center of interdisciplinary vitality. I wish to thank in particular the members of the Bryn Mawr-Haverford Committee on Interpretation for many invigorating conversations, and my colleagues in the Religion Department, from whom I have received a great deal of concrete aid in the final stages of writing and revision. The entire manuscript has benefited greatly from Richard Luman's learned suggestions for changes in style and substance. Anne McGuire offered a very generous, insightful, and tremendously helpful critical reading of the introduction and chapter 3, sharing with me her expertise in Gnosticism and Coptic philology. Michael Sells provided a number of thoughtful suggestions for revising the introduction and chapter 1, as did Deborah Roberts of the Haverford Classics Department. I am fortunate to have colleagues who have such patience and are willing to share so much of their time and energy.

The two anonymous readers for the University of California Press gave

the entire manuscript deeply informed readings and offered marvelously detailed recommendations for revision. I am also grateful to Anthony Long, Editorial Board Presenter for the Press, whose response stimulated an important reconceptualization of material in the first chapter. Classics editor Mary Lamprech's wise judgment was evident from the outset in the selection of readers, and every subsequent stage of the publication process has benefited from her meticulous, crisp, professional guidance. Manuscript editor Marian Shotwell improved the text with every correction and suggestion. All my readers have helped make this a better book and saved me from many errors; I am responsible for those that still remain.

Two Haverford religion majors, Kenneth Fromm and Robert Flynn, served with special distinction as my research assistants. Their help, along with that of fellow majors Ajantha Subramanian and Branavan Ganesan, was made possible by a generous Faculty Research Grant from Haverford College. My research and writing was also supported by a Summer Stipend from the National Endowment for the Humanities. Throughout the project, I received consistently excellent help from the staffs of the Classics, Divinity, and Sterling Memorial libraries of Yale University, as well as from Haverford College's Magill Library and Bryn Mawr College's Canaday Library.

Finally, I am indebted beyond measure to my wife, Ellen Dawson, who helped and sustained me in countless vital ways at every stage of thinking, research, writing, and revision.

A NOTE ON TRANSLATION AND CITATION

Generally speaking, I have made use of existing English translations; I have frequently made minor alterations in these without comment in light of the original ancient languages: such changes include modernization of diction and syntax and other adjustments in both for the sake of greater accuracy, literalism, or consistency of technical terminology. In those few places where I take issue with, or offer alternatives to, commonly accepted translations, I have explained myself in the notes. In cases where English translations were not available or were unacceptable for one reason or another, I have made my own. In all cases, regardless of the source of the translation, I have worked directly from standard critical editions of texts in their ancient languages, and my interpretations are based on those editions. Quotations in ancient languages have been transliterated. In general, single verbs are given in the present infinitive; single nouns and participles, as well as noun phrases, in the nominative. Verbal phrases and complete sentences are transliterated directly without alteration. Translations from scripture, except when based on the Septuagint,

are taken from the Revised Standard Version, with occasional modification.

I have used the following symbols for interpolations in quoted material: [ ] = my own interpolations (whether exegetical comments, references, or words and phrases from the ancient language of the original text); ( ) = interpolations by another editor or translator; {} = restorations of passages by another editor or translator. In some cases, my use of these symbols has required the alteration of the textual apparatus of the editions of the primary texts from which I am quoting. I have alerted readers to such adjustments in the notes.

Introduction

This book describes how some ancient pagan, Jewish, and Christian interpreters used allegory to endorse, revise, and subvert competing world views and forms of life. It departs from most standard discussions of the topic because it insists that ancient allegory is best understood not only as a way of reading texts, but also as a way of using that reading to reinterpret culture and society. After an opening discussion of various pagan etymologists, allegorists, and their opponents, I focus attention on three Hellenistic religious writers who represent different models of allegorical interpretation: the Jewish exegete Philo, the Christian Gnostic Valentinus, and the Christian Platonist Clement of Alexandria. These three authors claimed authoritative originality for their allegorical readings and compositions, which they used as a means of enabling certain privileged perspectives, variously construed as written text (Philo), mystical vision (Valentinus), and hermeneutical voice (Clement), to challenge cultural and religious precursors and contemporaries and to promote alternative ways of being in the world.

My approach to the interpretative practice of these writers stands in some contrast with three other influential views of allegory that, for convenience, might be labeled traditional, late modern, and postmodern.[1] Traditional approaches may be secular or sacred, though the religious version is prior and fundamental for later secular adaptations.[2] Traditional religious and theological commentators on allegory view it as a way of plumbing and expressing the spiritual depths of religious texts, especially the Bible.[3] On this view, allegorical readers discover the "deeper" or "more spiritual" meaning hidden beneath "the letter" of scripture, expressing their hermeneutical insights in the form of allegorical compositions, such as Dante's *Divine Comedy,* or allegorical commen-

taries, such as those on the Song of Songs.[4] The commentators on allegory that I call late modernist, echoing Wallace Stevens's bittersweet
praise of "supreme fictions," are typically skeptical of the traditionalist
confidence in the presence of allegorical meaning. For such theorists,
allegory represents an eternally frustrated effort to attain a meaning that,
while real and near, remains just out of reach. Those who follow the
beckoning mystery of this literary mode "to the end" discover that there is
no end, that complete hermeneutical initiation consists in the knowledge
that everyone is an outsider to textual meaning and truth.[5] Such a perspective comes very close to that of postmodern deconstructionists, who
positively celebrate what late modernists fear most, identifying allegory as
the trope par excellence of the semantic void, the figure that bears witness
neither to the available presence of hidden meaning nor to the intimation
of near, but ever-elusive, meaning, but to the absence of any meaning
whatsoever.[6]

In this book, I largely set aside these decidedly formalist perspectives in
favor of an approach that is more attentive to the historically specific ways
allegory's essential conflict of meanings actually engaged social and cultural practice in the ancient world. Ancient allegorical compositions and
interpretations constituted fields on which struggles between competing proposals for thought and action took place. The very tensions between literal and nonliteral readings that characterized ancient allegory
stemmed from efforts by readers to secure for themselves and their
communities social and cultural identity, authority, and power. But although this sociologically and historically oriented approach differs from
the three views of allegory sketched above, it also acknowledges and
draws upon important insights characteristic of each of them. The traditional claim that allegory discovers a deeper, hidden meaning is understood in this book as a particular strategy by which readers claimed
authoritative originality for their interpretations. For example, in one
form, the traditional view of allegory holds that a divine *logos* underwrites
a text's deeper meaning.[7] In my approach, such reliance on the *logos* is
understood as a particular way of exercising hermeneutical authority,
based on a claim to have obtained access to the primordial source of
authentic meaning and truth. The late modernist position, in which the
aura of meaning is tantalizingly near but always elusive, captures something of the apophatic reserve that tempers the mystical claims of Philo
and Clement. While each of these authors has sufficient hermeneutical
confidence to challenge and overturn precursors, each refrains from
professing absolute meaning and truth, even while insisting that such
knowledge (represented preeminently by the deity itself) is real and near
(Valentinus's mystical confidence is somewhat less circumspect). Finally,
the close connection between much ancient religious allegory and ap-

ophatic or "negative" theological sensibilities provides a partial parallel to the deconstructionist claim that allegory expresses an absence of meaning. But the parallel remains partial; for the ancient interpreters I will be examining (in contrast to postmodern readers), apophatic assumptions are not hermeneutical (or rather, antihermeneutical) ends in themselves, designed to foster an unending thrill of indeterminate interpretation.[8] Instead of reveling in the absence of meaning, these ancient allegorists tended to use apophatic claims rhetorically, as a way of justifying their own application of allegorical readings that were designed to show what the real meanings were. In effect, they combined an apophatic sensibility with the claim for hermeneutical originality: on the one hand, their recognition of apophatic limitations allowed them to declare the literal meaning of precursor texts to be mimetically inadequate (thus justifying their own application of allegory); on the other hand, their claim for originality enabled them to announce that their own new, nonliteral meanings successfully evaded the apophatic constraints that bound more ordinary discourse. Given these similarities and differences, then, I have drawn freely from all three approaches, combining their insights in eclectic fashion whenever they proved appropriate and illuminating, but always keeping in view the social and cultural functions of allegory.

The remainder of this introduction will be devoted to a more detailed description of the specific conception of allegory that informs this study. I begin by comparing and contrasting my notion of allegory with the related conceptions of metaphor, personification, and etymology. I then discuss allegory's possible roles in cultural accommodation and criticism. I go on to situate my approach to allegory with respect to ongoing debates about allegory's apologetic function and its relation to "symbol" and "typology." The introduction concludes with a brief overview of the organization and development of the specific claims that will occupy the following chapters.

I

My understanding of the basic literary character of ancient allegory is similar to classical rhetorical definitions of the procedure, which are based on the etymology of the Greek term itself. Derived from *allos* ("other") and *agoreuein* ("to speak in the agora," i.e., "publicly"), *allēgoria* means most simply "to say something other than what one seems to say."[9] Two special features of my use of the term "allegory" need emphasis. First, although the focus of this study is on allegorical reading or interpretation, "allegory" will be used as a generic term to refer to both allegorical interpretations and allegorical compositions. Second, interpretations and compositions designated as "allegorical" must have a narrative dimen-

sion. By "narrative," I mean nothing more complicated than a story that has a beginning, middle, and end, and depicts the interaction of characters and events over time.[10] For the purposes of this book, then, allegory always tries to tell a story: either the "other meanings" that allegory offers or the "literal meanings" that it plays off against must assume a narrative form; where there is no narrative at either "level" of meaning, some form of nonliteral or figurative reading may be present, but not allegory. When one reads a narrative "allegorically," thus producing an allegorical interpretation, one decides that a story appearing to be about one thing actually concerns something else.[11] Thus some ancient Christians read the story of the exodus of the Hebrews from Egypt and their entry into the Promised Land as an account of the soul's conversion from sin through the waters of baptism and its ultimate entry into the kingdom of heaven. In composing an allegory, one produces a story about one thing and in so doing actually conveys meanings about something else. For example, in *The Pilgrim's Progress,* John Bunyan composes the story of Christian's journey from the City of Destruction to the Celestial City—a story that, among other things, indirectly charts the course of the soul's progress from conversion to final redemption.

Although I distinguish compositional from interpretative allegory for purposes of analysis, this distinction is often blurred in some of the texts I will be examining.[12] Indeed, the very insistence on a distinction between composition and interpretation is itself an act of resistance against the radically revisionary consequences of an unfettered allegorical imagination.[13] For example, in the case of Valentinus's works, allegorical interpretation—the giving of nonliteral meanings to prior narrative texts (the Bible, Plato's *Timaeus,* Gnostic myth)—takes the form of new allegorical composition (Valentinus's own myth). Moreover, Valentinus makes a concentrated effort to efface any visible "seams" between his acts of composition and his acts of interpretation. When a nonliteral reading thus takes the form of nonliteral composition—when a reader interprets one narrative by subsuming it within another that displaces it—allegorical interpretation assumes its most subversive form.[14] In contrast, both Philo and Clement preserve, in quite different ways, a distinction between scripture as the original (divine) composition and their own commentary; neither aspires to the degree of innovation and personal authority that would subordinate or displace the original. Unlike Valentinus, both Philo and Clement look to some form of canon as the basis for their own interpretative authority.[15]

The distinction between the kind of commentary that preserves the identity and authority of canonical texts and the kind that effaces canonicity (and thus hides its own status as derivative commentary) is re-

flected in the different nuances of the terms "interpretation" and "reading." "Interpretation" is a term indebted to the traditional hermeneutical view of allegory as a procedure that uncovers a meaning hidden in a text; one "interprets" a text by drawing forth the meaning it somehow "contains." The term "reading" avoids these hermeneutical implications b, allowing instead for a process by which meaning might be found in places other than the text or by which something other than the retrieval of meaning as a hidden "object" might be going on. In this book, "interpretation" should be understood as a synonym for "reading," not the other way around. In many cases, when a text is seemingly "interpreted" through allegory, "meaning" is not being extracted from the text; instead, power is being exercised via one text over other texts and the world views they represent. This is true even, or perhaps especially, when ancient allegorists themselves choose to speak of their readings as the recovery of meaning rather than as the exercise of power.[16]

By emphasizing the narrative character of allegory, I intend to distinguish allegory from the intimately related categories of metaphor, etymology, and personification. I am aware that such discrimination, especially when presented in schematic fashion, runs the double risk of distorting the terms with which allegory is contrasted and minimizing the extent to which different nonliteral strategies inform one another in many complex allegorical works. But such distinctions seem necessary if the category of allegory is to retain any analytical significance. Allegory loses much of its usefulness as an interpretative tool whenever its characteristic narrativity is ignored or, as in much deconstructionist writing, it is allowed to become synonymous with figural language in general. Such expansion of the category may have its value in some contexts, but the circumscribed definition of allegory as an essentially narrative phenomenon is especially appropriate for the kind of analysis I am applying to the instances of ancient allegory that this book considers.[17]

Allegory bears the closest possible relationship to metaphor because, in a sense, it is composed of metaphors. But allegory and metaphor should not be simply identified. A metaphor is a trope that makes an implied analogy. Thus the metaphorical expression "War is a chess game" imaginatively identifies one object (war) with another (the game of chess), ascribing to the first some aspect of the second. It has become customary to distinguish between a metaphor's tenor, the idea expressed or the subject of the comparison, and its vehicle, the image by which that idea or subject is conveyed.[18] In "War is a chess game," the tenor is presumably something like strategy and cunning, the vehicle a game of chess. Ancient rhetoricians observed that allegory is clearly related to metaphor because both figures make a comparison. But some observed further that allegory

is an "extended" metaphor, that is, a metaphor that has been stretched into a narrative.[19] If I write a novel about a chess match between American and Soviet chess champions and in so doing seek to communicate another story about the disappearance of the cold war and the collapse of communism in Eastern Europe, I have extended my earlier metaphor into an allegory. Hence, while all allegories are metaphorical, all metaphors are not by themselves allegories. At most, they are potential allegories.

Much the same might be said of the trope of personification (or prosopopoeia), which endows nonhuman entities (e.g., plants, animals, inanimate objects, ideas, abstractions) with human attributes (e.g., human physiology, emotions, or language).[20] If I turn the concept of faith into a character (Faith) with human attributes such as voice and agency, as did the early Christian Prudentius in his *Psychomachia,* I will have produced a personification.[21] Personification is often a feature of many allegories, but, like metaphor, it should not simply be identified with allegory because it does not by itself have a narrative dimension; it offers character but no plot. However, plot may be implicit in the characterization a personification produces. One may personify a concept as the sort of character that is likely to do certain kinds of things. In addition, if agency, and by implication plot, is felt to be an inevitable concomitant of any truly human identity, some personifications would necessarily entail action and plot. Not surprisingly, then, personification is a common feature of allegory—namely, allegory's customary way of representing narrative agents. Even so, narrative is the element that must accompany personification for allegory to be present.[22] Many allegories and allegorical readings produce and decode personifications, but the mere presence of personification does not signal the presence of allegory.

Etymology, differing from both metaphor and personification, also needs to be distinguished from allegory. If one searches out the history of a word or name by distinguishing its components and tracing them back to their primordial forms in some ancestral language for the purpose of discovering an original or fundamental meaning, one is practicing etymology.[23] Because the fundamental meaning of a word that one discovers etymologically is likely to be quite different from the word's contemporary meaning, etymology is a typical feature of allegorical interpretation. It has often been presented by ancient interpreters as a "rational" or "scientific" way of justifying the attribution of another, less-than-obvious meaning to a word or of giving some sort of acceptable meaning to an otherwise incomprehensible expression. In this way, the etymologist could counter charges of hermeneutical willfulness with the claim to have uncovered the original foundations of meaning. Like metaphor and personification, etymology does produce an alternate meaning, but like these tropes, it too

lacks a narrative dimension. The two meanings generated by etymology do not by themselves constitute allegory.

As ways of giving words, names, or characters other meanings, metaphor, etymology, and personification are common tools of the allegorist. But only when the allegorist uses such tools to compose or interpret a narrative do we have allegory. Many ancient allegorical compositions and interpretations did in fact have narrative dimensions. Prudentius's *Psychomachia,* the earliest full-scale Christian allegory (ca. 400 C.E.), despite its dominant recurring opposition of psychological warfare, displays a clear narrative progression, relying on a reading of scripture that unifies the work as a single story with a clear beginning (creation), middle (redemption), and end (realization of the kingdom of God).[24] Likewise, much Christian allegorical reading of Hebrew scripture remained explicitly or implicitly dependent on the narrative of Jesus' life understood nonallegorically as the biography of a recognizably historical human being.[25] Indeed, there was considerable resistance when some Christians, having read the narratives of Hebrew scripture allegorically, attempted to apply the same allegorical hermeneutic to the New Testament account of Jesus' career; in such cases, allegory was felt to dissolve the narrative of a human life into a cipher for nonnarrative abstractions or generalizations.[26]

In allegory, then, indirect, nonliteral, or "other" meanings occur together with direct, literal, or "obvious" meanings of the narrative of the allegorical composition or of the text that is being read allegorically. Consequently, one can understand the character and function of allegory only in relation to its necessary "other," traditionally called the "literal sense" or "literal meaning." Whether as a mode of reading or as a kind of composition, allegory always appears with the literal sense, which it may accompany, revise, or displace. If allegory loses tension with the literal sense altogether, it simply becomes a literal sense itself—either the old literal sense it once challenged or the new literal sense readers now take it to be.[27]

My use of phrases like "literal sense," "level of meaning," or "meaning of the text" is not intended to indicate any essentialization or reification of meaning, or to suggest that texts somehow "possess" meaning the way individuals "possess" property (the connections between property and "proper" or literal meaning are hardly accidental). Instead, I understand "meaning" to be a construction of readers who seek to use texts to accomplish certain ends, to satisfy certain desires. "Meaning" is thus a thoroughly rhetorical category—it designates the way composers of allegory and allegorical interpreters enact their intentions toward others through the medium of a shared text. Consequently, although the "literal sense" has often been thought of as an inherent quality of a literary text that gives it a specific and invariant character (often, a "realistic" character),

the phrase is simply an honorific title given to a kind of meaning that is culturally expected and automatically recognized by readers. It is the "normal," "commonsensical" meaning, the product of a conventional, customary reading.[28] The "literal sense" thus stems from a community's generally unself-conscious decision to adopt and promote a certain kind of meaning, rather than from its recognition of a text's inherent and self-evident sense.[29]

An "allegorical meaning" obtains its identity precisely by its contrast with this customary or expected meaning. Because of this contrast at its very origin, allegory necessarily offers a challenge and possible alternative to that customary reading. Even the etymology of the term suggests such inevitable negation: to "say other" implies an antithetical stance toward a previous "saying"; the allegorical reader begins with resistance and denial: "You may say that this text means one thing; it does not mean that, but rather something else." Even when the allegorical reader does not explicitly reject the first meaning but simply adds the second to it, the mere presence of the addition implicitly denies the independence or exclusivity of the first meaning. Allegorical interpretation thus seems almost inevitably to challenge prior, nonallegorical readings. Naturally, those for whom that prior reading is meaningful and authoritative in its own right will resist the allegorical challenge, especially when challenge turns into outright replacement. But should a community of such "literalists" subsequently come to embrace the allegorical meaning as the obvious, expected meaning, that allegorical meaning would have become, in effect, the new "literal sense."

New literal meanings are often simply old allegorical innovations that have succumbed to the "lethargy of custom." For example, if a Christian community agrees with Paul that the rock in the wilderness struck by Moses is actually Christ (1 Cor. 10.4), then the literal meaning of the word "rock" is in fact "Christ"; the initial allegorical sense has become literal, now domesticated as the sense universally accepted, as customary and obvious as the "arm" of a chair. But before such domestication, an allegorical sense challenges the obvious sense. When the second-century Christian interpreter Marcion resisted the attempt of other Christians to give offensive passages of Hebrew scripture "other" meanings, he was defending his own "literal sense" in the face of the strong revisionary challenge that Christian allegorical readings presented. In the Pauline example, the literal sense is indistinguishable from allegorical readings that gain acceptance as the "actual," rather than the "other," meaning of a text, while in the Marcionite example, the reading that produces a potentially emerging plain sense (such as Paul's), before communal acceptance, plays the adversarial role characteristic of fresh allegorical interpretations.

II

I have said that allegorical readings resist a prior reading's claim to offer the one and only true meaning of the text, that allegorical readings always begin as counterreadings, starting with denial or negation. By challenging the literal sense, allegory may also revise prevailing cultural ideals. However, whether an allegorical reading of a text is in fact also a revisionary interpretation of culture depends on the extent to which the literal meaning of the text actually represents cultural ideals.[30] I want to suggest that religion, especially in the guise of a sacred text, can function as a counterhegemonic force, and, further, that allegory has been one of the principal means by which such challenges have been mounted. Although religion often functions to help legitimize cultural hegemony, this need not be the case.[31] Recent discussion of the hegemonic force of socio-cultural formations—their tendency to normalize and naturalize prevailing hierarchical relations of social dominance and oppression—has pointed to internal stratification and tensions that work as countervailing tendencies within the overall cultural forms of life.[32]

"Culture" is, then, a term that embraces a vast diversity of values, ideals, and systems of discourse. In my use of the term, I do not mean to suggest a view of culture as monolithic, with a single set of reigning assumptions. At best, culture is a general, abstract label for myriad competing, partially intertwined, partially separate cultures. When I refer to "reigning assumptions," I mean the very local varieties of patterns of value that give expression to dominant views; these patterns of value vary widely depending on place, time, and circumstance. Thus my notion of "reigning ideals" is formal until further specified. Likewise, the terms "conservative," "radical," and "moderate" are equally formal, until made representative of specified ideals, values, and goals. Culture is a field of competing assumptions, some of which reign in one sphere, others in a different sphere. Consequently, to be conservative with respect to one set of ideals might be to be radical with respect to another—and vice versa. Thus, one anti-imperial strain during the first century c.e. looks toward a possible revival of the Republic—an instance in which criticism of imperial ideology depends on the recovery of the countercultural potential of a conservatism turned radical.

Just as counterhegemonic forces exist within the various strata of secular society and culture, they can also exist between specific religious traditions and the wider culture; such was certainly the case with ancient Judaism and Christianity, both of which struggled against aspects of Hellenistic culture. Likewise, a religious community can struggle with itself, as emerging forces seek to subvert or overthrow well-entrenched,

traditional points of view (reflected, for example, in Christian reading of Hebrew scripture and Islamic reading of Jewish and Christian scripture). Such struggles between alternative world views and sociocultural practices are manifested in contests between literal and nonliteral readings of culturally important texts.

How, then, might allegory actually work as a culturally revisionary force? First, one must recognize that allegory is not inherently revisionary. If the literal sense is culturally shocking (which often is the case when a radical change in cultural ideals coincides with continued veneration of cultural classics), an allegorical reading might well serve to domesticate the text—to show that its literal meaning really is in step with cultural expectation. When the allegorical "nonliteral" reading neutralizes the culturally deviant meanings of the literal text, replacing them with culturally obvious meanings (e.g., a morally shocking scene from the *Iliad* is given an ordinary, scientific meaning), such a reading endorses prevailing cultural norms; the allegorical sense becomes in effect the proper literal sense.[33]

On the other hand, if the readily apparent sense of the text really is the culturally endorsed literal sense, an allegorical reading might provide a revolutionary challenge to prevailing cultural norms. If people really do believe that the gods have human bodies and personalities, then interpreting the quarrels of Olympian deities as representations of the contrary forces of nature becomes culturally offensive—indeed, it may be viewed as outright atheism (this, as we shall see, was precisely the charge leveled at some ancient allegorists). Thus we see that allegory can either protect culture by domesticating deviant texts or criticize culture by giving cultural classics deviant meanings. In the texts we will be examining, the coincidence of literal sense and cultural norms is often marked by the adjective *prepēs,* meaning "fitting," "appropriate," or "in place." Violations of this sense of the fitting, of cultural decorum, are often signaled by the adjective *atopos,* meaning "inappropriate," "monstrous," or literally "out of place."

Finally, there is also a third way that allegory can revise culture, a way sometimes used by allegorical readers who are proponents of scripturally based religions. Such readers may use allegory to enable scripture itself to absorb and reinterpret culture. In its most effective form, this revisionary interpretation of culture has two important features: textualization and originality. Rather than simply subverting preallegorical, literal readings, allegorical readings of this third sort bring meanings previously unrelated to scripture into a new and revisionary relationship with scripture as read in the preallegorical, literal manner. That is, precisely through an allegorical reading, other, formerly nonscriptural meanings may become "textualized" by being associated with the preallegorical, literal reading.

For example, the preallegorical, literal reading of Exodus might concern the escape of Hebrews from Egypt. If I draw on Platonic theories of the soul's origin and destiny in order to read this biblical story allegorically as an account of the soul's ascent from bodily distraction to mental purity, I may do so because I want to reinterpret Plato's account by placing it within a scriptural framework. But in so doing, I may in fact subtly alter the meaning that Plato's account has on its own terms by making the once-eternal soul now directly created by God. When functioning in this way, allegorical readings can subvert previously nonscriptural meanings (i.e., meanings that prior to the allegorical reading would not have been associated with scripture); the allegorical reading can enable the preallegorical or "literal" reading to critique or revise those nonscriptural meanings.

This sort of allegorical revision of culture may be made even stronger if one claims originality for the scripture to which one subordinates culture. In a truly revisionary reading of culture according to scripture, one will not only make cultural meanings scriptural, one will also make one's own sacred scripture prior to, and hence authoritative over, everyone else's not-so-sacred scripture. If one posits one's own text as prior to other texts and construes that priority as an authority bestowed by absolute and divine originality, all competing texts will be subordinated. Thus one might not only declare that scripture rather than Plato offers the most persuasive description of the soul's transformation, but also insist that Moses preceded Plato and that Plato derived all his best insights from original Mosaic wisdom.

The three religious allegorists examined in this study offer different versions of this third mode of allegory. The versions are different because only one interpreter—Philo—makes textualization his principal revisionary template; Valentinus replaces textualization with mystical vision, Clement with vocalization. But all three use allegorical readings to bring to bear on religious precursors and cultural ideals a revisionary force. In addition, all three make claims for originality in order to give their revisionary readings ultimate and unassailable authority.

III

The history of the study of allegory is characterized by extreme diversity and fundamental disagreement over allegory's nature and function. Scholars even question whether the category designates any clearly identifiable or reliably discernible literary form or mode of interpretation at all. Even so, one can identify several basic and recurring debates, and it may prove helpful to situate the understanding of allegory that informs this work in relation to three currently influential lines of scholarly analysis of the subject. These three lines intersect, but do not coincide with,

the three general perspectives discussed at the outset of this introduction. The lines of scholarly analysis can be summarized by a set of oppositions, the poles of which reflect particular definitions of allegory's essential character: defensive vs. positive allegory, allegory vs. symbol, and allegory vs. typology. Each of these oppositions is rooted in a "classical" debate, though in each case, the debate has in recent years moved away from its original formulation, crossing disciplinary boundaries and appearing in new idioms and sometimes inverted forms. But each debate, in both earlier and later forms, involves a fundamentally similar set of concerns. Thus, a nineteenth- and early twentieth-century debate among classicists over whether ancient pagan allegory was fundamentally "defensive" and apologetic or "positive" and philosophical, while still informing contemporary discussions in the field of classics, has reappeared in a different form in recent writings of some literary theorists who view allegory, along with other modes of nonliteral reading, as a form of literary revisionism. Likewise, the well-known, early nineteenth-century Romantic valorization of symbol over allegory endures in certain twentieth-century discussions of allegory, as well as in a radically inverted fashion in the contemporary deconstructionist insistence on the superiority of allegorical over symbolic modes of discourse. And a traditional, theologically motivated contrast between allegory and typology, stemming principally from the Protestant Reformation and advanced by Christian biblical scholars and theologians, has been recently reinvoked by contemporary theological advocates of "intratextual" (versus "extratextual") biblical hermeneutics.

My own approach to ancient allegory has been informed by aspects of all three debates, while diverging from them in a number of ways. Some classicists insist that ancient allegory was a defensive, apologetic effort to save venerated cultural classics from the rationalist, philosophical critique begun by Xenophanes and given impetus by Plato. Allegorical readers thus translated seemingly immoral myths of gods and goddesses into ethical and cosmological accounts.[34] Other classicists argue that ancient allegory, from its very origins, was a philosophically sophisticated hermeneutic designed to treat writers of myth and poetry as philosophers and scientists.[35] The debate about apologetic versus philosophical allegory, when combined with the question of the importance of discovering an original truth, turns into a debate about the revisionary function of allegorical reading. Thus, implicit in the argument of those classicists who claim that allegory sought to defend the poets from charges of immorality is the suggestion that allegorists sought to give the beleaguered poets Homer and Hesiod cultural power over rationalist philosophy. In contrast, those who argue that ancient allegory was a mode of positive philosophical reflection imply that ancient allegorists sought to give their own philosophy interpretative authority over traditional poetry. Defensive

allegory thus protects the cultural power of traditional classical literature in the face of rationalist assault; philosophical allegory protects the cultural power of philosophy by giving it the interpretative "last word" over classical Greek literature.[36] This debate continues to characterize discussions of allegory by classicists, though recent scholarship in the field has drawn on modern hermeneutical theories as well, and there has been at least one attempt to align ancient allegory with contemporary notions of "literariness" or "the literary as such."[37]

Contemporary discussions of allegory (and nonliteral reading in general) by literary theorists of revisionism often make reference to the work of classicists or draw on ancient hermeneutical models. However, while its general approach reflects something of the classicists' debate, the new literary theoretical discussion adds a certain twist, adumbrated by one ancient sarcastic remark about the "philosophical" intent of ancient allegorists. According to one critic, some Stoic philosophers used nonliteral interpretations to show "that even the earliest poets of antiquity, who had notions of these doctrines, were really Stoics."[38] In a similar vein, some modern theorists argue that creative readers resist the authority of their literary precursors by reading their works in such a way that the readers' own insights are shown to be the "actual" meanings of their precursors' texts; the precursor, despite coming earlier in time, is thus shown up as derivative, and the reader, freed from the burden of tradition, is able to carve out a literary or imaginative space for his or her own original literary creation. Sometimes, these theorists of revisionism emphasize the difficulty of the process, arguing that, in the end, most readers fail to overcome the influence of their predecessors.[39] In other cases, they point to successful allegorical displacement of precursors.[40] Theoretical discussion of these acts of literary resistance and aggression typically appeal to Nietzschean accounts of hermeneutical will to power, Freudian categories of repression and displacement, or Kafkaesque meditations on elusive meaning.[41]

In this book, I often agree with classicists who argue that allegory functions at times to defend literature from philosophical attack or to obtain philosophical insights from the pages of cultural classics. I also draw at numerous points on the work of contemporary revisionists who see nonliteral readings as struggles with textual precursors. However, in all cases, I try to turn these perspectives (apologetic, philosophical, revisionary) away from purely psychological, philosophical, or literary categories and more firmly toward social, cultural, and political realities.[42] I seek to determine not just whether ancient readers used allegory to defend poets from the charge of immorality, to discover hidden philosophy in ancient texts, or to give revisionary potential to literary texts, but whether they used allegorical readings of texts, especially scripture, to

endorse, criticize, or subvert sociocultural formations and political authority. Even so, this is more a matter of redirecting the insights generated by these debates than of setting them aside altogether.

The nineteenth-century Romantic contrast of allegory and symbol has been more historically influential than the contrast between defensive and positive allegory.[43] Reflecting culturally dominant literary and aesthetic judgments about the value of the symbol's intrinsic and "organic" relationship to that which is symbolized over allegory's artificial, sterile, or merely "mechanical" juxtaposition of image and meaning, Romantic theorists consistently denigrated allegory and praised the symbol. Unlike allegory's allegedly wooden translation of abstract ideas into sensuous images to which those ideas bore no essential resemblance, the literary symbol supposedly fused idea and image into an "organic" whole with quasi-sacramental significance. This Romantic contrast became so influential that modern studies of allegory typically begin with an effort to modify or overturn it.[44] Even more recently, as noted earlier, as part of a critical retrieval of Romantic poetics, some postmodern literary theorists have revalorized allegory, finding in the trope's "artificial" juxtaposition of idea and image a virtual equivalent of deconstruction's claim to have exposed the fullest implications of the "unmotivated" relation between textual signifiers and signified meanings.[45]

In my approach to ancient allegory, I replace the Romantics' quasi-theological concern with symbolic "translucence" with an interest in what might be called "direction of interpretation." What the Romantics viewed as allegory's "artificial" juxtaposition of idea and image, and postmoderns view as the arbitrary and unmotivated juxtaposition of signifier and signified, becomes in my perspective a religiocultural decision to use allegory for purposes of accommodation or transformation. Like some contemporary deconstructionist perspectives, this approach sets aside the Romantic valorization of symbol (as the trope that provides the best literary surrogate for the Christian doctrine of incarnation?) and reassesses the significance of allegory. But I seek to go beyond the literary formalism of deconstruction by insisting that allegory's "decisions" of mind are as much social and cultural as psychological or aesthetic. On the other hand, as mentioned at the outset, I endorse what is increasingly recognized as a strong link between deconstruction's insistence on allegory's expression of the absence of meaning and ancient apophatic (or "negative") theology.[46]

Endorsing the Romantic contrast between symbol and allegory, many modern Christian theologians and historians of biblical exegesis have made much of the Bible as a symbolic document, celebrating the religious potential of symbolic interpretation.[47] Indeed, one can argue that the

entire modern tradition of biblical hermeneutics, originating in the Romantic period, is devoted to this endeavor.[48] But other theologians have drawn an equally important contrast between allegory and typology (or figural interpretation). Typology, it is argued, is a mode of composition or interpretation that links together at least two temporally different historical events or persons because of an analogy they bear to one another. Because it is said to preserve the historical reality of both the initial "type" and its corresponding "antitypes," typology is said to differ from allegory, which dissolves the historical reality of type and/or antitype into timeless generalities or conceptual abstractions.[49]

The contrast between allegory and typology grew out of an ancient discrimination of various "levels" of meaning in scripture, a discrimination rooted in the difference between Hebrew scripture as "Old" Testament and early Christian literature as "New" Testament, a distinction produced in large part by christological exegesis of Hebrew scripture.[50] But the claim for the uniqueness of typological meaning and its essential distinction from, and incompatibility with, allegory arose much later, in large part as a result of Reformation polemic against the use of allegory.[51] Theological preferences for typological, rather than allegorical, ways of reading scripture reflect a desire to preserve the historicity of the persons and events depicted in Hebrew scripture, the "types" of which are thus not entirely negated and replaced by corresponding Christian "antitypes."[52] This desire in turn reflects concern to preserve the underlying continuity of Judaism and Christianity, the distinction of both from Greek (and modern, secular) culture, and the concrete reality of divine action and self-identification (i.e., revelation) in history.[53]

The valorization of the symbol on the one side and the rejection of both symbol and allegory in favor of typology on the other define two of the most important interpretative approaches to scripture in present-day theological hermeneutics. On the one side, contemporary theological advocates of symbolic discourse argue that such language preserves the experiential dimension of religious classics and provides a literary medium where theological and cultural realities can come together. Advocates of religious symbolism often aspire to the liberal Christian quest to make culture the form of religion, and religion the substance of culture. On the other side of the fence of contemporary theological method are those who have recently reinvoked the traditional contrast between allegory and typology under the rubrics of extratextuality and intratextuality.[54] "Intratextual" readings of scripture draw on typology to create a single story line out of the diverse and often contradictory elements of scripture, allowing the Bible to be read as a unified narrative stretching from Genesis to Revelation. Unlike allegory (and symbolism—which

these theologians view as only a slightly less egregious form of allegory), typological reading produces a unified biblical narrative that is not simply a code for other, nonliteral meanings; instead, this narrative is said to create its own world, its own reality, into which believers are invited to enter. "Intratextual" readings of scripture thus become "readings" of culture and experience—efforts to absorb nonscriptural realities into the world of the Bible.[55]

Quite apart from any theological merit the intratextualist proposal may possess, the notion that readers of sacred texts often seek to exercise counterhegemonic, reinterpretative power over culture proves to be an illuminating way of analyzing the character and function of much ancient religious allegory. However, the decision to divorce typology from allegory has obscured the underlying formal similarity of the two procedures by focusing on material theological considerations. If the literal sense is the product of an act of reading, allegorical (nonliteral) and nonallegorical (literal) readings can be understood as formally oppositional and mutually defining before they are defined as materially different. Consequently, in this book, typology is understood to be simply one species of allegory; the historical practice of giving texts other meanings (allegory) includes a certain subpractice of giving texts other meanings according to certain "rules" (typology).[56] On this view, typology is simply a certain kind of allegorical reading promoted as nonallegorical for specific theological and rhetorical reasons.

However, my own understanding of allegorical readings as either newly emerging "literal senses" or challenges to previously reigning "literal senses" suggests that allegorical readings might function intratextually; this, in fact, is the direct implication of the third kind of allegorical revision of culture I discussed above.[57] If an allegorical reading enables its implicit, prior, literal reading to reinterpret the world intratextually, such an allegorical reading would not cancel or displace but only provisionally suspend the prior, literal reading of scripture long enough to join non-scriptural meanings to scripture.[58] Such an allegorical reading would give scripture other meanings in order to make other meanings scriptural. Although one can easily imagine allegorical readings that overturn prior readings of scripture and replace them with nonscriptural additions, this need not be the case; allegorical readings might instead enable the particularities of scripture to interpret the surrounding, previously nonscriptural culture. Likewise, allegorical compositions might also perform such intratextual reinterpretations. Such compositions might offer readers a new vision of the world in which an old world view has been imaginatively reconfigured to conform to patterns established by a prior reading of scripture. My approach, then, endorses the intratextualist claim that texts can and do shape and reshape culture (though they need not do so), but it

drops the antithesis between allegory and typology, setting aside the specifically theological concern that helped underwrite that antithesis in the first place.

IV

The chapters that follow explore the various features and functions of allegory and related nonliteral procedures as they appear in the works of selected pagan interpreters (Cornutus, Heraclitus, Cicero, Seneca, Plutarch, and the Alexandrian grammarians) and of important Jewish and Christian religious figures who were part of the early Alexandrian allegorical tradition (Aristeas, Aristobulus, Philo, Valentinus, and Clement). The chronological organization of the chapters helps keep historical interrelationships clear and allows comment on important hermeneutical relationships between precursors and successors (e.g., Clement's domestication of Valentinus's radical Gnostic allegory). However, this organization is not designed to suggest any teleological line of development or narrative plot; my account of ancient allegorical practice is not itself meant to be allegorical. I do not try to tell a story so much as to describe a number of moments at which interpretative forces and counterforces emerge and enter into conflict with one another.[59] Indeed, part of my conclusion will be to suggest that some of these struggles are virtually inescapable features of the Western hermeneutical tradition, breaking out again and again in different forms, in varying sociocultural situations, with new implications. However, if there is a common feature in these struggles that recur throughout the history of interpretation, it may be the emergence and domestication of radical *gnōsis* in its countless forms.

The first series of struggles that I examine is located in the realm of pagan Hellenistic nonliteral exegesis of Greek myth and poetry, and the resistance to this practice. Chapter 1, "Pagan Etymology and Allegory," begins with Lucius Annaeus Cornutus, a Stoic interpreter of the first century c.e. who sought to discover the philosophical and scientific wisdom that ancient mythmakers had embodied in myths that the poets had preserved. While Cornutus's reading of these poets was mainly an exercise in etymological analysis for purposes of scientific and philosophical inquiry, his contemporary Heraclitus applied a genuinely allegorical reading to the *Iliad* and the *Odyssey* in order to defend Homer against the rationalist assaults of Platonists, Epicureans, and other philosophical critics. Both Cornutus and Heraclitus appealed to nonliteral readings in order to tap into the source of original and authoritative wisdom. But both interpreters used their nonliteral readings (etymology in the case of Cornutus, allegory in the case of Heraclitus) not for revisionary purposes, but in order to underwrite and defend reigning contemporary cultural

ideals and norms. Despite the popularity of etymological and allegorical interpretation in the ancient world, these strategies were not universally well-regarded; numerous pagan opponents objected to both procedures. The chapter thus concludes with a survey of representative opponents, ranging from those suspicious and skeptical of the techniques to those who rejected them altogether. In light of this chapter's survey of diverse pagan attitudes toward etymology and allegory, it seems evident that ancient Jewish and Christian use of these techniques was at least as much a considered hermeneutical strategy as a cultural inevitability.

The remaining chapters of the book offer accounts of three distinctly different modes of allegorical reading of scripture with revisionary aspirations that emerged in ancient Alexandria, widely regarded in antiquity, as well as by modern scholars, as the principal site of ancient allegorical interpretation. In various ways, Philo, Valentinus, and Clement used allegorical readings to reinterpret the texts and culture that surrounded them. These three writers stand within an identifiable literary tradition of allegorical reading: Clement quotes extensively from Philo's allegorical works and expends considerable effort refuting the interpretations of Valentinus, fragments of whose writings he preserves. While it cannot be demonstrated that Valentinus knew Philo's works, the close relationship between Valentinian Christianity and Alexandrian Judaism makes such knowledge quite likely. Despite their many differences, then, these three interpreters stand within a common literary and philosophical tradition—not only the general Hellenistic tradition of nonliteral hermeneutics, but the more specific early Alexandrian tradition of allegorical interpretation.

Even more important, they share one overriding goal: to convince readers that their allegorical interpretations tap directly into the original source of all meaning and truth, and, by contrast, to show up competing readings as mere derivations and deviations from this original, authoritative wisdom. Drawing on the shared repertoire of pagan Hellenistic interpretative techniques and strategies, Jewish and Christian exegetical precedent, and a deep current of apophatic theology, each of these allegorical readers formulated a distinctive view of the original and authoritative locus of meaning: for Philo, the sacred text of the Pentateuch; for Valentinus, his own mystical vision; for Clement, the speech of the divine *logos*. Text, vision, and speech were, then, the foundations for bold reinterpretations of culture that took the very different forms we might metaphorically describe as reinscription, revision, and revocalization.

While each interpreter emphasizes one interpretative category, each also draws on the other two categories. Philo makes text and writing the primary basis of his allegorical reinterpretation of culture, but he can also appeal to mystical vision and divine speech. Likewise, although Valen-

tinus gives personal mystical experience far more revisionary authority than does Philo or Clement, he can also characterize his mystical vision as a kind of writing and speaking. Finally, although Clement's dominant hermeneutical strategy depends on a transtextual hermeneutical voice or *logos*, like Philo, he can cast that voice into written forms, and like Valentinus, he can claim for the non-Valentinian Christian a superior mystical vision, in this case the reward of faith rather than *gnōsis*. Consequently, I will be examining three interpreters who offer distinctive emphases within a common set of interpretative strategies, metaphors, and faculties.

The reinterpretations of Philo, Valentinus, and Clement were first of all literary. Ancient readers were offered, as the fruit of the Alexandrian allegorical tradition, literary representations of alternative world views and forms of life. But these authors designed their representations to serve more than the literary imagination; all three searched for sources of social and cultural innovation, striving to use literary representation and revision to promote alternative ways of being in the world. Their revisionary readings of culture reflected the real-life activities of their communities and were intended to have real-life consequences for their readers. Each author wrote from within and for a specific religious community, as well as for a wider audience. These allegorists sought nothing less than to reshape and redirect the lives of those within their religious communities, as well as to suggest to outsiders the value of such association.

The appeal to a prior text from which all subsequent wisdom is derived appears in the fragmentary remains of the Ptolemaic Alexandrian Jewish writers Aristeas and Aristobulus and receives extensive development by Philo (ca. 20 B.C.E.–ca. 50 C.E.). This interpretative practice is described in chapter 2, "Philo: The Reinscription of Reality." Philo achieves a revisionary stance toward competing texts by insisting that the meanings of these texts are actually the same as the allegorical "other" meanings of scripture and then by claiming that those other meanings first appeared in scripture. Scripture thus consists of Moses' rewriting of nonscriptural ideas— ideas that Moses had before anyone else. As a result, Philo presents Moses' rewriting as a thoroughly original writing. Philo intends his interpretations not only to preserve, protect, and enhance the integrity of the Alexandrian Jewish community, but to make Judaism and its self-identifying scriptural narrative the paradigm for all historical meaning and the source of all true culture.

Philo's interpretations preserve a clear separation between sacred text and allegorical commentary. This distinction is all but erased in the second mode of Alexandrian allegorical revision, represented by the work of the Gnostic Christian Valentinus (ca. 100–ca. 175 C.E.), examined in chapter 3, "Valentinus: The Apocalypse of the Mind." In the works of

Valentinus, allegorical commentary becomes fused with scripture and other precursor interpretive traditions such as Platonic and Gnostic myth, as allegorical interpretation develops into allegorical composition, taking the form of Valentinus's original mythmaking. New composition becomes the principal vehicle of interpretation, and the compositional result of interpretation approaches the authority of a sacred text. Rather than separating his commentary from prior authoritative texts, Valentinus fuses text and commentary as the expression of his own original religious vision—a vision that assumes a revisionary stance toward competing texts by turning their characters and narrative sequences into new psychological and epistemological allegories of ignorance and knowledge, deficiency and fullness. For the Valentinians, history itself—from its catastrophic origin to its final redemption—existed within a paradoxical act of divine self-emptying (*kenōsis*) and self-knowledge (*gnōsis*). Valentinus's revisionary reading and composition was informed in part by an earlier Jewish Christianity in Egypt that focused on the "name of God," and its emergence was tied to the shifting fortunes and ultimate demise of Alexandrian Judaism and Jewish Christianity. Valentinian revision was also socially embodied in the liturgical life of Valentinian communities, which existed as "cells" within the larger, non-Valentinian Christian communities of which they were part.

Rather than collapsing the distinction between sacred text and commentary via the creation of original, hermeneutical myths, or construing scripture as an original text with which to inscribe the world, Clement (ca. 150–ca. 215 C.E.) discovers or inserts in scripture, as well as in the classics of Greek culture, an original pre-textual voice, a revisionary reading process described in chapter 4, "Clement: The New Song of the *Logos*." By appealing to a voice prior to and underlying all religiously significant texts and traditions, Clement is able to reject some elements of those texts while accepting others. Despite important differences between Philo's conception of meaning as scriptural and Clement's conception of meaning as vocal, Clement maintains a Philonic distinction between sacred text and commentary. Clement's mode of allegorical reading, like Philo's, is a reading that produces commentary on a preexisting authoritative text. This preexisting sacred text receives even further authority by virtue of the fact that it elicits commentary, and it lends its authority in turn to the interpretive works of the commentator. Clement's similarity to Philo on this point reflects both Clement's very non-Valentinian efforts to keep Christianity linked with scriptural Judaism and his "orthodox" domestication of the atextual, mystical authority of Valentinus's interpretative practice. Clement's social use of a controlled allegory and domesticated *gnōsis* is most evident in his efforts to define and protect the boundaries of the emerging "Church" from "heterodox," sectarian intrusion.

There has long been a tendency to view ancient Alexandrian allegory as a monolithic tradition stretching from Aristobulus, through Philo and Clement, to Origen, a particularly Eastern tradition interested (unlike the more historically minded Western tradition represented by Tertullian and Augustine) primarily in the apologetic or speculative goal of inserting philosophical meanings into texts that one would have thought were actually concerned with other things.[60] However, a closer look at the details of this early allegorical practice reveals instead an astonishing degree of interpretative diversity and conflict and shows us something of the high cultural stakes involved. Ancient allegorical practice gives us models of intratextual worlds (Philo), interpretation as new mythmaking (Valentinus), and experiential encounters with the perennial human meaning of cultural classics (Clement). Such models and examples, in both their approach to and divergence from our own concerns, may stimulate further reflection on the interrelationship of religion, textual interpretation, and cultural criticism.

ONE

Pagan Etymology and Allegory

The allegorical interpretations of Philo, Valentinus, and Clement emerged in the midst of ancient and diverse pagan hermeneutical practices. This chapter surveys some of the pagan allegorical and antiallegorical techniques, models, and attitudes available to these religious interpreters. We have already observed the close relationship between etymology and allegorical interpretation. This chapter begins, then, by considering the practice of etymology in the *Compendium of the Traditions of Greek Theology,* written by Lucius Annaeus Cornutus, a Stoic philosopher, grammarian, and pedagogue of the first century C.E. Cornutus uses etymological analysis of the names and epithets of deities to uncover the theological, philosophical, and scientific wisdom expressed in fragments of ancient Greek mythology preserved by the poets.

The second section of the chapter examines the considerably different interpretative model provided by the *Homeric Allegories* of Cornutus's contemporary, Heraclitus (the Hellenistic grammarian, not the pre-Socratic philosopher). Unlike Cornutus, Heraclitus interprets the *Iliad* and the *Odyssey* as though Homer had intentionally composed them as allegories. To convince his readers that Homer's poetry makes consistent allegorical sense from beginning to end, Heraclitus extends the nonliteral "other" meanings given to individual words or names to larger narrative units, and he seeks to bring his allegorical readings of various scenes into consistent relation to one another. Consequently, his approach moves well beyond Cornutus's relatively atomistic, nonnarrative use of etymology, providing an influential pagan example of allegory as defined in this study: a mode of nonliteral composition or interpretation that is narrative in character. In contrast to Cornutus, for whom etymology was essentially a means of "scientifically" extracting theological and philosophical knowl-

edge from ancient texts, Heraclitus uses his allegorical readings primarily to counter the charge that Homer's text violates a certain sense of what is morally fitting. As part of his defense of a beleaguered poet, Heraclitus declares Homer to have been the original philosopher and scientist from whom subsequent Greek thinkers derived all their best insights. In the discussions of Cornutus and Heraclitus in this chapter I also raise questions about the relation of their nonliteral interpretations to society and culture. Neither Cornutus nor Heraclitus is a cultural radical, writing in order to challenge the dominant culture. Instead, their works demonstrate some of the ways etymology and allegorical interpretation might be used to reinforce cultural ideals.

Finally, despite the prevalence of etymology and allegory in the ancient world, there were other hermeneutical choices available to ancient interpreters. The third section of the chapter investigates some of these choices, as well as the considerable ambivalence or opposition toward etymology and allegory in Greco-Roman culture. The writings of Cicero, Seneca, Plutarch, and various anonymous Alexandrian textual critics and philologists demonstrate that by no means was it a foregone conclusion that nonliteral reading was the best way to interpret ancient literature. This concluding survey of some opponents of etymology and allegory, together with the preceding consideration of some advocates, will illustrate different pagan hermeneutical models available to Philo, Valentinus, and Clement. It also suggests that Jewish and Christian reliance on allegorical techniques was enabled, but not mandated, by the wider Hellenistic culture.

ANCIENT MYTH AND STOIC ETYMOLOGY

Cornutus believed that ancient mythology contained a wealth of philosophical and cosmological wisdom. This mythology had been handed down in many forms, including the poems of Homer and Hesiod (e.g., *Epidr.* 24.45.23–24.46.1).[1] According to Cornutus, throughout the pages of the *Iliad*, the *Odyssey*, and the *Theogony*, readers encounter fragments of ancient myths that the poets have combined with their own novel literary creations. These ancient myths—whether Greek, Persian, Egyptian, Phrygian, Celtic, Libyan, or other (*Epidr.* 17.26.7–11)—contain the accurate observations of ancient thinkers (*hoi archaioi, Epidr.* 1.2.18) who "handed down" (*paradidonai, Epidr.* 3.3.16) their knowledge of reality in the symbolic form of mythical creations (*mythopoiiai, Epidr.* 17.26.8) or explanations (*mythologiai, Epidr.* 8.8.11). In particular, these thinkers expressed their insights in the form of special names for mythological heroes and deities.[2] In his *Compendium of the Traditions of Greek Theology,*

Cornutus identifies such fragments of myth embedded in literature and interprets their philosophical and cosmological truth.[3]

Cornutus explains that sometimes the poets preserved ancient myths in such a way that even though only fragments of the myths remained, their essential truth remained undistorted. But in other cases, the poets clearly failed to understand what the ancient mythmakers were trying to "hint at" (*ainittesthai*) and, like Homer, added their own "fictional accretions" (*ti proseplasthē*) to the genealogies contained in the transmitted myths (*Epidr.* 17.27.20–17.28.1).[4] Cornutus claims, for example, that although Hesiod managed to hand down some ancient theology intact, he also "corrupted a great deal of the true primitive theology" of ancient myth with his poetic embellishments (*Epidr.* 17.31.16–17) (by "theology," Cornutus refers to reflection on the elements of the cosmos, which Stoics viewed as divine). For example, though Hesiod claimed that Chaos was the first reality to come into existence, "the truth" is the Stoic insight "that fire was once everything and will be again in the course of the world cycle" (*Epidr.* 17.28.10–12). And though Hesiod's claim that Night is the daughter of Chaos is "quite reasonably said" (*Epidr.* 17.29.15), "you can," Cornutus tells his readers, "obtain a more perfect exposition than Hesiod's" (*Epidr.* 17.31.12–14). Consequently, the judicious interpreter seeking to uncover the wisdom symbolized in ancient myth must never "conflate the myths" or "transfer the names from one to another" (*Epidr.* 17.27.19–20).[5] In their complete, independent, and pristine form, the myths indirectly express profound messages; since they have sometimes been corrupted by later additions and alterations, any effort at comparative interpretation without prior textual criticism simply increases the chances of arriving at a false understanding.[6]

According to Cornutus, proper interpretation of ancient myths reveals that their authors' philosophical and scientific insights anticipated, or at least were consistent with, the wisdom of later Stoicism. We have just seen that Hesiod failed to grasp a basic point of Stoic cosmology—that everything began with fire, and everything will ultimately return to fire. In another instance, Cornutus finds Stoic scientific insights hidden in a fragment (*apospasma*) of ancient myth (*mythos palaios*) preserved by Homer in the form of the following question posed by Zeus to Hera: "Do you not remember the time I hung you from above and suspended two heavy masses from your feet?" (*Il.* 8.400 in *Epidr.* 17.26.14–15). Cornutus believes that Homer preserved this myth because of its true, inner meaning: "Zeus was said to have hung Hera by golden bonds from the ether (because the stars have something of a golden sheen) and to have fitted two heavy masses (a clear reference to earth and sea) to her feet. Thus, the air is stretched downward, unable to be torn away from either one" (*Epidr.*

17.26.17–17.27.2). Once the key etymology (Hera = air) is recognized, one can see that Homer has preserved an ancient meaning fully consistent with the contemporary Stoic understanding of how the physical elements compose the universe.

Cornutus uses his principal interpretative technique of etymological analysis in his second example of an ancient myth preserved in the *Iliad*— Homer's account of Thetis's rescue of Zeus "when the other Olympians wished to bind him: Hera, Poseidon, and Pallas Athena" (see *Il.* 1.396– 404; *Epidr.* 17.27.5–6). Cornutus analyzes the names Thetis and Briareos etymologically in order to uncover the scientific message that the ancient mythologists intended to convey:

> Clearly, each of these gods individually was continually plotting against Zeus, intending to interfere with this orderly arrangement. And that is just what would happen if the moist element seized power over everything and drenched it all; or, if the fire did and burned up everything; or, the air. But Thetis [*Thetis*], having properly disposed everything [*diatithenai*], set hundred-handed Briareos against the previously mentioned gods, which means, likely as not, the exhalations from the earth, which are distributed in all directions, picturing the division into all the individuals as taking place "through many hands." Consider whether it has received the name Briareos [*Briareōs*] because it raises [*airein*] what one might call the food [*bora*], as it were, of the parts of the universe. (*Epidr.* 17.27.7–18)

Cornutus devotes every page of the *Compendium* to similar etymological interpretations of the names of various gods, goddesses, and other figures that appear in ancient myth, liturgical ceremonies, or works of art.[7]

As a philosopher, Cornutus seeks to align himself (and presumably his students as well) with the ancient theologians: the interpretative ideal is to enable ancient protophilosophers to hand down their insights to their modern peers. Cornutus often constructs a partnership between the ancients (*hoi archaioi* or "they") and the moderns (*hoi neōteroi* or "we"). The ancients are the anonymous figures who, along with more recent poets and writers, "hand down" ancient tradition. The moderns are, of course, enlightened philosophical interpreters such as Cornutus:

> It has, as you know, been handed down from early times [*paradedomenon toinyn anōthen*] that Prometheus formed the human race from earth. But one must consider that Prometheus [*Promētheus*] is the name which was given to the foresight [*promētheia*] of the universal soul, which we moderns [*hoi neōteroi*] call "providence" [*pronoia*]. (*Epidr.* 18.31.19–18.32.3)[8]

One can follow Cornutus's construction of a bridge between ancients and moderns in *Compendium* 7. First, he summarizes the ancient myth:

> Finally, because Heaven was descending continually to have intercourse with Earth, Kronos is said to have castrated him and thus to have put a halt

to his outrage. But then Zeus expelled Kronos from the kingship and cast him down to Tartarus. (*Epidr.* 7.7.17–21)

Drawing on etymology, Cornutus next forges a link between the intention of the mythmakers and the philosophy of present-day interpreters:

> Through these stories they hint indirectly [*ainittesthai*] thàt the ordering at the beginning of the universe, which we claimed was called "Kronos" from "to accomplish" [*krainein*], checked the flow of the surrounding material which was at that time very great upon the earth, by making the exhalations finer. (*Epidr.* 7.7.21–7.8.3)[9]

Cornutus then connects this etymology of Kronos with an earlier etymology of Zeus—not to establish narrative continuity at the level of myth but to point to the cause-and-effect relationships in nature according to Stoic physics (which involves a personification of the world):

> But the nature of the world when it had gained its full strength, which we were saying is called Zeus, restrained the excessive instability of the change and put it in bonds, and thus gave a longer life to the world. (*Epidr.* 7.8.3–6)

Cornutus concludes by assuring his audience of the appropriateness of a different epithet for Kronos by drawing on yet another etymology:

> It is altogether reasonable [*pany eikotōs*] that they also call Kronos "Crooked-counseled" [*angkylomētēs*] since the things he will contemplate are "crooked" [*angkyla*]. That is to say, it is difficult to follow the sequence of the vast quantities of individual items which he produces. (*Epidr.* 7.8.6–9)

Once again, the appeal to what is "reasonable" or "fitting" is not designed to counter charges of immorality but instead to show the consistency of multiple names and epithets with the underlying meanings drawn from Stoic physics.

Etymological interpretation was especially favored by ancient Stoics, who gave it philosophical and linguistic justification. But just as our language of ego and id, drive and obsession, unconscious and subconscious, has long left the circle of Freudian specialists, so the practice of etymology ranged far beyond the bounds of Stoicism in the ancient world, becoming an important technique for interpreters of all philosophical and religious persuasions. Consequently, ancient interpreters who exploited etymological analysis hardly needed to refer to technical Stoic discussions; they could simply count on the wide cultural plausibility that this hermeneutical method enjoyed. Nevertheless, etymology was especially characteristic of Stoic exegesis and was often associated by non-Stoics with other ideas about linguistics and epistemology that were Stoic in origin and character. A review of some of these theories and their relation to the early Stoic practice of etymology will help explain the

connection between Cornutus's philosophical perspective and his etymological method.[10]

One can consider etymology from two perspectives: from an author's
point of view it is a way of representing meaning, while from a reader's
point of view it is a method of recovering the author's meaning. We shall
begin with the author and the production of meaning. Early Stoics opposed the views of the Sophists in the ancient debate over the "natural"
versus the "conventional" origin of language, arguing that the relationship between some words and things was "natural." Ancient and very wise
human beings imposed names that naturally imitated things in the following way.[11] They first absorbed repeated sense impressions of the same
realities. When gathered together in the memory, these impressions gave
rise to "conceptions" (*ennoiai*), which were then directly expressed in
language. The doxographer Aëtius of the first or second century c.e.
describes this process in which an original knowledge of the world led to
the formation of conceptions and the production of linguistic meaning:

> When man is born, the Stoics say, he has the commanding part of his soul
> like a sheet of paper ready for writing upon. On this he inscribes each one of
> his conceptions [*ennoiai*]. The first method of inscription is through the
> senses. For by perceiving something, e.g., white, they have a memory of it
> when it has departed. And when many memories of a similar kind have
> occurred, then we say we have experience [*empeiria*]. For the plurality of
> similar impressions is experience. Some conceptions arise naturally in the
> aforesaid ways and undesignedly, others through our own instruction and
> attention. The latter are called "conceptions" [*ennoiai*] only, the former are
> called "preconceptions" [*prolēpseis*] as well. Reason, for which we are called
> rational, is said to be completed from our preconceptions over the first
> seven years. (Aët. 4.11.1–4 [*SVF* 2.83])

Among all "conceptions," which are general concepts extrapolated from
specific sense impressions, some are culturally determined or result from
education ("conceptions"), while others are more immediately produced
by direct human experience of the world ("preconceptions").[12] The wise
name-givers/mythmakers thus perceived the world, received preconceptions, formulated conceptions, related them to one another, and expressed them by various names and words. For example, echoing common Stoic social theory, Cornutus links the presence of conceptions
(*ennoiai*) or general ideas with the possibility of harmonious human social
relations. He points out that a traditional epithet of Athena, "Giant-killer"
(*gigantophontis*), arose from an ancient wise man's perception that reason
(*logos*) overcomes divisive interpersonal relations:

> We may well suppose that the first men born from the earth were violent
> and hot-tempered against one another, for they were utterly incapable of

distinguishing or of fanning to flame the sparks of community spirit which was inherent in them. But the gods, by prodding and reminding them of their conceptions [*ennoiai*], proved victorious. Indeed, skill in reasoning [*logos*] conquered and subjected them. Thus it seems to have marched out and destroyed them, just as it did the Giants. For those people themselves changed and became different, and their offspring became fellow-citizens through the agency of Athena, "Guardian of Cities." (*Epidr.* 20.39.15–20.40.4)[13]

Diogenes Laertius, quoting Diocles Magnus, gives us some idea of the variety of ways that such conceptions might be formed:

It is by confrontation that we come to think of sense-objects. By similarity, things based on thoughts of something related, like Socrates on the basis of a picture. By analogy, sometimes by magnification, as in the case of Tityos and Cyclopes, sometimes by diminution, as in the case of the Pigmy; also the idea of the centre of the earth arose by analogy on the basis of smaller spheres. By transposition, things like eyes on the chest. By combination, Hippocentaur. By opposition [*kat' enantiōsin*], death. Some things are also conceived by transition, such as sayables and place. The idea of something just and good is acquired naturally. That of a being without hands, for instance, by privation. (D.L. 7.53 [*SVF* 2.87])[14]

Whether purely imaginative (i.e., a centaur or a creature with eyes on its chest) or factual (something that is white rather than black), conceptions are based on direct experience of reality.[15] In his *Compendium,* Cornutus draws on some of the modes of concept formation that Diogenes outlines. For example, he claims that it is well known that the name Ares (*Arēs*) comes from the conceptions of "seizing" (*hairein*), "killing" (*anairein*), and "bane" (*arēs*). He also suggests that Ares may have gotten his name "by opposition" (*kat' enantiōsin*), on the supposition that "those who so addressed him would mollify him" (*Epidr.* 21.40.19–21.41.3).

The conceptions of reality that lay behind such mythical names were captured in more basic linguistic forms that represented reality by imitating it. Such imitation might be onomatopoetic. For example, because *ph*, *ps*, *s*, and *z* are pronounced with a great deal of air, Stoics believed these letters were appropriately used in the words "shivering" (*psychron*), "seething" (*zeon*), "to be shaken" (*seiesthai*), "shock" (*seismos*), and "windy" (*physōdes*) (Pl. *Cra.* 427A). Cornutus indicates that the ancients called Zeus "Aegis-bearer" (*aigiochos*) because of "tempests" (*aigis*) that were themselves named from "to shake" (*aissein*) (*Epidr.* 9.9.10–11). Although this etymology contains a lexical link (*aigi*) between *aigiochos* and *aigis*, it may be more fundamentally grounded in the onomatopoetic "s" of *aissein*. Cornutus is more explicit with the name "Earth": "Because it has been compressed, the earth is called *chthōn*, by imitation [*kata mimēsin*]" (*Epidr.* 28.53.8–9). Imitation might also be synaesthetic (*mel*, "honey," is soft to

the ear as well as to the tongue) or gestural (when one says *nos*, "we," the gesture of the lips points inwards, but when one says *vos*, "you," it points outwards).[16] By such means, the wise name-givers/mythmakers produced a certain number of primitive, mimetically appropriate utterances, from which they then systematically fashioned a variety of names and ultimately language itself. Cornutus's mythmakers were just such wise men—"no common men," but men who were "competent to understand the nature of the cosmos, and were inclined to make philosophical statements about it through symbols and enigmas" (*Epidr.* 35.76.2–5). The key way they made such statements was to "etymologize" (*etymologein*), that is, create by etymology. Thus they "etymologized" the name "Heaven" (*Ouranos*) from "to be seen above" (*horasthai anō*) (*Epidr.* 1.2.3–4).

Names created by etymology are, of course, especially good candidates for etymological analysis. Through such analysis, readers simply reverse the process of linguistic construction, inferring from present linguistic forms the primordial mimetic elements from which the name was composed. Thus Cornutus draws on etymological analysis to recover the original conceptions that the ancient mythmakers enshrined in poetic names—conceptions that contain, at least embryonically, important insights of Stoic physics and ethics.[17] The process begins as early as the first chapter of the *Compendium*. There Cornutus describes a number of etymologically based references to "Heaven" (*Ouranos*) created by these ancient wise men. "Some poets," he says, "assert that Heaven is the son of Akmon, either because they are indirectly indicating [*ainittomenoi*] the indefatigable character [*to akmēton*] of its circuit, or because they had formed the preconception [*prolambanontes*] that it is immortal." In the latter case, "they introduce this through the etymology [*paristasi dia tēs etymologias*]. For we say that the dead are 'exhausted' [*kekmēkenai*]" (thus *a-kekmēkenai*, or simply *Akmēton*) (*Epidr.* 1.2.6–10). In general, early Stoic interpreters such as Chrysippus and some later Stoics such as Cornutus used etymology to reveal the "true meaning" of a name; that true meaning was the meaning that was either originally imposed or systematically derived from an original imposition.[18]

As the last section of this chapter will demonstrate, etymology was often viewed as bizarre and capricious by unsympathetic contemporaries of the Stoics, as well as by some Stoics themselves. But in its most rigorous form, Stoic etymological analysis was in fact loosely governed by principles. Those principles varied, depending on whether the original name-givers were assumed to have generated subsequent words by means of inflection (*klisis*) in declension or conjugation or by derivation proper (*paragōgē*) (e.g., "justice" from "just"). To determine instances of derivation by inflections of the same word, etymologists studied the declension of nouns and the conjugation of verbs. To uncover derivation proper,

they sought out some relation in meaning or sound between two words.[19] As one might expect, the process becomes more difficult the farther away one is from the original naming; Cornutus admits that "Athena's name is difficult to interpret etymologically [*dysetymologēton*] because of its antiquity" (*Epidr.* 20.36.1–2).

Stoic etymology appears to have been part of a more complex account of "meaning," though the evidence for this larger Stoic linguistic system is fragmentary and difficult to interpret. The Stoics seem to have held two views of meaning: nominal and propositional. In general, it seems that etymology was part of the Stoic theory of nominal meaning. Nominal meaning was a physical relationship between single names (*nomina*) and the objects they represented. In a process of primordial naming or dubbing by wise nomenclators, the "essence" or "content" of an object became the "meaning" of the word used to name it. Stoic etymologists presupposed such a view of the production of meaning when they sought to justify particular interpretations of relationships between words and meanings (e.g., Hera as "air") by appealing to more primordial and mimetic relationships between words and things (the name *Hēra* "participates in" the physical element *aēr*, a participation of physical and linguistic reality forged by the shared letters *ēr*).[20]

But this theory of naming was not the only way early Stoics conceived of linguistic meaning. Apparently as early as Chrysippus, Stoics also came to think of "meaning" as propositional—resulting not from single words or names but from propositions or statements. Propositional meaning was based on a distinction between nonmeaningful and meaningful (*sēmantikē*) utterance. A nonmeaningful utterance was a mere "verbal expression" (*lexis*), while a meaningful utterance was a "rational statement or proposition" (*logos*), that is, "meaningful speech issuing from an intention" (*phōnē sēmantikē apo dianoias ekpempomenē*).[21] A person deliberately saying something intelligible makes a meaningful utterance; a parrot repeating the words does not. Expression was meaningful when it signified what the Stoics called *lekta* ("things meant" or "meanings"). An example, borrowed from Seneca (and accompanied by my interpretative glosses), will illustrate what the Stoics meant by such "meanings."[22] If I look outside my window and see a man whose name is "Cato" walking down the street, my perception (the *phantasia* or "apprehensible presentation") of that man may lead me to say, "Cato is walking." My expression "says something" about Cato—namely, that he is walking; this "thing said about Cato" is the meaning of my expression. Unlike my verbal expression, my meaning is incorporeal and, strictly speaking, nonexistent. Nevertheless, it is real. It is also abstract, because in saying "Cato is walking," I have abstracted two components or "conceptions" from the original unitary "presentation" of a man in motion. I have first separated the man

from his motion (neither of which actually exists separately) and then brought together in my expression the abstract conception of walking and the abstract conception of Cato in order to signify the meaning "Cato is walking."

Consisting of words joined together (i.e., a syntactical unit), any meaning is either "incomplete" or "complete." An example of an incomplete meaning is a verb lacking a subject, for example, "is walking." Its incompleteness leads us to ask for more information: who or what is walking? A complete meaning, on the other hand, is a statement or proposition with three components: a predicate (e.g., "is walking"), a grammatical subject, which the Stoics called a *ptōsis* (e.g., "Cato"), and a referent in the real world (e.g., Cato walking). Thus "Cato is walking" is a complete meaning if someone says it about Cato as he walks.[23] When one joins the predicate "is walking" to "Cato" in order to make a statement about a real state of affairs, a meaning is produced. The Stoics make a distinction, then, between single nouns or names and the objects in the world that they represent (nominal meaning) and between sentences and the meanings that they signify (propositional meaning). Nouns fulfill different functions depending on whether they are used independently to denote objects in the world, or as cases combined with predicates to signify meanings.[24]

Cornutus's etymological interpretation in the *Compendium* relies on the nominal, rather than propositional, theory of meaning. Correspondingly, his approach to ancient myth focuses not so much on its narrative character or its syntax as on its nouns, especially its proper names. He is concerned with what has been called the metaphoric, rather than metonymic, axis of his mythical material.[25] In his view the ancient mythmaker is primarily a producer of personifications, turning conceptions of the elements of nature into anthropomorphic gods and goddesses. When he spins stories about these personifications—when he puts his characters into motion, so to speak—he produces allegories. Consequently, while poets such as Homer and Hesiod did not write allegories, ancient mythmakers did. However, Cornutus's own interpretative approach to these allegorical myths is more a matter of decoding names through etymological analysis than of translating in detail the narrative structure of the myths into another, nonliteral narrative. There are, in fact, too many myths, and they are preserved in too fragmentary a form for the individual narratives themselves to carry much weight. However, Cornutus's interpretations do presuppose a background set of Stoic cosmological beliefs that describe a progression from the generation of the *kosmos* by the action of the *logos* to its periodic dissolution in a grand conflagration or *ekpyrōsis*. This sequence is already well known; Cornutus's goal is to investigate in what ways ancient myths reflect this true story of the cosmos. However, the principal point of contact between the Stoic philo-

sophical account and the myths is provided not by the overt mythical plots but by the hidden meanings of names.

In summary, then, Cornutus's etymological interpretation of mythical names involves something like the following scenario. The mind of an ancient theologian receives "apprehensible presentations" from the world around him that physically alter his mind in various ways. These physical alterations are the essence of mental "conceptions," which he then expresses in the form of etymologically generated names as the deeper "meanings" of his myth.[26] For example, Cornutus's report (*Epidr.* 5) of the production of the name "Hades" implies first that one ancient wise man perceived the air that lies nearest the earth and gave it the name "Hades" (*Haidēs*); air was then personified as the god who is the brother of Hera and Poseidon. There are several possible conceptions that this name might convey. The name "Hades" and Hades' mythical association with the other deities (who have already been interpreted as the names of physical entities) may express the conception that air comes into being along with those other natural entities when the *logoi* in nature begin to flow (*rhein*) and produce (*krainein*) things (*Epidr.* 5.4.18–5.5.2). Presumably, the *H* in *Haidēs* would then be derived from the *h* of *rhein* and the diphthong *ai* from *krainein*. On the other hand, perhaps the name is intended to express the conception that the air in question is invisible (*aoratos*); that would explain why some etymologists "divide the diphthong," drop the *H*, and construe the name as *A-idēs* ("Un-seen"—*idein* being synonymous with *horan*) (*Epidr.* 5.5.2–4). Or perhaps *Haidēs* is a name given "by contradiction" (*antiphrasis*): the *Ha* and *d* would thus refer to "the one who pleases" (*ho handanōn*), for "Hades is where our souls seem to go at death, and death is what least pleases us" (*Epidr.* 5.5.4–7). Finally, the ancient mythmakers also called him Pluto (*Ploutōn*), which would be directly derived from the verb "to be wealthy" (*ploutein*), for all things are corruptible and therefore are "ultimately consigned to him as his property" (*Epidr.* 5.5.7–9).

Cornutus is then typical of many ancient Stoic readers of myth and poetry who, positing close correspondences between specific word forms and distinct meanings, sought to uncover those correspondences by etymological interpretation. But some Stoics also observed that in the everyday use of language the relations between words and meanings were indeterminate. Chrysippus noted that all too often the same word meant two things (i.e., was a homonym) or that two different words meant the same thing (i.e., were synonyms).[27] In addition, he observed that readers and listeners were themselves the principal producers of semantic indeterminacy, concluding that "every word is naturally ambiguous since the same can be taken in two or more senses."[28] In effect, propositional meaning and nominal meaning were potentially in opposition—no mat-

ter what the original nomenclators had decided names meant, later users of language might use them differently. Despite their mimetic confidence in etymology, then, even early Stoics were forced to conclude that a simple one-to-one correspondence between words and their meanings or referents could not be assumed; the Greek name "Athens" is plural, but there is only one city by that name; "immortal" relies on a privative prefix that implies that immortality is not a desirable thing but a privation; and far too many words fail to denote objects that physically share their grammatical gender; a "city" (*hē polis*), for instance, is not a feminine entity.[29]

Chrysippus's observation of semantic indeterminacy thus challenged Stoic confidence in the natural links between words, meanings, and things supposedly established by the original name-givers. A tension thus developed very early within Stoic linguistic theory between the mimetically grounded practice of etymology (which appealed to seemingly reliable ancient word-thing relations to certify contemporary word-meaning relations) and antimimetic semantic indeterminacy (due to unreliable word-meaning and word-thing relations). On the one hand, Stoic etymology directly illustrates the central Stoic belief, first suggested by the pre-Socratic Heraclitus, that because *logos* pervades everything, thought, speech, meaning, and reality are necessary co-implicates. On the other hand, a loose thread of semantic indeterminacy is also woven into the very fabric of Stoic linguistic theory. If pulled, this thread unravels the apparent nonlinguistic foundation of etymology. One might argue that despite its recourse to a word-thing relation that seeks to escape linguistic indeterminacy in a privileged prelinguistic origin, etymology fails to reproduce an originally nonlinguistic "apprehensible presentation" but instead describes the derivation of words in terms of the formation and derivation of conceptions, thus remaining at root a linguistic procedure.[30]

From one point of view, despite what Stoic etymologists believed about the "natural" links between words and the world, in practice they relied on a certain semantic indeterminacy: only if words really did not mean just one thing could etymologists depart from the "ordinary" or "literal" mythical meaning of certain words and names. Etymology demanded that customary or consensus readings not "fix" the meanings of words; only then might "Apollo" mean something other than the anthropomorphic deity typically understood to be the proper referent of the name. But while a certain semantic flexibility was needed to get the etymological project started, that project soon came to a determinate conclusion. As Cornutus's *Compendium* shows, the ancient mythmakers' names were not endlessly indeterminate; after the first, misleading mythological sense was set aside, one discovered that the words did indeed mean something—even if there was still more than one possibility to choose from. Once uncovered by etymological analysis, the mythmakers' nonliteral or

extraordinary language turned out to convey the primordial conceptions that had been impressed on their minds by existing realities such as the physical elements of earth, water, and fire. Consequently, although we might think of etymology as a mode of interpretation rooted in a moment of semantic indeterminacy and antimimesis, in the end it produced a new semantic and mimetic affirmation of the true meaning and reference of the text. In Cornutus's case, this true referent was the wisdom of ancient theology, which resembled contemporary Stoicism in its essential features. For Cornutus, etymological analysis enabled the reader to retrieve philosophical conceptions from fragments of ancient myth, making that myth relevant for the constructive work of contemporary philosophical education.

With this overview of the linguistic character and philosophical intentions of Cornutus's etymological practice in hand, we turn next to the question of the larger social and cultural purposes such a mode of interpretation might have served. In the Introduction, we noted three basic ways an allegorical reading can be revisionary. First, it can challenge the literal sense of an established text by offering an alternative meaning. Second, given its challenge to the literal sense, allegory can either endorse or revise culture. On the one hand, if allegory negates countercultural literal senses, it can actually domesticate a subversive text. Allegorical reading can be used to transform an initially revisionary and shocking text (e.g., one that presents divine beings in anthropomorphic guise) into a tamer and more acceptable account. When this happens, allegorical reading becomes an application of the sense of "the fitting" or "common sense"—of the reigning cultural assumptions concerning what is good and proper. On the other hand, if allegory replaces a literal cultural meaning with a countercultural allegorical meaning, it can criticize or revise culture; on such a reading, cultural classics become defamiliarized and nonsupportive of cultural expectations. Finally, allegory can be used to "textualize" cultural meanings. The target for this revision is not the text read allegorically but the allegorical meanings themselves—readers are led to view these meanings in a different light precisely because they are now attached to a new text. One can intensify this third mode of allegorical revision as textualization by claiming further that those cultural meanings came from thinkers who in turn derived them from the author of the text now being read allegorically. The text being read allegorically would then gain a privileged position over competitors and revise the reader's understanding of those competing ideas by placing them in subordinate relation to the allegorically read text.

How, then, does Cornutus's *Compendium* fit within this range of possibilities? On the whole, Cornutus's work seems primarily research-oriented; he is interested in finding the scientific wisdom in ancient

myths, not in defending writers against charges of immorality. However, he is clearly aware of such charges, and while he doesn't make their refutation the governing purpose of his work (as Heraclitus does), he nevertheless insists that what the ancient theologians have handed down in their myths is entirely "fitting." For example, having recognized that "Herakles is the universal *logos* in its aspect of making nature strong, in control, and indomitable" (*Epidr.* 31.62.1–31.63.2), one can recognize that the attributes of this god have, in "more recent stories," been mixed up with those of the human hero by the same name (*Epidr.* 31.63.7–12). Consequently, one should interpret the attributes of the hero (e.g., lion's skin, club, representation as an archer) as symbols appropriate to deity, though "transferred from the ancient theology to the hero" (*Epidr.* 31.63.12–14). One can also interpret other aspects of the story of the human hero as pointing toward divine attributes. Thus the mythical accounts of the hero are fitting and appropriate: the Coans "handed it down quite appropriately [*oikeiōs*] that Herakles cohabits with Hebe (*Hēbē*)." The appropriateness is proved by etymology, for the composer of the account thus shows that "intelligence is mature [*holoscheresteros*], having derived *Hēbē* from *hēban*, 'to be mature'" (*Epidr.* 31.64.3–5). Similarly, Cornutus insists that it was "fitting" (*prosēkein*) for the myths to say that Herakles served Omphale (*Omphalē*), for the point is that it is necessary for

> even the strongest men to submit themselves to reason and to do the things assigned by it, even if there happens to be a more feminine element concerned with inquiry and rational investigation involved in its oracular voice [*omphē*]. And it would not be surprising [*ouk atopōs*] that they called it "*Omphalē*." (*Epidr.* 31.64.8–14)

Similarly, when "Kronos is said to devour the children which are born to him of Rhea," "it is quite reasonably received thus [*pany eikotōs*], since all the things that come into being in accordance with the previously described process of motion disappear again by the same process as the cycle proceeds" (*Epidr.* 6.6.20–6.7.4).[31]

Cornutus composed his work for late adolescents who came to him for instruction in philosophy after having been trained by a *grammatikos* in classical Greek literature. He seems to have held a high view of his profession: he notes at one point that "Zeus is said to have engendered the Muse from memory since he was also the inventor of educational instruction, which is by nature received through disciplined study and secure retention, as something absolutely essential for right living" (*Epidr.* 14.14.3–7). He adds that "the basic element of education is diverting one's gaze from all else and fixing it on the divine" (*Epidr.* 14.15.17–18). Designed as a primer in philosophy, Cornutus's *Compendium*—like most

basic school textbooks—seeks to inculcate the ideals of the established culture.[32] Cornutus seems to have been culturally conservative, using his etymological readings not to overturn but to reinforce cultural ideals, especially traditional religious worship:

> Concerning the myths and the service which is given the gods, and concerning those things which are suitably done for honoring them, you will accept both the traditions of the fathers and the complete explanation, but only thus far: that young men be introduced to piety [*to eusebein*] but not to superstition [*to deisidaimonein*], and taught to sacrifice and to pray, to worship and to take oaths in proper fashion [*kata tropon*] and appropriate moderation in whatever situations may arise. (*Epidr.* 35.76.9–16)

Cornutus seems to have joined with many leading Stoic thinkers in the empire who supported a benevolent monarchy, as long as the emperor remained subservient to natural law and reason and respected the moral will and free speech of the citizenry. Evidence has been marshalled to suggest that Cornutus's etymological interpretation of "Apollo" might even have provided indirect philosophical justification for Nero's well-known aggrandizing self-depiction as Apollo: wearing his hair long in the back, singing to the lyre, and driving the chariot. If so, Cornutus's work might actually have contributed to Neronian imperial ideology.[33] Although Cornutus associated with opponents of Nero, the anonymous author of the *Life of Persius* depicts him as more moderate and circumspect than his politically subversive friends.[34]

While in most respects Stoic philosophers seem to have embraced the same social, cultural, and political assumptions as those held by other philosophers in the Hellenistic world, it is also true that Stoicism could support political subversion. Later Stoics of the Roman period were likely to find themselves numbered among the opponents of the Roman government. Stoics were behind the failed Pisonian conspiracy, designed to assassinate Nero and place C. Calpurnius Piso on the throne. Cornutus himself was exiled around 64 C.E., and his pupil Lucan (39–65 C.E.) was executed, as were Seneca and Thrasea—all for their roles in the plot against the emperor.[35] Philosophy in general was closely allied with subversion in the early Roman empire, and Stoicism in particular fortified its adherents to speak their minds to political leaders without fear of consequences, teaching them to despise the moral corruption fostered by subservience to another power. The Romans consequently made "philosophizing" or "Stoicizing" a crime, partly because these activities suggested an arrogant contempt for governmental authority.[36] It is possible that those who read and understood Cornutus's etymological interpretations of Apollo's symbolism, rather than taking it as endorsement of imperial

pretensions, might have been provoked to criticize Nero's presumption in claiming divine status for himself. Cornutus may have been more politically radical than the *Compendium* alone makes him appear.

But Stoicism did not automatically mean opposition to the principate. Stoics could be found on both sides of the struggle, and in some cases the same Stoic might support the government at one moment and be highly critical of it at another.[37] Stoics were often leading imperial allies: Athenodorus of Tarsus was adviser to Augustus, Seneca was tutor to Nero and later an imperial minister, and Marcus Aurelius was emperor.[38] Even Seneca waited to express his criticism of Claudius (in the *Apokolokyntōsis*) until after the emperor had died. In the *Compendium*, Cornutus does not promote free speech or political activity of any sort; on the contrary, he justifies punishment and criticism and tells those who err to repent.[39] He discusses power and rule as good things.[40] The final assessment seems to be that if Stoic philosophy did indeed offer both the ideals and the courage for cultural critique, Stoic etymological analysis sought to ground Stoicism firmly within the pages of acknowledged cultural classics. If Cornutus's work held any possibility for justifying resistance to imperial ideology, it seems to have come from certain tenets of his Stoic philosophy, not from the application of his etymological hermeneutic. It has even been argued that Stoic philosophy was possibly a cover for political struggles essentially devoid of philosophical import.[41]

READING HOMER AS AN ALLEGORICAL POET

We have seen that Cornutus analyzes certain literary works (as well as art and liturgical practices) because they preserve fragments of ancient myth. He does not interpret literature because the myths it contains are embarrassing or contradict prevailing notions of what is appropriate to say about deities. Instead, he seems to take it as simply obvious that ancient theologians expressed their insights in the form of strange, primitive stories about the deities. Of course, many myths would probably have struck him as embarrassing or shocking if he had thought that their authors had intended them as literal descriptions of the deities.[42] But there is almost no suggestion in the *Compendium* that Cornutus or his students were inclined to take the myths as anything other than strange, archaic stories filled with carefully constructed names and epithets intended to be etymologically unraveled. Cornutus's project is not, then, an apology for traditional anthropomorphic religion, but rather an investigation in what we would call comparative mythology for the sake of enhancing and confirming Stoic philosophy.

In contrast, Heraclitus's *Homeric Allegories* is a defense of Homer against the charge of immorality, leveled especially by Plato and Epi-

curus.[43] Unlike Cornutus, Heraclitus does not try to separate the poet's words from his sources in ancient mythology for purposes of interpretation. If something is in the *Iliad* or *Odyssey*, Heraclitus believes that Homer should be held responsible for it regardless of where he obtained it—for this is apparently the position taken by Homer's critics. Consequently, Heraclitus treats Homer the way Cornutus treated the ancient mythmakers. Like Cornutus's mythmakers, Heraclitus's Homer is portrayed as an original philosopher who chose to convey his philosophical insights by means of seemingly mythical compositions. But, in contrast to Cornutus, Heraclitus uses the term "myth" pejoratively, and the "mythical" character of the Homeric epics is only apparent. For Cornutus, "myth"—if uncontaminated by subsequent literary embellishment—is valuable allegorical philosophy; for Heraclitus, "myth" is impious and unfitting fable. Therefore, Heraclitus insists that readers would judge Homer's poetic compositions "mythical" only if they failed to read them properly, that is, nonliterally. If read literally, the Homeric epics do indeed deserve censure as "impious" and "unfitting" myth; when read "allegorically," however, they are seen to be not myths at all but indirect expressions of profound philosophical wisdom.

Since Heraclitus does not make Cornutus's source-critical distinction between poetic embellishments and mythical originals but treats the two Homeric epics as single, unified narratives, he commits himself to demonstrating that his allegorical readings actually make sense of the Homeric epics as single, coherent stories.[44] Simply showing by etymology how names and epithets reflect an underlying philosophical system will not do the job. Whatever the deeper significance of their names, characters must maintain their identities throughout the epics, and their nonliteral meanings must somehow cohere with their literal, narrative actions. Like Cornutus's assumption of the etymological intentions of the ancient mythmakers, Heraclitus's assumption of narrative unity is tied directly to a claim about authorial intention. Cornutus, we recall, insisted that the etymological analysis he performed was simply putting into reverse the etymological procedures by which ancient mythmakers created the names and epithets they did. The literary or poetic intentions of the authors of the source material, such as the *Iliad* or the *Theogony*, were secondary or even irrelevant; sometimes the intentions of the literary transmitters of myth matched those of the ancient makers of myth, and sometimes they did not. Fortunately, though, as long as the transmitter handed down the names intact (and the longer the process of transmission, the less likely this was), etymological analysis could recover the truth despite what Homer or Hesiod might have intended.

In contrast, Heraclitus locates the relevant intention directly in the poet himself, not in his sources. Heraclitus reads the *Iliad* and *Odyssey* as

though they were intentionally written by Homer as allegories of moral and scientific truths. In his own words, "since the trope of allegory [*allē-gorias tropos*] is common to all others, and is not ignored by Homer, why, having tolerated the despicable things he seems [*dokein*] to have [said] about the gods, shall we not provide a remedy by means of such a defense [*apologia*]?" (*All.* 6.1). Heraclitus justifies his allegorical apology on the grounds that Homer intended to write an allegory. Linking together in narrative fashion the meanings uncovered by etymological analysis, Heraclitus seeks to demonstrate that entire episodes in the two epics have coherent "other" meanings consisting of complex scientific or moral truths with their own internal coherence. Through such readings, Heraclitus hopes to defend Homer against the charge of impiety toward the gods.

According to Heraclitus, an allegorical approach to the epics is justified because Homer is both philosopher and poet, standing within a long tradition of philosophical poets and mythmakers. In his two epics, Homer draws on older myths not for their own sake, that is, to hand over either myth or fiction, but to fashion his own poetic narrative as an allegorical expression of those underlying moral and scientific truths that, as an accomplished philosopher, he has discerned on his own.[45] For example, in representing Hephaestus as lame, Homer "has not handed over [*para-didonai*] to us a lame Hephaestus in poetical fictions [*plasmata poiētika*] to please his audience, nor the mythical [*mythoumenon*] child of Hera and Zeus." To "tell such stories about the gods" would be "truly unfitting" (*aprepes ontōs*). Instead, "in these things, a certain philosophical conception [*philosophos nous*] is hidden by Homer" (*All.* 26.3–5). Heraclitus then proceeds to explain that "Hephaestus" refers to earthly fire, which, in contrast to celestial fire (ether), needs wood to keep burning. Thus Hephaestus is "symbolically called 'lame'" (*All.* 26.10). In this case, Heraclitus immediately shows that his allegorical reading is in fact the reading that Homer intended later interpreters to discover: "Homer says in other [verses]—not allegorically [*allēgorikōs*] but literally [*diarrēdēn*]—that it [the fire] is Hephaestus: 'the inner parts they pierced with spits, and held them over Hephaestus' [*Il.* 2.426]." Lest the reader naively conclude that because Homer says that Hephaestus represents fire, the god actually is fire, Heraclitus also explicitly points out the rhetorical trope that Homer is using when identifying the god and fire: "He says by transference [*meta-lēptikōs*] that the inner parts are cooked by Hephaestus" (*All.* 26.11).[46] At least on one reading of this line, the basis for Homer's allegorical composition (and Heraclitus's allegorical reading) is a belief about divine causality, not a materialistic conception of deity.

We can see, then, that as far as Heraclitus is concerned, allegory is no arbitrary exercise of hermeneutical power over the text; on the contrary, it is the appropriate—indeed, the necessary—hermeneutic for the sort of

text that Homer has in fact produced. According to Heraclitus, Homer himself even points this out by providing an example of just what sort of work he has written:

> As for Homer himself, he is not found using allegories that are ambiguous and sometimes contested. He hands over to us this clear example of the mode of interpretation [*tropos . . . tēs hermēneias*], in the verses in which Odysseus numbering the evils of war and battle, says: "Where the sword is like a sickle that strews the field with straw for very little grain, when the reaping is done and Zeus, the arbiter of battles, has inclined his scales" [*Il.* 19.222ff.]. For the thing said is agriculture, but the thing thought [or intended] [*to nooumenon*] is battle. Beyond all that, [in speaking allegorically] we say the thing indicated [*to dēloumenon*] by means of things different from one another. (*All.* 5.13–16)[47]

Homer thus tells his readers how he should be read. He composed allegories not to obscure the truth or make it ambiguous (as other allegorical writers such as the pre-Socratic Heraclitus sought to do—*All.* 24.3–6), but to make the truth clearly known. When Homer describes the allotment of portions of the cosmos to the deities (*Il.* 15.190–93), the poet "continually allegorizes these [elements] so that the obscurity that appears to rest upon these verses might become clearer by means of continuous exposition" (*All.* 41.12).

But Heraclitus contends that many of Homer's critics—especially Plato and Epicurus—have often misunderstood the genre of his work. Having taken his narrative at face value, they find many of his stories "impious" (*asebeis*) and "unfitting" (*aprepeis*), especially his depictions of the deities. Even though Homer has been the educational and cultural mainstay of Greeks from their early childhood until their deaths (*All.* 1.5–7), such readers heap scorn on the poet. Heraclitus seeks to refute such criticisms by offering correct, allegorical readings as an apologetic. To do this, he consistently separates Homer's narrative into two levels: a surface level of seemingly mythical poetry (the literal sense) and a deeper level of truth or philosophical insight (the allegorical sense).[48] When Heraclitus uses the verb "to allegorize" (*allēgorein*) transitively, he is referring to a single process, viewed either as the translation of ideas into poetic images or the selection of appropriate images by which to symbolize ideas.[49] Thus when Heraclitus says that Homer "allegorizes" a philosophical or scientific idea, he means that Homer has chosen to present the idea in a poetic or mythical form.[50] When he says that Homer has "allegorized" a myth (or character or event), he means the same thing—that Homer has used a myth (or character or event) to represent an underlying scientific or philosophical truth.[51] As an intentionally composed allegory, Homer's literal text "hints at" (*ainittesthai*) or "intimates" (*hyposēmainein*) more than

meets the eye. The frequent use of all these expressions (which are synonymous) points directly to Homer's intention to present his philosophy in the form of allegorical composition.

We can examine the details of Heraclitus's approach by attending closely to two allegorical readings he develops at length: the account of the plague in Book 1 of the *Iliad* and the binding of Hera in Book 15. In both cases, we will observe how Heraclitus struggles to keep literal and nonliteral narratives together. He devotes the first ten chapters of his *Homeric Allegories* to showing that in Homer's account of Apollo's assault against the Achaeans, the poet is actually allegorically describing the natural results of a plague. Of course, Heraclitus's allegorical reading is not intended simply to reveal the obvious point that a plague is under way, for Homer himself says explicitly that Apollo sends a plague on the Achaeans as punishment for King Agamemnon's insult to the priest Chryses and abduction of the priest's daughter Chryseis. Rather, Heraclitus's allegorical task is to show that the basic realities of a plague underlie just those particular details of the narrative that have been criticized for undermining proper conceptions of deity. Homer describes how Apollo, in response to Chryses' prayer for revenge, assails the Greeks with his arrows:

> Phoebus Apollo heard his [Chryses'] prayer and came down in fury from the heights of Olympus with his bow and covered quiver on his back. As he set out, the arrows clanged on the shoulder of the angry god; and his descent was like nightfall. He sat down opposite the ships and shot an arrow, with a dreadful twang from his silver bow. He attacked the mules first and the nimble dogs; then he aimed his sharp arrows at the men, and struck again and again. Day and night innumerable fires consumed the dead. For nine days the god's arrows rained on the camp. On the tenth the troops were called to Assembly by order of Achilles—a measure that the whitearmed goddess Hera prompted him to take, in her concern for the Danaans whose destruction she was witnessing. (*Il.* 1.45–56)

Here Homer depicts a god in human form who uses arrows to kill innocent Greeks (who had already approved of returning Chryseis to the priest in return for a ransom) indiscriminately, instead of punishing the guilty Agamemnon. Ancient critics thus condemned the passage for both its anthropomorphism and its injustice.

Heraclitus's allegorical reading of this scene involves more than simply giving words or names other meanings. Because he views Homer as a writer who composed entire narrative episodes as allegories, he faces the challenge of demonstrating the overall narrative coherence of his individual allegorical readings. He announces that he will set out his allegorical readings in the same order as Homer's own narrative, book by book:

My order of investigation [*taxis tōn logōn*] is the order of the Homeric verses [*hē tōn Homērikōn epōn taxis*]; in each song, by means of a refined [or subtle] science, the things being allegorized concerning the gods [*ta peri theōn allēgoroumena*] are demonstrated. (*All.* 6.2)

Heraclitus thus implies that his nonliteral readings will cohere with Homer's surface plot; although his primary goal is to neutralize offensive passages, he is clearly concerned to preserve as much of Homer's basic literal narrative as possible. Hence, Heraclitus's readings interweave aspects of Homer's literal narrative (especially the verbs) with allegorical elements (principally subjects). As a result, Heraclitus's reading does not simply displace Homer's literal narrative; rather, depending on how well it fits with the nonliteral elements, the literal narrative might prove either inaccurate (by "appearing" to be about some scandalous myth) or accurate (by being shown to be literally consistent with the allegorical meanings of accompanying passages). In this fashion, Heraclitus gives his allegorical readings narrative coherence by drawing extensively on existing features of Homer's own literal story line.

Heraclitus begins his allegorical reading of Homer's depiction of Apollo killing the Greeks with arrows by drawing on etymology to establish two levels of meaning.[52] Taking his cue from a popular liturgical chant ("Apollo is the sun and the sun is Apollo," *All.* 6.6), he rejects a series of historical and cultural interpretations of Apollo's epithets in favor of etymological readings that identify Apollo as the sun. Apollo's epithet Phoibus is not a matronym (from *Phoibē*, mother of Leto) but means "brilliant"; the epithet "far-working" does not come from *Hekaergēs* of the Hyperboreans but means that, like the sun, Apollo "works from afar" (*hekaergos*, from "one who works," *ergazomenos*, "from a distance," *hekathen*); the epithet *lykēgenetēs* does not refer to his birth in Lycia (Heraclitus notes that this is a recent myth that Homer could not have known), but to the "twilight" (*lykauges*) hour or the "year" (*lykabas*, a "path of light") that the sun begets; Apollo is called *chrysaoros* not because he carries a gold sword but because he is brilliant gold in color (*All.* 7.5–13). To this etymological evidence Heraclitus adds his later interpretation of the so-called battle of the gods (*theomachia*) (*Il.* 20.67–74; cf. *All.* 52–58). When properly interpreted, the theomachy also reveals Apollo's identity as the sun, since he is depicted in opposition to Poseidon, who (as Heraclitus will subsequently show) represents water because his name is derived from "drinking" (*posis*) (*All.* 7.14–15). So far, in establishing a series of etymologies, Heraclitus has done little different than Cornutus. But unlike Cornutus, Heraclitus does not propose or accept conflicting etymologies. He rejects those that do not establish, maintain, or even advance the particular set of correspondences that will produce an allegorical mean-

ing isomorphic with the literal narrative.[53] The identification of Apollo as the sun must work consistently throughout the entire episode.

To establish this consistency, Heraclitus proceeds to forge a series of connections between the two narratives that Homer's epic contains. Heraclitus does not use etymology to make the next link in the narrative chain. Instead, having appealed to a series of etymologies to warrant an allegorical replacement of one subject (Apollo) by another (the sun), Heraclitus reads Homer's literal statement about Apollo as a literal remark about a factual reality. Homer says expressly that Apollo was the cause of the deaths. Heraclitus does not attempt to give an allegorical equivalent for the action of killing as he did for the noun "Apollo"; he does not, for example, suggest that "Apollo kills" actually means "the sun shines," and then account for the apparent deaths by suggesting that "death" really means "sleep." His allegorical interpretation of Apollo as the sun preserves the literal action of killing. For Heraclitus, even though the *Iliad* is an allegory, not everything in it is allegorical—at least not at the same moment. Homer says Apollo is responsible for the deaths of the Achaeans, and though the subject is not really Apollo but the sun, and though even for Heraclitus the sun does not literally cause their deaths, the sun does accompany, and create conditions favorable for, literal, physical deaths. All of this squares well with the ordinary truth about plagues; they occur during the summer, when the sun is dry and red-hot rather than more moderate in temperature (*All.* 8.2–3). Heraclitus further supports the consistency and coherence of his reading by establishing from the text that Homer describes Apollo's attack in the summer months. He points out where the poet makes it clear that the Greeks fight their battles only during the summer months when the days are long, the nights warm, the weather good, and the sea calm (*All.* 8.7–10.2ff.). When troops seeking to quench their thirst stir up dust and the vegetation becomes scorched, one knows that summer has arrived (*All.* 10.4–7). At this point, then, Heraclitus draws upon the literal, historical sense of the text to support his allegorical reading.

Having set the stage for his interpretation, Heraclitus then takes a closer look at the details of the offensive passage, with the goal of enhancing the coherence of his reading by making more specific links between the details of the story and its underlying meaning. Homer's report that the arrows clanged on the shoulder of Apollo (*Il.* 1.46) is "not some mythical tale of noisy arrows but actually an expression that contains philosophical insight [*theōria philosophos*]" (*All.* 12.2). Heraclitus agrees that a literal sound occurred; he does not give an allegorical equivalent for the verb "clangs." Instead, he once again changes the specific subject, but keeps the general meaning of the verb: "arrows" refers to the heavenly bodies, and "clangs" refers more generally to sound. Sound was indeed

heard, but it was the music of the heavenly spheres, not the clanging of arrows. Similarly, when Homer says that Apollo's descent was "like nightfall," Heraclitus accepts the literal metaphor, explaining that the pestilential air produced by the sun was not clean and clear but murky. Indeed, the murky air explains why Apollo had to shoot his arrows from a distance ("he sat down opposite the ships"), that is, the sun shone its rays from afar. We can tell that the description of Apollo standing off at a distance and shooting should be understood allegorically because if its literal meaning were pressed, it would become illogical: after all, suggests Heraclitus, if Apollo were an enraged god shooting at someone, he would naturally want to get as close to his enemy as possible. But "at this point" (*nyn*) in his narrative, Homer is not writing history but making an allegorical point, and while he is "allegorizing the sun, he plausibly [*eikotōs*] sets forth the path of the pestilential arrows from afar" (*All.* 13.5). Homer thus creates plausible but unlikely fictions for the sake of conveying meanings allegorically. What is likely are those things that Homer intends to indicate in straightforward fashion. So it is plausible but unlikely that a god who is angry at human beings would shoot at irrational dogs and mules, which, as the narrative has it, were the first to die. What is likely (and therefore is not merely plausible but probable) is that Homer is here drawing on his scientific and medical knowledge in order to describe a common plague phenomenon: animals die before human beings, either because they are closer to the bad air near the ground or because their appetites become uncontrollable. Likewise, Homer draws on his medical knowledge when he notes that the arrows flew for nine days, for everyone knows that the odd days are the critical days of a plague (*All.* 14.6). We see, then, that Heraclitus does not dismiss Homer's literal narrative but brings it into accord with his allegorical intention.

According to Homer, Achilles and Hera save the Greeks from Apollo's "wrath," that is, from the sun-exacerbated plague. Heraclitus argues that it is appropriate for Achilles to help overcome the illness, since he reportedly had been trained by Cheiron (*Il.* 11.832), who had known Asclepius (*All.* 15.1). Note that Heraclitus does not allegorize Achilles (or any other human being in the episode); he simply gives him a literal role consistent with the allegorical realities taking place. Hera also is an appropriate savior, for by Hera, Homer has allegorized a natural element (*physikōs allēgorein*)—air (*All.* 15.2). Heraclitus uses etymology to make this identification: Homer does not call Hera "whitearmed" (*leukōlenos*) "without reason," but because of "what was actually taking place" (*apo tou symbebēkotos*): the bright (*leukos*) air was now replacing the noxious air of the plague (*All.* 15.6). To end the plague, Odysseus, on behalf of Agamemnon, appropriately offers sacrifices to the sun, which the poet confirms when he reports that the celebration and sacrifices ended at sunset (*Il.*

1.472–76). Homer says that the next morning, Apollo sent a favorable breeze, helping them return to camp (*Il.* 1.479), once again going out of his way to show "the particular [intervention] of the sun" (*All.* 16.3)— which Heraclitus elucidates by adding a brief description of how winds arise from the moisture made available by the sun's departure (*All.* 1.4).

Heraclitus thus concludes his reading of Apollo's attack in Book 1 of the *Iliad* triumphantly, declaring that he has "demonstrated the first allegory (*prōtē allēgoria*)." In Book 1, Homer has not given readers "the foolish fury of an enraged Apollo, but the philosophical conception [*ennoia*] of a scientific insight [*physikē theōria*]" (*All.* 16.5). Like the myth-makers in Cornutus's text, Heraclitus's Homer has important conceptions that Heraclitus's allegorical reading has now brought to light. Heraclitus then moves on to other events of Book 1 that need to be read allegorically—Athena's pulling of Achilles' hair to keep him from killing Agamemnon (*All.* 17–20), the revolt against Zeus by Hera, Athena, and Poseidon that Thetis foiled (*All.* 21–25), and Zeus's ejection of Hephaestus from heaven (*All.* 26–27). After providing allegorical readings of these episodes, Heraclitus then continues to work his way through other problematic portions of the two epics.

The revolt against Zeus is also worthy of close analysis because it too reveals how concerned Heraclitus is to preserve the coherence of his allegorical readings with Homer's literal narrative. The offending text (*Il.* 15.18–21, which describes how an enraged Zeus ties two anvils to the feet of Hera, suspending her from heaven with a golden cord) is one we have already seen Cornutus deal with. Like Cornutus, Heraclitus will show that the passage is actually an allegory of the four elements, but, unlike the Stoic etymologist, he also wants to demonstrate that the narrative sequence of the passage represents the proper cosmological sequence. Critics of the passage have failed to notice that not only do these verses attribute the "genesis of the universe" to the deity, but that "the order [*taxis*] of the verses also indicates the four elements continually discussed" by Homer (*All.* 40.2). Heraclitus then takes his readers line by line through the passage, demonstrating that the verses lay out the proper sequence of the generation of the cosmos (ether-air-water-earth), as well as referring to the clouds that separate ether from air:

> Do you not remember when you [Hera = air] were hung from on high
>   [the ether], and from your feet
>
> I suspended two anvils [water, earth], and about your wrists cast a
>
> band of gold that might not be broken? And in the air amid the clouds
> you did hang?
>
> (Il. 15.18–21)

Several questions arise. Why does Homer refer to a band of gold when a band of iron would be stronger and less expensive? Heraclitus answers that "it seems that the area between ether and air is especially similar in color to gold"; the gold chain thus marks the area "where ether ends and air begins, the place also marked off by clouds," just where Hera is said to have been suspended (*All.* 40.10–12). But there is a second question, generated by the appearance of narrative discontinuity: "How could Homer call the band 'impossible to break' when Hera is immediately released, if indeed one must attend to the myth?" (*All.* 40.14). Clearly Heraclitus worries about making his cosmological reading cohere with the literal narrative, but it is noteworthy that he does not ignore but rather highlights the problem. He is able to provide a solution by shifting the referent of "impossible to break" away from the chain holding Hera to the more general force that customarily holds together the cosmos: "The harmony of the universe is maintained by indestructible bands, and the alteration of the universe into opposites is difficult.[54] Homer rightly named 'impossible to break' what would never be able to be disjoined" (*All.* 40.14). Like the passage on the plague, this passage shows Heraclitus once again trying to integrate his allegorical readings with the literal narrative of Homer's epics.

The practice of etymological analysis as found in writers like Cornutus offered to ancient readers the possibility of finding other meanings for words, especially for personal names and epithets. But as noted in the Introduction, etymology by itself is not allegory, for it lacks a narrative dimension. This narrative component is the literary manifestation of a single intention, either of author or reader or of both. Heraclitus offers an example of such a genuinely allegorical perspective: he defends Homer as an intentional composer of allegory, and he offers his own allegorical readings as the recovery and reproduction of that authorial intention.

Did Heraclitus use his allegorical reading to challenge cultural ideals? It does not seem so. In fact, Heraclitus's *Homeric Allegories* reveals, in a different way than Cornutus's work, how nonliteral readings could endorse prevailing cultural ideals by supplying culturally appropriate (in this case, philosophically acceptable) allegorical meanings to culturally inappropriate texts. Moreover, although we have said that claims for originality can be the basis for cultural critique, such claims can also undergird cultural accommodation. Heraclitus's work shows how an allegorical reader could appeal to an authoritative origin to reinforce culturally conservative readings. Claims for originality are in essence claims for an authority bestowed by temporal priority and intellectual superiority, and that authority can be exercised for conservative, as well as radical, ends.

Heraclitus's fundamental goal is to show that Homer's epics are culturally fitting only if read allegorically:

> A violent and hostile case is brought from heaven against Homer for his
> contempt toward the deity. For he has been impious in all things if he has
> not allegorized. Sacrilegious myths, full of foolish combat against the gods,
> run throughout both works, so that if anyone should think that the exposi-
> tion is said poetically without philosophical insight, there being nothing la-
> tent in them in an allegorical figure, Homer would be a Salmoneus or Tan-
> talus, "having an uneducated tongue, most shameful affliction." (*All.* 1.1–3)

Heraclitus goes on to defend Homer's "fittingness" by claiming that his
philosophical insights are original and that they constitute the source
from which subsequent famous Greek thinkers derived their best insights. This double claim for Homer's originality and paradigmatic status
appears in Heraclitus's interpretation of the revolt against Zeus in *Iliad*
1.396–406 (*All.* 21–25). In the midst of battle, Achilles implores his
mother, Thetis, to go to Olympus to ask Zeus to help the Trojans punish
Agamemnon for his insolence. Recalling the time Thetis came to Zeus's
aid, Achilles thinks Zeus now owes his mother a favor:

> For instance, in my father's house I have often heard you proudly tell us
> how you alone among the gods saved Zeus the Darkener of the Skies from
> an inglorious fate, when some of the other Olympians—Hera, Poseidon
> and Pallas Athena—had plotted to throw him into chains. You, goddess,
> went and saved him from that indignity. You quickly summoned to high
> Olympus the monster of the hundred arms whom the gods call Briareus,
> but mankind Aegaeon, a giant more powerful even than his father. He
> squatted by the Son of Cronos with such a show of force that the blessed
> gods slunk off in terror, leaving Zeus free. (*Il.* 1.396–406 in *All.* 21)

While Heraclitus finds the attack on Zeus by his relatives scandalous, he
finds "the rescue of Zeus even more unfitting [*aprepestera*] than the plot
against him; for Thetis and Briareus released him from his chains, but
such aids—to be released by such allies—are unfitting [*aprepeis*]" (*All.*
21.6). But Heraclitus insists that critics of the story have failed to realize
that Homer is here offering philosophy beneath the narrative surface.
The apparently "impious" myth of the revolt against Zeus "is something
that has been allegorized [*allēgoroumenos*]," for "the principle of all things
and primordial nature is theologized [*theologeisthai*] in these verses" (*All.*
22.1). Heraclitus thus argues that the episode is fitting once the philosophical or scientific meaning of its impious literal language is properly
understood.

Before explaining just what this meaning is, Heraclitus makes extravagant claims for Homer's originality. Homer doesn't simply hand down
someone else's science through his poetry; his scientific teaching is based

entirely on his own original insights, which subsequent philosophers and scientists drew upon. Thus Heraclitus begins his allegorical reading of the revolt against Zeus with this announcement: "Homer is the initiator [archēgos] of the scientific beliefs [physika . . . dogmata] about the elements—having been the teacher of each one of those who follow him and of the conceptions [epinoiai] which they appeared [dokein] to discover" (All. 22.2). Thales, for example, argued that water was the primary element after reading Iliad 14.246 ("Ocean, from whom all are sprung") (All. 22.3–7). But it was Homer who first had the true conception (epinoia) of this scientific truth, and, like one of Cornutus's ancient wise men, he expressed his insight that water was "the genesis of all things" through an etymological coinage, "saying that the watery nature is Ocean [Ōkeanos], taking the name from 'to flow fast' [to ōkeōs naein]" (All. 22.7).[55] Similarly, when Anaxagoras made the claim that the foundational substance was the element earth combined with Thales' water ("so that water, mixed with a dry substance, from opposed natures might produce a single homogeneous nature"), he was simply echoing an insight that "Homer cultivated first." Once again, it was Homer who, in Iliad 7.99, "provided Anaxagoras the seeds [spermata] of his conception [epinoia] when he wrote 'Nay, may you one and all turn to earth and water'" (All. 22.8–9).

The opening of Agamemnon's prayer makes it unmistakably clear that when the greatest Greek philosophers proclaimed that there are four elements, they were merely repeating Homer's original scientific insights:

> Zeus, most glorious, most great, lord of the dark clouds, that dwellest in the heaven [aithēr] [Il. 2.412]; thou Sun, that beholdest all things and hearest all things, and ye rivers and thou earth, and ye that in the world below take vengeance on men that are done with life, whosoever hath sworn a false oath. (Il. 3.277–79 in All. 23.3; my emphasis)[56]

Homer here refers to ether by the name "Zeus," "either because he furnished life [zēn] to men or because . . . of his flaming and hot [zesis] nature" (All. 23.6). He allegorically calls air "the Hades below," for without the power to illuminate, air is dark and thus called "the invisible [aidēs]" (All. 23.9–11).[57] The beginning of Agamemnon's prayer thus describes the ether and the four elements (earth, air, fire/sun, and water). This lucid allegory was the source from which later thinkers such as the pre-Socratics Heraclitus and Empedocles derived their own obscure allegorical expressions of the four elements (All. 24). When Empedocles, for instance, speaks of "Zeus, brilliant, Hera nourishing, Aidoneus and Nestor, who wash with tears the mortal origin," he simply "imitates [mimeisthai] the Homeric allegory," referring to ether (Zeus), earth (Hera), air (Aidoneus), and water ("the mortal origin bathed in tears") (All. 24.6–7). Readers should not be surprised to discover that like his epigones, Homer

himself composed allegories: "Indeed, since those who explicitly claim to be philosophers use allegorical names [*allēgorika onomata*], it is no surprise that the one who declares himself a poet allegorized like the philosophers" (*All.* 24.8).

Once Heraclitus has made it clear that Homer is the originator of the scientific truth that four elements compose the world, the account of the revolt against Zeus can be properly understood as "attached to more scientific insights [*physikōterai . . . theōriai*]" (*All.* 25.1).[58] Scientists have observed that the universe will endure only as long as the four elements are ruled by harmony, with no individual element becoming tyrannical and seeking to overstep its proper bounds. If fire, for example, should rapidly boil over, there would be a "common conflagration [*ekpyrōsis*] of the universe, or if water should pour forth, the universe would be destroyed by a flood" (*All.* 25.5). Homer was the first to recognize this truth, and he expressed it in the verses that describe the revolt against Zeus, selecting names that were etymologically appropriate. When one reads the passage with this in mind, one can see that in these verses Homer does not discuss the petty feuds among gods and goddesses but rather "intimates [*hyposēmainein*] a certain approaching trouble in the universe" (*All.* 25.6):

> For Zeus, the most powerful nature, is plotted against by the other elements: Hera, the air; Poseidon, the watery nature; Athena, the earth, since she is the demiurge of the universe and the worker goddess. These elements are first united by means of mixing with one another. When a little confusion arose, providence [*pronoia*] was found to be an aid, whom [Homer] named "Thetis" with good reason, for it is she who fortunately lays down the ordering [*apothesis*] of the universe, establishing the elements in their own laws. Her strong [*briara*] and many-handed power became her ally; how otherwise would the many side-effects of her deeds be able to be eliminated except with great force? (*All.* 25.7–11)

Homer's original scientific conceptions have therefore led him to create a scientific myth, and Heraclitus's etymological analysis enables readers to retrace the line from Homer's poetic formulation back to his original scientific insight (i.e., from the name "Thetis" back to the conception of *pronoia* as an act of "ordering," *apothesis*). Thus Heraclitus concludes his allegorical reading of this episode of Homer with complete satisfaction: he has defended the poet against the charge of impiety by going on the offensive, demonstrating that what appears to be Homeric poetic fiction is actually original philosophy: "Thus the impious bondage of Zeus—inevitably subject to accusation—contains scientific insight in the form of allegory [*physikēn allēgorias echei theōrian*]" (*All.* 25.12).

It is unlikely that Heraclitus's defense constitutes any sort of cultural critique or revision. Hellenistic culture and society provided certain com-

monplace assumptions about fitting and unfitting speech and behavior that prompted Heraclitus to read the poets allegorically in order to defend them. Although the "world" that Heraclitus "discovered" in Homer was the intricate ethical and cosmological world view of eclectic Hellenistic philosophy, it was a world in which he and his philosophically minded readers were already well at home. From Heraclitus's perspective, the critics of Homer are quite mistaken in thinking that Homer was a failed moralist; he was instead a deep thinker writing philosophy by indirect means. Philosophically minded defenders of Homer like Heraclitus countered charges of immorality and impropriety by insisting that Homer was actually presenting a scientific and philosophical world view by means of the seemingly offensive portions of the *Iliad* and the *Odyssey*. To be offended by such passages was simply to miss the point.

Heraclitus certainly desired to preserve, protect, and honor Homer, and he inserted his own eclectic philosophical beliefs into Homeric texts as the texts' true meaning in order to show readers how "Homeric" such philosophy actually was. But for Heraclitus and his audience, an uninterpreted Homer was clearly a strange, offensive, and alien cultural "classic." It is unlikely that Heraclitus intended his allegorical readings to give Homer's text any revisionary power over the eclectic philosophy that constituted its underlying meaning. If such were the case, we would expect the Homeric text to exert some sort of interpretative control over its underlying philosophical meanings; discovering philosophy in just this particular text would then make a real difference in the character of that philosophy. But in Heraclitus's work at least, there appear to be no instances in which philosophy is itself shaped according to the demands of the Homeric text. The "world" that appears in Heraclitus's readings of Homer is invariably a philosophical world view that does not seem significantly challenged or altered by the text whose underlying meaning it is said to constitute.

Both Cornutus and Heraclitus provide interpretations that seem to endorse rather than challenge certain reigning cultural ideals. Heraclitus's readings in particular do not challenge literal senses that endorse cultural norms; instead, his readings neutralize culturally offensive texts by giving them philosophically acceptable nonliteral meanings. Neither writer appears to explore the third revisionary possibility of using allegorical readings of texts as a way of challenging cultural ideals. This possibility would have to await the practices of Jewish and Christian readers of scripture whose sectarian status kept them from being full and comfortable members of the dominant culture.

Up to this point, one might easily conclude that, variations aside, nonliteral interpretation was the pagan Hellenistic norm. But etymology and allegory were not the only hermeneutical tools antiquity possessed

and valued. Indeed, many prominent interpreters rejected both procedures altogether, recommending other ways of reading and composing narratives.

OPPOSITION TO ETYMOLOGY AND ALLEGORY

While the sense of the fitting could call forth an allegorical defense of the poets such as Heraclitus's, it need not. Offensive texts could be neutralized without recourse to etymology or allegory, and claims for originality and priority did not require allegorical modes of reading but only the charge of plagiarism. And there were those, at least as early as Plato, who resisted or even rejected etymology and allegory. Antiallegorical sentiments were common in the age of Cornutus and Heraclitus, as comments by Cicero, Seneca, Plutarch, and the Alexandrian textual critics suggest. Attitudes against etymology cut across party lines: both the non-Stoic speakers of Cicero's dialogue *On the Nature of the Gods* and the Stoic Seneca reject the practice. The Middle Platonist Plutarch reveals a deep ambivalence about the technique he calls "allegory" (which often seems to be identical with etymology). Although he reads Egyptian myths allegorically for their deeper meaning, he also largely rejects allegory as a way of reading the Homeric epics and other poetry. The Alexandrian textual critics also rejected allegorical reading, preferring to label offensive passages interpolations and remove them from the text, or to accommodate them in other, nonallegorical ways. A consideration of the variety of resistance to etymology and allegory shows that interpreters in the time of Philo, Valentinus, and Clement were able to neutralize morally offensive texts and discover hidden philosophy in poetry without recourse to nonliteral modes of interpretation. Consequently, the allegorical hermeneutic of Hellenistic Judaism and early Christianity was not an automatic outgrowth of pagan hermeneutical traditions.

In the three books of *On the Nature of the Gods* (*De natura deorum*), Cicero (106 B.C.E.–43 B.C.E.) presents a debate between the Stoic Balbus, the Epicurean Velleius, and the skeptical Platonist or Academic Cotta on the nature of the gods and the existence of divine providence.[59] Questions regarding the proper way to interpret religious myth arise repeatedly throughout the dialogue. Consequently, Cicero's treatise offers a compendium of some current Hellenistic views regarding the allegorical reading of traditional myths. In particular, it records some of the various negative assessments of nonliteral interpretations of myth and poetry prevalent in the first century B.C.E.

Cicero has the Epicurean Velleius (*Nat. d.* 1.36–43) and the Academic Cotta (*Nat. d.* 3.39–64) subject Balbus's Stoic theory of etymological analysis of mythical names and epithets to scathing criticism. Balbus's views on

the history of religion resemble those of Cornutus.[60] Like Cornutus, he argues that an original, true religion—a "true and valuable philosophy of nature"—has, over time, become corrupted into the immoral myths of the poets. With deep sarcasm, Balbus explains that, thanks to the poets,

> we know what the gods look like and how old they are, their dress and their equipment, and also their genealogies, marriages and relationships, and all about them is distorted into the likeness of human frailty. They are actually represented as liable to passions and emotions—we hear of their being in love, sorrowful, angry; according to the myths they even engage in wars and battles, and that not only when as in Homer two armies are contending and the gods take sides and intervene on their behalf, but they actually fought wars of their own, for instance with the Titans and with the Giants. These stories and these beliefs are utterly foolish; they are stuffed with nonsense and absurdity of all sorts. (*Nat. d.* 2.70)

But unlike Cornutus, Balbus does not draw a line between ancient theological myth and poetic innovation; instead, he wants to separate ancient nonmythical philosophy (as the source of true religion) from later mythical corruption, whether or not at the hands of the poets:

> But though repudiating these myths with contempt, we shall nevertheless be able to understand the personality and nature of the divinities pervading the substance of the several elements, Ceres permeating earth, Neptune the sea, and so on; and it is our duty to revere and worship these gods under the names which custom has bestowed upon them. (*Nat. d.* 2.71)

How does one keep the names without keeping the myth? The answer was provided by the early Stoics—Zeno, Cleanthes, and Chrysippus—who understood the reason behind those anthropomorphic deities who "have furnished the poets with legends and have filled human life with superstitions of all sorts" (*Nat. d.* 2.63). These deities have names that have been produced according to etymology.[61] For example, the "immoral fables" (*impiae fabulae*) that describe how Saturn tried to eat his sons and was in turn imprisoned by his son Jove contain a scientific meaning that etymological analysis can uncover (*Nat. d.* 2.63–64). Such analysis, in both Greek and Latin, reveals that Saturn's Greek name, Kronos, is derived from *chronos*, a "space of time." The Latin form "Saturn" comes from the fact that the god is "saturated" or "satiated with years" (*saturaretur annis*).[62] Such derivations indicate the correct interpretation:

> The fable is that he was in the habit of devouring his sons—meaning that Time devours the ages and gorges himself insatiably [*insaturabiliter*] with the years that are past. Saturn was bound by Jove in order that Time's courses might not be unlimited, and that Jove might fetter him by the bonds of the stars. (*Nat. d.* 2.64)

Only through such etymological analysis can otherwise "crazy errors and superstitions" be tolerated (*Nat. d.* 2.70).[63]

Velleius insists that Balbus's Stoic etymological analysis is actually atheistic because it reduces the gods to mere forces of nature. Thus, against Zeno, Velleius claims that

> in his interpretation of Hesiod's *Theogony* (or Origin of the Gods) he does away with the customary and received ideas of the gods altogether, for he does not reckon either Jupiter, Juno, or Vesta as gods, or any being that bears a personal name, but teaches that these names have been assigned by means of a certain kind of interpretation [*per quandam significationem*] to dumb and lifeless things. (*Nat. d.* 1.36)[64]

And against the first book of Chrysippus's work *Nature of the Gods*, Velleius argues that Chrysippus treats virtually everything as a god, including entities without any claim at all to such status (*Nat. d.* 1.39–40). Velleius contends further that in Book 2 Chrysippus "aims at reconciling the myths of Orpheus, Musaeus, Hesiod, and Homer with his own theology as enunciated in Book 1, and so makes out that even the earliest poets [*veterrimi poetae*] of antiquity, who had no notion of these doctrines, were really Stoics" (*Nat. d.* 1.41). Here Velleius makes it seem as though Chrysippus pretended that the poets themselves intentionally composed allegories, as Heraclitus assumed Homer had done. But there is no reason to think that Chrysippus did more than Cornutus was later to do; both simply used etymology to interpret certain names in some of the myths that the poets preserved and elaborated. Naturally, Chrysippus's etymological analyses, like those of Cornutus, uncovered aspects of Stoic philosophy embedded in the mythical details, as Velleius contends. But this was only to be expected, since both authors understood Stoic philosophy to be the subsequent development and refinement of the one true philosophy, aspects of which ancient wise men surely perceived and recorded, even though they did so in mythical form.[65] Velleius argues, however, that true knowledge of divinity was impressed on all human minds in the form of "preconceptions" (*praenotiones*):[66]

> We have then a preconception of such a nature that we believe the gods to be blessed and immortal. For nature, which bestowed upon us an idea of the gods themselves, also engraved on our minds the belief that they are eternal and blessed. If this is so, the famous maxim of Epicurus truthfully enunciates that "that which is blessed and eternal can neither know trouble itself nor cause trouble to another, and accordingly cannot feel either anger or favour, since all such things belong only to the weak." (*Nat. d.* 1.45)

In one sense, Velleius is claiming that his contemporaries can occupy the same place as Cornutus's ancient theologians and Heraclitus's Homer. They too can be original theologians, for the capacity of accurate theolog-

ical knowledge is something every human being enjoys. Contemporaries of Velleius, therefore, need no etymological analysis of mythical names. Indeed, poetic myth is a distortion, not an expression, of theological insight, for instead of unperturbed and unperturbable deities, the poets offer representations of the gods

> as inflamed by anger and maddened by lust, and have displayed to our gaze their wars and battles, their fights and wounds, their hatreds, enmities and quarrels, their births and deaths, their complaints and lamentations, the utter and unbridled license of their passions, their adulteries and imprisonments, their unions with human beings and the birth of mortal progeny from an immortal parent. (*Nat. d.* 1.42)

Velleius thus leaves readers with an unhappy choice: one must either accept the atheistic etymologies of the Stoics ("the dreams of madmen") or accept the "absurd outpourings of the poets," the "monstrous doctrines of the magi," the "insane mythology of Egypt," and "the popular beliefs, which are a mere mass of inconsistencies sprung from ignorance" (*Nat. d.* 1.42–43). The only sane choice is not to choose but to embrace instead the Epicurean position: poetry and myth are corrupt and theologically useless. In place of a vague, generalized Stoic deity that is active in, but ultimately indistinguishable from, the world, one should accept the existence of Epicurean gods, who may exist in personal form but are unmoved by passion and have nothing to do with the world.

Cicero has the Academic Cotta present an even stronger attack on Stoic etymology. Cotta insists that Balbus's interpretation of the gods as deified divine gifts is an illicit transformation of mere metaphors into realities: "When we speak of corn as Ceres and wine as Liber, we employ a familiar figure of speech, but do you suppose that anybody can be so insane as to believe that the food he eats is a god?" (*Nat. d.* 3.41). Likewise, personifications of moral virtues and passions are simply "abstractions, not personal deities"; they are either "properties inherent in ourselves" or "objects of our desire." Although they are sometimes valuable and worthy of respect, there is no reason to think them divine (*Nat. d.* 3.61). Finally, once one starts to interpret traditional gods and goddesses as virtues, vices, or natural forces, where is one to stop? One must go on to ask whether other, lesser mythological figures such as nymphs, Pans, and satyrs are also deities. Once a deity enters a family tree, does not the whole genealogy become divine in some sense (*Nat. d.* 3.44, 52)? And if one reinterprets the traditional deities, why not Egyptian or barbarian deities as well (*Nat. d.* 3.47)? "Either therefore this process will go on indefinitely, or we shall admit none of these; and this unlimited claim of superstition will not be accepted; therefore none of these is to be accepted" (*Nat. d.* 3.52).

Like Velleius, Cotta observes further that the Stoics themselves ac-

knowledge that ancient Greek myths, if taken in their literal form, undermine all religion. Where the Stoics go wrong is in trying to use etymology to "confirm them [the myths] by interpreting their respective meanings"; they should instead reject the monstrous myths outright (*Nat. d.* 3.60). Thus Cotta asks:

> Again, why are you so fond of those ways of interpreting myths and expounding names [*Iam vero quid vos illa delectat explicatio fabularum et enodatio nominum*]?[67] The mutilation of Caelus [= Uranus] by his son [Saturn], and likewise the imprisonment of Saturnus by his, these and similar figments you rationalize [*defendere*] so effectively as to make out their authors to have been not only idiots, but actually wise men. But as for your exposition of names, one can only pity your misplaced ingenuity! Saturnus is so called because he is "sated with years," Mavors because he "subverts the great," Minerva because she "minishes," or because she is "minatory," Venus because she "visits" all things, Ceres from *gero* "to bear." What a dangerous practice! With a great many names you will be in difficulties. What will you make of Vejovis, or Vulcan? Though since you think the name Neptune comes from *nare* "to swim," there will be no name of which you could not make the derivation clear by altering one letter: in this matter you seem to me to be more at sea than Neptune himself! A great deal of quite unnecessary trouble was taken first by Zeno, then by Cleanthes and lastly by Chrysippus, to rationalize these purely fanciful myths and explain the reasons for the names by which the various deities are called. But in so doing you clearly admit that the facts are widely different from men's belief, since the so-called gods are really properties of things, not divine persons at all. (*Nat. d.* 3.62–63)

The final pernicious result of such interpretation was to dignify harmful things with the names of gods and even to create forms for their worship—"witness the temple to Fever on the Palatine . . . and the altar consecrated to Misfortune on the Esquiline" (*Nat. d.* 3.63).

Such criticism of etymological analysis did not always come from non-Stoics; it could also come from the ranks of the Stoics themselves. For example, in *On Benefits* (1.3.2–10), Seneca (ca. 4–1? B.C.E.–65 C.E.) ignores the complex philosophical and linguistic theories of the Old Stoa that had sustained the etymologies and the high opinion of ancient mythologists as indirect philosophers.[68] He tells his readers that he will comment on the "Graces" described by the poet Hesiod, a comment he admits is really "foreign to the subject" of benefits.[69] The relevant questions are, according to Seneca, "why the Graces are three in number and why they are sisters, why they have their hands interlocked, and why they are smiling and youthful and virginal, and are clad in loose and transparent garb" (*Ben.* 1.3.2). After presenting several interpretations, Seneca offers one of his own, suggesting that it is equally arbitrary:

.

Why do the sisters hand in hand dance in a ring which returns upon itself? For the reason that a benefit passing in its course from hand to hand returns nevertheless to the giver; the beauty of the whole is destroyed if the course is anywhere broken, and it has most beauty if it is continuous and maintains an uninterrupted succession. In the dance, nevertheless, an older sister has especial honor, as do those who earn benefits. Their faces are cheerful, as are ordinarily the faces of those who bestow or receive benefits. They are young because the memory of benefits ought not to grow old. They are maidens because benefits are pure and undefiled and holy in the eyes of all; and it is fitting that there should be nothing to bind or restrict them, and so the maidens wear flowing robes, and these, too, are transparent because benefits desire to be seen. (*Ben.* 1.3.4–5)

Some such pedestrian nonliteral reading is always possible, implies Seneca, if anyone unduly enamored of the Greeks should think it necessary. But it is quite unacceptable to interpret the names of the Graces etymologically. Although "each one twists the significance of these names to suit himself, and tries to make them fit some theory," the fact of the matter is that "Hesiod simply bestowed on the maidens the name that suited his fancy" (*Ben.* 1.3.6).

According to Seneca, a prime example of such a "twister" of names is Chrysippus. Chrysippus says little about "the duty itself of giving, receiving and returning a benefit" (*Ben.* 1.3.8) (i.e., about Seneca's own moral concerns) and does not produce interpretations that illustrate moral teaching. Instead, he makes his readings the vehicle for his own teaching:[70]

Chrysippus says that the three Graces are daughters of Jupiter and Eurynome, also that, while they are younger than the Hours, they are somewhat more beautiful, and therefore have been assigned as companions to Venus. In his opinion, too, the name of their mother has some significance, for he says that she was called Eurynome because the distribution of benefits is the mark of an extensive fortune.[71] (*Ben.* 1.3.9)

Seneca's criticism is twofold. First, Chrysippus's etymology violates ordinary narrative sequence; he interprets "just as if a mother usually received her name after her daughters" (*Ben.* 1.3.10). Seneca's second charge is that Chrysippus acts "as if the names that poets bestow were genuine" (*Ben.* 1.3.10). "Surely," he exclaims, "no one will believe also that the names which Hesiod assigned to the Graces have any bearing upon the subject" (*Ben.* 1.3.6). But Chrysippus, like the later Cornutus, would have made just such an assumption about ancient mythological names that had been generated on the basis of the accurately perceived qualities of things. Seneca, however, holds an altogether different view of the poets as name-givers:

As a nomenclator lets audacity supply the place of memory, and every time that he is unable to call anyone by his true name, he invents one, so poets do not think that it is of any importance to speak the truth, but, either forced by necessity or beguiled by beauty, they impose upon each person the name that works neatly into the verse. (*Ben.* 1.3.10)

Seneca's judgment that names are selected because they work "neatly into the verse" owes virtually nothing to the Old Stoic confidence in the correspondence between expressions and meanings and the careful analysis of morphology that such correspondence entailed. His comment hides a revolution in Stoic sensibility; while Old Stoic etymology drew upon an ever-present correspondence between word (*logos*), meaning (*lekton*), and nature (*physis*)—a correspondence implied by Cornutus's etymologizing—Seneca's criticism ignores such correspondences, reflecting a loss of interest in the curious mixture of Stoic physics and logic that supported Chrysippus's, Balbus's, and Cornutus's etymological hermeneutic.[72] Cornutus, for whom the Old Stoa remained authoritative, had offered a much more extensive analysis of the Graces, including etymological analysis of each of their names (cf. *Epidr.* 15.18–20). But for Seneca, all that matters now is surface diction alone. Without the classic Stoic philosophical understanding of how words, meanings, and things mutually informed one another, traditional Stoic etymology becomes either trivialized or reduced to a matter of arbitrary moral illustration.

The Middle Platonist Plutarch's (ca. 45–125 c.e.) attitude toward non-literal interpretation of ancient myth stands somewhere between Balbus's unqualified approval and Cotta's complete rejection. On the one hand, in his treatise *On Isis and Osiris,* Plutarch suggests that a proper understanding of myth requires various forms of symbolic or allegorical interpretation. But in his treatise *How the Young Man Should Study Poetry,* he implicitly agrees with much of Plato's attack on allegorical reading for failing to neutralize the pernicious effects of immoral poetry. Consequently, he looks for other ways to preserve the poets' central place in moral education.[73] In this treatise, Plutarch shows young readers of poetry other ways of turning myth and poetry into a morally satisfying propaedeutic for philosophy.[74]

In his analysis of the myths of Isis and Osiris, Plutarch seeks to chart a middle ground between the extremes of atheism and superstition.[75] On the one hand, he argues that one should support popular religion, though not by following the atheistic Stoics who reduce divine beings to the status of mere natural or moral forces. On the other hand, one should not take the myths literally; such interpretations are absurd and unfitting superstition. What is called for are symbolic readings that allow one to

continue without superstition to revere popular gods as authentic deities. The key to making such symbolic readings lies in the following hermeneutical principle, which draws on Plato's contrast between *mythos* and *logos:* "We must not treat the myths as wholly factual accounts, but take what is fitting [*to prosphoron*] in each episode according to the principle of likeness" (*De Is. et Os.* 374E). This seems to suggest that interpreters need to match certain aspects of myth to philosophical and ethical meanings they already possess; whatever matches moral goodness and truth is to be retained as the authentic meaning.

Like Cornutus, Plutarch thus distinguishes between ancient mythology that contains philosophical truth and pure poetic fiction that does not. Consider, for example, the seemingly inappropriate myth of "the dismemberment of Horus and the decapitation of Isis" (*De Is. et Os.* 358E). Clearly such "most outrageous" episodes cannot literally have happened. But one should not assume that these myths are just bad poetry—the "flimsy stories and hollow figments such as poets and prosewriters weave and spread out before us, like spiders creating from themselves, as first principles which are quite unfounded" (*De Is. et Os.* 358E–F). On the contrary, ancient myth is not poetic fiction but "an image of a reality which turns the mind back to other thoughts" (*De Is. et Os.* 359A). So when ancient Egyptian mythmakers said that the sun-god rises from a lotus flower as a newborn babe, they actually "represent sunrise, symbolizing [*ainittomenoi*] the rekindling of the sun from amid moisture," and when they call Okhus, king of the Persians, "sword," they do so because "they compare [*pareikazontes*] the harshness and wickedness of his character with the instrument of death." If one performs this sort of reverent, philosophical reading of ancient myths—and if one continues to observe the sacrifices or the other rituals based on them—one can avoid all superstition (*De Is. et Os.* 355B–C).

Plutarch seems to approve of the sort of etymological interpretations we have seen the Stoic Cornutus employ, which he calls "allegorical." He praises Egyptian interpreters who repeat Stoic etymologies when they say that

> just as the Greeks explain Cronus allegorically [*allēgorein*] as time [*chronos*], Hera as the air [*aēr*], and the birth of Hephaestus as the change of air into fire, so among the Egyptians Osiris is the Nile uniting with Isis as the earth, while Typhon is the sea into which the Nile falls and so disappears and is dispersed, save for that part which the earth takes up and receives, becoming fertile through it. (*De Is. et Os.* 363D)

Similarly, when the Egyptians tell how Apopis, brother of the sun-god Helios, warred against Zeus and how Zeus defeated him with the help of

Osiris and made Osiris his son, calling him Dionysus, the interpreter can demonstrate that "the mythical aspect of this tale is connected with a physical truth [*physis alētheia*]" for

> the Egyptians give the name Zeus to the wind, to which the dry and fiery element is hostile; this element is not the sun, but has a certain affinity with the sun, and the moisture, quenching the excess of the scorching heat, increases and strengthens the exhalations by which the wind is nourished and flourishes. (*De Is. et Os.* 365D)

Plutarch thus seems to endorse the practice he calls "allegorizing," which in fact consists of rather typical applications of etymological analysis. But he resists taking the technique as far as the Stoics (who, thereby, turn the deities into mere natural occurrences), for this is simply atheism in disguise. Instead, Plutarch's Platonic sensibilities lead him to resist what he takes to be the materialistic (and thus atheistic) reductionism of Stoic etymology. While etymology is useful in avoiding superstition, it cannot be allowed to undermine the very deity of the gods. Despite his use of etymology when discussing the myth of Isis and Osiris, Plutarch criticizes Stoic etymological interpretations. For example, while one should not read words carelessly, one should also not indulge in the "mock seriousness" of Cleanthes, as when he reads the phrase "Zeus, Lord of Dodona," *Zeu ana Dōdōnaie*, (*Il.* 16.233) by taking the last two words, *ana Dōdōnaie*, as a single word, with *ana* meaning "up," "as though the vapor exhaled from the earth were 'updonative' [*anadōdōnaion*] because of its being rendered up [*dia tēn anadosin . . . onta*]!" (*De aud. poet.* 31E).[76] Plutarch echoes Seneca when he adds that Chrysippus is simply being "petty" when he "wrests the words ingeniously, yet without carrying conviction, as when he would force the phrase 'wide-seeing' son of Chronos [cf. *Il.* 1.498] to signify 'clever in conversation,' that is to say, with a widespread power of speech" (*De aud. poet.* 31E). Plutarch recommends that the young reader of poetry leave these sorts of inquiries to the grammarians, attending instead to what is more probable and morally useful (*De aud. poet.* 31F).

In the end, Plutarch tends to read the myths as collections of images pointing beyond themselves to a higher mystical reality. The Egyptian priests hint darkly at this hermeneutical insight when they claim that Osiris (who is identical with the Greek Hades and Pluto) rules over the dead. Popular religion misunderstands this claim, concluding too literally that the Egyptian priests are thinking of Osiris lying under the earth, among corruptible bodies. But this is a false understanding, for Osiris is actually incorruptible, far from earth in an eternal realm. Human beings seek knowledge of this hidden god, and the myth in which Isis searches for Osiris is itself an allegory of allegorical reading—of the need to search through the surface of myth to its underlying spiritual meaning:

The souls of men here, hedged in as they are by the body and its emotions, have no association with the god save for the dim vision of his presence which they achieve by the understanding gained through philosophy; but whenever they are freed and pass over to the formless, invisible, dispassionate and holy kingdom, then is this god their leader and king, for depending on him, they behold insatiably and desire the beauty which is, to men, ineffable and unutterable. This beauty, as the ancient story shows, Isis ever loves, and she pursues it and unites with it, filling this our world with all the beautiful and good qualities which have a part in creation. Such is the interpretation of these matters which is most becoming to the gods (*ho malista theois prepōu logos*). (*De Is. et Os.* 382E–383A)[77]

But what of readers who have not yet reached the heights of philosophical contemplation through their nonliteral reading of otherwise offensive mythology? What of young students just beginning their study of literature? These readers must understand that while one should avoid the Epicurean rejection of all poetry, it will still be necessary to separate out philosophical themes from mere myth (*De aud. poet.* 15D). But allegorical reading is not the way to achieve this end; distilling the good from the bad is not the same as reinterpreting the bad as the good. First of all, students need to recognize that poets often lie. The poets understood that audiences preferred entertaining fiction to harsh truth, so they gave their readers what they wanted. As a result, "we do not know of any poetic composition without myth [*amythos*] or without falsehood [*apseudēs*]" (*De aud. poet.* 16C). In contrast to Heraclitus's Homer, who tells readers to interpret his poems allegorically, Plutarch's Homer instructs readers to regard certain passages of his epics as fictional. For instance, if readers find themselves disturbed at Homer's account of the dead Achilles and Agamemnon stretching forth their hands, desiring to be alive (*Od.* 11.470, 390), they should recall the Homeric verse "Hasten eager to the light, and all you saw here / Lay to heart that you may tell your wife hereafter" (*Od.* 11.223), for this is Homer's way of letting readers know that the business about a visit to the shades "is fit stuff for a woman's ear because of the element of fable [*to mythōdes*] in it" (*De aud. poet.* 16E–F). Even when Homer, Pindar, and Sophocles are not deliberately deceiving, they often pass along false material unintentionally (*De aud. poet.* 16F) and sometimes describe things even they do not really believe (*De aud. poet.* 17C). Like Plato, Plutarch fears that readers will unwittingly be drawn into the emotions and passions of fictional, but highly dramatic, scenes (*De aud. poet.* 17D).

In effect, students must learn to assess poetry not as a straightforward prescription for action (it is, after all, "not greatly concerned with truth," *De aud. poet.* 17D), but as an imitative art analogous to painting that reproduces human life in both its good and bad aspects. One must be able

to applaud an appropriate rendering of an unfitting thing without com-
mending the thing itself:

> For by its essential nature the ugly cannot become beautiful; but the imita-
> tion [*mimēsis*], be it concerned with what is base or with what is good, if only it
> attain to the likeness, is commended. If, on the other hand, it produces a
> beautiful picture of an ugly body, it fails to give what propriety [*to prepon*]
> and probability [*to eikos*] require. (*De aud. poet.* 18A)[78]

Even the depiction of monstrous (*atopoi*) acts (e.g., Timomachus's painting of Medea slaying her children) can be acceptable, provided that the
"subject in hand has been properly imitated [*mimeisthai prosēkontōs*]" (*De
aud. poet.* 18A–B). As for the thing itself, readers should see whether the
poet condemns or praises it. Heraclitus, we recall, resorted to allegory
to deal with Agamemnon's seemingly unfitting treatment of the priest
Chryses. But Plutarch does not recommend allegory as a way of dealing
with this difficult scene. Instead, one should attend to the moral commentary that the poet himself appends to his descriptions: "For he in advance
discredits the mean and calls our attention to the good in what is said." In
the case of Agamemnon and Chryses, Homer "all but protests and proclaims that we are not to follow or heed the sentiments expressed, as being
monstrous [*atopoi*] and mean" (*De aud. poet.* 19B). Before depicting Agamemnon's harsh treatment of the priest, Homer "says in advance: 'Yet
Agamemnon, Atreus' son, at heart did not like it; harshly he sent him
away'" (*Il.* 1.24–25), meaning, says Plutarch, "savagely and wilfully and
contrary to what he should have done" (*De aud. poet.* 19B–C). And though
Homer puts in Achilles' mouth the bold words "Drunken sot, with eyes of
a dog and the wild deer's courage" (*Il.* 1.224–25), he also "intimates his
own judgement in saying, 'Then once more with vehement words did the
son of Peleus / Speak to the son of Atreus, nor ceased as yet from his
anger'" (*Il.* 1.222–23). With these additional words, Homer has made it
clear to readers "that nothing spoken with anger and severity can be
good" (*De aud. poet.* 19C). In various other ways, then (e.g., using adverbs
to evaluate action morally, adding closing lines that function as moral
verdicts), Homer enables his own text to evaluate itself.

If readers find themselves confronted with both good and bad lines,
they must always advocate the better side (*De aud. poet.* 20C). If Homer
gives descriptions of gods "being cast forth by one another, their being
wounded by men, their disagreements, and their displays of ill-temper,"
the reader should turn to other places where the poet speaks of divine repose and tranquillity, for these are "sound opinions about gods, and true,"
whereas the others are "fabricated to excite men's astonishment" (*De aud.
poet.* 20E–F). If the poet does not himself provide good lines as antidotes

to his bad ones, students must turn to other famous poets (*De aud. poet.* 21D). Sometimes one can change the sense from bad to good simply by considering the context more carefully (*De aud. poet.* 22Bff.),[79] by taking the words in another way (*De aud. poet.* 22C), or by correctly reading words that customarily have more than one meaning (*De aud. poet.* 22F).[80]

Plutarch is also aware of the claim by interpreters like Cornutus that mythmakers are simply translating their "conceptions" of the forces of the universe into the mythical names of gods and goddesses. But he wants to make a distinction between two kinds of conceptions: those about deities and those referring to things that deities provide or cause:

> When the poets employ the names of the gods, sometimes they apprehend in their conception [*ennoia*] the gods themselves, and at other times they give the same appellation [*homōnymōs prosagoreuontes*] to certain faculties [*dynameis*] of which the gods are the givers and authors. (*De aud. poet.* 23A)

In effect, Plutarch can produce the same meaning that Cornutus elicits through etymological analysis simply by saying that poets use the names of deities as metaphors. When Archilochus prays, "Hear my prayer, O Lord Hephaestus," he is clearly referring to the god. But when, upon the death at sea of his sister's brother, he says he might have moderated his grief "If upon his head and his body so fair, / All in garments clear, Hephaestus had done his office," he speaks not of the god but of fire (*De aud. poet.* 23B). In the case of Zeus, when one recognizes the presence of metaphor in poetic descriptions, "a corrective is to be found for most of the seemingly monstrous [*atopōs*] statements" regarding him (*De aud. poet.* 24A). It is easy to tell when the poet speaks literally about the deity, and when he speaks about the deity's actions; the literal sense is, as always, determined by cultural and religious propriety: "Wherever there is appropriateness, reason, and probability in the use of the name, let us believe that there the god himself is properly named [*kyriōs onomazesthai*]" (*De aud. poet.* 24B).

Finally, readers need to recognize instances in which the poets are exploring the complexity of human character. Unlike the Stoics, who insist on an absolute separation of vice and virtue, assuming "that the ignorant man is quite wrong in all things, while, on the other hand, the man of culture is right in everything" (*De aud. poet.* 25C), Plutarch thinks the poets have a more complex, nuanced sense of character, which their imitative art represents. Poetic imitation is effective because it draws on truth as well as falsehood; that is why it is neither direct copying nor pure fantasy. Consequently, imitation involves both vice and virtue, and the reader of poetry should neither commend everything he reads nor (like Stoic etymologists?) contrive "some specious quibbles to explain base

actions." Instead, readers should understand that the poets have a more sophisticated understanding of poetic imitation: for them,

> poetry is an imitation of character and lives, and of men who are not perfect or spotless or unassailable in all respects, but pervaded by emotions, false opinions, and sundry forms of ignorance, who yet through inborn goodness frequently change their ways for the better. (*De aud. poet.* 26A)

Whatever technique one uses, however, one should not turn to allegory in order to evade an unacceptable meaning; allegorical readings distort the author's own intention to lay things out in ways that reveal his own implicit moral judgment:

> By forcibly distorting these myths [*mythoi*] through what used to be termed "deeper meanings" [*hyponoiai*],[81] but are nowadays called "allegorical interpretations" [*allēgoriai*], some persons say that the sun is represented as giving information about Aphrodite in the arms of Ares, because the conjunction of the planet Mars with Venus portends births conceived in adultery, and when the sun returns in his course and discovers these, they cannot be kept secret. And Hera's beautifying of herself for Zeus's eyes [*Il.* 14.166ff.], and the charms connected with the girdle, such persons will have it, are a sort of purification of the air as it draws near the fiery element. (*De aud. poet.* 19E–F)

But to read in such allegorical fashion is to miss the lesson the poet is trying to convey, "as though the poet himself did not afford the right solutions":

> For, in the account of Aphrodite, he teaches those who will pay attention that vulgar music, coarse songs, and stories treating of vile themes, create licentious characters, unmanly lives, and men that love luxury, soft living, intimacy with women, and "changes of clothes, warm baths, and the genial bed of enjoyment [*Od.* 8.239]." (*De aud. poet.* 19F–20A)

Similarly, Homer makes his moral perspective clear when he has Zeus comment to Hera: "So you may see if you gain anything from the love and caresses / Won by your coming afar from the gods to deceive me" (*Il.* 15.32–33). Here, remarks Plutarch, Homer "has shown excellently well how the favor that women win by philters and enchantments and the attendant deceit in their relations with their husbands not only is transitory and soon sated and unsure, but changes also to anger and enmity, so soon as the pleasurable excitement has faded away" (*De aud. poet.* 20B). Thus Plutarch can conclude:

> The description and portrayal of mean actions, if it also represent as it should the disgrace and injury resulting to the doers thereof, benefits instead of injuring the hearer. Philosophers, at any rate, for admonition and instruction, use examples taken from known facts; but the poets accomplish

the same result by inventing actions of their own imagination, and by recounting mythical tales. (*De aud. poet.* 20B–C)

Plutarch points to a passage in the *Iliad* as a good example of such poetic invention for the purpose of pedagogy. In *Iliad* 24.130, Thetis "incites her son to pleasures and reminds him of love," a passage Plutarch admits "appears most shameful." As we shall see, Alexandrian editors removed this passage as non-Homeric because it was felt to be inconsistent with the behavior expected from goddesses and heroes. But Plutarch recommends reading the passage in a way that makes it "wholesome and profitable" even though it seems preposterous (*atopos*):

> But even there we must contrast Achilles' mastery of himself, that although he is in love with Briseis, who has come back to him, and although he knows that the end of his life is near, yet he does not make haste to enjoy love's pleasures, nor, like most men, mourn for his friend by inactivity and omission of his duties, but as he refrains from such pleasures because of his grief, so he bestirs himself in the business of his command. (*De aud. poet.* 33A)

As a moralist faced with too many unacceptable myths, Plutarch takes a position that largely rejects the extreme solutions of Stoic etymologists like Cornutus and allegorists like Heraclitus. He is unconcerned to demonstrate that a particular philosophy lies hidden on every page of Homer, behind every morally shocking myth. Instead, he wants to show that something of moral value can be found on the "surface" of the poetry. When a moral meaning is found, it should be supported by similar statements from philosophers, who themselves should then be credited as its original discoverers (*De aud. poet.* 35F). Plutarch here makes his own appeal to the authority of originality, elevating the philosophers over the poets.[82] By searching out philosophical parallels and recognizing the philosophical origins of poetry's moral insights, students are enabled to "bring the poet's work out of the realm of myth and impersonation" and thus whet their appetites for the direct study of philosophy (*De aud. poet.* 36D). Philosophy in the form of poetry prepares the young student to resist (and, ultimately, to break with) the past inculcation of immoral attitudes. A student comes to philosophy with a head full of

> what he has always heard from his mother and nurse, and, I dare say, from his father and tutor as well, who all beatify and worship the rich, who shudder at death and pain, who regard virtue without money and repute as quite undesirable and a thing of naught. (*De aud. poet.* 36E)

Breaking with this past and confronting philosophy directly would be too much, however—it would be like breaking the chains of Plato's cave and taking a direct look at the sun. Poetic philosophy provides a necessary mediation; through it, one can, in a kind of "reflected light," confront the

"dazzling rays of truth" without being "distressed" or "trying to get away from them" (*De aud. poet.* 36E). Plutarch thus offers a range of interpretative strategies to enable students to turn Greek poetry to moral advantage, avoiding what is morally shocking and endorsing what is appropriate, and thus being "transported by poetry into the realm of philosophy" (*De aud. poet.* 37B).

However, as Plutarch himself indicates, there was another way of dealing with the morally dubious passages in classical literature. Instead of resorting to etymology, allegory, or moralizing strategies, one could declare that the offending passages had never really been written by the author at all, but had been interpolated into the text by others. Sometimes, in order to secure a morally meaningful message, it may be necessary to emend the text (cf. *De aud. poet.* 33Cff.).[83] The philologists in Alexandria who edited the texts of Greek literature frequently adopted this strategy when confronted by unacceptable portions of "canonical" Greek literature.[84] Although they preserved allegorical readings by others, these Alexandrian textual critics did not subject the text of Homer to allegorical readings in order to lay bare a second, more fitting sense.[85] Instead, like many other literary scholars in the Hellenistic and Greco-Roman periods, they found other ways to preserve the "fittingness" of cultural classics, especially their literary fittingness or "Hellenicity" (*Hellēnismos*), their pure and correct Greek literary style.[86]

"Analogy" or regularity of inflection was one important criterion of literary propriety or Hellenicity. Because the best Greek authors were believed to have been rigorously consistent in their use of language, morphological regularity, rather than striking originality, was the key to admission into the Alexandrian "canon" or official list of outstanding classical authors. By first gathering from the writings of these authors words with similar primary forms and then classifying the similarities and differences in their inflections, Alexandrian editors were able to deduce the rules of regular inflection that governed different, but clearly related, word forms.[87] As a criterion of Hellenicity, morphological regularity was far more than a matter of philological theory or aesthetic preference; it was also the practical presupposition of Alexandrian textual editing. Morphological irregularities detected in the works of typically regular Greek authors were considered clear signs of corruptions that had slipped into scribal copies of the author's autograph.[88] In order to identify such irregularities, the Alexandrian editor needed first to establish the paradigms of normal usage, from which careless scribes (but never the author) might have deviated. The problem of deviations was, of course, compounded when an editor faced not only corruptions in a single text but the variants presented by multiple manuscripts or created by the evolution from Homeric to Attic Greek.[89]

Although the recurrence of similar grammatical forms enabled Alexandrian editors to determine the authenticity of words and phrases in the texts of the Greek poets, thematic considerations also influenced their editorial and interpretative decisions. We have already seen that in the wake of Plato's scathing criticisms of Homeric representations of the gods (which followed the lead of earlier attacks by Xenophanes) Greek literary critics such as Heraclitus sought to defend the poet against charges of thematic "unfittingness."[90] This critical and interpretative principle was especially important for the work of the Alexandrian editors.[91] Homer was not only likely to have written in a morphologically consistent way; he was also likely to have said certain things and unlikely to have said others. The Alexandrian sense of what was "fitting" for Homer was thus as much a matter of thematic content as of linguistic form.[92]

To a great extent, then, ancient Alexandrian assessment of the authenticity of Greek literature was governed by often implicit, but nevertheless determinative, assumptions about what was proper and fitting speech and behavior for gods and goddesses, heroes and heroines. Like the search for formal linguistic regularity at the level of individual words and phrases, the search for the fitting at the thematic level of character and plot was fueled by a desire for consistency and a distaste for deviance. Consistency of grammatical form and consistency of speech and action that reflected conventional religious and cultural values were closely related critical and hermeneutical ideas. As a result, texts displaying unfitting (*aprepēs*) or wholly monstrous (*atopos*) deviance were either assimilated to existing grammatical paradigms and prevailing cultural norms or else marked as spurious.[93]

The scholia on the Homeric epics and Greek comedies show how this sense of the fitting led to textual athetization. In contrast to commentary on heroic epic, which sought to eliminate violations of the sense of the fitting, commentary on Greek comedy exploited such violations for comic effect. Several examples drawn from both sorts of scholia will demonstrate the way the sense of the fitting led to Alexandrian nonallegorical editorial and interpretative decisions. In Book 3 of the *Iliad*, Helen is led to her bedroom by the goddess Aphrodite, who has just rescued Paris from the hands of Menelaus and deposited him there to await her:

> When they reached the beautiful house of Paris,
> the maids in attendance betook themselves at once to their tasks,
> while Helen, the great lady, went to her lofty bedroom.
> There the goddess herself, laughter-loving Aphrodite, picked up a chair,
> carried it across the room and put it down for her in front of Paris.
> Helen, daughter of aegis-bearing Zeus, sat down on it,
> and turned her eyes aside and began by scolding her lover.

> (*Il.* 3.421–27)

Aristonicus, an Alexandrian grammarian of the Augustan age, reports that Zenodotus (ca. 325 B.C.E.–234 B.C.E.) had replaced lines 423–26 with a single line that he inserted between lines 422 and 427, producing this shorter version:

> When they reached the beautiful house of Paris,
> the maids in attendance betook themselves at once to their tasks,
> but she [Helen] made Alexander, drawn from a mist, sit opposite
>   [replaces 423–26]
> and turned her eyes aside and began by scolding her lover.

Aristonicus then explains that Zenodotus made the alteration because "it appears unfitting [aprepes] to him that Aphrodite fetches [bastazein] a chair for Helen."[94] To Alexandrian sensibility, it was unthinkable that a goddess would violate the dictates of the divine-human and intrahuman hierarchies, performing the task not only of a mortal, but of a mere servant-woman. Homer could never have written such a thing, and therefore the line should be removed from the authentic text. More than violation of common expectations of divine behavior is at stake here; a critical concern for authenticity lies behind Zenodotus's charge of "unfittingness." Alexandrian editors were not bowdlerizing Homer simply to protect delicate Alexandrian sensibilities but were trying to recover what Homer himself actually wrote. Yet in the end, the authentic Homer was invariably the "fitting" Homer.

Like goddesses, Homeric heroes also have their appropriate stations; they cannot perform just any common task. Because Homer could scarcely have had Odysseus tell Achilles that he had been ordered "both to open and to close the door" of the Trojan horse (Od. 11.525), such a line "should be marked for deletion as unfitting [perigrapteon hōs aprepē]. For it is the task of a doorman."[95] Similarly, both goddess and hero fail to play their proper roles in this scene from the final book of the Iliad that we have already seen Plutarch consider:

> Achilles' lady Mother [Thetis] sat down close beside him,
> stroked him with her hand and spoke to him.
> "My child," she said, "how much longer in lamentation and misery
> are you going to eat your heart out, forgetful even of your food
> and bed? Is there no comfort in a woman's
> arms—for you, who have so short a time to live
> and stand already in the shadow of Death and inexorable Destiny?
>   (Il. 24.126–32)

Although some modern readers might be moved by the pathos of the scene in its context, ancient Alexandrian scholars were offended by its disregard of decorum and perplexed by its lack of common sense. Aristonicus tells us that lines 130–32 were athetized because "it is unfitting

[*aprepes*] for a mother to say to her son that 'it is good to take comfort with a woman' "; "it is also altogether most inexpedient [*asymphorōtaton*] [to take such comfort], and especially for those setting out to war, for they need vigor and spirit"; and finally, "to say that your death is near" just before battle is "untimely [*akairos*]."[96] The lines must go, another scholiast concludes, "for they are inappropriate [*anoikeioi*] for a hero and a goddess," whether Thetis "says these things to gain for him a full posterity" or "to carry him away from sorrow."[97] All of these improprieties and illogicalities, conclude the editors, rule decisively against the authenticity of the passage.

Similar offenses against the fitting are generated by an especially problematic Homeric description of a god's behavior. In *Iliad* 24.22–31, Homer describes the divine response to Achilles' relentless dragging of Hector's body behind his chariot:

> This was the shameful way in which Achilles in his wrath treated Prince Hector.
> The happy gods looked on and felt compassion for him.
> They even hinted to the sharp-eyed Hermes that he might do well to steal the corpse,
> an expedient that found favor with the rest, but not with Hera,
> or Poseidon or the Lady of the Flashing Eyes [Athena].
> These hated sacred Ilium and Priam and his people just as much now as when the trouble first began and Paris fell into the fatal error
> of humiliating the two goddesses at their audience in his shepherd's hut
> by his preference for the third, who offered him the pleasures and the penalties of love.
> But when at length . . .
>
> (*Il.* 24.22–31)

The scholiast notes that seven of eight lines (23–30) have "not unreasonably" been marked as inauthentic by one earlier editor, but he defends the retention of line 23 on both syntactical and thematic grounds: line 23 ("The happy gods looked on and felt compassion for him") connects smoothly with line 31 ("But when at length . . ."), and it is "credible that all [the gods] take notice of the object of compassion." But the seven lines in between are a different matter: because they "bespeak excessive anxiety for Hector," they "are appropriately athetized." The scholiast agrees with Aristarchus that the suggestion that Hermes became a thief "is not fitting for gods [*theois ou prepon*], and [that] it is unreasonable [*alogos*] to bring in the subsequent lines concerning the opinion of the gods about the theft [25–31] and the words of Apollo denouncing the gods publicly [33–54]." The fact is simply that "these [lines] are immediately convicted as not being Homeric; for it was not necessary that the gods have the same anger as Achilles."[98]

When they did not athetize offensive texts, Alexandrian editors generally invoked a variety of nonallegorical interpretive strategies to discover a more subtle propriety. One could, for example, defend questionable Homeric lines by showing that the heroes or deities were consistently
depicted with heroic or divine attributes. Although Zenodotus athetized
lines depicting Aphrodite as a servant who carried a chair for Helen (*Il.*
3.424–25), Aristonicus, probably echoing an observation of Aristarchus,
discovered in the passage a more subtle consistency that preserves Aphrodite's divine attributes, and he commented: "It remains unnoticed [by
Zenodotus] that she [Aphrodite] is likened [earlier in the narrative] to an
old woman [*Il.* 3.386], and she occupies herself [in this passage] with
things appropriate to this appearance."[99] By appealing to the consistency
of an assumed role, Aristonicus thus preserves Zenodotus's criterion of
the fitting (i.e., what is proper to a deity) as well as the lines of the poet.
Aphrodite had earlier appeared in the form of an old serving maid well
known to Helen, and her later assistance with the chair simply shows that
she is "staying in character"—her adopted role of servant does not violate
her divine nature.[100]

Not surprisingly, what is unacceptable in heroic epic is often routine
fare in Attic comedy, which exploits sensitivity to what is unfitting for
comic effect. Rather than rationalizing or minimizing the shameful attributes and actions of gods and goddesses, scholiasts on Aristophanes
delight in pointing them out to the reader. For example, in the *Plutos*,
when the wife of Chremylus asks Carion (who had sought to gather up for
himself the food and drink left over from a religious ritual), "Did you not
fear the god [i.e., Asclepius]?" (*Plut.* 684), and Carion responds, "Indeed I
did, lest he should cut in first [*nē tous theous egōge mē phthaseie me*], /
Garlands and all, and capture my tureen" (*Plut.* 685–86), the scholiast
observes that the phrase *mē phthaseie me* and what follows is "a joke at the
god's expense, as though he were a thief."[101] And Hermes, whose association with a contemplated theft in *Iliad* 24.24 offended Homeric scholiasts,
appears in the scholia on the *Plutos* in precisely this guise:

> *Carion:* How could we use you if we took you in?
> *Hermes:* Install me here, the Turn-god [i.e., "hinge," *strophaios*] by the door.
> *Carion:* The Turn-god? Turns and twists we want no more.
>
> (*Plut.* 1152–54)

Although one scholiast suggests that Hermes was called *strophaios* "from
being inclined to shuffle," another reports that *strophaios* "is a surname of
Hermes because he is set up at the door to keep off all other thieves [*hoi
alloi kleptai*]."[102] What the Homeric scholiast wants to eliminate, the Aris-
tophanic scholiast volunteers—and both decisions reveal the force of the
culturally normative sense of the fitting.

Thus we see that while a notion of the fitting was comically exploited by Aristophanes and elucidated by his scholiasts, the same cultural ideal helped Alexandrian editors determine which lines of Homer should be athetized and which needed to be reinterpreted and assimilated according to various nonallegorical interpretative techniques. The sense of the fitting enabled comedians to turn an embarrassing poetic text to comic effect, while at the same time prompting grammarians and philologists to make the Homeric epics more culturally acceptable. In both comedy and epic, this sense of the fitting was intimately bound up with standard Hellenistic expectations about the proper roles of deities and various kinds of persons, as well as with conceptions of social hierarchy in the high-culture, urban world of ancient Alexandria.[103] In the midst of their own socially and politically favorable circumstances, the Alexandrian philologists not surprisingly (and probably unconsciously) drew upon the standards of Alexandrian courtly society to define the sense of the fitting that in turn shaped their editorial and interpretative decisions.[104] As a result, impropriety was imputed to Homeric descriptions that were in fact accurate representations of life in the archaic Heroic age. Occasionally, the Alexandrian critics did display historical sensitivity by drawing on their limited understanding of ancient "Homeric usage" or custom to establish textual authenticity and meaning—but this was the exception rather than the rule. Instead, far more often, either contemporary norms or the ideals of archaic texts devoid of contemporary relevance determined their editorial judgments. Alexandrian philologists were not inclined to disengage the Greek classics from their own contemporary Alexandrian world view in order to use those texts to create another, different vision of reality. Unconcerned with any revisionary potential that depictions of a long-past, archaic age might offer, they meticulously edited at least some portions of their classics to conform to the norms of their own contemporary culture.

The preceding survey of pagan advocates and opponents of etymology and allegory suggests some of the possibilities available to Hellenistic Jewish and Christian interpreters. Philo, Valentinus, and Clement were well aware of the strategies we have discussed, and they made use of many of them in their own allegorical interpretations. While Philo and Clement in particular made considerable use of the sort of etymological analysis found in Cornutus's *Compendium,* they both treated the texts they interpreted more along the lines of Heraclitus's reading of Homer: for Philo, Moses had written the Pentateuch as an allegory, and for Clement, the divine *logos* spoke allegorically in biblical and pagan literature. While their tendency was to interpret texts rather than edit or emend them, both Philo and Clement could also make textual alterations in the manner of the Alexandrian grammarians.[105] Valentinus, in contrast, puts himself in

the place of Cornutus's ancient theologians or Heraclitus's Homer as an original source of theological insight. He then gives expression to that insight not in the form of commentary (and certainly not in the form of scholarly editing), but through the creation of original mythological compositions that allegorically reinterpret his precursors. More traditionally minded Christians like Clement thus said of Valentinus what Cornutus had said of Hesiod and other poets—that they had corrupted the deposit of ancient theology through their own idiosyncratic poetic embellishments and additions. But from Valentinus's point of view, such complaints merely typified the deference to past authority that always marks the domestication of authentic *gnōsis*. Authentic *gnōsis* always entails the absorption by the self of what is other, and the replacement of what is past with what is future. But before we consider this *gnōsis* and its later domestication, we must first examine the ancient Jewish allegorical interpreter Philo, whose devotion to the literal text was every bit as serious as that of the antiallegorical Alexandrian grammarians.

TWO

Philo: The Reinscription of Reality

Following the exegetical precedent of his predecessors Aristeas and Aristobulus, Philo of Alexandria (ca. 20 B.C.E.–ca. 50 C.E.) read scripture allegorically in order to associate with the Pentateuch meanings previously unconnected with it. The first part of this chapter surveys these Ptolemaic Jewish interpreters, who represent most of what we know of the shadowy tradition of allegorical interpretation out of which Philo emerged. From the works of Aristeas, Aristobulus, and others like them, Philo learned that allegory might be used to systematically associate nonscriptural, Hellenistic meanings with scripture, just as if Moses had in fact been the true author of the classics of Greek culture. He also learned that Moses' writing could thus become the basis for a revisionary stance toward the dominant, Hellenistic culture.

The second part of the chapter examines in some detail the hermeneutical model that Philo took over from his Ptolemaic predecessors and developed further. Philo first reduces classical wisdom to anonymous conceptual form, and then, by reading scripture allegorically, presents that wisdom as the true, underlying meaning of scripture. Moses is also given absolute chronological priority over all classical authors and thus becomes the truly original philosopher. One can grasp this revisionary process by thinking of writing and rewriting: Philo's allegorical reading transforms Moses' writing (i.e., the Pentateuch) into a rewriting of classical meanings and then paradoxically presents that rewriting as an original writing. The analogy of a palimpsest may help us visualize this complex mode of revision. A surface that once contained writing but was erased and written upon again is said to contain a palimpsest—that is, a second writing or re-writing. When read allegorically, scripture can also be viewed as a re-writing, for to give a writing "another meaning" is, from the

opposite point of view, to say that some other meaning has been written. If that other meaning was once written in a nonscriptural work and then is also found in scripture, one might conclude that the meaning had now been "rewritten" by the writer of scripture. For example, although one could say that the "other" meaning of a certain passage of scripture is identical to Plato's theory of the soul, one might say instead that Plato's theory of the soul has been rewritten by Moses, that is, that it was once written by Plato in the *Phaedrus* but is now written by Moses in Genesis. Genesis thus becomes a palimpsest that is written over the now-erased text of the *Phaedrus*. One might then go even farther and claim that Plato's theory of the soul, although written by Plato, was written by Moses first; the Mosaic "palimpsest" would then become the original, rather than the secondary, writing. The Platonic theory would then become a Mosaic theory, and Plato would be reduced to a mere epigone or plagiarist.

Philo seeks to use just this sort of allegorical reading of scripture to reinterpret the cosmos, world history, and Alexandrian social reality, as well as classical philosophical and literary wisdom, by viewing them all through the lens of Moses' original Pentateuch. The resulting new view of the world also implied a certain kind of behavior, for Philo insists that the original Pentateuch was also a law to be enacted. The third section of this chapter thus explores the ways in which Philo's revisionary interpretation of culture was reinforced by an insistence on fidelity to the religious practices enjoined as law by scripture. Without this evidence drawn from the realm of social practice, Philo's allegorical correlation of Hellenistic meanings with the text of scripture might be read as a way of Hellenizing scripture, accommodating the particularities of the Pentateuch to the demands of culture. However, Philo's emphasis on lexical details and his concern to "textualize" reality strongly suggest, contrary to much received opinion, that his allegorical readings are designed to reinterpret Hellenistic cultural ideals according to the demands of scripture. And when the connection between literary revision and social practice is kept in view, it becomes unmistakably clear that for Philo allegorical interpretation is an effort to make Greek culture Jewish rather than to dissolve Jewish identity into Greek culture. Philo's concern for the specific practice of Judaism in Alexandrian society reveals that for him allegorical interpretation is central to Jewish communal identity and survival in a hostile environment.

JEWISH ALLEGORY AND HELLENISM

Jewish reading of scripture in Ptolemaic Alexandria does not appear to have been significantly influenced by the interests and practices of the Alexandrian grammarians and editors. This is initially surprising since

the high point of Alexandrian philology coincided with the emergence of creative and interpretative literature written in Greek by Alexandrian Jews of significant social, intellectual, and political status. But Jewish interpreters were engaged in an enterprise fundamentally different from that of the scholars of the Museum and Library. Alexandrian editors of the Greek poets, determined to salvage the remains of a quickly receding classical heritage, sought to purify ancient texts by assessing passages whose authenticity could no longer be taken for granted.[1] But Alexandrian Jews were not preoccupied with authenticating an authoritative text that was believed to have become corrupted.[2] Rather than attempting to edit old classics for a new age, they were seeking to interpret the new age in light of their own old classic—the Septuagint version of the Pentateuch. Such a reading (and, ultimately, revision) of culture required more than commentary on scripture; Alexandrian Jewish writers of the Ptolemaic period also turned to classical and Hellenistic literary models such as drama, epic, chronography, and romance to reinterpret the world around them.[3] Just like the Jewish commentaries on scripture, these Alexandrian Jewish works also sought to revise Hellenistic life and thought in light of the authoritative text of the Greek Pentateuch.

Alexandrian Jewish texts that explicitly comment on scripture consistently draw upon the hermeneutical procedures favored by Greek etymologists and allegorical interpreters. This is especially true of the *Explanations of the Book of Moses* by Aristobulus and the so-called *Letter of Aristeas to Philocrates* by Pseudo-Aristeas.[4] An examination of the understanding of allegorical composition held by these Jewish commentators and the ways their allegorical readings functioned in the context of Ptolemaic society demonstrates that both authors considered scripture to be the original written version of all wisdom—precisely the mode of revisionary reading that Philo was to pursue with even greater vigor.

Like Heraclitus, Aristobulus and Aristeas view allegorical composition as a rhetorical strategy. Consequently, scripture—as an instance of allegorical composition—is a means of communicating a message, despite any obscurities it may initially present to a reader. Aristeas and Aristobulus assume that the Pentateuch is an extended message from Moses, oblique but ultimately perspicuous, in which he often speaks of moral or cosmological topics by means of images and narratives of other things. For example, Aristobulus writes that Moses, "by using words that refer to other things" (*eph' heterōn pragmatōn logous poioumenos*), proclaims "arrangements of nature and preparations for great events" (Euseb. *Praep. evang.* 8.10.3). Aristeas makes a similar point when he has the high priest Eleazar observe that the inner message of scripture that justifies its odd dietary demands lies deeper than the insights of mere human reason. Although various biblical restrictions concerning "food and drink and

touch and hearing and sight" seem to contradict human reason's conclusion that such things are in reality "similarly constituted, being all admin-
istered by a single power," the high priest argues that "in each and every
case there is a profound logic for our abstinence from the use of some
things and our participation in the use of others" (*Aris. to Phil.* 143).
Human logic might conclude that because all is divinely given, all is
permitted, but a deeper, divine logic explains why discrimination is necessary. Moses' peculiar legal prescriptions reflect that deeper logic, which
Eleazar unveils through his allegorical reading.

Because the ancients thought the purpose of most literature was to
communicate a message, they tended to use the categories of rhetoric as
the basis for their literary criticism. Since literature was understood as a
fundamentally rhetorical exercise—as a kind of speech delivered in writing to an audience of readers—lack of clarity or obscurity was a significant
literary vice. This was true even for indirect modes of discourse such as
allegory. This rhetorical understanding of allegorical composition and
reading was the widely prevailing norm throughout antiquity.[5] It continued into the early Middle Ages as well, as shown by a dialogue written
by Fulgentius (ca. 467–532 c.e.) in which the author has the ghost of Virgil interpret the concealed meanings of his own *Aeneid*.[6] Since many ancient commentators could agree that poetry often expressed clear meanings (especially moral meanings) indirectly, debate sometimes centered
on whether the poet's intended meaning was for instruction or merely
for entertainment. Thus the Epicurean Philodemus of Gadara (ca. 110
b.c.e.–40/35 b.c.e.), although admitting that Homer "knew the facts,"
wonders whether or not he wrote "for educational purposes."[7] On the
whole, the ancient conception of fiction assumed that an author began
with a message and then embodied it in image and narrative. No one
seriously thought that a writer might use a story or subject to symbolize
something only generally related to it in some way other than as an
expression of an intended message.[8] The modern notion of "symbolic,"
as distinct from allegorical, discourse—a Romantic distinction between
language that is evocative and expressive (symbolic) and language that
offers a sterile translation of image into idea (allegorical)—was not opera-
tive in the ancient world. Scripture readers like Aristobulus and Aristeas
do not read the Pentateuch "creatively" or "imaginatively"; instead, they
read the text allegorically in order to retrieve Moses' deliberately hidden
message.

The actual Mosaic messages embodied in odd scripture passages, especially those describing God anthropomorphically or presenting strange
dietary regulations, become clear to Aristobulus when he reads the text
as if it had been composed as an allegory. In Moses' indirect rhetoric,
God's "hands" represent divine power (Euseb. *Praep. evang.* 8.10.7–9),

God's "standing" refers to the establishment of the cosmos (*Praep. evang.* 8.10.9–12), God's "voice" means the establishment of all things (*Praep. evang.* 13.12.3), and God's "descent" upon Mount Sinai graphically depicts the ubiquity of divine majesty (*Praep. evang.* 8.10.12–17). Aristeas reads the Mosaic text the same way: Moses permits the eating of some fowl and not others to signify (*sēmeiousthai*) two kinds of moral behavior (*Aris. to Phil.* 148), using dietary regulations in general to set forth (*ektithesthai*) figurative (*tropologōn*) indications of justice and injustice (*Aris. to Phil.* 150). With the phrases "parting the hoof" and "cloven foot," Moses hints at the need for moral discrimination and at the distinctiveness of the Jews (*Aris. to Phil.* 150–52), and he alludes to memory with the phrase "chewing the cud" (*Aris. to Phil.* 154).

Like both classical allegorists and Alexandrian philologists, Alexandrian Jews sought to refute inappropriate or unfit readings.[9] Aristobulus is distressed by "those devoted to the letter alone" (*tōi graptōi monon proskeimenoi*) (*Praep. evang.* 8.10.5), whose readings reflect a "fictional and anthropomorphic [*mythōdes kai anthrōpinon*] way of thinking about God" (*Praep. evang.* 8.10.2) common to those without "insight and understanding" (*Praep. evang.* 8.10.5). Such readings are inappropriate because they discover nothing "elevated" (*megaleion*—i.e., "fitting") about God (*Praep. evang.* 8.10.5). Aristobulus exhorts his readers instead "to receive the interpretations according to the laws of nature [*pros to physikōs*][10] and to grasp the conception of God that agrees with them [*hē harmozousa ennoia peri theou*]"—that is, that is fitting (*Praep. evang.* 8.10.2). Those who do so will be "able to think well" and consequently to "marvel at his [Moses'] wisdom and at the divine spirit in accordance with which he has been proclaimed as a prophet also" (*Praep. evang.* 8.10.4). As an allegorical reader, Aristobulus decides that he will examine each meaning (*sēmainomenon*) in sequence; any failure on his part will reflect only his own hermeneutical weakness in fathoming the sublime Mosaic insights (*Praep. evang.* 8.10.6).

Like Aristobulus, Aristeas anticipates that readers of scripture may be swayed by seemingly unfit meanings, and he thus warns them not to accept "the contemptible view that it was out of regard for 'mice' and the 'weasel' and other such creatures that Moses ordained these laws with such scrupulous care." "Not so," Aristeas insists—"these laws have all been solemnly drawn up for the sake of justice, to promote holy contemplation and the perfecting of character" (*Aris. to Phil.* 144). He assures his readers that "nothing has been set down through scripture heedlessly or fictionally [*mythōdōs*]" (*Aris. to Phil.* 168). These references to a sense of the fitting make early Alexandrian Jewish reading of scripture look much like Heraclitus's readings of Homer. But the Jewish writers tend to dismiss the issue of unfittingness (presumably raised by other Jewish exegetes)

rather than make it central to their work; they do not display quite the degree of defensiveness that pervades Heraclitus's *Homeric Allegories.*

While Ptolemaic Jewish literature does not seem to reflect the influence of Alexandrian philology, it does seem to have benefited from royal encouragement and approval—a point that Aristeas underscores by linking the translation of the Septuagint to Demetrius of Phaleron who, he asserts, was librarian at Alexandria.[11] Aristobulus and Aristeas probably wrote during the reign of Ptolemy VI Philometor (180 B.C.E.–145 B.C.E.), and Philometor's personal interest in the Jews of Alexandria is well documented.[12] During Philometor's reign, Alexandrian Jews seem to have secured their own neighborhood in the city and established formal organization as a *politeuma.*[13] Echoing typical Jewish synagogue dedication formulae ("on behalf of King Ptolemy") and following Greek models of literary dedication, Aristobulus dedicated his work to Philometor (*Praep. evang.* 8.9.38), possibly seeking thereby to honor the king by implicit comparison with his ancestor Ptolemy II Philadelphus (285 B.C.E.–247 B.C.E.).[14] Aristobulus's work thus testifies to the increasing social and political status of Jews under Philometor's rule.

Aristeas's narrative also gives evidence of such status.[15] Apart from the overall story, which stresses in a variety of ways the degree to which Alexandrian royalty were interested in the Jews and their sacred text, the author himself, clearly a Jew despite his Gentile literary persona, reveals his close relation to the royal administration by showing intimate knowledge of the details of Ptolemaic bureaucracy, especially features of court protocol.[16] Aristeas's inside knowledge almost certainly came from holding a high position at the Ptolemaic court.[17] Both Aristobulus and Aristeas seem to be highly placed Jews in Alexandria, writing under generally favorable social and political conditions. Although those conditions were to change dramatically by Philo's generation, the tradition of Jewish allegorical reading of scripture, insofar as we can reconstruct it from fragmentary remains, seems to have remained essentially the same from the time of these early Ptolemaic interpreters to that of Philo.[18] We will see the further resiliency and flexibility of such a mode of reading, especially its apparent usefulness in the tense social and political context of Roman Egypt, in our examination of Philo's interpretative practice. For the moment, however, we must ask about the purpose of Jewish allegorical reading of scripture in the more favorable circumstances of the early Ptolemaic period.

Aristobulus and Aristeas sought to reinterpret their Alexandrian Greek host culture by allegorically uncovering the true meaning of the Torah. This reinterpretation of culture by reading a sacred text involved two related, yet distinguishable, processes: subordination of the host culture's authoritative authors and their writings and allegorical reading of scrip-

ture that attached formerly nonscriptural meanings to scriptural words and narratives. Even though subordination and allegory are two facets of a single revisionary process, it is useful to distinguish them for purposes of analysis. Alexandrian Jewish readers deliberately construed the significant writings of their Greek host culture as subsequent, and hence subordinate, to original scriptural insights. By reading their own scripture allegorically, these interpreters correlated meanings from their Hellenistic host culture with the scriptural text, so that cultural meanings became scriptural. Jewish interpreters could combine the two processes by reading the host culture's texts allegorically. For example, an allegorical reading of a line from Homer could give it "another meaning"—one that might have nothing to do with Homer's "intended meaning" but instead would be identical to the meaning of scripture (whether or not scripture was also read allegorically). In such a case, Jewish readers subordinated Homer not by explicitly denying Homeric originality (e.g., by claiming that Homer plagiarized Moses), but by denying it implicitly through the correlation of the allegorical meaning of Homer with the true meaning of scripture.

But like Heraclitus, who promoted the priority and authority of Homer over Plato and other philosophers, Aristobulus also asserts the priority of Moses and his writing over Greek authors and their literature. If for Heraclitus, a "philosophical" Homer is always prior to all other philosophers, for Aristobulus, Moses is always prior to all Greek writers. Aristobulus asserts that among those who were "able to think well" and thus to understand Moses' intention are "the philosophers already mentioned and many others, including poets, who took significant material from him and are admired accordingly" (*Praep. evang.* 8.10.4). Plato, writes Aristobulus, "imitated our legislation" and "investigated thoroughly each of the elements in it"; Pythagoras "transferred many of our doctrines and integrated them into his own system of beliefs" (*Praep. evang.* 13.12.1); Solomon speaks "more clearly and better" regarding wisdom than do the Peripatetics (*Praep. evang.* 13.12.11). Aristobulus then summarizes some of the ideas taken by classical epigones from Moses' creation account in Genesis:

> And it seems to me that Pythagoras, Socrates, and Plato with great care follow him [Moses] in all respects. They copy him when they say that they hear the voice of God, when they contemplate the arrangement of the universe, so carefully made and so unceasingly held together by God. And further, Orpheus also imitates Moses in verses from his (books) on the Hieros Logos. (*Praep. evang.* 13.12.4)

Aristobulus then cites a long "Orphic" poem to prove the last claim.

Aristobulus supports his assertion of the subordinate and derivative

character of Greek poetry and philosophy with examples of radically revised Greek texts: Homer and Hesiod, "having taken information from our books, say clearly that the seventh day is holy" (*Praep. evang.* 13.12.13), as does Linus the mythical singer (*Praep. evang.* 13.12.16). Aristobulus even subjects one such verse to further allegorical reading: Homer's statement that "on the seventh morning we left the stream of Acheron" actually signifies "that away from the forgetfulness and evil of the soul, by means of the sevenfold principle in accordance with the truth, the things mentioned before are left behind and we receive knowledge of the truth" (*Praep. evang.* 13.12.15).

As it turns out, at least some of the verses that Aristobulus quotes have been altered (or even fabricated) in order to ensure that they echo scriptural praise of the Sabbath (though it is not clear whether Aristobulus altered them or took over a source that did so).[19] That Aristobulus may have made such alterations as part of his interpretative revision is certainly possible, since he describes in detail one particular change. He quotes the first nine lines from Aratus's *Phaenomena,* changing all occurrences of "Zeus" to "God" and providing this justification:

> I believe that it has been clearly shown how the power of God is throughout all things. And we have given the true sense [*sēmainein*], as one must, by removing the (name) Zeus throughout the verses. For their (the verses') intention [*dianoia*] refers [*anapempesthai*] to God, therefore it was so expressed by us. (*Praep. evang.* 13.12.7)

Once again, the sense of the fitting is at work; Aristobulus makes the replacement so that there will be "nothing unsuited [*ouk apeoikotōs*] to the things being discussed" (*Praep. evang.* 13.12.7). Unlike the Alexandrian editors, Aristobulus is not worried at this point about morphological regularity. Adherence to such grammatical principles would have required him to choose between "Zeus" or "God" on philological grounds, perhaps even making an emendation without regard to meaning. In contrast, practical acceptance of semantic indeterminacy (in this case, synonymy) warrants a replacement of one word by another ("God" for "Zeus") based on recognition of the identity of the "actual" signified meanings. Aristeas also makes the same interpretative move by playing on the supposed etymology of Zeus—*Zēn* from *zēn* ("to live") and *Dis* from *dia* ("through" or "by means of"):[20]

> God, the overseer and creator of all things, whom they [the Jews] worship, is he whom all men worship, and we too, Your Majesty, though we address him differently, as *Zēn* and *Dis;* by these names men of old not unsuitably [*ouk anoikeiōs*] signified that he through whom all creatures receive life and come into being is the guide and lord of all. (*Aris. to Phil.* 16)

Alexandrian Jews such as Aristeas and Aristobulus are implicitly arguing that classical Greek wisdom is best understood as derivative Mosaic insight, and their subordination of Greek philosophical and poetic texts to the Pentateuch suggests that these Jewish interpreters would like to give those texts a new author. But this reauthorization, perhaps unexpected by those accustomed to viewing Hellenistic Judaism as an exercise in cultural and religious assimilation, turns into a virtual rewriting when the meanings of non-Jewish texts become the allegorical meanings of the Pentateuch. The allegorical reading of the Pentateuch brings the Greek world within the interpretative grasp of the Jewish text by making Hellenistic ethics or cosmology the content of scripture. Hellenistic Jewish writers make this point not only by directly commenting on scriptural passages, but also by discussing liturgical practices described in scripture. For example, as part of his reading of the Exodus account, Aristobulus insists that Greek astronomical observations about the positions of sun and moon are reflected in the Jewish dating of Passover. And Aristeas suggests through his description of the translation of the Septuagint that Ptolemaic Greek ideals stand in a subordinate relation to both Jewish scripture and Jewish religious practice. Aristeas implies that the excessive deference of the Ptolemaic king to the Jews (emphasized by having him volunteer to eat the same kosher meal as the Jewish translators), and the Jewish translators' insistent linkage of common Hellenistic aphorisms on kingship to dependency on God suggest that interpreting the world means reading it through the lens of Jewish scripture, belief, and practice.[21] Allegorical reading thus transforms Jewish scripture from a parochial closed book into an interpretative lens capable of permitting readings that construe the wider Greek culture in specifically Jewish terms.

Even if one acknowledges the ability of Jewish allegorical reading of scripture to embrace and subordinate nonscriptural cultural meanings, one might still wish to construe this interpretative process (and that of much of Hellenistic Jewish literature) as an apologetic effort by Jews to emphasize their fundamental religious identity with Greek contemporaries at the level of philosophical belief.[22] But in the case of the *Letter of Aristeas*, such a view does not fully account for the implications of Aristeas's linkage of scriptural interpretation both to the power of the Jewish God (whose will Aristeas's text makes explicit) and to the social boundaries of the Jewish people. The embassy to Jerusalem to fulfill the royal desire for a translation of scripture cannot be made until all Jewish slaves in Egypt are freed:

> For inasmuch as the legislation which we propose not only to transcribe but also to translate is laid down for all Jews, what justification shall we have for

our mission when a large multitude subsists in slavery in your realm? Rather with a perfect and bountiful spirit release those who are afflicted in wretchedness, for the same God who has given them their law guides [*kateuthunōn*] your kingdom also, as I have learned in my researches. (*Aris. to Phil.* 15)[23]

The telling point is not that the Jewish God and the Greek God are actually identical. Because strict Jewish monotheism makes this a given in any discussion, such an equation does not determine the specific import of Aristeas's remarks. Instead, because the Jewish God is the only God (and consequently, from a Jewish perspective, the only real God the Greeks could have), informed and prudent Greeks will obey that God's injunctions and respect that God's people. Aristeas does not fail to point out that the Jewish God did not just "guide" King Ptolemy but in fact compelled him to release the Jewish slaves:

God fulfilled our whole desire and constrained [*synanagkazōn*] him to liberate not only those who had accompanied his father's army, but also any that were there previously or had been brought into the kingdom subsequently. (*Aris. to Phil.* 20)

Before the meaning of Jewish scripture can be "led out" to Greeks through translation by Jewish translators, Jewish slaves must be led out from Egyptian slavery in a new, contemporary exodus.[24]

Rather than synthesizing scriptural and nonscriptural meanings, Hellenistic Jewish writers thus subordinate formerly nonscriptural meanings to scripture. Their allegorical reading brings the Greek world into the text in the form of the text's underlying meaning, and the specific characteristics of the text, as well as its links to social and religious practice, reinterpret that meaning. From the Jewish point of view, it is not the meaning of scripture that is hidden and uninterpreted, but the meaning of the world. How can the world, in all its Greek character, be the same world so adequately described in Jewish scripture? How, for instance, in its scientific reality can it be a world that is properly understood in terms of the Jewish Passover? Hellenistic Jews do not respond to such questions with the simple claim that truth is to be found in both Greek texts and scripture. Their claim is much bolder, and from a classical point of view thoroughly presumptuous. Jewish interpretative subordination is in fact a hermeneutical usurpation in which classical writers are demoted to the status of Mosaic epigones, condemned merely to echo his original and sublime insights. Authentic Greek culture is actually Jewish.[25] Aristeas, Aristobulus, and other now-forgotten Ptolemaic Jews bequeathed this reading of scripture as a revisionary interpretation of Greek culture to Philo, who developed it on an even grander scale.

REPRESENTATION AND TEXTUALIZATION

In the midst of interpreting a passage of scripture concerning Joseph's dreams, Philo is led by scriptural echoes to consider the story of Abraham's near sacrifice of his son Isaac. Philo is perplexed when Moses says that Abraham "came to the place [*topos*] of which God had told him: and lifting up his eyes he saw the place [*topos*] from afar" (Gen. 22.3–4).[26] The two occurrences of "place" create a paradox because "place" is the object of the verbs "came" and "saw," yet the impression of proximity conveyed by "coming" and "seeing" is contradicted by the suggestion of distance created by the modifier "from afar" (*makrothen*). Philo thus faces two equally perplexing possibilities: Is Abraham simultaneously in a place while seeing it from afar? Or is he in a place that is really somewhere else? Although Philo might have addressed these paradoxical alternatives by determining whether "from afar" modifies Abraham's seeing or the place that he sees, he focuses instead on the noun "place," wondering whether one and the same place can really be meant both times.

Philo does not pursue the possibility that Moses uses the word "place" both times with its meaning of "a space occupied by a material body" to denote the same geographical location, first as low background and then again as elevated foreground—a resolution of the paradox that makes realistic narrative sense if we imagine Abraham slowly approaching the foot of Mount Moriah and then looking up upon his arrival. Instead, Philo suggests two other possibilities:

a. "Place" is a homonym (*homōnymia*) with the two meanings "Word" (*logos*) and "God."

b. Although used twice, "place" has the single meaning of "Word" (*logos*).

When "place" is given these meanings, the verse now reads one of two ways (with the meaning of the modifier *makrothen* italicized):

a. He came to the Word of which God had told him; and raising his eyes, he saw God *from afar* (i.e., raising his eyes, he, from afar, saw God).

b. He came to the Word of which God had told him; and raising his eyes, he saw the Word *far away* (i.e., he saw that the Word was far away from God).

Because Philo's two readings require *makrothen* to mean both "from afar" and "far away," even had Philo chosen to investigate what *makrothen* modifies rather than what *topos* means, he would eventually have been led

to recognize the presence of a homonym. In version *a, makrothen* as "from afar" modifies the phrase "he saw God" (i.e., it characterizes the location from which Abraham sees God), thus emphasizing the great distance between that location (which is the Word, the place to which Abraham has come) and God. In version *b, makrothen* as "far away" modifies the Word that Abraham sees, which is also where he is, as the repeated term "place" indicates. Consequently, both versions have the same underlying or allegorical meaning: despite his spiritual progress, Abraham has not reached unmediated knowledge of the remote God but only the "place" of the mediating Word.[27]

In what sense has Philo's reading of this verse of scripture been "allegorical"? His interpretation of this verse involves two interrelated, but distinct, nonliteral readings—the first of a single word and the second of a complete sentence. First, nonliteral meanings of "place" (as "Word" and "God") are generated in contrast to the literal meaning of "place" as "the space occupied by a material body." Then, using the new meanings for "place," two different nonliteral readings of the entire scripture sentence are generated in contrast to the initially perplexing literal reading. It seems that the ordinary potential of one word to have (by virtue of ordinary linguistic usage) or to be given (by a reader) multiple meanings is the condition for the very possibility of Moses' allegorical use, and Philo's allegorical reading, of "place." As a writer of allegory, Moses is able to use "place" to indicate something other than "the space filled by a material body" because words do not have single meanings or referents. As a reader of allegory, Philo is alert to the possible meanings of Moses' indirect language. Both Moses' composition and Philo's reading rely on the paradoxical capacity of scriptural language to be simultaneously representational and nonrepresentational.

Philo suggests that scripture's capacity for representation derives from the scene of Adamic naming in the Book of Genesis and from the preservation of that naming in the Septuagint translation (LXX) of Hebrew scripture into Greek.[28] According to Philo, God wants to test Adam's ability to confer names that would "bring out clearly the peculiar natures [*idiotētai*] of the things [*hypokeimena*] which bore them" (*Op.* 149).[29] Prelapsarian man passes this test easily, matching names (*klēseis*) to bodies (*sōmata*) and things (*pragmata*) through his accurate perception of their essential natures (*physeis*) (*Op.* 150); Adam thus linguistically re-presents the original presentations of the peculiar natures of the things around him. Philo is, of course, using Stoic concepts and terms to depict Adam's perception and naming. The objects that Adam perceives emit physical "presentations" (*phantasiai*) that embody their essential natures. These presentations travel through the air, entering Adam's sense organs (in this case, his eyes) and imprint themselves on his mind, as a seal imprints its

image on wax. Stoics distinguished between nonapprehensible (*akatalēp-tikai*) and apprehensible (*kataleptikai*) presentations. Some presentations are nonapprehensible either because they do not proceed from a real, existing object in the world or because they are so indistinct that they fail to agree with or correspond to the object from which they proceed. However, the presentations Adam received were clearly apprehensible. The objects from which the presentations proceeded were real and exist-ing, and these presentations agreed with those objects and were clearly and distinctly imprinted on Adam's mind.[30]

Although Adamic naming is linguistic in its outcome, its origin is nonlinguistic. The visual presentations that were "apprehensible" were things, not words. Adamic names are thus perfect linguistic representa-tions of nonlinguistic realities. The connotations of the English word "sense" capture both the source and the product of Adamic names: the source is Adam's "sense" (as "sensation") while the product of his sensa-tion is a name that has an appropriate "sense" (as "meaning"). As well as having a "sense," Adamic names also have a "denotation"—that is, a rela-tion to the things to which they have been applied. Philo argues that scrip-ture's account of Adamic naming is superior to any other theory of lan-guage's origin. The links that Adam simultaneously perceives (as physical "sensation") and forges (as linguistic "sense") between names and things manifest a consistency, harmony, and universal validity that can come only from having a single, authoritative name-giver. Philo compares this Edenic linguistic triumph to alternative Greek theories of language's origin. Unlike the numerous wise name-givers among the Greeks, who would inevitably have produced incongruous and ill-matched names, Adam, as the first and only name-giver, was able to "bring about harmony between name and thing, and the name given was sure to be a symbol [*symbolon*], the same for all men, of any thing [*tygchanon*] to which the name was attached or of the meaning [*sēmainomenon*] attaching to the name" (*L.A.* 2.15). To underscore the superiority of Adamic naming, Philo uses *sēmainomenon* to stand for the substantial meaning constituted by Adamic names—the "essence" or "nature" of the thing named, the nature that was "manifested" (*dēloumenon*) and perceived by Adam, or what was previously called a "sense." Philo appears to imagine that when Adam perceived the first dog, he received a presentation of the very essence of dog and cried out (presumably in Hebrew) in a moment of perfect insight and apt naming: "Dog!"

The Adamic congruity between name and essence lives on in the names given by Adam's progeny. Isaac re-dug his father Abraham's wells, giving them the same names that his father had given them (Gen. 26.18), for he knew that "if he should change the names, he would change the things at the same time." Philo adds that the case is the same with "geo-

metrical figures, for each of them has its own name [*klēsis*], and if anyone changes this, he changes the nature of the thing [*hē tou hypokeimenou physis*]"—in other words, a new name would refer to a different thing (*QuGen.* 4.194).[31] In the mimetic world of Eden, Adamic language represents reality directly and accurately because reality itself has provided the first name-giver with its own self-description in the form of accurate impressions.

Adamic naming is not only reiterated by name-giving patriarchs like Abraham and Isaac; Moses' linguistic competence ensures that it is also preserved in Hebrew scripture. More important for Philo's Greek-speaking audience, however, is the confidence that the language of the Septuagint, by replacing Hebrew words with precise Greek equivalents, preserves Adamic and Mosaic correspondences between words and things. This correspondence simultaneously accounts for both the dependability of the Greek text and its linguistic crudity. Philo contends that the Septuagint was not a paraphrase in which different Greek words were used to render the same Hebrew words, but a strictly literal, word-for-word translation. The process of translating the Septuagint was thus quite unlike the flexible mental "translation" a speaker makes in his or her own language when he or she selects various and sometimes quite different expressions in order to convey the same idea. By consistently matching the same Greek words with the same Hebrew words (and thus implicitly retaining the Adamic links between those Hebrew words and their original referents), the Septuagint translators have wisely sacrificed the smooth literary style admired in their Hellenistic milieu in order to avoid the distressing ambiguity that stylistic exploitation of Greek synonyms and homonyms might have created. In contrast to the ambiguities of ordinary Greek language, "the Greek words used [in the Septuagint] corresponded literally [*synenechthēnai d' eis tauton kyria kyriois onomasi*] with the Hebrew, exactly suited to the things manifested [*ta dēloumena pragmata*]" (*Mos.* 2.38–39). Philo contends that the Septuagint translators were aware that "they could not add or take away or transfer anything, but must keep the original form [*hē ex archēs idea*] and shape [*typos*]" (*Mos.* 2.34). Philo seems to think that the original Hebrew text was like a geometrical diagram; changing the diagram (e.g., from ◯ to △) automatically changes the meaning (from "circle" to "triangle"). Thus the form or shape of the Hebrew text must not be altered in translation.[32]

Philo is certain that the Septuagint translators, by sacrificing style to substance, have preserved scripture's true meaning, handing down their Adamic-Mosaic hermeneutical heritage intact. Because they were not mere word-changers but "prophets and priests of the mysteries" who consorted with "the purest of spirits, the spirit of Moses," they were able to select just the right Greek equivalents for the original Hebrew words.

Consequently, Philo is confident that the Greek words of the Septuagint preserve the correspondences that the Hebrew words maintained with their original "senses." He seems certain that these scripturally rendered correspondences ultimately go back to the perfect perceptions and names of Adam, the originator of all language. The making of the Septuagint— aided by an inspired original author (Moses) and inspired translators—is a virtual extension of Adamic naming. We have the following representational chain:

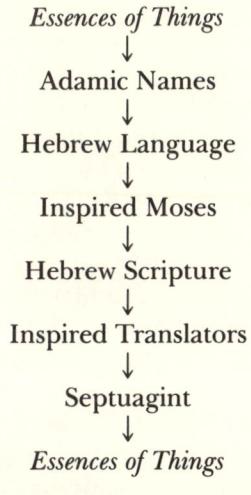

Essences of Things
↓
Adamic Names
↓
Hebrew Language
↓
Inspired Moses
↓
Hebrew Scripture
↓
Inspired Translators
↓
Septuagint
↓
Essences of Things

Apparently lacking the linguistic skill as Hebraist to judge the matter for himself, Philo reports the conclusions of those fluent in both Hebrew and Greek: reading the new Greek translation is just as good as reading the Hebrew original because the Greek and the Hebrew texts are "one and the same, both in subject matter [*pragmata*] and words [*onomata*]" (*Mos.* 2.40). Philo thus shares a classical Greek linguistic sensibility evident at least as early as the pre-Socratic Heraclitus and expressed in Plato's *Cratylus:* language is mimetic or representational, consisting of words that correspond directly to their subject matter. Despite Philo's recognition of semantic ambiguity in ordinary human languages,[33] at the Origin (Eden) and in the divinely guaranteed access to the Origin (scripture), words directly convey meaning and represent reality.

But readers of Philo's interpretation of the Abraham and Isaac story might wonder whether Philo as a practical reader of scripture has actually followed his own linguistic presuppositions. After all, the linguistic chain sketched above does not seem to permit the presence of a scriptural homonym like "place." And surely the original name-giver Adam did not produce synonyms (upon seeing the first dog, he did not say both "dog" and "hound"), for then there might just as well have been two original

name-givers—or more. Nor did the inspired Septuagint translators seem to struggle with such semantic indeterminacy. Philo insists that the translators provided perfect Greek equivalents for the original Hebrew words, and he does not suggest that they debated which of several possible meanings they should translate into Greek. Philo's appeal to the semantic and referential richness of "place" thus seems to stand in some tension with the privileged linguistic status he attributes to scripture.

In contrast to his depiction of language's representative power in Eden and in the individual cells of the seventy Septuagint translators, Philo's comments on the Genesis scenes of creation, temptation, and fall reveal a failure of linguistic representation and suggest that the origin of that failure lies in the necessary deficiency of human knowledge. Recognizing the same two stories of creation in Genesis 1–3 that modern biblical scholars have identified as the work of the Priestly Writer (P) and the Yahwist (J), Philo understands "Adam" to be a composite figure whose identity shifts between an ideal, nonmaterial Adam of Genesis 1 and a material Adam of Genesis 2–3. The first, ideal Adam of Genesis 1, copied after the image of God, desires to be like his divine archetype, and this desire marks his difference and distance from the divine: "For the image of God is an original pattern [*archetypos*] of which copies are made, and every copy [*mimēma*] desires [*pothein*] that of which it is a copy, and to be present with it" (*L.A.* 2.4).[34] Yet ideal Adam's desire to be similar to, and present with, the divine is necessarily frustrated at its very origin, for as a Platonist, Philo believes it to be axiomatic that "every image [*pasa . . . eikōn*] by its deceptive resemblance [*homoiotēs euparagōgos*] falsifies the original [*to archetypon*]" (*Praem.* 29). Because, then, the very creation of ideal Adam constitutes a primordial difference between human beings and God, human existence becomes a perpetual effort to represent an absent deity rather than to enjoy unmediated divine presence. Philo's account of ideal Adam, the model for material Adam, suggests that material Adam may not have had the capacities necessary to create a perfectly mimetic language, even though the scene of Adamic naming follows shortly upon his creation.[35]

No sooner than material Adam unambiguously names the animals, he paradoxically becomes the victim of a temptation that succeeds because of language's failure to convey meaning without ambiguity. Material Adam falls because the serpent deceives the woman by exploiting language's semantic indeterminacy. The Septuagint reports God's command: "From every tree which is in Paradise you may eat [*apo pantos xulou tou en tōi paradeisōi brōsei phagēi*]; but of the tree of the knowledge of Good and Evil—of it you shall not eat, but in whatsoever day you eat of it, you shall surely die" (Gen. 2.16–17). Philo first accurately distills this command (summarizing Genesis 2.17 in the phrase "except from one"): "[God] says,

'From every tree which is in Paradise you may eat except from one.'" He then reports the serpent's version of this command: "God said, 'Do not eat of any tree of Paradise' [*ou mē phagēte apo pantos xulou tou en tōi paradeisou*]." Philo observes that the serpent here "put forward an ambiguity [*aporia*, or perhaps *amphisbētēsis*] of words." On the one hand, the expression *ou mē phagēte apo pantos* ("do not eat from any") means "do not eat even from one"—a false version of the command because God did not forbid eating from every single tree in the garden. On the other hand, *ou mē phagēte apo pantos* can mean "do not eat from all," that is, "do not eat from every one (but perhaps from some)." This version is of course true because God's prohibition was not universal but applied only to a single tree. With an "artful lie," the serpent thus uses the ambiguous phrase *apo pantos* in order to make a statement that, though potentially true, could easily be taken by the woman in a false sense. The serpent, Philo concludes, "spoke a falsehood in a very clear manner" (*QuGen.* 1.34).

Successful temptation through language's semantic ambiguity hardly increases confidence in the mimetic capacity of Adamic language. On the contrary, Philo's description of the temptation is more consistent with his allegorical reading of "place" than with his account of Adamic naming. The serpent's words do not directly correspond to the essences of things; instead, like *topos*, *apo pantos* bears at least two different meanings. Unlike the naiveté of Adamic naming, the serpent's cunning closely parallels the indirection of scripture itself. Although the Septuagint's *apo pantos* faithfully translates the original Hebrew idiom, it has not preserved a semantically and representationally determinate Adamic language, but a language that is ambiguous even in the original Hebrew. The move from Adamic naming to scriptural language is a move from single names to complete statements or propositions, from nouns that supposedly reproduce the natures of things to syntactical units that make affirmations about things. Semantic and referential certitude seems to have suffered in this move; the ambiguity of the serpent's words is an ambiguity of syntax rather than of names.

Finally, the actual fall of tempted material Adam (an event that Philo says "could not but be," *Op.* 151) radicalizes the initial difference between the ideal Adamic model and the divine creator, raising further questions about material Adam's ability to recognize and name reality. Formerly, created Adam (as both ideal Adam and material Adam) desired to overcome his difference from his creator. But succumbing to the serpent's temptation, material Adam exchanges a desire for the Same (that is, for the God who has established the world of archetype and copy correlation) for a desire for the Other (*pothein . . . hekaterōi*)—for the woman, despite enormous similarity to Adam, is different from him (and different from God). Material Adam sees in the woman a figure "like his own and a

kindred form"; she, in turn, sees "no living thing more like herself than he" (*Op.* 151–52). A union born of desire for the *relatively*—rather than the *truly*—Same follows. Abandoning his former state, in which he was "growing like [*homoioun*] to the world and like God, and receiving in his soul the impressions [*charaktēres*] made by the nature of each" (*Op.* 151), Adam yields to another desire (or "desire for fellowship with the other"), which leads to pleasure, violation of the law, mortality, and wretchedness (*Op.* 152). The disjunction opened by creation, once potentially able to be minimized if not overcome through increasing "likeness," is now opened wider: recognizing their nakedness, the man and the woman conceived "an alienation [*allotriōsis*] . . . toward the whole world" (*QuGen.* 1.40).

Their alienation is pervasive; formerly able to name the objects around him because he literally internalized their essential natures, Adam is now decisively severed from the world. There were, however, earlier indications that Adam's knowledge, limited by the primordial distinction between creator and created being, was incomplete; for despite his ability to name the animals, prelapsarian Adam was unable to name either God or himself (*L.A.* 1.91). "Why should we wonder," Philo concludes, "that the Existent [*to on*] cannot be apprehended [*akatalēpton*] by men when even the mind [*nous*] in each of us is unknown to us? For who knows the essential nature [*ousia*] of the soul [*psychē*]?" (*Mut.* 9–10). The antimimetic implications of the creation of ideal Adam and the temptation and fall of his material, name-giving counterpart, as well as the contrasting mimetic confidence of the idealized scenes of Adamic naming and the translation of the Septuagint, leave their traces in Philo's reading of the story of Abraham and Isaac. On the one hand, his reading of the text quickly becomes allegorical, as "place" assumes multiple nonliteral meanings and referents. "Place" assumes two different meanings, failing to deliver a univocal meaning even as Abraham fails to enjoy unmediated divine presence. Within Philo's interpretive work, an antimimetic countercurrent persistently runs against the stream of classical mimesis. But on the other hand, out of that polysemous situation, Philo does extract clear and determinate meanings and referents for the word "place" that together constitute Moses' hidden message. As an allegorical reader of scripture, Philo shares with his Hellenistic culture a paradoxical fascination with both the promise and the limits of linguistic representation.

Philo finds Mosaic representation problematic because he believes that the human capacity to know God and the world is limited. He declares repeatedly that deity is "inconceivable [*aperinoēton*] and incomprehensible [*akatalēpton*]" (*Mut.* 15), "save in the fact that he is. For it is his existence which we apprehend [*katalambanein*], and of what lies outside that existence nothing" (*Deus* 62). At best, human beings can know *that* God is, not *what* God is; divine existence is knowable, but divine essence is not.[36]

Scripture itself acknowledges these limitations, insisting that God is unnameable and beyond description (*Mut.* 15). When scripture appears to
offer such descriptions, it does so merely as a pedagogical concession.
Anthropomorphic or anthropopathic representations of God are aimed
at spiritually deficient readers who are unable to approach God in any
other way. Philo points to the ambiguity of scripture's characterization of
God by contrasting a nonrepresentational "way of truth" and a representational "way of concession" (see *Som.* 1.237). For those who cannot con-
ceive of a God without a body and thus need anthropomorphic representations if they are to be spiritually educated at all, scripture depicts a God
with "face, hands, feet, mouth, voice, wrath and indignation . . . weapons,
entrances and exits, movements up and down and all ways" (*Som.* 1.235).
The truth of the matter, however, is that deity never changes. God simply
provides an "audiovisual aid" in the form of an anthropomorphic representation (*eikōn*), which is mistakenly understood by some to be God's
original form (*archetypon eidos*) rather than the mere copy (*mimēma*) it
actually is (*Som.* 1.232). Through the terror created by certain anthropomorphic depictions, the "duller sort" learn spiritual self-control (*Som.*
1.236–37); they are eventually able to exchange their fear of God for the
abstract love (*erōs*) that Plato describes in the *Symposium* (cf. *Deus* 69).
Unlike classical interpreters of the Greek poets such as Heraclitus, Philo
seldom views anthropomorphic depictions with embarrassment as "unfitting" elements to be quickly allegorized away. Instead, he more often views
them as pedagogical devices, transferring the responsibility for unfittingness from the text and its author to spiritually ill-prepared readers "who
have made a compact and a truce with the body" (*Deus* 56).

The impossibility of direct knowledge of God is part of a general
human inability to obtain certain knowledge. In Philo's view, language
users routinely fail to establish clear and determinate correspondences
between words, meanings, and things. As in the case of inadequate theological discourse, this more mundane linguistic failure stems from an
epistemological limitation. In contrast to prelapsarian Adam, who, per-
ceiving the nature of each thing, captured its "sense" in a perfect name,
postlapsarian human beings are unable "to see the nature of each [thing]
[*tēn hekastou physin idein*]" because of "the vastness of the darkness which
overspreads the world of bodies and things" (*Ebr.* 167). Although we, like
Adam, perceive the impressions (*phantasiai*) of things, we receive different impressions from the same objects at different times and consequently lack a basis for certain knowledge and judgment: "Since the
mental impression is variable, the judgment we form of it must be variable
also" (*Ebr.* 170). Our language simply passes along the results of this
indeterminate perception (*Det.* 131).[37] Philo criticizes those who believe
that human speech can overcome such epistemological limitations (*Her.*

72).[38] Human language lacks the subtlety necessary to register the distinctiveness of things, in contrast to the ability of Adamic names to "bring out clearly the distinctive natures of the things which bore them [*hai tōn hypokeimenōn idiotētai*]" (*Op.* 149). Postlapsarian discourse enjoys no such Edenic epistemological clarity: "No single thing presents itself to us in its own absolute nature but all contain interlacings and intermixtures of the most complicated kind" (*Ebr.* 189). Human language is thus incapable of directly describing deity and only marginally adequate for describing anything else because of a defect in perception that necessarily followed upon the very creation of human beings.

Although the Adamic capacity for accurate knowledge is denied to ordinary human beings, it lives on in the extraordinary Moses. Like Adam, Moses has accurate knowledge of what he wishes to communicate. Unfortunately, the only language available to Moses is a postlapsarian language with all the deficiencies noted above. But Moses is not like "most men," because his perceptions are superior to the language at his disposal. His name-giving flows from an accurate "knowledge that has to do with things"; consequently, he "is in the habit of using names that are perfectly apt and expressive" (*Agr.* 1–2). Even so, Moses is forced to use ordinary language to express his extraordinary insights. As a result, his message is always clear and determinate once it is perceived, but it lies hidden in very indirect linguistic expressions marked by various forms of semantic indeterminacy.

Because God is essentially unknowable and language is not representationally reliable in any case, Moses cannot use language in a literal or proper sense (*kyriōs*) to represent the divine. If it is to be applied to God, language must be "abused" by the trope that Philo, following Greek grammarians and rhetoricians, calls "catachresis" (*katachrēsis*).[39] The Latin term for "catachresis" is *abusio* ("abuse"), which effectively expresses the function of the trope—to force language away from its customary usage. The trope of catachresis occurs when an existing word with an ordinary or customary meaning is used to denote something that has hitherto lacked its own word.[40] Catachresis consequently uses an old word to do the job of a neologism, namely, provide a way of speaking about something new.

The rhetorician Quintilian offers a Latin example that contrasts catachresis with synonymy, synecdoche, and metaphor. *Gladius* and *ensis* are synonyms for "sword." *Ferrum* and *mucro* may be used by synecdoche for "sword"—one may be killed either by "steel" (*ferrum*) or by a "point" (*mucro*): each word represents a part of the whole. When used as metaphors for "sword," *ferrum* and *mucro* thus become synonyms; when used in their ordinary, proper sense, they are not. But both synecdoche and synonymy are different from catachresis. Although *ferrum* and *mucro* may

be used to denote a sword, a sword does in fact have its own proper name—in fact, it has at least two, *gladius* and *ensis*. But according to Quintilian there exists no general term in Latin for those who commit murder with any sort of weapon. Hence the word *sicarii*, which is properly used only of those who murder with a dagger (*sica*), is used catachresti-cally for all those who murder with any sort of weapon. *Sicarii* in its extended or "abused" sense thus functions as would a neologism such as *armacidi*—a word one might invent to mean "those who kill with weap-ons," drawing on *arma* ("weapon").

Of course, the plight of a Latin speaker who wants a word for "mur-derers with weapons" is not as great as that of a theologian like Moses who wants a word for deity, for the Latin speaker knows about murderers and weapons of all sorts, but the theologian does not have comparable knowl-edge of God. Philo concludes that the inability to perceive the nature of God means that "no personal name [*onoma kyrion*] even can be properly [*pros alētheian*] assigned to the truly Existent" (*Mut.* 11). So in response to Moses' request for God's name, Moses is told only that "I am he that is" (Exod. 3.14), which is not a name but another way of saying that "my nature is to be, not to be spoken" (*Mut.* 11). Yet in deference to the human desire to have a title (*prosrēsis*) with which to refer to deity, God

> allows them to use by license of language [*katachrasthai*], as though it were his proper name [*hōs an onomati kyriōi*], the title of Lord God [*kyrios ho theos*] of the three natural orders, teaching, perfection, practice, which are sym-bolized in the records as Abraham, Isaac and Jacob. (*Mut.* 12)

Scriptural representations of God's activities also demand catachresis. Scripture may have God profess to destroy humankind "because I was wroth in that I made them" (Gen. 6.7), but "wrath" is a term used more metaphorically (*tropikōteron*) here than one might expect, for "the passion of wrath is an attribute properly predicated [*to kyriologoumenon*] of men" (*Deus* 71) and can be predicated of God only by catachresis. Similarly, when scripture suggests that God is visible (as in Deuteronomy 32.39, where God proclaims: "See, see that I am"), these words are not said literally (*ou kyriologeisthai*), but as a distortion (*katachrēsis*); the reader is to refer the language to God's subordinate powers (*Post.* 168). Catachresis is evident not only when God is the subject; it appears throughout scriptural language.[41] Moses refers to the animals that Adam is about to name as "helpers." But Philo observes that these animals "are not properly [*ou kyriōs*] called our helpers, but [are so called] by a straining of language [*katachrēstikōs*]" (*L.A.* 2.10). Moses in fact often resorts to catachresis, bending fallen human language beyond its ordinary usage in order to speak of something else. By using a word for something that has hitherto lacked a word, catachresis produces a forced or artificial homonym. For

example, we call the end of one of our legs a "foot." We might also decide to call the abstract, level area that the bottom of a mountain occupies its "foot." "Foot" thus becomes a homonym, one word with several different meanings. According to Philo, Moses' language is filled with homonyms, and as an allegorical reader Philo exploits the semantic richness of such homonyms, as he did in his reading of "place" in the Abraham and Isaac story. In addition to containing ordinary homonyms and words used by catachresis, scripture is also full of synonyms; Moses often talks about the same thing in different terms. While catachresis, homonymy, and synonymy are different, together they reflect the fact that Moses speaks rhetorically in scripture by using a variety of linguistic forms to embody oblique, but ultimately determinable, messages.

As scriptural reader, Philo is interested in uncovering this indirectly expressed message. But homonyms and synonyms threaten to mislead him. As a single word with two different meanings—for example, a swimming "pool" and a game of "pool"—a homonym suggests identity where there may be complete difference. The word "pool" hides the radical difference between its two meanings behind its single lexical form. As for synonyms, because by definition they share at least one meaning (but generally not all meanings), they may mislead in two different ways. As two words with shared meanings but entirely different lexical forms (e.g., "home" and "domicile"), synonyms may suggest complete difference where there is actually a high degree of similarity. But synonyms may also, by virtue of their perceived similarities, suggest a greater degree of similarity than actually exists.

Anxious to uncover Moses' message, Philo is determined not to let lexical forms mislead him and his readers. Human beings are all too ready to succumb to such confusion; human speech itself is "unable to present with clear expression those distinctions [*hai idiotētai*] in things which baffled its vague and general vocabulary" (*Her.* 72). As a "second Adam," Moses is an accurate language user, and scripture readers should be careful not to misconstrue his specific, though indirectly expressed, message. Readers must be sensitive to the peculiar dual character of Moses' allegorical writing: they must be aware of scripture's lack of reliable representation on a first reading, but confident in the certainty of scripture's representation on a second. Philo seeks to eliminate the false identifications and differences suggested by the mere lexical forms of synonyms and homonyms in order to recover the authentic Mosaic message.

In the case of scriptural synonyms, Philo seeks to show that just because one verse contains a word like "home" and another verse a word like "domicile," the reader should not suppose that Moses is necessarily talking about different things. Readers must learn to recognize when Moses is using synonyms to talk about the same thing in two different ways. On the

other hand, Moses may have wished to emphasize the meanings not shared by synonyms; he may have used the terms "home" and "domicile" not to say one thing two ways but to say two different things. Words that may be synonyms in the ordinary use of language may function quite differently in Mosaic rhetoric. The allegorical reader of scripture cannot simply assume that words that are synonyms in ordinary usage will be used synonymously in scripture as well.

Moses often uses synonyms to suggest the richness of their common meaning or referent. Scripture's many synonyms for divine wisdom, such as the manna and the rock in the wilderness (*Det.* 115–18) or the royal road and the word of God (*Post.* 102), help suggest the rich and multi-faceted character of that wisdom (*L.A.* 1.43). Philo may then emphasize the shared meanings of lexically distinct words. For example, the key to a correct understanding of Genesis 6.3 (following an LXX variant that reports that the "angels" of God took wives from among the daughters of men) lies in discovering that "soul," "daemon," and "angel" are synonyms, "different names for the same one underlying thing [*hypokeimenon*]" (*Gig.* 16). Elsewhere Philo observes that "heaven" and "field" of Genesis 2.19 are synonyms by which Moses "allegorizes the mind" (*allēgorōn ton noun*) (*L.A.* 2.10). Like Moses, God also uses synonyms. When God condemns the fallen Adam henceforth to eat "grass" and "bread," God "uses the terms grass and bread synonymously [*synōnymōs*]; the meaning [*pragma*] is the same" (*L.A.* 3.251)—that is to say that Adam has become an evil man infatuated with sense perception.

Yet in other cases, Philo desires to discern the differences hidden by synonymy, that is, to highlight elements of the semantic fields not shared by the two words. In some cases, what appear to be synonyms even turn out to be antonyms. Moses calls Noah a "cultivator" (Gen. 9.20) rather than "soilworker" because, contrary to popular belief, "cultivation" and "working the soil" are not synonyms but direct opposites (*Agr.* 3). Like-wise, although "people who have not acquired real accuracy will perhaps suppose" that "cattle-rearing" and "shepherding" are "synonymous de-scriptions [*synōnymousa . . . prosrēsis*] of the same pursuit," Philo's allegori-cal reading demonstrates that such expressions "denote different things [*pragmata*] when words are rendered in the light of their deeper meaning [*di' hyponoiōn*]" (*Agr.* 28); those "resorting to allegory" (*allēgorountes*) find "a wide difference in meaning to underlie apparent identity" (*Agr.* 27). Similarly, although "Lord" (*kyrios*) and "Master" (*despotēs*) in Genesis 15.2 ("Master and Lord, what will you give me") are rightly said to be syn-onymous (*Her.* 22), Philo adds that even "though one and the same thing [*hypokeimenon*] is denoted by both, the connotations [*epinoiai*] of the two titles [*klēseis*] are different" (*Her.* 23). Philo then uses etymology to qualify the synonymy between *kyrios* and *despotēs*, observing that the different

connotations of the two epithets derive from their different roots. *Despotēs* is derived from *desmos* ("bond"), from which *deos* ("fear") is also derived. Thus *despotēs* denotes a terrifying, fear-inducing Lord. In contrast, *kyrios* is derived from *kyros* ("power"), to be contrasted with *akyros* ("insecure," "invalid"). Thus *kyrios* connotes a secure and valid rule, to which the term *despotēs* adds additional meaning (*Her.* 23), which is why Philo claims that Moses uses the expression as a whole to recommend a combination of caution and confidence (*Her.* 22). Philo's reading of synonyms indicates his view that scriptural language does not necessarily directly relate words to meanings or referents. If one would know Moses' message, the difference between that message and the words used to express it must never be ignored and their identity never taken for granted.

Like synonyms, homonyms are capable of misleading scripture readers, in this case by suggesting a similarity in meaning or reference when none exists: "Many are deceived by the application of the same terms [*homōnymiai*] to denote different things" (*Mut.* 201). Philo thus tries to show the differences hidden by homonyms, arguing that "for us, for whom it is natural to allegorize and who seek other things beyond that which is seen, it is fitting and proper to examine and question the names, and not to be deceived or taken in by homonyms" (*QuGen.* 4.243). He adds elsewhere: "It is a thoroughly scientific proceeding [*physikōtaton*] to show how one and the same name [*hē homōnymia*] has different shades of meaning" (*Post.* 60). He wants readers to recognize that even if "pool" appears in two different verses, it may not mean the same thing at all, but very different things. Without such analysis, "the difference between the things signified [*hē en tois pragmasi diaphora*] is obscured by their passing under the same name [*hē en tois onomasi koinōnia*]" (*Agr.* 26).

We have already seen Philo bring this perspective to bear on a single verse from the story of Abraham and Isaac in order to separate out the various meanings of the homonym "place." Similarly, understanding Genesis 3.15 (LXX 3.16), "He shall watch your head, and you shall watch his heel," requires realizing that the phrase "shall watch" has two meanings—"guarding/preserving" and "destroying" (*L.A.* 3.189). Likewise, "Hebron" means "union," but "union may be of two kinds, the soul being either made the body's yokefellow, or being brought into fellowship with virtue" (*Post.* 60). When homonyms are produced by the repetition of names in scripture, such as Enoch, Methuselah, Lamech (*Post.* 40–48), Philo immediately makes distinctions in the meanings (*sēmainomena*) of the names (*Post.* 44),[42] discovering through etymologies that the repeated names point to reiterations of the contrasting Cainite and Sethian types of soul.

As his allegorical reading of Abraham's "place" suggests, Philo's awareness of homonyms often reflects his apophatic theological perspective.

Considering the phrase "the glory of God came down upon Mount Sinai" (Exod. 24.16), Philo observes that the word "glory" is a homonym. While "glory" denotes the powers of God, it also denotes "only a belief in and counting on the divine glory, so as to produce in the minds of those who happen to be there an appearance [*phantasia*] of the coming of God, who was not there" (*QuEx.* 2.45). Philo makes a similar point when commenting on Moses' reception of the title (*klēsis*) "Tent of Testimony" for his own tent (Exod. 33.7). The verse stresses that Moses' tent was merely "called" (*kaleisthai*) the "Tent of Testimony" in order to distinguish it from the "Tent of the Existent One," which "really is, and does not merely receive the title" (*Det.* 160); for only God truly possesses being; all other things "exist in semblance only, and are [only] conventionally said to exist." The human virtue allegorically represented by Moses' tent is less real than the divine virtue or "Tent of the Existent One" and hence "must be accorded not existence but only a title [*klēsis*], seeing that it is a copy and likeness [*mimēma kai apeikonisma*] of that divine virtue" (*Det.* 160). On one side of Philo's Platonic divide lies archetype, reality, and vision; on the other, copy, unreality, and language. It is therefore no accident that Philo sees the mutual implications of Adam's status as a copy (*mimēma*) and as originator of language.

Earlier we examined a scripture sentence concerning Abraham and his place. The following passage from the same treatise, which discusses not one man in two places but two Gods in one place, will again illustrate the interrelationship of mimesis, antimimesis, and allegory, as well as the direct connection between Moses' limited knowledge of God and his deliberate use of catachresis. In the text, God announces: "I am the God who appeared to you in a place of God" (*egō eimi ho theos ho ophtheis soi en topōi theou*) (Gen. 31.13; *Som.* 1.227). Once again, Philo discovers a homonym in the text, this time "God" rather than "place." Philo's monotheism leads him to argue that this homonym is an instance of catachresis because the second instance of "God" improperly denotes the *logos*. Philo states:

> He that is truly [*alētheiai*] God is one, but those that are improperly so called [*en katachrēsei legomenoi*] are more than one. Accordingly scripture in the present instance has indicated him who is truly [*alētheiai*] God by means of the articles, saying "I am the God," while it omits the article when mentioning him who is improperly so called [*katachrēsei*], saying "who appeared to you in a place" not "of the God," but simply "of God." (*Som.* 1.229)

Here scripture "gives the title of 'God' to his [i.e., God's] chief *logos*, not from any superstitious nicety in applying names, but with one aim before him, to use words to express the things themselves [*pragmatologein*]" (*Som.* 1.230). In the case of both homonyms and synonyms, Philo refuses to allow language to mislead readers as to the real nature of the subject

matter that Moses is presenting. Philo's effort to separate such variable lexical expressions from the subject matter they are used to convey is consistent with his conception of scripture as a rhetorical composition. Moses has a message that he has put into various oblique lexical forms; as an allegorical reader of Mosaic compositions, Philo interprets such forms in order to recover this message. There is one final striking feature of this passage on the "two Gods," which characterizes the earlier passage from the Abraham and Isaac story as well—the specificity of Philo's interest in the lexical expressions themselves. Philo does not disregard the details of Moses' lexical expression in order to uncover his allegorical meaning. In this case, the different meanings hidden by the homonym "God" are signaled by a small lexical distinction: the absence of the definite article. Philo's allegorical reading of scripture constantly seeks to correlate allegorical meanings with minute details of lexical expression, for the revisionary capacity of this mode of reading depends upon the ability of scripture to redefine or rewrite its "other" meanings.

The principal nonliteral meaning that Philo discovers in scripture concerns either the moral education of the human soul or the order of the cosmos in which the soul's progress from vice to virtue takes place. The allegorical reading "attentive to human character or virtue" (*ēthikōs*) is actually part of the larger, natural order of things uncovered by an allegorical reading "attentive to the order of nature" (*physikōs*).[43] Both readings bring the reader into direct contact with Moses' most profound insights, which according to Philo impress themselves on the reader's soul the same way the essences of things impressed themselves on Adam's soul—like a seal on wax (*Agr.* 16). As Philo views them, Mosaic psychological and cosmological insights do not lend themselves to description under the ordinary constraints of time, space, and identity. And for Philo, honoring such constraints is the basic feature of the sort of reading he calls "literal." Consequently, in order to describe Moses' hidden wisdom about the soul and the cosmos, Philo must reduce the attraction of the literal reading of scripture precisely by evading these constraints.

For example, Philo evades the temporal character of historical events in order to interpret both the exodus and its annual remembrance at Passover as an ever-present process of the sanctification of the human soul. Passover, of course, emphasizes the contemporary significance of the past historical event of the exodus.[44] Philo's literal reading of that historical event relates the contemporary liturgical practice to its historical prototype while preserving the unique temporal aspects of both (*Spec.* 2.146). But Philo also agrees with other allegorical readers of scripture who claim that the scriptural account of the historical exodus (though it occurred "at that time" and is celebrated "once in every year") has another, underlying meaning concerning any soul's progress in virtue at any

time: "the Crossing-festival hints at the purification of the soul" (*Spec.* 2.147). Philo's literal reading connects the historical event and the contemporary liturgical remembrance while preserving the specific character of each. But his allegorical reading momentarily suspends the temporality of the past historical exodus (which happened once) and the present-day liturgical celebration (which happens once a year) in order to point out the ever-present possibilities for human existence that they imply.[45]

Philo's allegorical readings minimize the spatial aspects of ordinary "literal" description as well. In his reading of the Genesis description of Paradise, Philo relocates the trees from Eden to the soul, paradoxically returning the soul to Eden. Genesis 2.9 describes the origin of the various trees in Paradise: "God caused to spring out of the ground every tree fair to behold and good for food, and the tree of life in the midst of the garden, and the tree of knowledge of good and evil." Contending that Moses thus indicates the kinds of "trees of virtue God plants in the soul" (*L.A.* 1.56), Philo explains the statement's underlying meanings. By "fair to behold," Moses denotes the theoretical aspect of virtue, by "good for food" the practical aspect. The "tree of life" is generic virtue, from which all specific virtues flow, and its preeminence is denoted by its location in the middle of the garden, which is the soul. Read allegorically, Genesis 2.9 thus means the following: God caused to spring out of the soul every theoretical and practical virtue, generic virtue in the center of the soul, and the tree of knowledge of good and evil (see *L.A.* 1.56–59). Philo observes next that while Moses says "expressly" or "literally" (*rhētōs*) where the tree of life is located, he is silent about the location of the tree of knowledge (*L.A.* 1.60). He concludes that this tree must lead a kind of "homonymous" existence, for it is "both in the garden and outside it, in literal fact [*ousiai*] in it, virtually [*dynamei*] outside it" (*L.A.* 1.61). The tree thus has an allegorical, indeterminate existence permitted it by the absence of the ordinary spatial constraints of a realistic narrative. Its location is determined not by the topography of Eden but by the disposition of the soul—by the two attitudes a human soul might take toward the generic virtue represented by the tree of life. If the dominant faculty of the soul (mind) receives the impressions (*typoi*) of generic virtue, that mind "becomes the tree of life." In this case, the mind and the tree of life are actually in the garden, and the tree of knowledge is also in the garden (for it functions as the tree of knowledge of *good*). But if the mind receives impressions of vice, it "becomes the tree of knowledge of good and evil," and because vice has been exiled from Eden, both the vice-receptive mind and the tree of knowledge (functioning now as the tree of knowledge of *evil*) are virtually not in the garden (see *L.A.* 1.61). In order to read this text as the story of the education of the soul, then, Philo blurs the boundaries of ordinary narrative space.[46]

Philo also evades the constraints of literalism by suspending the personal identity of important biblical characters. Read allegorically, these characters become, either individually or in combination, personifications of various types (*tropoi*) of souls or of faculties (*dynameis*) within the soul (see *Agr.* 22). For example, concerning Genesis 24.66 (Abraham's servant "related to Isaac all the things which he had done"), Philo asks: "Why, when [the servant] had been sent on a mission by one person [Abraham], did he give a response to another?" By reading allegorically, Philo discovers that Abraham and Isaac are "one and the same thing, that is, [one is a symbol] of taught virtue, [the other] of natural [virtue]." According to this reading, Abraham and Isaac are in effect synonyms for virtue although their names have different connotations. Consider these patriarchs, Philo says, "not as mortal men who question each other now, but as formless types of soul [*aneideoi tropoi psychēs*] . . . which wisdom harmonizes and fits together to bring about partnership and unity" (*QuGen.* 4.144; see *Mos.* 1.76). Such "types of soul" (*ēthē* or *tropoi*) are also represented by Ham and Canaan, sons of Noah (*QuGen.* 2.77). But while Ham and Canaan represent two different sorts of souls, Philo treats them elsewhere as synonymous counterparts to Abraham and Isaac, an interpretation provoked by Genesis 9.27, which leads Philo to ask: "Why, when Ham sins, does (scripture) present his son Canaan as the servant of Shem and Japeth?" (*QuGen.* 2.77). It turns out that, just as Abraham and Isaac represent two sorts of virtue (natural and practiced), Ham and Canaan denote two sorts of vice (passive and active). So when Noah curses Canaan for Ham's sin (i.e., makes Canaan a servant of Shem and Japeth), he is in effect ignoring his sons' literal individualities in order to make an allegorical point: "Virtually [*dynamei*] he [Noah] does curse his son Ham in cursing Canaan, since when Ham has been moved to sin, he himself becomes Canaan, for it is a single thing [*hypokeimenon*], wickedness, which is presented in two different aspects, rest and motion" (*Sob.* 47). Just as the two trees in Eden lose determinate location in Philo's allegorical reading, so do Ham and Canaan, like Abraham and Isaac, lose determinate identity. Philo's allegorical readings turn specific characters who speak and act according to ordinary narrative realism into the impulses and faculties of the inner world of the human soul. Along with the suspension of narrative time and space, the reading of scriptural characters as personifications of psychological dispositions and faculties provides scripture with an underlying meaning of immediate, universal spiritual relevance.

Although Philo's allegorical reading of scripture suspends the ordinary narrative constraints of space, time, and personal identity in order to uncover Moses' psychological and cosmological wisdom, Philo does not wish to reject literal readings. He is equally reluctant, however, to sacrifice nonliteral readings in order to preserve literal meaning. Philo's dual

allegiance requires him to convince his audience that both literal and nonliteral readings are plausible interpretations of the same text that do not cancel one another. Of course, if one tries to read a text allegorically and literally without provisionally suspending one reading or the other, the two readings will indeed cancel one another, or at least create considerable confusion. Philo seeks to avoid this outcome by correlating the two aspects of scriptural language as closely as possible.

Both Moses' writing of the story of Abraham and Isaac as allegory and Philo's allegorical reading of that story depend on a logically prior meaning that makes possible the very notion of "another" meaning. Allegorical composition and reading constantly play themselves off against a substratum of words that are not meant or read allegorically (at least not at the same time or according to the same allegory). For example, despite Philo's allegorical reading of Abraham as "mind," Moses' words still describe the patriarch Abraham as a character in his own right who maintains his identity throughout various incidents and actions recorded in the Pentateuch. Philo describes Abraham's emigration as "one of soul rather than body" (*Abr.* 66), seemingly presenting the patriarch's journey as a representation of any soul's potential spiritual and philosophical progress. The patriarch is a personification of a universal and ever-present moral and spiritual possibility. But Philo's language also reminds readers that Abraham is the specifically identifiable patriarch who migrated with his father Terah from Ur of the Chaldeans to Haran ("he departed with all speed first from Chaldea, a land at that time blessed by fortune and at the height of its prosperity, and migrated to Haran"). Philo believes the two readings of this migration can peacefully coexist:

> The migrations as set forth by the literal text of the scriptures [*hē . . . rhēte tēs graphēs*] are made by a man of wisdom, but according to the principles of allegory [*hoi en allēgoriai nomoi*] by a virtue-loving soul in its search for the true God. (*Abr.* 68)

While Philo varies the emphasis of this bifocal reading throughout his treatises, he insists on keeping both story lines going at once. Literal readings and nonliteral (or allegorical) readings are mutually defining polarities, each constituting at any given moment the character—indeed, the very possibility—of the other's existence. Philo is confident that his exposition of the scriptural depiction of Abraham has simultaneously honored the literal and nonliteral meanings:

> So in both our expositions, the literal as applied to the man [*hē . . . rhēte hōs ep' andros*] and the allegorical as applied to the soul [*hē di' hyponoiōn hōs epi psychēs*], we have shown both man and soul to be worthy of our affection. (*Abr.* 88)

Close attention to the way Philo relates literal and allegorical readings shows that his principal goal is to protect the integrity of the literal textuality of scripture and to enable that textuality to embrace the Hellenistic meanings of his cultural milieu, especially cultural values concerning the soul and its moral and philosophical education. For example, Philo notes an allegorical reading of Genesis according to which Abraham represents mind (*nous*) and Sarah represents virtue (*aretē*) (*Abr.* 99). But this reading seems impossible to Philo because virtue, as a good, must be essentially active and masculine, yet *aretē* is a grammatically feminine noun (*Abr.* 101). Philo notes that the problem may lie in "the deceptiveness of the nouns" (*Abr.* 101), so he distinguishes the male gender of the allegorical referent ("virtue itself") from the grammatically feminine gender of the allegorical lexeme *aretē:* "If any one is willing to divest the things [*pragmata*] of the terms [*klēseis*] which obscure them and observe them in their nakedness in a clear light, he will understand that virtue is male" (*Abr.* 102)—even though male virtue is denoted by the feminine *aretē,* itself represented by the female Sarah. Philo's specific effort to connect the allegorical meaning/thing (i.e., virtue itself, located in a realm beyond language) to the lexical details not just of the scriptural text (containing "Sarah") but of the allegorical "subtext" (containing *aretē*) illustrates his general concern to demonstrate the literal textuality of his nonliteral meanings. Despite insisting on a disjunction between "meaning" and "language" to account for a gender discrepancy, Philo still feels it necessary to justify and explain away the apparent conflict between the two.

In another instance, Philo finds himself faced with a scripture sentence from Leviticus that can be understood in two different ways, depending on where the reader chooses to divide it (*Plant.* 113). According to Philo, the Greek text of Leviticus 19.23 reads: *ho karpos autou tria etē estai aperikathartos ou brōthēsetai.* Faced with a standard Alexandrian editorial problem, Philo presents the alternatives.[47] If the sentence is divided after *estai,* it means: "Its fruit shall be for three years. Unpruned it shall not be eaten." But if divided after *aperikathartos,* it means: "Its fruit shall be for three years unpruned. It shall not be eaten." Not surprisingly, Philo resolves this Alexandrian philological problem by allegorical means. He does not make a choice between the two possible punctuations but accepts the syntactical ambiguity. He carefully distinguishes lexical expression (*lexis*) (*Plant.* 113) from meaning (*to sēmainomenon*) (*Plant.* 114), arguing that each lexical expression yields its own distinct meaning. Focusing on the first half of each sentence, Philo offers the following interpretations. "Fruit" refers to the benefits of instruction; "three years" indicates past, present, and future—in other words, all of time. According to the first choice of punctuation, the first half of the line thus means that the

benefits of instruction are eternally incorruptible (*Plant.* 114). But the second choice of punctuation leads to a different allegorical possibility. The word *aperikathartos* ("unpruned") can be applied either to fruit that needs pruning and has not received it or to fruit that has already been pruned. Using the latter possibility, taking "pruning" as "purifying" and retaining the allegorical equations from the first reading, Philo offers this second reading: the benefits of instruction remain wholly pure forever (*Plant.* 116). Philo was originally led to these intricate readings because the verse from Leviticus describing the "pruning" of fruit conflicted with his everyday experience. Philo had seen gardeners prune trees, but had never seen anyone prune grapes, figs, or other fruit (*Plant.* 112). So the words of scripture did not seem to correspond to the things they purported to represent, forcing Philo to realize that "this again is one of the points to be interpreted allegorically, the literal meaning being quite out of keeping with the facts" (*Plant.* 113). But Philo's nonliteral readings are scrupulously attentive to the very specific lexical details of the text— rather than ignoring these details while on his way to a nonliteral reading, he preserves two versions of the lexical details, finding a satisfactory meaning for both.

Philo is concerned not only when the text of scripture seems to contradict reality but also when it contradicts itself. In *On Sobriety* 21ff., Philo finds the following passage from Deuteronomy to contain a disturbing inconsistency:

> If a man has two wives, one loved and the other hated, and the beloved and the hated each bear a son to him, and the son of her that is hated is the firstborn, it shall be that on the day on which he allots his goods to his sons, he shall not be able to give the right of the firstborn to the son of her whom he loves, and set aside the firstborn, the son of her whom he hates, but he shall acknowledge the firstborn, the son of her whom he hates, to give him a double portion of all that he has gotten; for he is the beginning of his children and to him belong the rights of the firstborn. (Deut. 21.15–17 in *Sob.* 21)

Philo observes that scripture always uses the term "first-born" or "elder" for the son of the hated wife, never for the son of the beloved, thus creating this sequence:

a. hated (first-born)—beloved (second-born) (*Sob.* 22)

But he also notes that in the passage from Deuteronomy, the expression "if . . . the beloved and the hated each bear a son" clearly puts the giving birth by the beloved before that by the hated in the syntax, producing a different sequence:

b. beloved (first-born)—hated (second-born) (*Sob.* 22)

Now, there is of course no contradiction between *a* and *b* if the first-born of sequence *a* may be considered the second-born, and the second-born of sequence *b* may be considered the first-born. Philo offers just such a reading (*Sob.* 23ff.). The beloved mother of the first-born (sequence *b*) is a symbol of pleasure, which the multitude love. But love of pleasure is shameful; consequently, her son is in fact the "second-born" (i.e., of secondary value or dishonorable) "pleasure-loving tendency [*tropos*] in the soul." In contrast, the second-born son of the hated mother (sequence *b*) is in fact the first-born because his hated mother is a symbol of prudence, which is hated by the multitude but honored by the few. Her son is therefore the "first-born" (i.e., of primary value or honorable) "virtue-loving tendency in the soul."

Sequence *a* reflects scripture's literal linking of two women and the order of the births of their children according to ordinary common sense; sequence *b* reflects the literal order of mothers and their children as they appear in the linguistic sequence of scripture. When read allegorically, sequence *b* concerns the erring soul's attitude toward pleasure and prudence: the erring soul *hates* prudence, thus failing to exercise its primary (*first-born*) capacity. Instead, it *loves* pleasure, exercising its secondary (*second-born*) capacity. The sequence of *b*'s allegorical meaning is consequently the same as the lexical sequence of *a*:

hated (first-born)—beloved (second-born)

As a result, Philo has vindicated both sequence *b* (the lexical sequence of the text) and sequence *a* (the "real-life" sequence of the text). Moreover, what at first might appear to be a spiritually unsatisfying legal prescription regarding inheritance rights becomes through Philo's allegorical reading a clear justification of both the husband's apparent hatred and his choice of beneficiary. The hatred is a disposition not of the benefactor but of the pleasure-loving and virtue-hating masses, while the choice of beneficiary is made because the husband values prudence over pleasure. The allegorical meaning thus remains faithful to all the literal details of lexical sequence while turning an ancient legal injunction into an analysis of the moral possibilities for contemporary existence. In the end, despite the allegorical reading, the literal legal injunction remains intact.

Philo's movement from the literal details of the text to nonliteral interpretation is often triggered by an apparent absence of meaning, as, for example, in the seemingly inscrutable Genesis 4.15: "He . . . that slays Cain shall loosen seven punishable objects." The text of Genesis does not make clear "what the seven objects are, nor how they are punishable, nor in what way they become loose and unstrung" (*Det.* 167). This unclarity convinces Philo that the literal "language is figurative and involves deeper meanings" (*Det.* 167). So he launches into a discussion of the soul's seven

irrational parts, suggesting that Cain represents the eighth part (the mind) to which the others are subject. When the eighth part is destroyed, the seven become subject to punishment, having lost their ruling power. Philo adds to this purely nonscriptural, Stoic meaning the scriptural illustration of the flood story, which describes Noah or "the reasoning faculty" selecting "from among the clean beasts seven, male and female" those to be saved (Gen. 7.2), and then returns to the rest of his allegorical reading. Taking its point of departure from a close reading of the literal text, Philo's allegorical commentary is thus textually validated by the key word "seven," which occurs in another scriptural context. Although Philo's own interpretation is not literal, but "allegorical," it is a sort of "intratextual allegorization" in which he strives to validate scriptural meaning in some sense by scripture rather than by his imagination or by Stoic philosophical doctrine alone.

The intratextual character of Philo's allegorical reading is suggested further by his discussion (*Det.* 177) of the second half of Genesis 4.15: "The Lord God set a sign upon Cain, that everyone that found him might not kill him." Like the first half of the verse, the second is rather opaque: it has not been made clear what the "sign" is. But Philo turns again to the possibility for interpretation suggested by the larger scriptural context. He observes that elsewhere in scripture Moses is "in the habit of showing the nature of each object by means of a sign, as in the case of events in Egypt when he [God] changed the rod into a serpent, and the hand of Moses into the form of snow, and the river into blood" (*Det.* 177). Observing the Septuagint's use of *sēmeion* in Exodus 4.8–9 and also here in Genesis 4.15, Philo asks: How then does the *sēmeion* of Cain reveal the nature of Cain? Philo responds: It does so by suggesting that Cain will not be killed. Once again, Philo's interpretation turns on an intratextual reference, this time negative: "For nowhere in the Book of the Law has his death been mentioned" (*Det.* 178). But this verse also has a nonliteral or figurative message, and Philo draws on an analogy with the *Odyssey* (12.118) to present it: "This shows in a figure that, like the Scylla of fable, folly is a deathless evil [*kakon athanaton*], never experiencing the end that consists in having died, but subject to all eternity to that which consists in ever dying" (*Det.* 178). Philo's reading of these half-verses is striking; although his treatment of the second is a precise inverse of his treatment of the first, both halves are curiously literal as well as allegorical. In the first half-verse, a literally obscure text is interpreted by an appeal to a nonscriptural cultural meaning (the Stoic doctrine of the nature of the soul) and then confirmed intratextually (by reference to the flood story). In the second half-verse, a text is first explained literally by intratextual means (by reference to the exodus signs) and then given further meaning and significance by the presentation of its cultural implication in the form

of a general maxim (to which the Homeric text can equally give rise). In both cases, Philo's desire to preserve the intratextual character of his interpretation is evident, since he does not logically need the cultural references in order to produce the desired meaning. But Philo wants to convince the reader that they are in fact necessary, suggesting that the cultural meaning is actually the true meaning of scripture.

Philo sometimes finds the literal meaning of the text unacceptable because it is incongruous with expected human behavior. Exodus 2.23 says that the Hebrew people groan over sufferings in Egypt after the death of the king of Egypt—a reaction "contrary to expectation": "For one would expect, when a tyrant dies, those over whom he has tyrannized to be glad and rejoice" (*Det.* 94). Thus, "taken literally the sentence is contradictory to reason" (*Det.* 95). "Contradictory to reason" means, of course, that it conflicts with the literal narrative context in which it occurs. But Philo notes that when one applies the first part of the verse to "the powers that sway the soul," the second part that describes the Israelite reaction makes sense: the pharaoh, or the powers that produce a licentious life, has died, but the Israelites groan because, suddenly freed from those powers, they are unwilling to face the prospect of living up to new moral standards, preferring pleasurable old Egyptian vice to new, austere demands for virtue. So Philo has not disregarded the literal character of half a verse in order to save the other half but instead has invoked the cultural meaning of "pharaoh" (the powers that sway the soul) in order to save both halves of the literal text and render them mutually consistent. Once again, Philo's nonliteral reading actually protects the lexical details of the literal narrative. Philo's approach suggests that we might profitably make a distinction between the literal *meaning* of a text (its conceptual "content") and its literal *shape* (its lexical particularities). Philo seeks to preserve the specificity of the literal shape, whether that shape yields immediate "literal" meanings (i.e., customary concepts) or secondary "nonliteral" meanings (nonstandard concepts).

The preceding examples indicate that when correlating scripture's lexical expression and literal narrative sequence with its allegorical meaning, Philo tenaciously guards the specific lexical details or shape of a text whose constraints he otherwise seems so ready to evade. Given our earlier discussion of Heraclitus, it might be tempting to attribute Philo's allegorical readings to a desire to avoid unfitting or embarrassing passages. But although he clearly does acknowledge on occasion that some readers may find a literal reading "unfitting" (e.g., *Mut.* 60), the defensive reaction against the lack of propriety commonly expressed by Hellenistic critics of the poets is largely absent from Philo's interpretative texts. Even when words like "monstrous" (*atopos*) and "inappropriate" (*aprepēs*) do appear, they are generally used by Philo to condemn not the text itself but read-

ings or readers that he finds absurd. The expressions *to prepon, to atopon,* and their various synonyms do indeed appear often enough, but generally in the course of confident boasting or criticism of others rather than hermeneutical evasion.[48] Again and again, throughout his allegorical readings, Philo, like his Hellenistic Jewish predecessors, simply declares that the text offers a meaning that is fitting and appropriate. Philo's assertion of the fitting character of scripture is part of his insistence on the meaningfulness and significance of its lexical expressions.

Philo correlates allegorical meanings and scriptural expressions so that those expressions can reshape, redefine, or "rewrite" formerly nonscriptural, cultural meanings. The old classical wisdom has been replaced by a God who as poet/maker (*poiētēs*) writes/creates the new wisdom of scripture, a poem or cosmos that forever surpasses the poetical fictions and myths of the traditional classical past. God surpasses the authors of the classical tradition precisely as a writer who engraves divine truth into the created cosmos: "In the poetry/creation [*poiētikēi*] of God you will find no fiction of myth [*mythou . . . plasma*], but truth's inexorable canons as though engraved on stone [*stēliteumena*]" (*Det.* 125). With this metaphor of divine writing or engraving, Philo seeks to subsume and surpass the entire Greek poetic tradition. He does the same to the Greek philosophical tradition by asserting that the "royal road" (Num. 20.17) and the word of God (= both cosmic *logos* or law and written Pentateuch) are synonyms representing "true and genuine philosophy" (*Post.* 102). Philo thus boldly claims that all authentic Hellenic literary and philosophical values are the product of God's cosmological and scriptural writing.

Philo sometimes subordinates his Hellenistic inheritance to scripture by having scripture directly proclaim Hellenistic philosophical wisdom, particularly Stoic ethical teaching. Although the content of this teaching is essentially the same as the wisdom that Philo discovers by reading the text "ethically," in these instances Philo has scripture present the teaching directly without the benefit of allegorical reading. Thus when Rebecca calls the servant who asks for water *kyrios* ("Sir," "Master") (Gen. 24.18), she expresses the famous Stoic paradox "that only the wise man is free and a ruler, though he may have ten thousand masters of his body" (*Post.* 138). Similarly, Genesis 12.4 ("Abraham journeyed even as the Lord spoke to him") indicates that the fundamental Stoic mandate "to live according to nature"—"the aim extolled by the best philosophers"—is actually a possibility created by scriptural legal injunctions. The Stoic life according to nature occurs "whenever the mind, having entered on virtue's path, walks in the track of right reason and follows God, mindful of his injunctions, and always and in all places recognizing them all as valid both in action and in speech" (*Mig.* 128). The result is that "the actions of the wise man are nothing else than the words of God" (*Mig.* 129). These

scriptural references do not seek to promote Stoicism as such. Not only are the Stoics seldom mentioned by name, but according to Philo's readings, scripture contains elements from a variety of classical philosophical systems. For example, the correlation of Abraham, Isaac, and Jacob with education by teaching, perfection, and practice (*Mut.* 12) echoes an Aristotelian formulation. But regardless of the specific kind of philosophy proclaimed, scripture is able to make such ethical proclamations primarily because Moses, the author of scripture, embodied all virtues and transferred them from his person to his writing (*Mos.* 2.8–11). Thus for Philo, scripture does not always require an allegorical reading to unveil Hellenistic philosophical meaning; it often presents its message concerning ethical wisdom directly.

Just as he subordinates Greek meanings to scripture, so Philo explicitly subordinates the classical sources of those meanings, often by quoting or paraphrasing the sources anonymously in new contexts that make them echo scriptural meanings. For example, Philo rejects a certain "mythical fable" of the Greeks preserved by Ovid (*Met.* 5.642ff.) concerning the hero Triptolemus, who reportedly sowed corn seed over the earth; Philo insists instead that it is God who provides all sources of nourishment (*Praem.* 8–9). Yet having quickly dispensed with Ovid's tale, Philo then forces Plato to agree with him against Ovid by providing a new context for Plato's claim that "learning is recollection":

> For none of the works of God is of later birth, but all that seems to be accomplished by human skill and industry in later time was there by the foresight of nature lying ready half made, thus justifying the saying that learning is recollection. (*Praem.* 9)

Philo thus reduces the essential basis of Platonic epistemology to an anonymous "saying" whose only value consists in bearing witness to the creative providence of God.

In other instances, Philo simply forces classical texts to corroborate or bear witness directly to the meaning of scripture. Philo contends that "one of the old writers has testified" to the difficulty of attaining virtue suggested by 1 Samuel 1.15 (LXX 1 Kings 1.15), quoting lines anonymously from Hesiod's *Works and Days* (*Ebr.* 150). In another place, as discussed above (see p. 105), Philo suggests that "the poet's words" "No mortal is she, but a deathless ill" (*Od.* 12.118) "may fitly apply" to the peculiar sort of wickedness illustrated by Cain, and he adds a colorful but anonymous phrase ("More to be thrown out than dung," from the pre-Socratic Heraclitus) to characterize the lifeless corpse of wickedness (*Fug.* 61). Philo then observes that the peculiar evil of Cain, thus explicated, is expressed also by Plato: "This truth found noble utterance in the *Theaetetus* [176A–B]" (*Fug.* 63). All of these classical texts are cited as witnesses to the

meaning of Genesis 4.15 as read by Philo. In one remarkable passage, Philo even quotes Homer by name and with reference to a specific place in a specific work, only to indicate his subordinate status as confirmer of antecedent truth: "The same idea [as the one presented by scripture] is suggested I think by Homer in the *Iliad* at the beginning of the thirteenth book [13.5–6]" (*Cont.* 17). He then quotes several lines. In other cases, an anonymous citation can be used to make the same point. After explaining that Moses in Genesis 17.17 used the phrase "said in his mind" in order to indicate swiftness of thought, Philo adds that "this is, I think, the reason why the poet most highly esteemed among the Greeks says, 'like a bird's wing or a thought' [Hom. *Od.* 7.36]" (*Mut.* 179). Through all these carefully arranged citations, Philo appropriates the prestige of Homer, the pre-Socratic Heraclitus, and Plato through direct quotation while undercutting their authority by forcing them to confirm and endorse meanings already firmly tied to scriptural expressions. When the meanings to be correlated remain on a literal level, Philo can simply assert that scripture already treats the topics. Thus airborne souls are called "angels" by Moses, but "demons" by "other philosophers" (*Gig.* 6); some Greeks call Abraham, Isaac, and Jacob "the Graces" (*Abr.* 54); and the "just" person who lived during the great flood is called "Noah" by the Hebrews, but "Deucalion" (from *dikaios,* "just") by the Greeks (*Praem.* 23).

The subordination of classical sources to scripture receives a decisive turn when Philo underscores Moses' temporal priority and spiritual authority, explicitly asserting that Moses, as author of scripture, precedes the classical authors in time and surpasses them in wisdom (see *Mos.* 1.21). The pre-Socratic Heraclitus took his opinions from Moses "like a thief" (*QuGen.* 4.152) and constructed his book *On Nature* out of Mosaic insights (*QuGen.* 3.5). Similarly, although Zeno "lived under the direction of virtue to an unsurpassed degree" (*Prob.* 53), the "fountain from which Zeno drew . . . was the law-book of the Jews" (*Prob.* 57), and the Stoic maxim "Live according to nature" is enjoined by "Zeno, or rather an oracle higher than Zeno" (*Prob.* 160). Although Hesiod says that the world is created and not eternal, "long before [*makrois de chronois proteron*] Hesiod, Moses the lawgiver of the Jews said in the Holy Books that it was created and imperishable" (*Aet.* 18–19). Even Socrates himself is finally eclipsed in Philo's allegorical reading of Genesis 11.32c ("Terah died in Haran"). Philo argues that there is a single mode (*tropos*) of self-knowledge called "Terah" by the Hebrews and "Socrates" by the Greeks—for the Greeks "say that 'Know Thyself' was likewise the theme of life-long pondering to Socrates, and that his philosophy was concerned exclusively with his own self" (*Som.* 1.58). But Socrates' historicity marks his subordination to Terah and to the text that depicts him as the primary emblem of classical wisdom; for while Socrates "was a human being," Terah

was self-knowledge itself, a way of thinking set before us as a tree of great luxuriance, to the end that lovers of virtue might find it easy, as they pluck the fruit of moral knowledge, to take their fill of nourishment saving and most sweet. (*Som.* 1.58)

Here an individual becomes subordinate to the state of being he represents. For Philo, these states are like Platonic Forms, superior to the individuals who participate in them, just as virtue itself was superior to Sarah. But it is not the conventional Platonism of this subordination of particular to ideal that warrants attention, but the way Philo turns that conventional philosophical motif against Greek philosophy and culture, subordinating them to his own sacred text. Unapprehensible by human nature, God anticipated the Delphic Oracle by telling Moses to "know thyself" (*Spec.* 1.44). Thus in various ways does Philo subordinate classical meanings, texts, and authors to scripture. His allegorical reading of scripture brings the images and concepts prevalent in his Hellenistic culture into direct relation to scripture. In fact, by reading scripture allegorically, Philo treats scripture as a rewriting of previously written cultural ideals.

The origin and driving force of this rewriting is Moses, who functions in three related ways: as one who is himself "written upon" by God at Sinai, as a writer of scripture, and as an author of laws for proper behavior.[49] Moses prepares for the Sinai theophany by leaving the city and entering the desert, in order to purify his soul: he cannot receive God's divine writing or engraving until "the marks which his old transgressions have imprinted [*ensphragisthentes typoi*] on him have gradually grown faint, melted away and disappeared" (*Dec.* 11). On Sinai itself, Moses and the people "saw the voice" (*Dec.* 47), for the divine word is also a deed or act. When the text says that the voice proceeded from the fire, it indicates symbolically that those who obey God's word/deed "will live forever as in unclouded light with the laws themselves as stars illuminating their [now purified] souls" (*Dec.* 49). God's word/deed takes the concrete form of engraving on tablets (*Dec.* 50), but it is already clear that it has been simultaneously engraved on Moses' purified soul. Moses' experience of the divine is thus a reception of a kind of divine writing; he hears a voice that is also a deed, and the word/deed is also an engraving. Because Moses could not find in ordinary fallen language the means to learn and express wisdom, he "prints and impresses [*sēmeioumenos kai ensphragizomenos*] on his understanding the lessons of true wisdom" (*Det.* 38). By virtue of such impressions, Moses becomes one of the "living laws" even before composing the written laws.[50] In his own person, Moses functions as a kind of seal designed to impress the law (in the shape of his life) on those who would become his followers. Moses

has set before us, like some well-wrought picture, a piece of work beautiful and godlike, a model [*paradeigma*] for those who are willing to copy it [*mimeisthai*]. Happy are they who imprint, or strive to imprint, that image [*typos*] in their souls. (*Mos.* 1.158–59)

Moses' life represents the law in its original form as a life engraved with the forms of wisdom.

Moses as a living law then transforms himself into a literally written law when he composes the Pentateuch. Readers of Philo's treatises will recall how often Philo conveys his sense of the Pentateuch as a written text, and, more specifically, as originally written rather than secondarily transcribed from original speech.[51] Philo's Moses is a writer rather than a speaker, and the Pentateuch is fundamentally a text to be read rather than a voice to be heard.[52] In writing the Pentateuch, Moses simply elaborates the Ten Principles, which were "engraved" (*stēliteuesthai*) or "written" (*graphesthai*) on stone tablets "by the finger of God" (*Mig.* 85).[53] The point of reading the written or engraved scripture is the same as that of using the "living law" of Moses as a seal—to impress or "characterize" one's soul with the discriminations of the law. Receiving these correct impressions enables one, like Moses, to know when one word has two meanings or two words have one meaning and explains why Philo's efforts to discern the differences masked by the similarities of homonyms and synonyms is so important— it is crucial that the soul of the scripture reader be brought into contact with the actual Mosaic message conveyed by the words of the text. To read the scriptural text is to impress its writing on one's soul so that the "substantial realities" represented by scriptural language become "graven, as though on stone [*stēliteumena*], on the heart of the wise" (*Conf.* 74).

The scripture that Moses writes is not only a text to be read; it is also a legal code to be enacted. Jews are to write this code into their lives. God's engraving of the number seven (a number filled with cosmological import) on the tablets of commandments, the minds of the readers, and the order of their lives brings together the various forms of divine writing discussed above (*Op.* 128). The Israelites are to be more than mere readers of scripture; they are to translate their scripture reading into action in the world. Religious practices, even if not explicitly written in scripture, are in fact unwritten laws, and these practices or customs, like the written text, are to be engraved in the souls of those active in a sociopolitical practice or *politeia*. The enacted text of the law is the final goal of the original divine writing. That writing began in the darkness on Mount Sinai when God wrote the law on the soul of Moses. As a living law, Moses writes his virtuous life on those who make him their model, and as an author, he writes out the law for readers to rewrite on their own souls and to enact in their own lives: "The most holy Moses . . . loves and teaches the

truth which he desires to engrave and stamp [*egcharattein kai ensphragizes-thai*] on all his disciples, dislodging and banishing false opinions to a distance from their understanding" (*Spec.* 1.59), in order to enhance "the commonwealth of the laws" (*hē kata tous nomous politeia*) (*Spec.* 1.63).

Although applicable first of all to the Jewish community, divine writing has a universal grounding because the ultimate divine lawgiver is also the creator of all human beings and the entire cosmos. Divine "right reason," the source of all other law (*Prob.* 47), "is an infallible law engraved not by this mortal or that [such as Solon or Lycurgus] and, therefore, perishable as he, nor on parchment or slabs, and, therefore soulless as they, but by immortal nature on the immortal mind, never to perish" (*Prob.* 46).[54] Creation itself is the primordial divine writing, and the metaphor of engraving emphasizes the permanence of the cosmos: "All that is fixed and permanent in circumstances and condition is graven as on stone [*stēliteumenon*] in the keeping of God alone" (*Conf.* 106). The text of scripture corresponds to the text of the cosmos; to imitate one is to imitate the other. The tablets of the universe are engraved by the God who engraved Moses' soul. Through divine creation and through Moses' writings, this God continues to "write upon" the souls of all human beings. The actual written text of the Pentateuch with its specific narratives and legal injunctions gives definition and character to this divine engraving.

By allowing Moses to rewrite the moral and philosophical wisdom of Hellenistic culture, Philo has in effect allegorically subordinated classical meanings and texts to scripture. Because Moses came before the classical authors, his rewriting paradoxically becomes original writing, and the classical writers become his weak imitators. Philo's allegorical reading seldom contradicts competing classical sources. Instead, whatever of value they contain has been anticipated by the author of the master text of the Pentateuch. Furthermore, the rewriting of classical precursors is available not simply in individual scriptural texts but in the Pentateuch as a coherent whole. Classical precursors are the victims not of a fragmentary rewriting but of a single, unified book. Hellenistic culture is being absorbed by a single book, and Philo's intratextual interpretation underscores the unity of that master text. Philo also shows an explicit interest in that book's relation to his own religious community. One Philonic allegorical reading of a passage in Exodus suggests that God takes special interest in the fate of the Jewish nation. Philo reads the account of the burning bush in the wilderness as a "description of the nation's condition as it stood at that time," and he presents the allegorical meaning of this description as a consolation to the Hebrews:

Do not lose heart; your weakness is your strength, which can prick, and thousands will suffer from its wounds. Those who desire to consume you

will be your unwilling saviors instead of your destroyers. Your ills will work you no ill. Nay, just when the enemy is surest of ravaging you, your fame will shine forth most gloriously. (*Mos.* 1.69)

This social and political prophecy, hidden beneath the literal narrative of a burning bush that remains unconsumed by fire, speaks most obviously about the ancient exodus from Egypt. But such an allegorical reading had social and political implications for Philo's contemporary audience as well.

THE WORLD WITHIN THE TEXT

Philo not only correlates allegorical meanings with lexical expressions and intratextual references in order to subordinate nonscriptural, cultural meanings to scripture. His interpretative practice also has a social and political function; his interpretative texts are designed to do, as well as say, certain things. It has been argued that Philo's allegorical reading of scripture sought to internationalize Judaism by eliminating all its distinctive features, producing a philosophy acceptable to both Jews and Greeks.[55] But this suggestion fails to account for Philo's interpretative practice in the context of the Jewish community in Alexandria. On the contrary, we have already observed Philo's efforts to protect the distinctive features of scriptural expression and to link allegorical meaning to those features. Rather than seeking to transform those features into a general philosophy, Philo redefines general philosophy in terms of scripture's distinctive features. Through such subordination and reinterpretation, Philo seeks to preserve the particularity of Jewish religious, social, and political identity by defending the literal text of scripture and by insisting that the law be literally observed, even though it may be read allegorically. And Philo takes the further, far bolder step of giving this particular obedience a universal scope. Taken as a whole, the law that the Jews obey forms a story that stretches from creation to judgment and defines not simply Jewish history but the entire course of world history. Philo was convinced that Gentiles would not only acknowledge Jewish identity as defined by obedience to Mosaic law but also would one day recognize that the sacred text that shapes Jewish identity also shapes their own. Consequently, Philo's allegorical reading of scripture revises Greek culture by subordinating it to Jewish cultural and religious identity; his interpretation is not a synthesis but a usurpation. Just as Philo preserves the linguistic integrity of scripture's lexical expression in order to reinterpret Greek meanings (e.g., philosophical and ethical concepts), so he insists on obedience to the written laws of the Pentateuch as the definition of authentic culture.

The Jews occupied a prominent place among the many different

mpeting for power in ancient Alexandria.[56] The Romans had
lly respected and defended the rights enjoyed by Jews as mem-
_.._ ,_.:teumata (i.e., quasi-independent and self-regulating communal
organizations) in the major cities under imperial control. The rights given
to the Alexandrian Jews as a *politeuma* by the Ptolemies had been confirmed by Augustus and were reportedly engraved on a stele placed in the
middle of the city. Despite such rights of limited self-government, the
Romans continued to exercise jurisdiction over the Jews. This was illustrated in 10–12 c.e. when Augustus summarily abolished the head office
of the Alexandrian Jewish community (the ethnarch), handing over the
administration of the *politeuma*'s affairs to a council of "elders." The more
customary Augustan policy of defending Jewish rights was continued by
Tiberius, flouted by Gaius Caligula, then partially reaffirmed by Claudius.
Following their typical administrative policy for the Greek-speaking East,
the Romans regarded all non-Greeks in Egypt, including the Jews, as
Egyptians. Although some Jews in Alexandria possessed Greek citizenship, the majority did not.[57] Since the vast majority of Alexandrian citizens were Greek, Alexandria itself was viewed by the Romans as a Greek
city.[58] Indeed, in order to placate Greek nationalist sentiment, the Romans maintained the fiction that the Alexandrian *polis* was autonomous
by referring to the city as Alexandria "near" Egypt (*ad*, not *in*, *Aegyptum*).[59]
Philo's wealthy family was intimately involved with the Roman government. After Philo's death, his nephew Tiberius Julius Alexander obtained
the rank of *eques* and became the prefect of Egypt, necessarily leaving
behind his Jewish identity in the process.[60] As a leader of the Alexandrian
Jewish community, Philo dealt frequently with members of the local
Roman and Greek power structures. He knew from experience that
protecting Jewish interests in the face of hostile challenges from Greeks
and Egyptians depended on good relations with Rome. Philo's embassy to
Gaius Caligula illustrates that he was prepared to act dramatically in
response to those challenges.

The Alexandrian Jewish community was composed of several different
factions, principally a small elite of highly Hellenized intellectuals and a
large group that despised both Greek culture and Roman rule and was
influenced by revolutionary impulses emanating from Palestine. The
hatred that 3 Maccabees has the Jews display toward their Ptolemaic
rulers is probably a thin disguise for Jewish hatred of Roman rule under
Augustus.[61] Between the elite and revolutionary groups there was also a
group of "orthodox" Jews who were content with preserving the social
and political status quo.[62] This group may well have included the finan-
cially influential figures, as well as the literal readers of scripture, who
occasionally surface in Philo's treatises.[63] It is likely that Philo's efforts at
rapprochement and negotiation with Rome and with the Greeks reflected

the interests only of a small minority consisting of the elite group and perhaps some of the orthodox contingent. He leveled a fair amount of polemic against the "Jewish mob," which was often threatening insurrection. These threats became reality when Claudius succeeded Caligula in 41 c.e. Although Claudius returned to the Augustan policy of toleration for the Jews in Alexandria, the previously attacked Jews took advantage of their sudden change in fortune, assaulting the Greeks of the city.[64] After the final settlement of the question of Jewish status in Alexandria by Claudius, these new nationalist Jews, rather than those represented by Philo, became dominant.[65] In contrast to the militant stance of the Jewish nationalists, Philo's group had sought the rights and benefits of Greek education and culture that *polis* life could provide. But the desire of the Jews to reap the benefits of Greek education elicited intense animosity from the "authentic" Greeks of Alexandria.

The Greeks were also divided, disputing among themselves as to which of them had authentic Greek status and citizenship and which did not, and together despising Jewish intellectuals who sought to achieve status equal to their own. The Greeks viewed such Jews with a scorn usually reserved for the Egyptians. Intra-Greek friction was exacerbated by Augustus's definition in 4/5 c.e. of a new class of inhabitants, *hoi apo gymnasiou* ("those who belong to the gymnasium"). The *gymnasioi* were Greek-speaking and Greek-educated Egyptians living outside the three *poleis* whom the Romans decided to treat (partially) as Greek for legal purposes. Together with the *mētropolitai*—Hellenized inhabitants of the chief Egyptian towns (*mētropoleis*)—these persons were legally Egyptians, yet highly privileged owing to their education. Greek *gymnasioi* found themselves caught between the true classical definition of Greek nationality—membership in a Greek *polis*—and the new Roman criterion of Greek origin—a gymnasium education. Their ambiguous status was reinforced by Roman legal casuistry; like all Egyptians, they were forced to pay the poll tax (*laographia*) introduced in 24/23 b.c.e.; yet unlike the common peasants, they paid at a reduced rate. Such inner stratification led to strife and resentment as a result of the jealousy and insecurity generated by status inconsistency and social ambiguity, for while Greek education was a widely acknowledged mark of cultural superiority, payment of the *laographia* denoted severe cultural inferiority. Jews were especially galled by the fact that the Romans regarded these Greek-speaking Egyptians as Greek while considering the Jews Egyptian, thus making them subject to payment of the *laographia.* Conversely, Hellenized Egyptians resented the Jews' attempt to obtain the rights of Greek citizens, especially when Jews such as Philo denied them similar status as "Alexandrians."

In addition to these more or less formal legal and social distinctions, we also find the sort of economic stratification in Alexandria typical of large

Hellenistic seaports. Philo reports that there were investors, shipowners, merchants, artisans, and peasant farmers (*Flacc.* 57). For the most part, these groups could be expected to side with Roman and Greek interests that were conducive to the shipping trade on which their livelihood depended. While anything that seriously threatened their financial interests would probably mobilize such persons to respond in some way, they were primarily concerned to preserve social stability. Alexandrian Greeks in this group thus helped reinforce the alliance with Rome, and they also supported Roman efforts to collect the *laographia*, in order to protect their own status by ensuring the "purity" of the gymnasium. Although Jewish members of this economic class resented paying the poll tax, they wanted to preserve social stability.

Evidence from 3 Maccabees shows that Greeks and Jews could in fact work together in business life, despite severe social tensions.[66] In the countryside, one could find landowners, vine dressers, shepherds, livestock farmers, and boat owners, as well as the ever-present poor, who shared the oppressive burden of life under Roman rule whether they were Jews or Egyptians.[67] Philo's references to these rural groups are infrequent, and his writings suggest that his own immediate social world was that of refined, Hellenistic, intellectual Jews in the city. His reports on the Therapeutae do indicate, however, that he was familiar with varieties of Judaism outside the city. Philo's interpretative writings emerge from the web of social, political, and religious relationships generated by these various groups.

In contrast to modern historical-critical exegesis of scripture, which begins with the assumption that the ancient communities that produced the text were radically different from our own, for Philo exegesis of the Pentateuch was first of all commentary on the actual history of the community to which he belonged. For a Jew living under foreign domination in Egypt, dealing with the Pentateuchal accounts of ancient oppression in Egypt and deliverance by Moses surely had an immediacy and contemporary relevance that we can scarcely imagine. This fact is suggested by the number of anti-Semitic histories of Egypt that offered highly polemical versions of the portions of Egyptian history that involved the Jews. Chaeremon, a Greco-Egyptian priest and teacher of Nero who probably accompanied the Alexandrian delegation to Rome in 41 c.e., wrote a history of Egypt similar to that attributed to Manetho, an Egyptian priest of an earlier age.[68] Another Alexandrian writer of the first century b.c.e., Lysimachus, also wrote such a history.[69] Serious sociocultural and religious clashes between Greeks and Jews in Alexandria thus led to competing interpretations of the early history of the Egyptian Jews. A number of such anti-Semitic histories included specific vilification of Moses.[70] Consequently, it is not surprising that the acrimonious controversy be-

tween Philo and the Greek nationalists took the form of competing interpretations of the literal scriptural narratives of Moses' life. In general, the
Greek nationalist faction represented by the writers of anti-Semitic histories sought to convince the Romans that the Jews were aliens, promulga-
tors of a crude and barbaric religion, haters of humanity, and despisers of
the gods. We are not likely to appreciate the social and political force of
Philo's *Life of Moses* if we do not keep such attacks constantly in mind. In
the context of such Greek slander, Philo's claim that Moses and his literal
laws most perfectly embody the ideals of Greek culture and provide the
foundation for a superior social organization becomes a political and
social claim directly relevant to the social circumstances of Jews in Alexandria.

One of Philo's contemporaries, Apion, was the author of an anti-
Semitic tract. Apion was an Alexandrian grammarian, a Hellenized Egyptian with Greek citizenship. He was probably head of the Alexandrian
library, and he also taught rhetoric in Rome during the reigns of Tiberius,
Caligula, and Claudius. Philo's debate with Apion (or at least with the anti-
Semitic position he represented) surfaces at several places in the *Life of
Moses*. Along with his predecessors in anti-Semitic polemic, Apion had
argued that the ancestors of the Jews were Egyptians by race who had
been justly expelled from Egypt because they carried contagious diseases
(Joseph. *Ap.* 2.8). This charge reflects Apion's general insistence on the
illegitimate status of Jews in the midst of the competing social groups in
Alexandria. The crux of Apion's complaint is of course not historical; he
is complaining about contemporary Jews, whom he terms "aliens" (*Ap.*
2.71), who are illegitimately seeking rights he believed were only properly
held by Alexandrian Greeks. Apion is astonished "at the idea of Jews
being called Alexandrians" (*Ap.* 2.38), asking, "Why, then, if they are
citizens, do they not worship the same gods as the Alexandrians?" (*Ap.*
3.66).[71] One example of the length to which these anti-Semitic writers
could go is Apion's story about Jews in Jerusalem who kidnapped "a
Greek foreigner" and sacrificed him in the temple and "while immolating
the Greek, swore an oath of hostility to the Greeks" (*Ap.* 2.95). Clearly
Apion is attempting to shock and disgust the Greeks (and indirectly the
Romans) by means of such vilification, while preserving and defending
his own ambiguous social status. Defensive about his own questionable
status, he continually ridicules the Jews precisely for cultural inferiority—
they "have not produced any geniuses, for example, inventors in arts and
crafts or eminent sages" (*Ap.* 2.135).

In response to such charges, Philo offers in the *Life of Moses* an alternative account of the origin and nature of the Jews, implying that they enjoy
a social prestige that contradicts their status as represented by authors like
Apion as well as their actual status in Alexandria: Jews are "settlers and

friends who are anxious to obtain equal rights with the burgesses and are near to being citizens because they differ little from the original inhabitants" (*Mos.* 1.35). Such is Philo's ideal. But the king of the Egyptians did not acknowledge the ideal, and Philo finds in the contemporary oppression of Jews in Alexandria an "antitype" corresponding to the "type" of their ancient suffering in Egypt (see *Mos.* 1.36). Philo's disputes with the Greek nationalists indicate that his commitment to the literal narrative of the biblical text as history is deeply related to the polemical context in which he actually writes his interpretative works. Apion's attacks on Jewish history take place necessarily at a very literal level; no amount of allegorical reading could answer them without simply turning over Jewish history to the anti-Semitic interpreters, and Jewish communities to the social and political forces they represented. Classical allegorical readers could give up the literal reading of unfitting Homeric narratives because their social survival was not at stake. To the extent that Philo spoke for the Alexandrian Jewish community, he had no such option. He clearly understood that allegorical readings that ignored or denigrated the literal narrative fostered or at least acquiesced in the capitulation of Jewish identity in the face of Greek cultural pressures. Such capitulation might result from a failure to defend the literal text as history; it would certainly come from failure to obey the laws that the literal text prescribed.

In the *Life of Moses* Philo responds to Apion's challenge by showing that the highest Hellenistic ethical ideals were first embodied in Moses and subsequently set forth in the specific form of Jewish laws.[72] As a result, Moses emerges as the true philosopher-king, promulgating laws for a true *politeia.* In the process, Moses is far from being a mere occasion for the display of Greek ideals; Philo ties Moses' virtues to his specific deeds as the Septuagint or Jewish oral tradition records them. If the Greeks are Philo's audience, they seem to be invited by the *Life of Moses* to become Jewish. But the highly Hellenized Jews who are probably the actual audience are being told that the most authentic way to be Greek is to be authentically Jewish—which means, at a minimum, obeying Jewish law.

Philo's insistence on obedience to the law appears in a much-discussed passage in which he criticizes over-zealous allegorical readers for failing to obey the laws that they read allegorically:

> There are some who, regarding the written laws[73] as symbols of intellectual things, are overpunctilious about the latter, while treating the former with easy-going neglect. Such men I for my part should blame for handling the matter in too easy and offhand a manner: they ought to have given careful attention to both aims, to a more full and exact investigation of what is not seen and in what is seen to be stewards without reproach. As it is, as though they were living alone by themselves in a wilderness, or as though they had become disembodied souls, and knew neither city nor village nor household

nor any company of human beings at all, overlooking all that the mass of men regard, they explore reality in its naked absoluteness. These men are taught by the sacred word to have thought for good repute, and to let go nothing that is part of the customs fixed by divinely empowered men greater than those of our time. (*Mig.* 89–90)

Philo's charge of apoliticism against the allegorical readers makes sense in light of the Alexandrian social conflicts that swirled around him. In the midst of Alexandrian struggles with the Roman imperial government, Jewish literal readers probably supported Jewish rites and customs (which were inherently tied to the literal text of the Pentateuch), while Jewish allegorical readers were perhaps more willing to give in on such matters. But Philo insists that allegorical readers must obey the Mosaic laws literally even though they read them nonliterally.

Philo uses metaphors of body and soul to criticize the allegorical readers in this passage though elsewhere he uses the same metaphors to praise the Therapeutae (*Cont.* 78). Against the allegorical readers, Philo suggests that because the letter of the law is like the body and its inner meaning like the soul, we should value the former no less than the latter since we "have to take thought for the body, because it is the abode of the soul" (*Mig.* 93). Unlike the extreme allegorical readers, the Therapeutae view scripture as "a living creature with the literal ordinances for its body and for its soul the invisible mind [*nous*] laid up in its wording." But the Therapeutae clearly seek to pierce through the body/letter to reach the soul/mind (*Cont.* 78). Philo's praise of the Therapeutae's hermeneutical aspirations thus explains why his criticism of the over-zealous allegorists remains muted; like the other allegorists, Philo wants to move beyond the mere letter.[74] But the difference between moving through the letter to the spirit and replacing the letter by the spirit remains fundamental. Philo joined the ranks neither of the extreme allegorical readers nor of the Therapeutae, and his political efforts to preserve Jewish rights in Alexandria are consistent with a concern for the literal text of the laws not shared by the excessive Jewish allegorical readers. Unlike those who sought to "explore reality in its naked absoluteness," Philo joined the society of "the mass of men," forsaking the extreme allegorical readers who imagined themselves to live apolitically, "as though they were living alone by themselves in a wilderness, or as though they had become disembodied souls, and knew neither city nor village nor household nor any company of human beings at all" (*Mig.* 90). Hence Philo's allegorical reading does not entail one possible and logical set of apolitical and antisocial consequences. Rather than leading to social and political disengagement or submission, allegorical reading can be a means of social and political revision and subversion.

Consequently, although Philo praises Moses for embodying typical Hellenistic virtues—"self-restraint, continence, temperance, shrewdness, good sense, knowledge, endurance of toil and hardships, contempt of pleasures, justice, advocacy of excellence"—he gives praise for embracing such virtues and censure for neglecting them "according to law" or "as the law directs" (*Mos.* 1.154). Philo thus links Hellenistic virtues to obedience to Jewish law. Yet Jewish law does not parochialize the virtues; the striking thing about the Jewish lawgiver is that "each element" of the entire cosmos "obeyed him as its master" (*Mos.* 1.156). Consequently, Moses need not be enrolled on any particular citizen list because he is a "world citizen" (*Mos.* 1.157). His life is a model for all to imitate, the "form of virtue" that all are called to desire to possess (*Mos.* 1.159). But despite his universal, even cosmic, significance, Moses is not a cipher of moral virtue in general; instead, his moral virtues bear witness to the fact that he himself is "a reasonable and living law" (*Mos.* 1.162). Philo thus insists that Moses' virtue is the outgrowth of the laws he instantiates. In contrast, writes Philo (with his nephew in mind?), most men, given a little prosperity, "look down on their relations and friends and set at naught the laws under which they were born and bred, and subvert the ancestral customs to which no blame can justly attach, by adopting different modes of life, and, in their contentment with the present, lose all memory of the past" (*Mos.* 1.31). But such was not Moses' path. Even though he "reached the very pinnacle of human prosperity," Moses "was zealous for the discipline and culture of his kinsmen and ancestors" (*Mos.* 1.32).

Adherence to their ancestral discipline and culture provided protection for the ancient Israelites. The outsider Balaam was unable to curse the Hebrews—"not because their dwelling-place is set apart and their land severed from others, but because in virtue of the distinction of their peculiar customs they do not mix with others to depart from the ways of their fathers" (*Mos.* 1.278). However, just as the particularity of Mosaic legal injunctions does not negate their universal import, so too the peculiarity of Hebraic customs does not mean that the Hebrews have no right to define true *politeia*. When Balaam looks out over the Hebrew encampment, Philo remarks that he was "astounded at their number and order, which resembled a city [*polis*] rather than a camp" (*Mos.* 1.288). Philo's definition of universal Hellenistic ideals in terms of Jewish particularity is also suggested by Balaam's advice to Balak to have the harlots tempt the young Israelite men by causing them to leave "the ways of [their] fathers" (*Mos.* 1.298). Philo here links a commonplace of Hellenistic ethics—the problem of reason's subversion by passion—with the specifically Jewish concern to follow the customs of the ancestors. The young men lose their bodies to "pleasure" when they lose their souls to "lawlessness and unholiness" (*Mos.* 1.301).

Perhaps the clearest example of Philo's attempt to reinterpret the social and political order in terms of Jewish particularity is his description of the translation of the Pentateuch. Philo is clear that the whole point of the translation is not to demonstrate how Greek the Jewish ethos really is, but precisely the opposite: to show how Greek culture is best understood as deficient Judaism. The translation is the work of those who were more than mere translators but were "prophets and priests of the mysteries" (*Mos.* 2.40). Philo uses this elitist language of the Greek mysteries to convince his Hellenized Jewish readership that the pinnacle of Greco-Roman religious culture was now available in the form of their very own Jewish scripture—if only they could understand its deeper meaning and significance. Understanding scripture requires attending the synagogue, which is now the true home of classical virtue: "For what are our places of prayer throughout the cities," Philo asks, "but schools of prudence and courage and temperance and justice?" (*Mos.* 2.216). Philo announces that God answered the prayers of the translators so that "the greater part, or even the whole, of the human race might be profited and led to a better life by continuing to observe such wise and truly admirable ordinances" (*Mos.* 2.36). Philo thus discusses the Septuagint in conjunction with the present social status of the Jews and their hopes for the future. Both Jews and non-Jews in Alexandria, ordinary citizens and nonrulers, come to the island of Pharos "even to the present day" (*Mos.* 2.41) to celebrate the making of the translation, even "though our nation has not prospered for many a year" (*Mos.* 2.43). Philo then looks to the future: "It is but natural that when some people are not flourishing their belongings to some degree are under a cloud. But, if a fresh start should be made to brighter prospects, how great a change for the better might we expect to see!" (*Mos.* 2.43–44). This passage has been read as indicating the temporal priority of a Jewish revelation consisting of a generic "international philosophy," and as thus constituting Philo's explanation that the Greeks did not in fact recognize this international Jewish philosophy as their own because the Jewish nation was beleaguered and, finally, all but destroyed.[75] This interpretation might seem convincing if one assumed that the *Life of Moses* was directed essentially to pagan Greek intellectuals as an apologetic.[76] But the preceding discussion has suggested that the proper context for the *Life* is more likely (1) an intra-Jewish dialogue in which Philo supports and enhances Jewish identity by stressing obedience to Jewish law because it contains all the riches of Greek wisdom and (2) a polemical interchange between Philo and Greco-Egyptian anti-Semitic attackers of the literal history of the Jews. Given this context, Philo's interpretative work hardly seems designed to translate Jewish law into a generic, universal philosophy. On the contrary, it translates Greek ideals into Judaism in all of its particularity.

It has been suggested, however, that any traces of such "particularity" or a "nationalistic standpoint" in Philo's works simply reflect Philo's answer to the question of what might happen to true philosophy if the people elected to promote it no longer existed.[77] But this judgment, which subordinates the specific people to the general philosophy, does not do sufficient justice to the clear prediction by Philo that non-Jewish nations will in fact one day honor particular Jewish laws alone. Philo tells his Hellenistic Jewish readers that renewed prosperity will not come from casting aside Jewish ways for Greek culture, but from stubbornly guarding their peculiar ways until the Gentiles convert:

> I believe that each nation would abandon its peculiar ways, and, throwing overboard their ancestral customs, turn to honoring our laws alone. For, when the brightness of their [the laws'] shining is accompanied by national prosperity, it will darken the light of the others as the risen sun darkens the stars. (*Mos.* 2.44)

Philo's eschatological hope that the Gentiles will ultimately come to obey Jewish law is partly grounded in the fact that the law is stamped with the seal of nature itself.[78] The Septuagint translators of Hebrew scripture, following the order of the books of the Bible, began with the creation of the cosmos, not with the account of the chosen people and their laws (*Mos.* 2.37). But one should not therefore conclude that the law is somehow secondary to a purely natural theology, for it was Moses himself—living law and lawgiver—who had placed the creation account first. Philo argues that the very way in which Moses organized his exposition— "relating the history of early times, and going for its beginning right to the creation of the universe"—was designed to show that "the Father and Maker of the world was in the truest sense also its Lawgiver" and that "he who would observe the laws will accept gladly the duty of following nature and live in accordance with the ordering of the universe" (*Mos.* 2.48). Here Philo makes the point illustrated by both the nature of his allegorical reading and the social functions of his writings: the well-ordered life is a Jewish life that by its very nature (i.e., because God is Creator as well as Lawgiver) is the life that the non-Jewish world will eventually come to recognize as the goal of its own moral striving.

The link between scripture and creation enables Philo to highlight the narrative of scripture as the key to a life as well ordered as the cosmos. Philo construes Jewish scripture as a story that unfolds from a clear beginning to a clear end. He argues in the *Life of Moses* that this narrative pattern consists of two basic parts: a "history" consisting of a creation story and a genealogy, and the "commands and prohibitions" (*Mos.* 2.46– 47). It has been well observed that this pattern corresponds exactly to the pattern of the group of treatises known collectively as the *Exposition of the*

Law.[79] Such a pattern is mentioned again in the last work of the *Exposition* entitled *On Rewards and Punishments*. In this text Philo separates the narrative pattern into three, rather than two, principal sections: creation, history, and legislation (first general, then specific) (*Praem.* 1–2). Combining Philo's various summaries of the narrative pattern of scripture, we can outline the narrative of the *Exposition of the Law* as follows (with the categories capitalized and the titles of individual treatises italicized):

Life of Moses
I. HISTORY
   A. Creation Story
     An Account of the World's Creation Given by Moses
   B. Genealogy
     1. *On Abraham, i.e., the life of the wise man made perfect through teaching, or the first book on unwritten laws*
     2. *On Isaac* (lost)
     3. *On Jacob* (lost)
     4. *On Joseph, i.e., the life of the statesman*
II. LEGISLATION (= "Commands and Prohibitions")
   A. General
     On the Decalogue
   B. Specific
     1. *On Special Laws*
     2. *On the Virtues, which together with others were described by Moses, or On Courage and Piety and Humanity and Repentance*
     3. *On Rewards and Punishments*

This overall pattern need not be the product of a unified apologetic to pagan Greek readers interested in Judaism, as is sometimes claimed.[80] One proponent of such a view cites a passage from the *Exposition* in which Philo explains in detail aspects of Jewish law and custom that all Jews would already know quite well (and that would thus presumably be redundant information for them), but that would perhaps catch the interest of pagan readers:

> But while the Law forbids bodily labor [on the Sabbath], it requires the better types of activity, which are those carried on by words and teachings with respect to virtue. For it enjoins the spending of that time in philosophizing for the improvement of the soul and the dominant mind. So on the Sabbath there stand open throughout all cities ten thousand places of instruction in prudence, self-control, courage, justice, and the other virtues, in which the people sit quietly and in order, with ears alert and all attention, by reason of their thirst for the refreshing words, while one of those more skilled stands and expounds the noblest, helpful principles by which the whole life shall advance to better things. (*Spec.* 2.61–62)[81]

While it might be possible to conclude that this passage is directed at Greeks unfamiliar with synagogue practices,[82] a more likely conclusion is that Philo is portraying classical virtues as features of Jewish practice for a Jewish audience. On this reading of the description, Philo does not seek to persuade Greeks to become Jewish, but to convince Jews that they can assimilate some measure of classical pagan culture even (or especially) while attending synagogue. Admittedly, Philo describes synagogue practice in a way that would appeal to a Greek readership. But Philo does this so that his actual Jewish audience will "overhear" a description of their customary life that reveals its uncustomary (i.e., Greek) cultural and ethical significance. Philo's rhetorical strategy seems analogous to the way Christian "apologies," though formally addressed to emperors, were designed to be read by Christian intellectuals. Through this indirect description of synagogue practice, Philo leads his Jewish readers to see what they usually do and say in a new light, and thus he enables them to enjoy greater self-esteem.[83]

We have seen that Philo defended certain literal details of scripture in the controversy with anti-Semitic Greek nationalists like Apion. But the larger scriptural story running from divine creation to eschatological rewards and punishments also functions socially and politically by its stress on its *telos*—the final judgment of God. By 38 C.E., Flaccus, the Roman governor of Alexandria, had helped the Alexandrian nationalists drive the Jews into their first ghetto in history and incited the Alexandrian populace to attack them. If Philo saw the world (and particularly the specific world of Alexandria in 38–41 C.E.) as a moment within a larger history defined and ordered by this narrative framework, one would expect the end of that narrative to play a role in Philo's writings. And indeed it does. As Flaccus displays in his moral regress the obverse of Moses' ascent in virtue, so he receives at the hands of the Jewish God a punishment that one could receive only if life were in fact defined by that scriptural narrative (see *Flacc.* 125ff.).[84] Indeed, Philo may well intend his account of his embassy to the emperor Gaius Caligula to be a serious warning to the Romans to join the winning side of history. In the *Legatio ad Gaium*, written late in his life, Philo looks back on his defense of Alexandrian Jews who were attacked for their resolute refusal to accept the emperor Gaius Caligula's claim to be divine, and he describes the embassy that he led in order to persuade the emperor to alter his policies toward the Jews. The work, probably directed to Claudius (or perhaps Nero), seems to be designed to prove to Roman officials that they run great physical risks in attacking the Jews.[85] Through his invective against the emperor Gaius (*Leg.* 78–115) and his encomium of Gaius's predecessors Tiberius and Augustus (*Leg.* 141–62), Philo draws on his rhetorical skills to place the affairs of emperors under the judgment of

God as foretold in Hebrew scripture.[86] After presenting Gaius as a self-contradictory perversion of classical ideals of deity and kingship, Philo then argues that there is an alternative to Gaius—an alternative of good rulership as evidenced in the true nature of the Julian house established by Augustus and Tiberius. In particular, Philo explains how Augustus supported Jewish rights and customs. He underscores Augustus's insight into and tolerance of Jewish customs as part of a long-standing policy of the Romans. Philo strengthens the parallel he is drawing between Augustus and his reader Claudius in several ways: he minimizes Julius Caesar's role (though it was undoubtedly he who was really responsible for the policy) in order to idealize Augustus's policy, and while alluding to Claudius's own expulsion of the Jews in 41 c.e.,[87] he observes that Augustus did not eject the Jews from Rome or deprive them of their Roman citizenship (*Leg.* 157). This last remark might well be an indirect appeal to Claudius to protect the civil status of Jews (i.e., their rights as a *politeuma*) in Alexandria.[88] And despite the dictates of the imperial cult, Augustus financed Jewish "sacrifices of whole burnt offerings" as "a tribute to the most high God" (*Leg.* 157). As Philo describes it, Augustus's policy toward the Jews reflects his role as "source and fountain-head of the Augustan stock in general" (*Leg.* 149)—stock of which Claudius is a part and that offers a goal toward which he should aspire, a goal ignored by his predecessor.

Philo's rhetorical encomium of Augustus (and of Tiberius) is thus simply the counterpart to his invective of Gaius—neither is ultimately concerned with the emperors themselves, for whom Philo had no high regard, but with the presentation of an ideal of kingship that might result in a favorable policy toward the Jews. Philo simply presents an appeal as well as a threat to Gaius's successor Claudius. This threat is part of the larger purpose of the work as announced in the prologue: to demonstrate God's providence in protecting the Jews and God's vengeance upon those who assault them—"honors for things good and punishment for things evil" (*Leg.* 7). Romans who wish to avoid such vengeance must reject the ploys of the Greek nationalists and see through their manipulation of the Roman prefect Flaccus (who under pressure had declared the Jews to be "foreigners and aliens," *Flacc.* 54). They must support the Jewish *politeuma*'s claims—for in Philo's eyes the present Alexandrian Jewish *politeuma*, founded originally by Moses, was the prefiguration of a universal (yet still Jewish) *politeia*.

Philo's interpretative work was thus not confined to the allegorical reading of scripture. His rhetorically crafted invectives and encomia and his biographies of the patriarchs, like his reading of scripture, functioned as a means of interpreting all of Alexandrian reality—social, cultural, and political. Scripture provided the interpretative lens through which Philo

viewed his world. For Philo, the nature of true *politeia* was itself derived from and supported by his reading of scripture. This true *politeia* would escape God's curses and receive God's blessing—as had its early political and ethical leaders, the patriarchs—for it is the true "world city" or *kosmopolis,* the city of God on earth (*Mos.* 2.51). In contrast, the Greek nationalists (and any emperors who might be misled by their appeals) speak only for a parochial human city. Rather than an effort to transform Jewish texts and history into Greco-Roman philosophy and sociopolitical structures, Philo's work was a bold hermeneutical and sociopolitical bid for the right of Jews to define authentic Hellenism. Rather than simply giving scripture "other" meanings, Philo read scripture as Moses' rewritten version of the host culture's meanings. The resulting reinscription of the world was brought about by Philo's allegorical reading of Jewish scripture, a reading through which he announced that all authentic intellectual and cultural wisdom, as well as the plot of world history, had been written first by Moses.

Reinscription, however, was not the only way Alexandrian religious interpreters could represent culture as different and more desirable. About a century after Philo, a Christian Alexandrian—Valentinus—drew on the allegorical tradition for purposes of cultural revision. But for him, the reshaping of culture was a matter not of textual reinscription but of a personal, mystical vision and creative, mythopoetic composition. History and culture were now forced to submit not to scripture, but to the visionary power of the human imagination.

THREE

Valentinus:
The Apocalypse of the Mind

Born around 100 c.e. in Phrebonis, a coastal town in the Egyptian Delta, Valentinus lived and taught during the first half of his life in the city of Alexandria, before moving to Rome sometime between 136 and 140 c.e.[1] He was educated in Greek learning (*paideia*) in Alexandria and taught there at the same time as the Christian philosopher Basilides.[2] According to their followers, each of these two Christian thinkers stood in a distinguished apostolic teaching tradition. Valentinians claimed that Valentinus had been a "hearer" (i.e., student) of Theudas, a disciple of Paul; and followers of Basilides declared that their leader had been instructed by a certain Glaucias, an "interpreter" (*hermēneus*) of Peter.[3] We know almost as little of Valentinus's writings as of his life, for—with the exception of his meditative homily known as the *Gospel of Truth*—only a few fragments of his works remain.[4] What we do have conveys a striking impression of bold originality and deep piety. On the one hand, Valentinus reads the sacred texts and traditions he inherits with surprising freedom, authority, and innovation. On the other hand, a deep christocentric piety suffuses his gospel meditation as it distills the complicated mythology of earlier Gnostic texts into a concentrated exposition of spiritual loss and salvation.

Valentinus performed his allegorical revisions upon previously existing Gnostic mythology, as well as upon other philosophical texts and religious writings, some of which would become part of the canonical New Testament. The Gnostic myths that were the target of his revisionary readings were themselves compositions arising from allegorical interpretations of Hebrew scripture, Platonic dialogues, and various other texts. Although aspects of all these texts inform Valentinus's own literary style, he rarely quotes any of them directly, and even when he does quote, he does not distinguish quoted or borrowed material from what he creates

on his own. Instead, he absorbs his sources almost entirely into his own imaginative compositions: his allegorical reading of precursor texts becomes a process of new mythmaking. Consequently, the interpreter of Valentinus's writings faces bewildering layers of interpretation, each layer seeking to hide its interpretative character. The first part of this chapter (which focuses on the fragments) separates these layers in order to uncover the ways in which Valentinus revises his precursor texts. We will examine the process by which these revisions become new mythical compositions.

Not only is Valentinus different from both Philo and Clement because he erases the line between text and commentary, as interpretation becomes new composition; his mode of allegorical interpretation is also distinctive because it is authorized by his claim for personal authority. Unlike Philo, Valentinus does not rely on a single sacred text as a paradigm for textual and cultural revision. And even though, like Philo and Clement, he draws upon prevailing Jewish and Christian Middle Platonic philosophical speculation about the divine *logos,* he does not make the divine voice his privileged metaphor. Instead, he authorizes his writing by appealing to his own experiential knowledge of the divine, for which I will use the term "vision." The second part of this chapter focuses on the character of this vision as expressed in the *Gospel of Truth.* This vision holds in tension ignorance and knowledge, forgetfulness and remembrance, blindness and insight, and finally seeks to transcend altogether the categories of text and voice, writing and speech. Walter Benjamin observed that Kafka "listened to tradition, and he who listens hard does not see."[5] Kafka, we might say, failed in his visionary quest because he deferred to the past. Philo listened to tradition in the form of a text, Moses' primordial inscription. Through that text, he sought to textualize all of reality, to reinscribe culture, remaking it in a Jewish image. Clement, as we shall see, also listened to tradition, not in the form of a text, but in the form of the primordial voice of the *logos.* The *logos* that had spoken in the classics of his Hellenic heritage now sang a new song in the pages of New Testament scripture. But Valentinus's listening soon took him beyond such deference to the past, to a transformative revision—a personal re-seeing of reality, focused on the metaphor of the divine name. In his new vision, the very distinction between matter and idea on which the notion of representation ultimately rests finally collapses. At the very borderline between matter and idea, Valentinus discerns a point of mutual interpenetration, and he thus declares their previous distinction to be the pernicious result of human misperception. By challenging the very notion of representation itself, his vision dramatically inverts and finally dissolves customary perceptions and evaluations of reality, truth, good-

ness, and beauty. It also seeks to dissolve our basic notions of temporality and narrativity.

In the last part of the chapter, I turn to the possible social functions of Valentinus's allegorical reading as composition. For whom did he write—and why? It seems as though we must locate Valentinus's reflections on the divine name within the history of Judaism and Jewish Christianity in Alexandria. The catastrophic fate of these forms of religious life and practice provides the backdrop for visionary reinterpretations of all of reality, and especially human history, as a single divine act that addresses the problems of personal, social, and historical evil. Valentinian Christians entered into this divine drama when they underwent the ritual of baptism.

ALLEGORICAL INTERPRETATION AS COMPOSITION

The allegorical interpretations that we have examined so far preserve a clear distinction between the narrative being interpreted and the contribution of the interpreter. In their interpretations of allegorical compositions by mythmakers or Homer, both Cornutus and Heraclitus make it clear that they are simply trying to elucidate what the composers of the allegories intended to say. Neither writer offers his interpretations as the creative or idiosyncratic product of his own imagination, but simply as a clearer version of what ancient authors sought to communicate in myth or epic poetry. In similar fashion, Philo did not blur the line between what was written in the Pentateuch and what he offered by way of interpretation. Indeed, throughout his exegetical treatises, he typically quotes a biblical verse or verses and then supplies his comment, working his way in this fashion through the Pentateuch.

But ancient allegorical interpreters did not always maintain such a clear distinction between text and commentary. Instead, allegorical interpretation sometimes takes the form of new composition: the allegorical interpreter gives "other" meanings to the narrative he is interpreting, but at the same time makes those other meanings represent characters and events in a new story, into which he surreptitiously weaves the old story. In its most subtle (or, from the point of view of the devotees of the old story, insidious) form, this mode of allegorical interpretation as composition seeks to efface all evidence of its origin as commentary. This mode of interpretation strives for originality (indeed, the relevant narratives often turn out to be myths of origin). To achieve the appearance of originality, aspects of commentary must be suppressed—for commentary is necessarily derivative. The interpreter thus offers the new story with its own integrity and does not explicitly say that this new story is derived from one

that precedes it. Curiously enough, this mode of interpretation as com-position gains much of its effectiveness precisely because the new story contains oblique, sometimes nearly subliminal, echoes of the old story. A former reader of the old story who encounters the new one is likely to say to himself or herself: "This seems vaguely familiar; where have I heard it before?" The allegorist thus garners the unwitting sympathy, and per-haps even support, of readers who, were they to see how seriously their former favorite story has been undermined, displaced, or absorbed, might otherwise be shocked at the interpreter's audacity.

For a paradigmatic example of the process I have just described, one need look no further than the Christian Bible. In its reading of Hebrew scripture as Old Testament, the New Testament offers an unparalleled example of allegorical interpretation as composition. Consider first the opening verses of Genesis:

> In the beginning God made the heaven and the earth. But the earth was invisible and unfurnished, and darkness was over the deep, and the Spirit of God moved over the water. And God said, "Let there be light"; and there was light. And God saw the light, that it was good; and God divided between the light and the darkness. And God called the light "day," and the darkness he called "night." And there was evening and there was morning, the first day. (Gen. 1.1–5, LXX)

When Philo set about interpreting this text, he certainly gave it a set of allegorical meanings. To him, Moses is not describing the creation of the material universe at all, but rather the intelligible universe that contains the patterns for the subsequent material creation:

> First, then, the maker made an incorporeal heaven, and an invisible earth, and the essential form [*idea*] of air and void. To the one he gave the name of "darkness," since the air when left to itself, is black. The other he named "deep," for the void is a region of immensity and vast depths. Next (he made) the incorporeal essence of water and of life-breath [i.e., *pneuma* or "spirit"] and, to crown all, of light. This again, the seventh in order, was an incorporeal pattern [*paradeigma*], discernible only by the mind, of the sun and all luminaries which were to come into existence throughout heaven. (*Op.* 29)

In this interpretation of the opening verses of Genesis, Philo preserves a clear line between the original text and his comments. But several genera-tions after Philo, another allegorical reader of this passage erased that line altogether. This interpreter wants his audience to hear in his new myth the echoes of these verses from Genesis because he wants his audience to realize that the earlier story in Genesis is not really the separate, indepen-dent story it might appear to be; instead, it is merely part of a new, more comprehensive story:

In the beginning was the Word [*logos*], and the Word was God. He was in the beginning with God; all things were made through him, and without him was not anything made that was made. In him was life, and the life was the light of human beings. The light shines in the darkness, and the darkness has not overcome it. There was a man sent from God, whose name was John. He came for testimony, to bear witness to the light, that all might believe through him. He was not the light, but came to bear witness to the light. The true light that enlightens every person was coming into the world. (John 1.1–9)

The evangelist is clearly reading the opening verses of Genesis allegorically: for example, what one might assume was physical light has now been given another meaning—the *logos* or Son of God, soon to be explicitly identified as Jesus of Nazareth. But the evangelist does not want his readers to think that he is simply giving them an interpretation of Genesis; rather, he is giving them Genesis properly understood, that is, Genesis as absorbed by a larger story. And as Jewish readers were quick to point out, this is no longer the former Genesis story at all. Their response has been anticipated by this author, however. He indicates that some people will want to cling to the old story alone, and he hints at the benefits of refusing to do so:

He [the *logos*] was in the world, and the world was made through him, yet the world knew him not. He came to his own home, and his own people [the Jews] received him not. But to all who received him, who believed in his name [i.e., who became Christians], he gave power to become children of God; who were born, not of blood nor of the will of the flesh nor of the will of a man, but of God. (John 1.10–13)

Later in this chapter, we will have occasion to ponder further the allegorical changes that Valentinus makes to notions of the divine "name" and the process of divine rebirth. For now, I simply wish to point out that John's allegorical reading of Hebrew scripture as a new story provides a useful illustration of the kind of interpretation as composition that Valentinus will bring to bear on his precursor texts (which include Genesis and the Gospel of John). It is precisely this revisionary freedom toward one's precursors that marks the presence of an authentically "Gnostic" spirit. Conversely, deference to the past, whether to canonical texts or other traditional authorities, marks the domestication of *gnōsis*—even, or especially, when one claims, as Clement will, to possess the "true" *gnōsis*.

In order to see how Valentinus's revisionary reading works, we will need to break it down into its main constituent elements. This will necessarily be to some extent a hypothetical endeavor, for Valentinus has deliberately obscured those "seams" and "joints" that would make it easy for us to see just where and how he brings allegorical interpretation to

bear on a text, and where and how that interpretation assumes a compositional form. We can, however, distinguish three basic layers of the process: (1) the "original" myths of scripture or Platonic dialogue; (2) the pre-
Valentinian Gnostic allegorical readings of these original texts, which take
the form of mythological compositions; and (3) Valentinus's own allegorical readings of both 1 and 2, which take the form of a new "Valentinian"
mythology. Before we look closely at some examples of level 3, it will be
useful to characterize in general terms the nature of the second layer of
Gnostic mythology that Valentinus is reinterpreting.

Gnostic myths are exceedingly different from one another; each often
contains its own complicated cosmogony and salvation history. There is,
however, a group of texts that appear to offer varying depictions of
portions of a basic shared myth. This myth centers around the redemp-
tive actions of a divine savior named Seth (after the biblical child of Adam
and Eve). In its most general outline, this myth tells of a divine and
unknowable first principle that contemplates itself, generating in the
process a second principle. The second principle in turn produces a series
of other emanations (or aeons), including four "luminaries" (containing
the heavenly prototypes of Adam, Seth, the "seed of Seth," and another
group that goes under various names). The last aeon to be emanated,
Sophia (wisdom), seeks to know the transcendent first principle in an
inappropriate way, for which she finds herself (or, in some versions of the
myth, her product or offspring) cast out of the divine realm (or "entirety"). Sophia's offspring, a malevolent chief ruler (demiurge, craftsman), is often named Ialdabaōth. Along with his own offspring (rulers,
angels, powers), Ialdabaōth tries to trap and seize for himself the divine
power contained in his mother, Sophia (for she, unlike her offspring, is
exclusively from the divine realm). To do this, he and his assistants create
Adam, Eve, and the rest of the human race, as well as the material
universe. Sophia seeks to regain the stolen divine power that Ialdabaōth,
via Adam and Eve, has now dispersed into the generations of human
beings, especially the race of Seth, Adam and Eve's son. The descendants
or "offspring" of Seth in the myth await a savior from the divine realm
who will come to them, give them knowledge (*gnōsis*) of their true origin
and nature, and teach them how to return to their divine home. The
historical Gnostics who wrote and used different variations of this myth
believed that this promised savior had in fact arrived, enlightened them,
and set them on the path back to their divine home. The savior figure
from the divine realm is different in various versions of the myth (e.g., a
preexistent Christ, Word, Seth, Barbelo) but in the versions that we
possess is generally connected in some fashion with the historical figure
Jesus of Nazareth.[6] Such is the general outline of Gnostic mythology. This

summary gives only the barest sketch of the basic plot and the main agents that figure in most versions of the myth; different versions add considerably more characters and narrative detail, including intricate subplots.[7] For the remainder of my discussion, I will use two representative interpretations of various portions of this myth: *The Secret Book According to John* (*Apocryphon of John*) (long version, NHC II and IV) and *The Reality of the Rulers* (*Hypostasis of the Archons*).

Valentinus bases his revision of Gnostic myth on his perception of the essential "dynamic" or "movement" underlying its baroque narrative. One must be cautious in using temporal expressions to characterize this "deep sense" since Valentinus seeks to dissolve the temporal, narrative features of his predecessors' myths. This dynamic is best thought of as a transformative "occurrence" consisting of three "moments": original fullness, subsequent lack, and ultimate recovery or fulfillment. When understood in a linear, narrative fashion, this transformative process corresponds to the well-known tripartite Christian narrative (in its general outline, it also corresponds to a Plotinian neo-Platonic narrative of emanation and return). This Christian narrative is generated by a spiritual problem (fallenness, sin, evil), which in turn implies the loss of a superior antecedent state (paradise, creation, image of God) and looks for a subsequent solution (salvation, redemption, kingdom of God). Valentinus appropriates and alters this thoroughly traditional narrative structure in order to transform Gnostic myth through a series of metaphorical associations and substitutions that are tantalizingly complex in their allusiveness and resonance. Drawing especially on the metaphors of names and naming (and associated images and themes), Valentinus's allegorical reading attempts to neutralize the sequential, narrative aspects of both the precursor Gnostic myth and the tripartite Christian narrative by calling into question the notion of temporality that necessarily underlies all narrative sensibility. He seeks to purge from Gnostic myth much of its sequential, narrative structure and many of its distinctive characters and events, in order to produce a much more austere account of loss and recovered fullness, understood in part as the presence and absence of naming and the possession and loss of names.

With this overview of Valentinus's allegorical interpretation of Gnostic myth now in hand, we turn to some specific instances of his revisionary readings. Drawing on the fragments of his now-lost works, I will focus on one specific portion of the Genesis narrative, its Gnostic revision, and Valentinus's reinterpretation: the creation of Adam and his naming of the animals. Before we begin, it may prove helpful to have before us the texts from Genesis and the *Timaeus* that are the central objects of Gnostic and Valentinian reinterpretation.

In the beginning God made [*poiein*] the heaven [*ouranos*] and the earth. But the earth was invisible [*aoratos*] and unfurnished [*akataskeuastos*], and darkness was over the deep, and the Spirit of God moved over the water. And God said, "Let there be light"; and there was light. And God saw the light, that it was good; and God divided between the light and the darkness. And God called the light "day," and the darkness he called "night." And there was evening and there was morning, the first day. And God said, "Let there be a firmament in the midst of the water, and let there be a division between water and water," and it was so. And God made the firmament, and God divided between the water which was under the firmament and the water which was above the firmament. And God called the firmament "heaven," and God saw that it was good; and there was evening and there was morning, the second day. (Gen. 1.1–8, LXX)

And God said, "Let us make [*poiein*] a human being [*anthrōpos*] according to our image and likeness [*kat' eikona hēmeteran kai kath' homoiōsin*]." . . . And God made [*poiein*] the human being [*ho anthrōpos*], in the image of God [*kat' eikona theou*] he made him; male and female he made them. (Gen. 1.26–27, LXX)

And God modeled [*plassein*] the human being [*ho anthrōpos*] of dust of the earth, and breathed upon his face [*prosōpon*] the breath of life [*pnoē zōēs*], and the human being became a living soul [*psychē zōsa*]. (Gen. 2.7, LXX)

And the Lord God said, "It is not good that the human being should be alone, let us make [*poiein*] for him a help suitable to him." And God modeled [*plassein*] yet farther out of the earth all the wild beasts of the field, and the birds of the sky, and he brought them to Adam, to see what he would call them, and whatever Adam called any living creature, that was the name of it. (Gen. 2.18–19, LXX)

And when the father that engendered [the cosmos] perceived it in motion and alive, a thing of joy to the eternal gods, he too rejoiced; and being well-pleased he designed to make it resemble its model [*paradeigma*] still more closely. Accordingly, seeing that that model is an eternal living being [*zōon aidion on*], he set about making this universe, so far as he could, of a like kind. But inasmuch as the nature of the living being was eternal [*aiōnios*], this quality it was impossible to attach in its entirety to what is generated; wherefore he planned to make a moving image [*eikōn*] of eternity [*aiōn*], and, as he set in order the heaven [*ouranos*], of that eternity [*aiōn*] which abides in unity, he made an eternal image [*aiōnios eikōn*], moving according to number, even that which we have named time. (Pl. *Tim.* 37C–D)[8]

These texts tell of the divine creation of human beings and the cosmos according to the model of archetype and copy, in which the copy is an image of the archetype. Genesis describes how a human being is fashioned "in the image [*eikōn*] of God," its archetype. Plato describes how a divine demiurge fashions a cosmos that, in order to resemble its archetype (the eternal living being), is given time as a "moving image" (*eikōn*) of that

archetype. Both texts speak of the creation of "heaven" (*ouranos*) as well. The Gnostic authors of *The Secret Book According to John* and *The Reality of the Rulers* interpreted both these myths allegorically by absorbing them into a new myth, in which many of the old events remain the same, but the characters, as well as the overall plot, change dramatically. *The Reality of the Rulers* changes the Genesis account of the creation of the human being by God into an account of the human being's creation by malevolent sub-deities ("authorities" or "rulers"). In order to capture a divine image that they see reflected in the waters, the rulers fashion a human being "according to the image of the god." In the passage from *The Reality of the Rulers* given below, some of the more explicit echoes of Genesis are italicized:

> As incorruptibility gazed down into the region of the *waters*, its *image* was shown forth in the *waters;* and the authorities of the *darkness* became enamored of it. But they could not lay hold of that *image*, which had been shown forth to them in the *waters*, because of their weakness—since merely animate beings cannot lay hold of those which are *spirit*-endowed; for they were from *below*, while it was from *above*. This is the reason why incorruptibility gazed down into the region . . . so that, by the parent's will, it might join the entirety unto the *light*. The rulers laid plans and said, "Come, *let us create a human being that will be soil from the earth." They modeled their creature as one wholly of the earth. . . . They took {some soil} from the earth and modeled {their human being}, after their body and {after the image} of god* that had been shown forth {to them} in the *waters*. They said, "{come, let} us lay hold of it by means of our modeled form, {so that} it may see its male counterpart { . . . }, and we may seize it by means of our modeled form"—not understanding the power of god, because of their powerlessness. *And it [the chief ruler] breathed into his face; and the human being came to be animate* and remained upon the ground many days. But they could not make him arise because of their powerlessness. Like storm winds they persisted (in blowing), that they might capture that *image*, which had appeared to them in the *waters*. And they did not recognize the identity of its power. Now, all these events came to pass by the will of the parent of the entirety. Afterward, the *spirit* saw the animate human being upon the ground. And the *spirit* came forth from the Adamantine realm; it descended and came to dwell within him, *and that human being came to be a living soul. It called his name Adam since he was found moving upon the ground*. (*RR* 87.11–88.16)

In this passage, the Gnostic author has radically revised the Genesis account, principally by making the rulers, rather than God, the agent of Adam's creation. Moreover, here Adam is depicted as deficient, unable to move; and although the rulers try, they are not able to overcome this deficiency. Only a purely divine power (the spirit from the Adamantine realm) can energize Adam, which it eventually does by coming to dwell within him. The divine spirit also gives this human creature its name, as well as the capacity to give names:

> A voice came forth from incorruptibility for the assistance of Adam; and the
> rulers gathered together all the animals of the earth and all the birds of the
> sky and brought them in to Adam to see what Adam would call them, that
> he might give a name to each of the birds and all the beasts. (*RR* 88.17ff.)

This account from *The Reality of the Rulers* represents the kind of Gnostic
myth against which we must read the extant fragments of Valentinus's
mythical compositions. In these fragments, we discover that Valentinus
treated prior Gnostic myths as they had treated their own precursors: he
read them allegorically and turned his reading into a new mythical composition (one might compare John's reading of Genesis, which in turn
reinterprets prior Babylonian creation myths).

We will begin our consideration of Valentinus's revisionary mythmaking by closely examining two fragments (C and D). Together, these fragments set up three analogous relationships: between Adam and a higher
divine power, a portrait and an actual living face, and the world and a
higher divine realm. This analogical structure is the conceptual basis for
Valentinus's transformation of Gnostic myth. We will examine two features of this transformation: the fusion of various divine agents in Gnostic
myth along with a corresponding concentration of divine power in Adam,
and the reduction of Gnostic narrative to a seemingly nonnarrative dynamic of fullness, deficiency, and fulfillment. First, it will be useful to have
the entire texts of both fragments before us. The first fragment (C) draws
a striking analogy between Adam's creation (his "modeling") and the
creative activity of human artists:

> And even as fear [*phobos*] overcame the angels in the presence of that
> modeled form [*plasma*] because it uttered sounds superior to what its mod-
> eling [*plasis*] justified, owing to the one who had invisibly deposited in it [or
> him] a seed [*sperma*] of higher essence and who spoke boldly [or freely]
> [*parrhēsiazesthai*]: so too in the races of worldly people, human works [*erga*]
> become objects of fear [*phobos*] for their creators—for example, statues and
> images [*eikones*] [probably paintings] and everything that (human) hands
> make in the name of a god [*eis onoma theou*]. For Adam, modeled [*plastheis*] in
> the name of a human being [*eis onoma anthrōpou*], made them stand in fear
> [*phobos*] of the preexistent human being [*proōn anthrōpos*]; for precisely the
> latter stood in him. And they were stricken with terror and quickly con-
> cealed [or marred or destroyed] [*aphanizein*] the work [*ergon*]. (Frag. C)[9]

The second fragment (D) introduces an analogy between two kinds of
hierarchical relationships: a (lesser) portrait and a (greater) living face,
and a (lesser) cosmos and a (greater) living realm:

> However much an image [*eikōn*] [in this case, a portrait] is inferior to a living
> face [*zōon prosōpon*], just so is the world worse than the living realm [*zōos
> aiōn*]. Now, what is the cause of the (effectiveness of the) image [*eikōn*]? It is

the majesty [*megalōsynē*] of the face that has furnished to the painter a prototype [*typos*] so that it [the portrait?] might be honored by [or through] its [or his] name [*di' onomatos autou*]. For the form [*morphē*] was not reproduced with perfect fidelity [*authentikōs*], yet the name filled up [*plēroun*] the lack [*hysterēsis*] within the act of modeling [*en plasei*]. And also the invisible [aspect or dimension?] of god [*to tou theou aoraton*] contributes toward the faith [*synergein . . . eis pistin*] of the one who has been modeled [*ho peplasmenos*]. (Frag. D)[10]

Using a series of repeated images and metaphors, fragments C and D set up five hierarchical relationships. I have summarized the five relationships below, capitalizing the items being related.

1. Divine artists model ADAM (a *plasma*) in the name of a HUMAN BEING (the *plasma* then terrifies its creators) (frag. C).
2. Human artists produce WORKS (*erga*) in the name of a GOD (the *erga* then terrify their creators) (frag. C).
3. A human artist produces a PORTRAIT (*eikōn*) honored by the name (and majesty) of the LIVING FACE (frag. D).
4. The WORLD is inferior to the LIVING REALM (frag. D).
5. Modeled ADAM is inferior to the invisible of GOD (and/or NAME) (frag. D).

Reduced to their essentials, the preceding five remarks set up the following relationships:

1. Adam   Human Being
2. Works   God
3. Portrait Living Face
4. World   Living Realm
5. Adam   God/Name

We are justified in considering the two fragments together not only because they share so much language and imagery, but also because they share a core analogy between artists and their works (2 and 3 above). In fragment C, artists recoil in terror when they confront their own artworks created "in the name of a god." In fragment D, a portrait painter's work is honored by the name (and majesty) of the living face it depicts. The parallel between the two analogies suggests that we are being offered two views of the same essential phenomenon. The "name" of a god that generates the angels' fear and the name (or "majesty") that gives the portrait its honor are two ways of describing a divine archetype that exceeds its representation (and, as we shall see later, overcomes that representation's deficiency). In both cases, the "name" indicates a divine power that is both terrifying and awe-inspiring. Both instances of the artist/artwork relationship also point to the basic theme of the other three

relationships: the similarity and dissimilarity between a representation (or image) and that which is represented. In fragment C, the relationship between the artists and their works (*erga*) is itself presented as analogous to the relationship between the demiurgical angels and their work, the *plasma* Adam. Like their human counterparts, the demiurgical artists are terrified at what they have fashioned, for it, like ordinary artistic productions, is fashioned "in the name" of something or someone greater—in the case of Adam, the name of "a preexistent human being." In fragment D, Valentinus hints that the two relationships between portrait and living face, and world and living realm are analogous to the relationship described in fragment C between the (lesser) Adam and the (greater) preexistent human being. The hint comes at the very end of the fragment, where "Adam" is introduced obliquely with the phrase "act of modeling" (*en plasei*) and more directly with what can be considered Adam's key epithet: "the one who has been modeled" (*ho peplasmenos*). Now that we are oriented to the basic analogical structure and the way the same essential contrast governs both fragments, we can turn to an examination of the ways in which the fragments function as allegorical revisions of prior Gnostic myth.

In this revision, Valentinus seeks to assimilate the various divine agents of Gnostic myth and to enhance the status of Adam. In effect, he tries first to concentrate the power of various divine beings and then to grant a great deal of that power to Adam. Fragment C thus takes the reader back to that moment in the Gnostic narrative when the chief ruler and the other authorities fashioned the human being in order to trap the divine image reflected in the waters. We recall that in the Gnostic account, the creature produced by the rulers is deficient: like Plato's material objects, he is two steps removed from that according to which he is modeled, for he is created after the image (on the waters), which itself is only the reflected image of the divine being (incorruptibility). The Gnostic account further underscores Adam's deficiency by noting that he cannot move but remains prone until energized by the divine spirit.

In contrast, Valentinus's revision emphasizes Adam's power. Rather than lying immobile on the earth, Valentinus's Adam utters "sounds superior to what its modeling justified." (Here, by the way, is fragment C's first suggestion of the hierarchical relationship between Adam and a higher divine force that is analogous to the two relationships described in fragment D.) We are told that Adam speaks with unanticipated grandeur, frightening the demiurgic rulers (now called "angels"), and we are told he is able to do so "owing to the one who had invisibly deposited in him a seed of higher essence and who spoke boldly."

In this new account of Adam's creation and his newly obtained capacity of speech, Valentinus has first preserved, but then conflated, the divine

agents described in the Gnostic myth. Moreover, he has transferred their divine power to Adam himself, under the metaphor of the divine name. We recall that the Gnostic myth presents two divine figures who come to the aid of Adam: a "spirit" from the Adamantine realm and a "voice" from incorruptibility ("Adamantine realm" and "incorruptibility" are typical Gnostic expressions for the divine realm and its character). Valentinus transforms the Gnostic spirit into an agent who deposits a seed and speaks boldly (or perhaps into the seed itself), and the voice into a preexistent human being, in whose name Adam speaks. Thus, by referring to a seed depositor and a preexistent human being, Valentinus initially preserves the two Gnostic divine agents. But he soon collapses them into a single divine category—the name of the preexistent *anthrōpos*—and then closely associates this name with Adam. The fragment depicts a close relationship between Adam and the seed depositor, a relationship that embraces both similarity and difference. Adam is clearly described as distinct from the agent who deposits a seed and speaks boldly. On the other hand, the agent puts the seed of higher essence within Adam, and even before mentioning the seed, Valentinus says that Adam himself was the one who uttered the superior sounds. It appears that Valentinus is thus working to give Adam divine powers, which Adam is then justified in claiming as his own.

Valentinus then equates Adam's possession of the seed of higher essence with his capacity for "bold speech." This equation also marks Valentinus's assimilation of the Gnostic spirit and the Gnostic voice; the spirit, reinterpreted as seed depositor and seed, and the voice, reinterpreted as the name of the preexistent *anthrōpos*, are both given to Adam as his possession (the seed is deposited *in* Adam; the preexistent *anthrōpos* stands *in* Adam). And that possession or presence of the divine becomes evident in Adam's own bold speech (*parrhēsia*).

Valentinus enhances his concentration of divine power in Adam by changing the Gnostic (and biblical) notion of Adam's "creation in the image of God" into a creation "in the name of a [preexistent] human being." By changing the locus of divine power from "God" to a preexistent "human being," Valentinus enhances the status of humanity as such: Adam is powerful not because of his unaided, modeled nature, but because of something beyond him that nevertheless is paradoxically not something other than what he essentially is. Likewise, by changing "image" to "name," Valentinus changes what in the Gnostic version was a metaphor of lack or deficiency into a metaphor of fullness and plenitude. The Gnostic account had described Adam's demiurgic creation after the image seen in the water, and the resulting creature was immobile, having "spirit" without "soul." But Valentinus's Adam is not plagued by such a deficiency; he arrives on the scene speaking boldly and terrifying his

creators. We are told that the bold speech of the seed depositor in Adam caused fear (*phobos*), and later, that Adam, because of the preexistent human being who provided the name in which he was modeled and who also stood in him, made the rulers stand in fear (*phobos*). Both the bold speech of the one who put the divine seed in Adam and the *anthrōpos* who stands in Adam thus cause fear on the part of the rulers. This identity of effect suggests an identity of cause: the seed depositor (formerly the Gnostic spirit) who supplies Adam with a "seed of higher essence" might well be the preexistent *anthrōpos* (formerly the Gnostic voice) who supplies Adam with the name.

This identification is rooted in the analogy of artistic creation in the first fragment that forms a bridge between the opening example of the seed and bold speech and the closing example of the name of the human being. According to the analogy of artistic creation, just as the rulers create a *plasma* (Adam) who frightens them because speaking in him is a higher seed depositor, in the same way artists create "works" (*erga*) that frighten them because they are made in the name of a god. The analogy thus equates frightening bold speech with the frightening presence of the name within the *plasma* Adam. The resulting interchange of divine and human capacities is indicated by the chiastic structure of the fragment's governing analogy:

DIVINE angels model a *plasma* in the name of A HUMAN BEING

HUMAN artists create *erga* in the name of A GOD

Both activities result in fear (*phobos*). By repeating this effect, Valentinus apparently wishes readers to think of fear as the result of a "name," and thus to link the name in which Adam was modeled to his bold speech. Furthermore, the chiasm invites readers to recognize the divinity of the preexistent *anthrōpos* through its implicit *ad maiorem* argument: if mere works of art frighten so much, and even they are created in the name of a god, how much more must the incomparably greater divine act of creating the *plasma* Adam, who terrified even divine beings, result from an even greater, more divine name—not the name of a mere god, but of the preexistent human being. In another fragment (H), Valentinus clearly identifies "bold speech" as a divine attribute. There, quoting Matthew 19.17, he refers to the divine Father's speech: "And one there is who is good! His manifestation of the son is bold speech."[11] Like God the Father, Adam also enjoys *parrhēsia*. Valentinus thus appears to equate Adam's possession of a divine seed, the *parrhēsia* it makes possible, and the name of *anthrōpos* that stands within him.[12] This series of identifications marks the simultaneous assimilation of Gnostic divine agents and the concentration of divine power in Adam.

Finally, Valentinus emphasizes Adam's divine power in his revision of the Gnostic (and biblical) account of Adamic naming. Valentinus's new version places the emphasis not on naming but on powerful self-expression. When Adam now speaks, he not only names the animals, as he did in Genesis and Gnostic myth; he also terrifies the rulers, thus further diminishing the status they enjoyed in the Gnostic account. In contrast to the Gnostic account, in which a divine spirit gives Adam an etymological, mimetic name based on the Hebrew of Genesis (*adam* from *adamah*, "earth") and a divine voice helps Adam name the animals, Valentinus stresses Adam's own power of speech. In this version, Adam's naming is not a linguistic reproduction of perceived essences (as it was for Philo, and for the Gnostic myth), but rather a bold self-expression that underscores the powerful, transcendent quality of the Adamic self whose true nature is defined by the preexistent *anthrōpos*. The angels recognize Adam's divinity, which reminds them of their own deficiency. We will find this same motif central to Valentinus's *Gospel of Truth:* ignorance—and, by extension, creation—is a direct concomitant not merely of the superiority, but of the unknowability, of the higher divine realm.

We have seen that Valentinus's presentation of Adam's capacities stresses the fullness of divine presence within him, in contrast to his deficient status in the Gnostic account: the preexistent human being in whose name Adam was modeled actually stands within Adam himself. A second key goal of Valentinus's revisionary reading of Gnostic myth is to transform the detailed narratives of those myths into a more fundamental dynamic of fullness, lack, and fulfillment. Fragment D links the theme we have just described (the assimilation of characters and the enhancement of Adam's status) to this three-part dynamic when it explicitly refers near its end to a "completion of a lack within the act of modeling" by "the name." Prior to this statement, we have been told that both portrait (image) and world are inferior to their archetypes, the living face and the living realm. Once again, there is both similarity and dissimilarity between archetype and image. Similarity is denoted by the metaphors of "honor" and "name," dissimilarity by the metaphors of "lack" and "inauthenticity." One honors a portrait to the extent that it captures the "majesty" of its archetype; when this happens, viewers say something like "What a wonderful portrait—it really captures the character of Socrates." As the fragment puts it, "it is the majesty of the face that has furnished to the painter a prototype [*typos*] so that it might be honored by his name." But no portrait is ever quite right; there is always something about it that remains untrue to the person whom it depicts, as Valentinus observes: "The form [*morphē*] was not found with perfect fidelity" (or perhaps, "was not authentically reproduced").

So far, the fragment has stayed largely within the linguistic world of

Plato's *Timaeus*, though it also echoes Genesis (especially the "face" and "living soul" of Genesis 2.7). But with the verb "modeling" and the substantive "the one modeled," the closing lines introduce another figure, recognizable because of its characterization in fragment C—the *plasma* Adam: "The name completed the lack within the act of modeling. And also the invisible of god contributes toward the faith of the one modeled." From fragment C, we learned that Adam was modeled in the name of a preexistent human being, who represents original divine presence or fullness. We learn now from fragment D that Adam's difference from his divine archetype (the preexistent human being), just like the portrait's difference from the living face or the world's difference from the divine realm, is a deficiency or lack. Yet no sooner is the notion of lack introduced than it is overcome; the very deficiency of a portrait gestures toward the antecedent fullness of a majestic face as its prototype, form, or name. As the portrait is honored by the name of the previously existing living figure whose representation it is, so Adam is able to utter "superior sounds" because he is modeled "in the name of" a preexistent human being (frag. C). In the midst of creation, then, whether cosmic or artistic, there is deficiency; that deficiency is precisely the measure of difference between person and portrait, or between preexistent human being and Adam. But in the midst of deficiency there is also (potential) fulfillment, for although the "form" was "not reproduced with perfect fidelity" (in either portrait, world, or modeled Adam), yet the name (= "god's invisible"?) completes the lack within the act of modeling. Just as the modeling of Adam testifies to the antecedent power of the name, it also expresses simultaneously both lack and compensation for that lack.

In thus recasting Gnostic myths about a deficient Adam into a more subtle dialectic between deficiency and fulfillment, Valentinus has also appropriated Plato's struggle with the problematic relation between creation and its divine archetype. Plato's demiurge does the best he can in the face of the "necessary" recalcitrance of the physical order, producing an image that, while deficient, is valid up to a point. In contrast, his Valentinian counterparts, the demiurgical rulers, succeed only in producing a creature who through his bold speech reminds them of their mimetic failure. Defined by the difference between copy and original, this failure can be compensated only by the original itself. Only the divine name, the name of *anthrōpos*, can fulfill the resultant deficiency: all human or demiurgical acts of creative imitation, in their inevitable failures, point to the necessary role of divine power. Thus while intensifying the lack described by Plato Valentinus simultaneously offers a stronger vision of its fulfillment. Together, then, these two fragments display Valentinus's revision of Gnostic, biblical, and Platonic mythology into an oscillation between actu-

ality and potentiality, defined by the "moments" of the presence, absence, and recovery of the divine name.

Valentinus ponders the deeper meaning of Gnostic myth from several other points of view, drawing on metaphors other than the divine name in his revisions. In particular, he appeals to metaphors drawn from the life of Valentinian believers and from relations between God (as Father) and God (as Son). In the following exhortation to Valentinian Christians, Valentinus uses the imagery of life, death, and asceticism to suggest the dynamic of fullness-lack-fulfillment:

> From the beginning you (plur.) have been immortal, and you are children of eternal life [*zoē aiōnia*]. And you wanted death to be allocated to yourselves so that you might spend it and use it up [*analiskein*], and that death might die in you and through you. For when you nullify [*lyein*] the world and are not yourselves annihilated [*katalyein*], you are lord over creation and all corruption. (Frag. F)[13]

Immortal from the beginning and now seemingly subject to time, decay, and death, Valentinian Christians are urged to envision a process by which the world will be nullified for them and corruption will end. The triad of fullness, lack, and completion to which fragments C and D pointed is now represented by the triad immortality, death/corruption, and eternal life: the "children" in the beginning are immortal, they then engage death in such a way that death itself is overcome, and they finally become (or rather, find themselves revealed to be) children of "eternal life." The midpoint of this triadic progression is central: this is the point at which the self is engaged in spending and using up death, negating what is not the self, thereby recovering (i.e., realizing) the self's fundamental immortality.

There seems to be a close parallel between the career of Adam and the lives of these children of light (i.e., Valentinian Christians). Adam's deficiency was revealed in the act of modeling, even as it was overcome in that same act by the name. Likewise, the deaths of the children of eternal life, although a deficiency when viewed from an ordinary point of view, are simultaneously a fulfillment since the giving up of life is actually a kind of spending of death to purchase life. We are led to draw this analogy between Adam and the children of eternal life because of Valentinus's use of the words "life" and "living." We have already seen that he associates Adam's true nature as preexistent *anthrōpos* with the "living" (*zōon*) face and the "living" (*zōos*) realm by the introduction of Adam into the end of fragment D. Now, in fragment F, we are told that the true nature of the children is an "eternal life" (*zōē aiōnios*) of immortality and corruption. It appears that Adam's creation, as an act of both lack and fulfillment, may be the paradigm for the life of Valentinian Christians. From a com-

monplace (i.e., non-Valentinian) point of view, that "life" appears to be a steady act of dying, an ever-intensifying lack or deficiency. In Adam's case, such deficiency was inherent in the very act of "modeling" or embodiment in mortal flesh. But from the perspective of Valentinian *gnōsis*, the life that otherwise marches on toward death is the emergence of true (i.e., eternal) life, a progressive fulfillment of its own deficiency. The two acts of life— "dying" and "using up death"—are in fact the same: the distinction is the result of perspective, and awareness of this perspective the reward of authentic *gnōsis*.

The notion that Valentinian Christians will be able to overcome the corruption to which earthly embodiment subjects them corresponds to the idea that they will have their inner essences purified by the divine Son:

> And one there is who is good! His manifestation through the son is bold speech [*parrhēsia*]. And through him alone can a heart become pure, when every evil spirit has been put out of the heart. For the many spirits dwelling in the heart do not permit it to become pure: rather, each of them performs its own acts, violating it in various ways with improper desires. And in my opinion the heart experiences something like what happens in a caravan-sary.[14] For the latter is full of holes and dug up and often filled with dung, because while they are there, people live in an utterly vulgar way and take no forethought for the property since it belongs to someone else. Just so, a heart too is impure by being the habitation of many demons, until it experiences forethought. But when the father, who alone is good, visits the heart, he makes it holy and fills it with light. And so a person who has such a heart is called blessed, for that person will see god. (Frag. H)[15]

The unpurified heart of the Valentinian, subject to corruption, needs a purificatory visit by the divine Son. This "manifestation of the son" in the heart is identified with the divine Father's own "bold speech"—almost certainly the same as the "bold speech" of the one in whose name Adam was modeled (frag. C). Indeed, just as Adam's modeled state is a paradigm for the Valentinian believer's strange dealing with death, so Adam's state is equally paradigmatic for the Valentinian's need for holiness: just as Adam needs "the name" to complete "the lack within the act of modeling" (frag. D), so the Valentinian Christian needs the speech of God (which is simultaneously the appearance of the Son in one's heart and one's own vision of God) to transform his or her inner essence. This fragment thus looks beyond the present condition of the impure heart (or, as fragment F puts it, of "dying") to that "moment" when purification will take place and the Valentinian will "see God," even as the fragment also glances retro-spectively at that antecedent divine being who speaks freely and who "alone is good." We learn from yet another Valentinian fragment that the divine Son is able to purify the corrupt heart precisely because he himself lacks all corruption:

> He was continent, enduring all things. Jesus digested divinity: he ate and
> drank in a special way, without excreting his solids. He had such a great
> capacity for continence that the nourishment within him was not corrupted,
> for he did not experience corruption. (Frag. E)[16]

The food digested by Jesus does not become excrement, like that found in
the "caravansary" or animal yard of the heart corrupted by demons and
evil spirits (frag. H). Instead, Jesus' incorruptibility overcomes the lack,
just as the name overcomes the lack in the embodiment of Adam, and
children of eternal life use up death. Their "nullification" of the world
corresponds to Jesus' "nullification" of the corruptible character of his
nourishment.

MYSTICAL VISION AND ALLEGORICAL REVISION

We turn next to an exploration of Valentinus's meditation called the *Gospel
of Truth,* paying particular attention to the modes of revision already
found in the fragments. The following discussion will address two basic
topics: the *Gospel*'s allegorical revision of prior Gnostic accounts of the falls
of Sophia, Adam, and Eve and its use of the divine name as an organizing
metaphor for its own thematic composition. We shall discover that the
Gospel, like the fragments, strives to neutralize the sort of narrative sensibility that depends on memory and anticipation, offering instead a rhetorical mode that seeks to collapse and absorb narrative temporality into an
atemporal revelation that occurs in the mind rather than in history.[17]

Gnostic myth recounts a fall before the fall described in Genesis. Because of her efforts to know the unknowable first principle without the aid
of her male consort, Sophia was expelled from the spiritual realm. She
then gave birth to the malicious demiurge Ialdabaōth, who, along with his
own progeny, was responsible for the created order. The Gnostic *Secret
Book According to John* describes the catastrophe this way:

> Now, the wisdom belonging to afterthought, which is an aeon, thought a
> thought derived from herself, (from) the thinking of the invisible spirit, and
> (from) prior acquaintance. She wanted to show forth within herself an
> image, without the spirit's {will}; and her consort did not consent. And (she
> wished to do so) without his pondering: for the person of her maleness did
> not join in the consent; for she had not discovered that being which was in
> harmony with her. Rather, she pondered without the will of the spirit and
> without acquaintance with that being which was in harmony with her. And
> she brought forth. (*BJn* [Codex II] 9.25–35)

What Sophia brought forth was a certain misshapen product—Ialdabaōth—which she immediately cast outside the boundary or limit of the
spiritual realm.

Valentinus reworks this Gnostic myth in the following passage from the *Gospel of Truth:*

> Inasmuch as the entirety had searched for the one from whom they had emanated, and the entirety was inside of him—the inconceivable uncontained, who is superior to all thought—ignorance of the father caused agitation and fear. And the agitation grew dense like fog, so that no one could see. Thus error found strength and labored at her matter [i.e., the material universe] in emptiness. Without having learned to know the truth, she took up residence in a modeled form, preparing by means of the power, in beauty, a substitute for truth. (*GTr* 17.4–20)

Valentinus's account of the appearance of Error retells the Gnostic myth of Sophia's inappropriate mimetic efforts, her fall from the pleromatic realm, and her subsequent production of Ialdabaōth. But Valentinus has once again simplified the Gnostic narrative by assimilating characters, replacing Sophia and Ialdabaōth with "Error," a single personification of ignorance of the divine Father and its psychological manifestations. Such ignorance of the Father is more than an epistemological failure with psychological accompaniments; it is also an ontological reality. Error's presence is the very modeled form in which she "takes up residence" (recall fragment D's insistence that in the case of the first human being there was a deficiency "within the act of modeling"). Ignorance or error (*a-gnōsis*) is a state of nonexistence whose very nonexistence paradoxically takes on a phenomenal or material character the beauty of which may hide the fact that it is only a "substitute" for truth and reality.[18] Valentinus's revision thus reduces Gnostic "fallen Sophia" to a personification (Error) designed to embody a number of dispositional, epistemological, and ontological states (ignorance, agitation, fear, blindness, emptiness) that no longer characterize a single mythical figure but rather the entirety of aeons or emanations as a group.

Valentinus's new myth also tries to blur the narrative aspects of Gnostic myth. Despite his recourse to active verb forms (Error "labors" and "prepares," *GTr* 17.15, 19; "beguiles" and "takes captive," *GTr* 17.34–35; "becomes angry" and "persecutes," *GTr* 18.22–23), Valentinus undercuts the credibility of these descriptions as quickly as they are offered, assuring his audience that "the agitation and forgetfulness and the modeled form of deception were as nothing," that Error has "no root" (*GTr* 17.24–25, 30), and that "the forgetfulness" characterizing Error "is not apparent" (*GTr* 17.36–37) since as soon as the Father is known, "there will no longer be forgetfulness" (*GTr* 18.10–11). The "actions" of Error simply provide striking metaphors for the horror of a certain materially impressive kind of unreality: Valentinus wishes readers to take with utter seriousness the

paradox of the "emptiness" in which Error "labors" at her "matter" (*GTr* 17.14–16).

Valentinus's new myth of Sophia's fall as the emergence of Error informs his subsequent revision of the Gnostic account of Adam and Eve's fall. First, it will be useful to have in mind the details of the biblical myth that lies behind both the Gnostic and the Valentinian version:

> Now the serpent was more subtle than any other wild creature that the Lord God had made. He said to the woman, "Did God say, 'You shall not eat of any tree of the garden'?" And the woman said to the serpent, "We may eat of the fruit of the trees of the garden; but God said, 'You shall not eat of the fruit of the tree which is in the midst of the garden, neither shall you touch it, lest you die.'" But the serpent said to the woman, "You will not die. For God knows that when you eat of it your eyes will be opened, and you will be like God, knowing good and evil." So when the woman saw that the tree was good for food, and that it was a delight to the eyes, and that the tree was to be desired to make one wise, she took of its fruit and ate; and she also gave some to her husband, and he ate. Then the eyes of both were opened, and they knew that they were naked; and they sewed fig leaves together and made themselves aprons. (Gen. 3.1–7)

The Reality of the Rulers reinterprets this biblical myth in order to argue that the fruit of the tree of knowledge (*gnōsis*) eaten by Adam and Eve actually revealed their own lack of knowledge:

> And the carnal woman took from the tree and ate; and she gave to her husband as well as herself; and these merely animate beings ate. And their imperfection was shown forth in their lack of acquaintance; and they knew that they were naked of the spiritual element, and took fig leaves and bound them upon their loins. (*RR* 90.13ff.)

Valentinus offers the following version of these events in the *Gospel of Truth:*

> It is to the perfect that this, the proclamation of the one they search for, has made itself known, through the mercies of the father. By this the hidden mystery Jesus Christ shed light upon those who were, because of forgetfulness, in darkness. He enlightened them and gave them a way, and the way is the truth, about which he instructed them. For this reason error became angry at him and persecuted him. She was constrained by him, and became inactive. He was nailed to a tree and became fruit of the father's acquaintance. Yet it did not cause ruin because it was eaten. Rather, to those who ate of it, it gave the possibility that whoever he discovered within himself might be joyful in the discovery of him. And as for him, they discovered him within them—the inconceivable uncontained, the father, who is perfect, who created the entirety. (*GTr* 18.11–34)

In this revision of the Gnostic account, Valentinus once again assimilates characters. This time, he identifies Adam and Eve's act of eating the forbidden fruit with personified Error, thus dropping Adam and Eve, like the Gnostic Sophia, as individual characters in favor of a more general description of ignorance of God. He then depicts this Error (now represented by the forbidden fruit) as the destroyer of Jesus. Valentinus's interpretation has here become a new story concerning the battle between Error and Jesus. Jesus wins this battle, however, for in the midst of his destruction by Error (historically speaking, his crucifixion), he becomes an antidote or "counter-fruit," providing a restorative *gnōsis* of the Father. Valentinus makes this point by drawing on the Gospel of John, where Jesus declares, "I am the way, and the truth, and the life; no one comes to the Father, but by me" (John 14.6). Jesus, says Valentinus, "shed light upon those who were, because of forgetfulness [which comes, we recall, from Error], in darkness. He enlightened them and gave them a way, and the way is the truth, about which he instructed them" (*GTr* 18.17–21). In response to Jesus' teaching and enlightenment, Error "became angry at him and persecuted him. She was constrained by him, and became inactive. He was nailed to a tree [cf. Gen. 2.17] and became fruit of the father's acquaintance" (*GTr* 18.22–26). Jesus thus becomes a new kind of fruit, an antidote to the poisonous fruit of Eden; this new fruit "did not cause ruin because it was eaten" (cf. Gen. 3.7) but gave the possibility of mutual self-discovery on the part of God and the Valentinian believer (*GTr* 18.26–35). The pronominal ambiguity in the concluding lines of this passage leads the reader from an awareness of the christological character of salvation to its deeper theological foundation: the fruit of salvation is mutual knowledge between Jesus and the believers, and, ultimately, between the believers and the Father of the entirety.

Those who have ruined themselves by eating the fruit of Error's forgetfulness are saved through the mercies of the Father who has uttered forth ("manifested," frag. H) his Son Jesus in an act of divine *kenōsis* or self-emptying. This divine self-emptying is both Error's most intense "persecution" of the Son (his death on the cross) and Error's final self-annihilation (cf. dying to use up death, frag. F). In other words, the moment of Error's death is also the moment of her complete self-knowledge. Her self-knowledge is a self-emptying or *kenōsis* because she suddenly learns she has no self—that she is mere "modeling," pure "substitution," "fabrication" or "fiction," empty signifier without a signified. As a result of this self-knowledge, Error becomes "inactive"; her previous agency is now unveiled as a lie, her material appearance and beauty the result of a terrible misperception on the part of all who are not God—aeons, emanations, human beings. Error thus vanishes in a split second of mutual discovery and self-discovery: the Valentinian believer

discovers himself or herself to be in the Son (or Father), and the Son (or Father) is revealed to be in the believer.

Valentinus's revision of the Gnostic myth of the falls of Sophia, Adam, and Eve has several implications. By making the fruit of Genesis (as Error) actually "cause ruin" rather than simply reveal ignorance (as was the case in Gnostic myth), Valentinus indirectly gives greater importance to the new fruit of Jesus that overcomes that ruin; the importance of the historical figure of Jesus is highlighted elsewhere in the *Gospel of Truth* where his teaching activity in the social and historical world is described (cf. *GTr* 19.18ff.). With this emphasis on the figure of Jesus, Valentinus's revisionary reading of Gnostic myth "Christianizes" that account far beyond the Christian trimmings previously applied by Gnostics to non-Christian Gnostic myth.[19] Valentinus's battle between Error and the crucified Jesus draws on a classic Christian revisionary problem/solution pattern that Clement will later use to read Hebrew scripture in light of his Christian assumptions. This interpretative pattern not only allows Valentinus to revise scripture and Gnostic myth, but also enables him to structure the logic of his own gospel meditation in a way that features personified Error rather than Adam or Eve as the chief protagonist.

Another feature of Valentinus's interpretative allegory is that, in contrast to the mythology that it interprets and revises, it does not seek to be structured by a steady sequential progression from origin to goal. Rather than taking place sequentially in time, "actions" seem to occur within one another, as physical states of being dissolve into one another in metaphysical space, within the all-inclusive field of the Father.[20] We should imagine looking through a kaleidoscope rather than watching a motion picture (or if we think of watching a motion picture, we should think of scenes fading in and out or dissolving into one another). Both the *Gospel*'s theme and its syntax reflect and foster this curious nonlinear, "antinarrative" quality. For example, the prologue of the work establishes a thematic tension between search and discovery, lack and completion, that later statements in the body of the text elaborate.[21] The prologue speaks first of discovery, of those who "have received grace" (*ji pihmat*) and are filled with "joy" (*telēl*) upon receiving the Word's emanation from the Father:

> The proclamation [or gospel] of the truth is a joy for those who have received grace from the father of truth, that they might learn to know him through the power of the Word that emanated from the fullness that is in the father's thought and intellect—the Word, who is spoken of as "savior": for, that is the term for the work that he was to accomplish to ransom those who had fallen ignorant of the father. (*GTr* 16.31–17.1)

Later in the body of the text, this opening description of fullness and presence is reiterated and elaborated by three further claims. Those in

the prologue who "received grace" are now called "the perfect" (*jēk abal*), the gracious emanation of the Word is now called "the mercies of the father" (*nimntšanhtēf nte piōt*), and the "joy" of those who received grace is now matched by a "rejoicing" (*reše*) at the "discovery" (*čine*) of the father:

> It is to the perfect that this, the proclamation of the one they search for, has made itself known, through the mercies of the father. By the hidden mystery Jesus Christ shed light upon those who were, because of forgetfulness, in darkness. (*GTr* 18.11–17)

We see, then, that both in the prologue and later on in the text, the *Gospel* proclaims an achieved fullness or completion. But the second half of the prologue, as well as statements later in the body of the text, introduces the motif of searching. The passage we quoted from the prologue immediately goes on to say that those who have received grace are nevertheless "searching" (*kōte*), motivated by their energetic "hope" (*helpis*): "the term proclamation [or good news] refers to the manifestation of hope, a discovery for those who are searching for him" (*GTr* 17.1–4). Later, the *Gospel* again characterizes those who have discovered something as still straining in hope:

> This is the account of the good news [or proclamation] about the discovery of the fullness, for those who strain toward the salvation coming from above. Their hope [*helpis*], towards which they strain [*samt*], is straining (toward them). (*GTr* 34.35–35.4)

Not only can we find alternating expressions of search and discovery in the *Gospel*, but these oppositional themes are even more directly implicated in one another than might at first appear. Even as both the prologue and later statements suggest discovery by describing a group of perfect ones who have received grace, this discovery is immediately undercut in each passage by the intrusion of searching. In the first part of the prologue, "those who have received grace" have received it so "that they might learn to know [*souōn*] him"—one receives only in order to strive for something still unattained. In the later statement, "the perfect" still "search for" (*kōte*) the Word—once again, possession does not produce contentment. The same tension between possession and aspiration or lack, though in the reverse sequence, appears in the second half of the prologue and the corresponding statements in the body of the text. In the second half of the prologue, "those who are searching" do so in the immediate presence of a "discovery" (*čine*) or "manifestation" (*ouanh*), and in the corresponding later statement, "those who strain towards salvation" do so together with "the discovery of the fullness" (*tčine nte piplērōma*), for that towards which they strain "is straining (towards them)" (*essamt*).

Thus, the *Gospel of Truth* unfolds in a manner that does not mark a clear

linear progression from search to discovery. Instead, it insists on a seemingly unresolved tension, dialectical interplay, or oscillation between the
two. In this way, the *Gospel* as allegorical composition strives to overcome
the narrative dimensions of the myths that it interprets. We have seen how
Valentinus reads precursor myths allegorically in order to make allegorical replacements (e.g., Error for Sophia) so that the groundwork might be
laid for his own mythical composition. In this composition, even the
remaining characters (Error, Jesus) become allegorical figures of yet another "story" of blindness and insight that seeks not to be a story or
narrative at all.

The oscillation just described between the themes of search and discovery is echoed by a similar interaction between representations of absence
and presence. In Valentinus's revision of Gnostic Sophia as the manifestation of Error, there is a "movement" from presence to absence and then
back to presence. At the outset, the entirety is present, but the entirety
manifests a lack, having "searched for the one from whom they had emanated" (*GTr* 17.5–6). But this lack produced by ignorance is destined to
receive completion: "Inasmuch as forgetfulness arose because the father
was unknown, from the moment the father comes to be known [*souōn*],
there will no longer be forgetfulness" (*GTr* 18.7–11). This oscillation appears in similar mythical guise later in the text when Valentinus proclaims
that although Error is "a fallen (?) thing," it "can easily be made upright
through the discovery [*čine*] of him who came to that which he would
bring back" (*GTr* 35.18–21). Lack will find completion in the "restoration" or "repentance" (*metanoia*) of Error (*GTr* 35.22). Once again, it is
tempting to construe Valentinus's dialectic of absence and presence, lack
and completion, in linear terms, especially when we sense that the alter-
nations echo the tripartite narrative of basic Christian myth. But Valentinus intends readers to understand Gnostic and biblical narratives not so
much as stories but as representations of modes of being—of the ever-
present possibilities of spiritual blindness or insight, nonexistence or
existence.

Valentinus supplements the thematic paradoxes we have noted by
exploiting odd syntactical constructions to work against the linear narrative sequence of Gnostic precursor myths. In particular, he often interchanges active and passive constructions. The medium for these various
interchanges is always the "fullness of the entirety," or "the Father." We
return to a passage considered earlier, this time with an eye not to its
character as a revisionary reading of Gnostic themes, but to its syntactical
and rhetorical character:

> He [Jesus Christ] was nailed to a tree and became fruit of the acquaintance
> of the father. Yet it did not cause ruin because it was eaten. Rather, to those

> who ate of it, it gave the possibility that whoever he discovered within
> himself might be joyful in the discovery of him. And as for him, they
> discovered him within them—the inconceivable uncontained, the father,
> who is perfect, who created the entirety. Because the entirety was within him
> and the entirety was in need of him—since he had retained within himself
> its completion, which he had not given unto the entirety—the father was
> not grudging; for what envy is there between him and his own members?
> (*GTr* 18.24–40)

The ambiguous genitive phrase "acquaintance of the father" (*picaune nte
piōt*) suggests both the Father's knowledge of others and their knowledge
of him. The second possibility seems endorsed by the assertion that "those
that ate" "might be joyful in the discovery of him" (*aurese nhrēi nhn pičine
ntaf*), but the activity of those searching and discovering is immediately
restated as the Father's discovery of them "within himself" (*ntafčntou
nhētf*). Yet even as the Father plays the role of seeker, he also acts as the
one sought: "As for him, they discovered him within them" (*ntaf aučntf
nhētou*). The Father is the perfection of fullness, dialectically completing
the lack that motivates the seekers, for "he had retained within himself its
[the entirety's] completion" (*eafamahte mpijōk nteu nhētf*). The seekers are
"members" (*melos*) of the Father, but as his "own" members they are also
the perfect, "joyful" in their "discovery" because "the father was not
grudging" (*nefr phthoni en nči piōt*). By means of metaphorical substitution
and pronominal ambiguity, this account turns back in upon itself, as the
seekers find and the finders seek.[22]

Such syntactical and rhetorical features reinforce the thematic oppositions to narrativity examined earlier. We have already seen that as soon as
the actions of Error and Jesus are described in the most vivid narrative
form, they are psychologized and transformed into metaphors of mutual
search and discovery, as the Father discovers the entirety within himself.
This discovery is simultaneously the entirety's discovery of the Father
within itself and an individual Christian's discovery of the Father within
himself or herself:

> Inasmuch as the completion of the entirety is in the father, the entirety must
> go to *him*. Then upon gaining acquaintance, all individually receive what
> belongs to *them*, and draw it to themselves. For whoever does not possess
> acquaintance is in need, and what that person needs is great, inasmuch as
> the thing that such a person needs is what would complete the person. (*GTr*
> 21.8–18; my emphasis)

As Valentinus's allegorical reading of prior narratives (Genesis, Gnostic
myth, the *Timaeus,* the Gospels) merges imperceptibly into the creative
allegorical composition that is the *Gospel of Truth,* the specific characters of
precursor texts (Adam, Eve, Sophia, Ialdabaōth, Jesus) dissolve into more

fundamental, abstract, multilayered representations of fullness, lack, and completion. These representations are simultaneously the psychic history of the divine first principle and of each individual Christian. The transition from lack to completion, from forgetfulness to knowledge, is instantaneous—one need not go anywhere or do anything: "Inasmuch as forgetfulness [*tibše*] arose because the father was unknown, from the moment the father comes to be known, there will no longer be forgetfulness" (*GTr* 18.7–11); "Inasmuch as the lack [*šta*] came into being because the father was not known, from the moment that the father is known the lack will not exist" (*GTr* 24.28–32). Directly challenging deeply ingrained narrative desires, Valentinus does not give us an Aristotelian plot with beginning, middle, and end, a story with identifiable individuals and their interactions. Instead, he offers an allegory of blindness and insight at odds with its own narrativity, in which temporal metaphors represent degrees of similarity and difference rather than moments of sequential progression.

The interpretative energies unleashed in the *Gospel of Truth* are simultaneously the basis for, and the expression of, the deep religious and philosophical concerns of the text as a composition in its own right. Valentinus can express his own distinctive vision only by rereading his precursors. As we have already seen, that vision takes the form of a composition whose own events and characters point allegorically beyond themselves toward nonnarrative states of being and nonbeing. We turn next, then, to an investigation of the *Gospel* as an allegorical composition in its own right—to its character as an allegory of spiritual blindness and insight. One of the principal organizing metaphors for this allegory is the divine name, and it will be useful to explore first the kinds of speculation about the divine name on which Valentinus might have drawn.

When Valentinus in the early second century C.E. declares that Adam was created "in the name of the *anthrōpos*" and that "the name of the Father is the Son," he is able to do so because he stands within an already developed tradition of speculation about the divine name. Evidence for the importance of various "divine" or "sacred" names in Alexandrian Christianity appears first in the form of a strange scribal practice. When Christian scribes in early second-century Egypt wrote the name "Jesus" in their papyrus manuscripts, they did not write *Iēsous* but simply $\overline{ie}$.[23] Fourteen other words received a similarly special abbreviation: *christos* ("Christ"), *kyrios* ("lord"), *theos* ("God"), *pneuma* ("spirit"), *anthrōpos* ("man"), *stauros* ("cross"), *patēr* ("Father"), *huios* ("Son"), *sōtēr* ("Savior"),[24] *mētēr* ("mother"), *ouranos* ("heaven"), *Israēl* ("Israel"), *Daveid* ("David"), and *Hierousalēm* ("Jerusalem"). Scribes abbreviated these *nomina sacra* or "sacred names" either by suspension (writing only the first two letters, such as $\overline{ie}$ for *Iēsous*) or by contraction (writing only the first and last letters,

such as $\overline{\imath s}$ for *Iēsous*); a horizontal line drawn above the abbreviation indicated that the word was sacred and presumably not to be pronounced as customarily written. This special system did not, it appears, arise by accident but instead emanated from a single authoritative teaching center, almost certainly Jerusalem.[25] The special significance given to these words by Christian scribes derives from traditional Jewish reverence for the Tetragrammaton (YHWH), or name of God.[26] Yet, surprisingly, the *nomina sacra* are almost exclusively limited to Christian manuscripts; when given the opportunity to use them, as illustrated by Jewish copies of the Pentateuch dating from the early second century B.C.E. to the early first century C.E., Jewish scribes invariably chose instead either to write out the word in full or in the case of the Tetragrammaton to write out the four consonants in Hebrew. The spoken equivalent of the Tetragrammaton, "lord" (Greek *kyrios;* Hebrew *adonai*), was also not abbreviated, but written out in full.[27] Consequently, the presence of the abbreviated *nomina sacra* is an identifying feature of early Christian papyri from Egypt, specifically marking them off from Jewish manuscripts, from which they might otherwise be indistinguishable.

The *Epistle of Barnabas* provides the earliest direct evidence for a *nomen sacrum* in a literary text. *Barnabas* was probably written in Alexandria, where it was included in the New Testament (it follows the Book of Revelation in the Codex Sinaiticus). The author of this text interprets the number of Abraham's followers, 318, as "Jesus" and "cross":

> Learn fully then, children of love, concerning all things, for Abraham, who first circumcised, did so looking forward in the spirit to Jesus, and had received the doctrines of three letters. For it says, "And Abraham circumcised from his household eighteen men and three hundred [Gen. 17.23, 27; 14.14]. What then was the knowledge [*gnōsis*] that was given to him? Notice that he first mentions the eighteen, and after a pause the three hundred. The eighteen is *iōta* ten, *ēta* eight—you have Jesus—and because the cross was destined to have grace in the *tau* he says "and three hundred." So he indicates Jesus in the two letters and the cross in the other. (*Barn.* 9.7–8)[28]

Knowledge of the system of numerical equivalents for the Greek alphabet is needed to unravel this enigmatic text. The Greek letter tau (*t*) equals 300; it also has the shape of a cross. The letters iōta ēta (*iē*) together equal 18 and form the first two letters of Jesus' name in Greek (*Iēsous*). The suspension $\overline{\imath\bar{e}}$ for *Iēsous* appears forty-five times in the second-century Christian papyri from Egypt. Since *Barnabas* probably dates from the early second century, and its author does not present his numerological reading as his own invention, this particular interpretation probably stems from a tradition going well back into the first century C.E. Such an early appearance makes it likely that *Iēsous* was the first *nomen sacrum*.[29]

The surprising absence in the papyri of eucharistic words as *nomina sacra* suggests that the Egyptian Christian environment was relatively unaffected by Pauline and Johannine influences.[30] Instead, the early prevalence of *anthrōpos* as a *nomen sacrum* suggests the influence of very early gospel traditions of the sayings of Jesus, which often included the title *huios anthrōpou* ("Son of man"). This title, which originated among Aramaic-speaking Jewish Christians, was not used by Paul and was soon replaced in Christian literature by other titles.[31]

The use of *nomina sacra* in Alexandrian Christianity probably derived from a precedent established in Jerusalem; only the Jerusalem apostolic center is likely to have provided the early authority and technical precedent needed to set out rules for Christian scribes.[32] Although fraught with problems as a historical source, the New Testament book of Acts purports to describe this early Christian center. According to Acts, the divine name was a prominent feature of Jerusalem Christianity. The apostles in Jerusalem claimed to possess the power of the divine name, manifested in "bold speech" (*parrhēsia*) (Acts 4.29), miracles (Acts 4.7, 10, 12, 30), and authoritative teaching (Acts 4.17, 18; 5.28, 40, 41).[33] Salvation itself, according to this Jerusalem teaching, can be in no other name than that of Jesus (Acts 4.12). Of course, the name of God had already been identified with the name of Jesus at least as early as the (Palestinian?) tradition that Paul invokes in Philippians 2.9–11:

> Therefore God has highly exalted him and bestowed on him the name which is above every name [the Tetragrammaton?], that at the name of Jesus every knee should bow, in heaven and on earth and under the earth, and every tongue confess that Jesus Christ is Lord, to the glory of God the Father.

This traditional confession seems to be part of an early Christian baptismal formula reflecting the notion that the name of God was given to Jesus after his resurrection. Later we shall see that Valentinus's student Theodotus also declares that the divine name descended on Jesus at his baptism (Clem. *Ex. Theod.* 22.4–6).[34]

This ascription of the divine name to Jesus in the early Christian community grew out of a transformation of traditional Jewish reverence for the name of God into a Christian messianic reading of certain passages in Hebrew scripture.[35] An especially early and striking instance of such a reading (in this case, of Joel 3.5) appears both in Peter's Pentecost speech in Acts and Paul's letter to the Romans. Peter declares that in the "last days," before the "day of the Lord," amid many other signs and wonders, "it shall be that whoever calls on the name of the Lord shall be saved" (Acts 2.21). Similarly, Paul assures his readers that anyone who "believes with his heart" that God resurrected Jesus, and "confesses with his lips" that Jesus is Lord will be saved, for "every one who calls upon the name of

the Lord will be saved" (Rom. 10.9, 13). Echoing Paul's Philippian hymn, Peter connects the crucified and resurrected Christ with "the name" as the source of an apostolic healing:

> Be it known to you all, and to all the people of Israel, that by the name of Jesus Christ of Nazareth, whom you crucified, whom God raised from the dead, by him this man is standing before you well. . . . And there is salvation in no one else, for there is no other name under heaven given among men by which we must be saved. (Acts 4.10–12)

Like Peter, James also appeals to the divine name; in the presence of Barnabas and Paul, he reports that Peter has "related how God first visited the Gentiles, to take out of them a people for his name" and adds confirmation from the prophets, who speak of a restorative act of God in which "the rest of men may seek the Lord, and all the Gentiles who are called by my name" (Acts 15.14, 17). These passages and many others like them suggest that earliest Christianity in Jerusalem forged a connection between the divine name and the figure of Jesus as the key to the basic Christian interpretative appropriation of Hebrew scripture and Jewish messianic promises.[36]

Christian use of the category of "name" soon became widespread in the Greek-speaking world. The Book of Revelation, in speaking of those "sealed on their foreheads" (Rev. 7.3) with the name (Rev. 22.4), especially with the names of the Lamb and his Father (Rev. 14.1), and of the one upon the white horse whose name "The Word of God . . . no one knows but himself" (Rev. 19.12–13), alludes to baptismal "sealings" and probably presupposes the existence of the *nomina sacra*.[37] Christian texts popular in Alexandria and strongly informed by Judaism, such as *1 Clement* and the *Didachē*, also reflect this Jewish name speculation. *1 Clement* speaks of God's "name, the source of all creation" (*1 Clem.* 59.3; cf. 58.1), and the *Didachē* of thanks given to God for the "Holy Name, which thou [God] didst make to dwell [*skēnoun*] in our hearts" (*Did.* 10.2). The latter usage is echoed by John 1.14: "And the word [formerly, the name?] became flesh and dwelt [*kataskēnoun*] among us."[38] John in particular virtually identifies Jesus and the name in John 17.6: "I [Jesus] have manifested thy name to the men whom thou gavest me out of the world; thine they were, and thou gavest them to me, and they have kept thy word" (cf. John 17.11–12, 26). The *Shepherd* of Hermas, which like *Barnabas* was part of the New Testament in Egypt, declares that "the Tower [the Church] has been founded by the utterance of the almighty and glorious Name" (Herm. *Vis.* 3.3.5; cf. Herm. *Sim.* 9.14.3) and that "the name of the Son of God is great and incomprehensible, and supports the whole world" and thus "he supports" "those who bear his name with their whole heart" (*Sim.* 9.14.5–6).[39]

The *Gospel of Truth* draws on similar early Christian traditions of the divine name. We turn next to its use of the name as an organizing metaphor for its mystical vision. Since the *Gospel of Truth* is not well known except by specialists and since the passages in which Valentinus meditates on the name are exceedingly intricate, it will prove helpful to have the relevant portions of the text before us in full before we begin a close examination of them. There are at least three important discussions of names and naming in the *Gospel.*

I

Those whose names he foreknew were called at the end, as persons having acquaintance [= *gnōsis*]. It is the latter whose names the father called. For one whose name has not been spoken does not possess acquaintance. How else would a person hear, if that person's name had not been read out? For whoever lacks acquaintance until the end is a modeled form of forgetfulness, and will perish along with it. Otherwise, why do these contemptible persons have no name? Why do they not possess the faculty of speech? So that whoever has acquaintance is from above: and if called, hears, replies, and turns to the one who is calling; and goes to him. And he knows how that one is called. Having acquaintance, that person does the will of the one who has called; wishes to please him; and gains repose. One's name becomes one's own. Those who gain acquaintance in this way know whence they have come and whither they will go; they know in the manner of a man who, after having been intoxicated, has recovered from his intoxication: having returned into himself, he has caused his own to stand at rest. He has brought many back from error, going before them unto their ways from which they had swerved after accepting error because of the depth of him who surrounds every way, while nothing surrounds him. It was quite amazing that they were in the father without being acquainted with him and that they alone were able to emanate, inasmuch as they were not able to perceive and recognize the one in whom they were. (*GTr* 21.25–22.33)

II

All the ways are his emanations. They know that they have emanated from him like children who were within a mature man but knew they had not yet received form nor been given name. It is when they receive the impulse toward acquaintance with the father that he gives birth to each. Otherwise, although they are within him they do not recognize him. The father himself is perfect and acquainted with every way that is in him. If he wills, what he wills appears, as he gives it form and name. And he gives it name, and causes it to make them come into existence. (*GTr* 27.11–31)

III

Now, the name of the father is the son. It is he who in the beginning named what emanated from him, remaining always the same. And he begot him as a son and gave him his name, which he possessed. It is he in whose vicinity the father has all things: he has the name, and he has the son. The latter can

be seen; but the name is invisible, for it alone is the mystery of the invisible, which comes into ears that are wholly full of it, because of him. And yet the father's name is not spoken. Rather, it is manifest in a son. Thus, great is the name! Who, then, can utter his name, the great name, but him alone who possesses the name—and the children of the name in whom the father's name reposed and who in turn reposed in his name! Inasmuch as the father is unengendered, it is he who alone bore him unto himself, as a name, before he had put the aeons in order, so that the name of the father might be supreme over them as lord. And this is the true name, confirmed by his command in perfect power. For this name does not result from words and acts of naming, but rather his name is invisible. He alone gave him a name, for he alone saw him, and it was he alone who was able to name him: for what does not exist has no name—indeed, what would a nonexistent be named?—but what exists, exists along with its name. And he alone is acquainted with him and <. . .> for him alone to give him a name. He is the father: his name is the son. So he did not hide it within action, rather it existed. The son alone gave names. So the name belongs to the father, just as the name of the father is the son, the beloved. For where would he find a name except from the father? Yet perhaps someone will say to another, "Who could name one that preexisted before him? Do not children get names from their parents?" First, we must consider the question of what sort of thing a name is. For he is the true name. Thus it is he who is the name from the father; for it is he who exists as the most lordly name. Accordingly, he did not get the name on loan—unlike others, all of whom individually get their names according as they are created. But this one is the most lordly name. There is no other being that bestowed it upon him. Rather, he is unnameable and indescribable until such time as the perfect alone has spoken of him. And it is the latter who is able to speak his name and see him. So when it pleased him that his uttered name should be his son, and when he who had emanated from the depth gave him his name he spoke of his secrets, knowing that the father is without evil. Precisely for this reason he produced him—so that he might speak concerning the place from which he had emanated and his realm of repose, and that he might glorify the fullness, the greatness, of his name, and the father's sweetness. (*GTr* 38.7–41.3)

We can begin to make our way into this complex set of assertions about names and naming by keeping before us one basic affirmation about the *Gospel* that will hold true despite the need for qualifications at certain points: the thoroughgoing monism of Valentinus's vision is the key to all that follows.[40] For Valentinus, dualism or "division" is a false notion, a fundamental misperception about reality. There is only one reality—the inconceivable, uncontained Father—who is an unfathomable depth that "surrounds every way [or aeon], while nothing surrounds him" (*GTr* 22.25–27).[41] What, then, constitutes the distinction between spiritual entities (aeons, emanations) and the divine Father? Or between the material

realm of ordinary human existence and the spiritual realm? The answer to both questions is the same: both sets of distinctions are the direct, unavoidable consequence of the Father's own act of self-contemplation. The spiritual realm has emanated "from the fullness that is in the father's thought and intellect" (*GTr* 16.34–36). This is another way of saying that the Father's own act of self-contemplation has produced (hypostatized) as its by-product certain lesser centers or regions of contemplation (variously called ways, aeons, selves, or places). Because of the Father's unknowability, these areas of contemplation are by definition forced into a state of *a-gnōsis*. Such an unfortunate, but necessary, result of divine self-knowledge is implied by the logic of the *Gospel:* after noting that the entirety (i.e., the collection of aeons) searches for the one in whom it exists, Valentinus observes parenthetically that the one searched for, the "inconceivable uncontained," nevertheless remains "superior to all thought" (*GTr* 17.8–9). Because the Father is superior to all thought, the aeons cannot escape their "ignorant" condition.

Valentinus is baffled and perturbed by this fact: why is the presence of the divine at one's own origin not an adequate basis for one's knowledge of God? "It was quite amazing," he exclaims, "that they [the aeons] were in the father without being acquainted with him and that they alone were able to emanate, inasmuch as they were not able to perceive and recognize the one in whom they were" (*GTr* 22.27–33). Although the aeons were within the divine, this location was also necessarily the site of a primordial absence of the divine. The aeons are paradoxically the victims of their own identities. Their own constitution as selves independent from the deity was made possible by the deity's own act of self-realization, but that act also withdrew the divine presence from them. As a result, the aeons find themselves in the exasperating situation of being constituted as individuals precisely by the distance from that which is the basis of their true identities—their source or "root" (*GTr* 17.30; 41.15–28). Valentinus's psychological characterizations of this process make it clear that the fate of the aeons is also the human fate; indeed, what happens within the divine *plērōma* is what happens in the human realm, understood, however, from a more profound point of view. Human beings are, then, like the aeons; they find themselves yearning for those sorts of personal relationships by which their identities might be fashioned or revealed. "Unknown to certain people," they wish "to become known, and so become loved, by them" (*GTr* 19.10–14).

Since the deity's self-constitution is the reason why all other beings lack full and authentic existence, the deity would seem to be responsible for the human predicament of error and forgetfulness. Although Valentinus is clearly troubled by this possibility of divine shortcoming, he nevertheless insists that the appearance of Error "was not humiliating" to the

"inconceivable uncontained" (*GTr* 17.21–22). The Father cannot be held responsible because, quite literally, forgetfulness did not arise "in the father's company," thus "surely then not because of him!" (*GTr* 18.2–3). In the divine company can only be acquaintance. But were not the not-yet-emanated but soon-to-be-forgetful aeons "in his company"? Only in a manner of speaking, for their forgetfulness actually resulted from failing to keep that company. Thus a familiar regression of causes begins. What, then, was the cause of that primal failure to keep that company? What, in effect, is the origin of evil? Valentinus provides a thoroughly paradoxical answer: evil arises from the transcendence and self-knowledge of a divine first principle who nevertheless "alone is good" (frag. H) and "without evil" (*GTr* 40.29; 42.7). Ever since that primordial lack, the Father has "retained within himself" the entirety's "completion" (*GTr* 18.36–37). Although the Father has not given that completion to the entirety, he has not refrained because he begrudges them such fulfillment—"for what envy is there between him and his own members?" (*GTr* 18.39–40). Just when the text seems about to explain this paradoxical state of affairs, gaps in the papyrus appear: "For if this realm had {. . .} them, they would not be able to {. . .} the father, retaining their completion within himself, in that it {was} given them in the form of return to him and acquaintance and completion" (*GTr* 18.39–19.7). We learn that the outcome is to be "return," "acquaintance" (*gnōsis*), and "completion," but the syntax needed to bring this conclusion into a fully satisfying relation with what has preceded is missing. Readers of the text are thus left with the unnerving knowledge that all humanly recognizable "reality" is the misleading aftermath of a hidden catastrophe "at the highest levels." As a consequence, they are enjoined to call into question their current sense of "reality." What human beings have always taken to be real is false; ignorance of the Father has left them with only a beautiful "substitute" (*GTr* 17.20) for truth and reality that, for all its outward charm or terror, is mere "emptiness" (*GTr* 17.16), "as nothing" (*GTr* 17.23).

But just as there is lack and deficiency, so there is the possibility of possession and fulfillment. Human misperceptions are potentially reversible and corrigible at any moment: "Inasmuch as forgetfulness arose because the father was unknown, from the moment the father comes to be known, there will no longer be forgetfulness" (*GTr* 18.7–11). Human beings are, after all, still "in" the Father, and his name is in them even as they are in his name. The first two selections on names and naming quoted above connect this peculiar status of the individual self to notions of name and "form." Each aeon or self has emanated from the fullness of the Father. Emanation is a metaphor for the "ignorance" of the Father, for the "act" of emanating or coming forth is one long step in the direction of increasing absence—a *kenōsis* of name, form, and existence. What is

needed is a "return" (another metaphor for *gnōsis*), a step back in the direction of form and name, true reality and personal identity. Only then does a person's name become his or her "own" (*GTr* 22.12–13)—when he or she hears it called out by the Father from the living book, inscribed with human names or identities even before human beings emanated (*GTr* 21.25–27). The Father thus has knowledge of human beings' true identities prior to their emanation, before they lapse into deficiency, and he goes ahead of their error to redirect their paths back to him. Having "inscribed these things in advance" (*GTr* 21.23), he "has brought many back from error, going before them unto their ways from which they had swerved after accepting error" (*GTr* 22.20–25).

The third and most complex selection on naming quoted above lends considerable nuance to the Father's call of the names of the once-pre-inscribed and now-wayward aeons. Just like each aeon, the Father also has a name, which is his "Son." Like its prototype, the Jewish Tetragrammaton, the Father's "name" is his essential nature or character and as such is necessarily "invisible" and "unutterable" by others. Indeed, even the Father himself cannot utter his own name but must manifest it in the visible form of the Son. Perhaps here we should think of this divine utterance as productive, along the lines of the Hebraic notion of *davar* (as "word/thing/deed"). Like those names elected and preinscribed by the Father, so the name of the Father emanated. The emanation of the Father is the Son, but the Son emanated "prior to" the emanation of the aeons, in order to be "lord" over them (*GTr* 38.36–38). As the utterance of the Father's ineffable name, the Son as "lord" echoes the Jewish spoken form of the unpronounceable Tetragrammaton (Hebrew *adonai*, "lord").[42] The divine name-as-Son is "lord" both because of his temporal priority (he preexists the aeons; cf. Phil. 2.9–11) and because of his spiritual authority (his name is the "proper" or true name that perfectly captures the essence of the mysterious Father). "Proper" or "lordly" names are not mere "words" or the results of ordinary "acts of naming." They are not the products of purely conventional decisions about meaning and referentiality. Instead, "proper" or "lordly" names depend on intrinsic connections (i.e., Cratylean or Adamic shared natures) between words and things. If the name-as-Son were simply an ordinary name applied to the divine first principle, it would have to be used improperly or by catachresis—"loaned" from one realm to another. The Coptic *njaeis nren* ("lordly name") simply translates the Greek *kyrion onoma* and should be understood in contrast to the Coptic *apoušep* ("on loan"), which translates the Greek *katachrēstikōs*.[43] Consequently, as a name that is *kyrios*, the name-as-Son is the most literal name there could be, not a catachresis for the Father. The "lordly name" expresses the Father's nature as "without evil," as fullness rather than emptiness. The "lordly name" is "a fullness of

name" that is each individual's own potential fullness, name, form, reality, and identity. Like the prodigal sons and daughters they are, the aeons are enjoined to "come to themselves" (cf. Luke 15.17). Divine self-constitution as self-naming through the manifestation of the Son is the inverse of the human self-naming as self-constitution that occurs when human beings "hear" the Father's self-naming as the calling of their own names. This experience or realization lies behind Valentinus's conclusion that "the father is without evil."

The emanated Son provides the link between the name of the Father (the Father's true reality) and the names of the emanated aeons (their own true realities). The name is unspeakable and invisible, existing only when the Father "pronounces" it, not as a mere word but as a visible Son. We have seen that the manifestation of this name as the Son necessarily entails a lack. The Father emanates as the Son ultimately to the point of near self-annihilation in order to provide the antidote to the aeons' ignorance that unavoidably accompanied their genesis. At the point of greatest ignorance, members of the entirety are like the error they "embody"—nothing but empty "modeled forms" without substantial reality. This is the point of greatest terror or existential shock. Each aeon cries out in horrified self-discovery: "I have come into being (only) in the manner of shadows and apparitions of the night." To this Valentinus can only exclaim: "O the light's shining on the fear of that person, upon knowing that it is nothing!" (*GTr* 28.26–31). Such terror, fear, disturbance, instability, indecision, division, futility, and empty ignorance (*GTr* 29.1–8) can only be compared to one's worst nightmare, in which one is "running toward somewhere—powerless to get away while being pursued—in hand-to-hand combat—being beaten—falling from a height—being blown upward by the air, but without any wings . . . being murdered, though nobody is giving chase—or killing one's neighbors, with whose blood one is smeared" (*GTr* 29.11–25).

Similarly, at the point of fullest divine self-naming or emanation of the name-as-Son, the Father also undergoes a lack. Valentinus does not take the Lurianic step of depicting total divine contraction but, in a typically Christian mediation, defers that role to the Son. As a relatively distinct hypostasis, the Son thus performs the Father's act of self-*kenōsis*. To do so, the Son must "take up" the "incomprehensible" "living book of the living" (*GTr* 19.34ff.)—that total divine essence in which all names are inscribed. But to "take it up" requires that he "accept the sufferings" (*GTr* 20.11). Before Jesus, "no one had been able to take it up, inasmuch as it was ordained that whoever should take it up would be put to death" (*GTr* 20.3–6). But the divine Son is willing to do what Moses could not do—look upon the face of God and die (Exod. 33.20). The Son realizes that although the one who sees God must die, only the one who loses his life

saves it. Recognizing, then, that "his death would mean life for many" (*GTr* 20.13–14), Jesus as the Father's proxy extends the *kenōsis* of the Father to the point of self-annihilation. "Wrapped" in the book (*GTr* 20.24)—invested with the name of the Father—Jesus' death exchanges corruptibility for incorruptibility. He exchanges the most extreme departure from the fullness of the Father (the Son-as-emanated) for the divine fullness shared with the Father (the Son-as-name) (cf. frag. E). For Valentinus, then, the meaning of Christ's crucifixion and resurrection lies in a self-negation of God the Father in his name-as-Son that paradoxically provides the fullness to overcome the Father's own deficiency. The Son embodies the Father's self-contraction to a point of maximal lack that is also the first moment of return. This is the moment at which the prodigal has so dissipated himself that he is forced to "come to himself," the moment at which the members of the entirety "learn about themselves, recovering themselves from the father" and "returning" (*GTr* 21.5–8).

The name of the entirety constituted the writing of that living book that was inscribed in the Father's thought and intellect. As the book is taken up by Jesus, the Father similarly names himself and calls out the names of the entirety (who have the living book inscribed in each of their hearts). Here is the moment at which each Valentinian self, as well as the divine Son, is both born and given up to death. Or perhaps we should say dies and is reborn, for what "dies" is what is powerfully unreal and nonexistent, while what is born truly exists. At this point, we should recall the children of eternal life who live only by using up death (frag. F), as well as the name of the preexistent *anthrōpos* that fills up the lack within the act of Adam's modeling (frag. D). At the same time that Jesus on the cross enters upon the "empty ways of fear" with soteriological effectiveness, one awakens from one's own nightmare state of perceived reality into the luminous state of actual reality. Because Jesus is resurrected, one's nightmare assailants have now vanished:

> Such are those who have cast off lack of acquaintance from themselves like sleep, considering it to be nothing. Neither do they consider its other products to be real things. Rather, they put them away like a dream in the night, and deem acquaintance with the father to be the light. That is how each person acted while being without acquaintance: as though asleep. And the person who has acquaintance is like one who has awakened. And good for the person who returns and awakens! And blessed is the one who has opened the eyes of the blind! (*GTr* 29.32–30.16; cf. frag. H)

Immediately after this passage, Valentinus gives his audience another glimpse of the old Gnostic myth that his new allegory of nightmare and awakening is displacing (we have already seen him revise a portion of this myth in fragment C):

> And the quick spirit hastened after that person when the person had
> awakened; having helped the one who lay prostrate on the ground [i.e.,
> modeled Adam], it made that one strong enough to stand up; for that
> person had not yet arisen. (*GTr* 30.16–23)

The death of the old self is, finally, not the death of the self at all, but the
death of an image, an echo, a facade, a pretense—mere *plasma;* it marks
the final annihilation of that "beautiful modeled form" that was never
truth, never reality, but only the poorest substitute.

Collapsing the very distinctions that generate its own narrative movement, the idiosyncratic rhetoric of Valentinus's allegorical composition
suggests that its author seeks to reflect in the style of his writing the
atemporal stance of a visionary who has left behind the realm of time and
"lack"—the realm of appearance, multiplicity, discord, and death. Yet
the very stylistic and rhetorical articulation of those to-be-dissolved (yet
never-quite-dissolved) distinctions suggests that the visionary author of
the *Gospel of Truth* still writes from within the realm of the lack. Indeed, it
may not be too misleading to say that his writing is itself a kind of
reiteration of lack or absence. Despite his apparent desire, Valentinus's
creative allegorical composition does not free itself from the temporality
of Gnostic and scriptural precursors; the *Gospel of Truth* is not atemporal,
mythopoetic vision. Valentinus dissolves the distinction between sacred
text and commentary, desiring to produce a "text of truth," as though his
self-referential allegory had itself become a version of that "living book of
the living," consisting of texts that are neither vowels nor consonants to be
spoken but "texts of truth which speak and know only themselves" (*GTr*
23.8–10). Yet he still preserves a distinction between his lexical expression
and its meaning, even if such a distinction is not true of the Father's self-
expression as the name or Son.

If Valentinus's rhetoric, in imitation of the Father's speech that produces the true, noncatachrestic name-as-Son, seeks to close the gap between expression and meaning, it does so only by generating and exploiting a semantic indeterminacy more radical than Philo's. Philo allowed
only enough semantic indeterminacy in scripture to make it possible for
Moses to have meant something else; but once identified, Moses' other
meaning turned out to be stable and determinate. And we shall see that
Clement also used allegorical readings to discover in scripture a coherent
and meaningful message that the allegorical composer of scripture (in
this case, the *logos* rather than Moses) had hidden in indirect language.
But Valentinus's allegorical discourse does not resemble these versions of
the ancient rhetoric of persuasion as much as it resembles a postmodern
rhetoric of tropes; he is not engaged in isolating a clear, retrievable

message under initially obscure language, but in exploiting linguistic ambiguity in search of that toward which language itself gestures.

Yet Valentinus's prose does not produce unmitigated antimimesis, generating a semantic indeterminacy that proliferates endlessly, each word disseminating an endless series of other meanings. He is not, despite initial appearances of unrestrained metaphorical innovation, a deconstructionist *avant la lettre*.[44] Instead, Valentinus assumes a visionary stance that escapes, or rather confronts and then surpasses, the alternatives of mimesis and antimimesis.[45] Valentinus's use of metaphors that lack determinate meaning does not lead to an antimimetic, semantic regression because the resulting semantic indeterminacy is not linear (i.e., his signifiers are not extended infinitely in time and space, endlessly differing from one another and deferring meaning; instead, they are self-reflexive). We must imagine, then, neither an endless chain of signifiers nor an arbitrary end to such a chain, but rather something like an expanding and contracting balloon: when full, a balloon is different than when empty, but whether expanded or contracted, it remains the same balloon. The entirety is in the Father, and the Father is in the entirety, but one is not simply the other; indeed, each lacks the other. Although Valentinus's words surrender determinate meanings, they do so in reciprocal fashion; meaning is neither endlessly deferred nor randomly disseminated. Instead, Valentinus's signifiers seek to produce, or, better, bear witness to, a new state of being that is a state of the full presence, not absence, of the divine. In the end, this state of being is the speaker's own; as visionary, Valentinus's ultimate concern is neither for textuality nor for language in general, but for the personal subject or self. The *Gospel of Truth* does not celebrate the death of the subject but its irreducible identity and reality.

Valentinus's meditation on the name of the Father underwrites the identity and reality of the divine subject—and, by implication, the human subject as well. We saw the fragments claim that the oscillation between mimetic fullness and antimimetic deficiency was rooted in the creation of a modeled Adam who lacked the completion that only its ideal prototype could provide. The *Gospel* now claims that the same dynamic pervades the very interstices of deity itself. Inscribed in the very identity of the Father, the gap between fullness and lack is first marked by the distinction between the Son as an "entity" or emanation of the Father and "the Son" as the Father's name or true essence (*GTr* 38.7–24). The distinction between the Son as an entity and as a name in the assertion that "what emanated" was "named" is at once seemingly erased by the claim that the one who produced the emanation remained "always the same" (*GTr* 38.9). Likewise, Valentinus's exploitation of pronominal ambiguity makes it uncertain whether the Father, in giving the Son "his name," gave the Son the

Son's name (which is distinctively the Son's) or the Father's own name (the divine name or Tetragrammaton). Yet even as Valentinus insists on the difference between the names of Father and Son (the name of the Father, unlike the Son, is invisible), he still claims that the visible Son is the "manifestation" (*ouanh*) of the invisible name (*GTr* 38.23).

With such subtle identifications among differences and distinctions among identities, Valentinus wrestles with both the possibilities and limits of linguistic representation of divine reality. For Valentinus, as for Philo, deity is "unnameable and indescribable"—that is, "until such time as the perfect alone [i.e., the Son] has spoken of him" (*GTr* 40.16–19). The Son provides the only access to the high God: it is the Son "who is able to speak his name and see him" (*GTr* 40.20–23; cf. 39.23). The Son can name the unknowable Father simply by virtue of his existence since "the name of the father is the son" (*GTr* 38.7). Once again, name and entity, first distinguished, nearly coalesce: "For what does not exist has no name—indeed, what would a nonexistent be named?—but what exists, exists along with its name" (*GTr* 39.11–16). Yet name and entity do not fuse, and in their difference we can hear a faint echo of Philo's apophatic reservation about language's mimetic capacities. Different from the Father—a difference that Valentinus's vision shows to be unreal and that his rhetoric seeks to efface (while inadvertently reiterating)—the Son emanates for a thoroughly rhetorical task:

> Precisely for this reason he [the Father] produced him [the Son]—so that he might speak concerning the place [*topos*] from which he had emanated and his realm of repose [*pefma nmtan*], and that he might glorify the fullness, the greatness of his name, and the father's sweetness. (*GTr* 40.30–41.3)

This rhetorical gesture of the Father in speaking forth the Son, whose own rhetorical task consists in revealing the Father, is finally part of a much larger act of divine self-knowledge. That act is both the cause of human unreality and the key to the true realization of humanity. When problem and solution are thus seen as a single phenomenon, precisely this vision marks the end to simple division of word from thing, of language from reality; a new, unitary, monistic vision emerges, and anti-mimesis ends. The *Gospel of Truth* is not simply an exercise in protodeconstruction, unless one is ready (as most deconstructionists are not) to grant a kind of realized presence or fullness to that Other to which *différance* gestures in its trace. Nor is the Father's name-as-Son a Philonic instance of catachrestic language—language borrowed from one realm and "loaned" to another, to make do. Instead, it is an instance of true or authentic language, in which the "speaking" of a name is the manifestation of a reality.

The preceding literary analysis suggests that despite the pronouncements of Valentinus the visionary, Valentinus the writer does not dissolve

the tension between mimetic and antimimetic perspectives. Valentinus's mystical or visionary claim to have attained a state in which this tension dissolves into a sui generis third category, like any spiritual or mystical claim, lies beyond the grasp of literary analysis, deep within autobiographical experience, and depends on that personal experience for its final authority. Unlike Philo, who appeals to the authority of a sacred text, and Clement, who defers to the authority of a sacred voice, Valentinus relies on his own heart's visionary experience. There alone is the true origin of the wisdom that others routinely attribute to authoritative texts. In a sermon entitled *On Friends*, Valentinus claims that the wisdom common to both classical Greek literature ("things written in publicly available books") and Christian literature ("the writings of god's church"), whether conceived as speech ("utterances") or writing (the "written" law), is first available in the hearts of "the people of the beloved" (frag. G).[46] One does not need to go to derivative sources, for the truth originally lies in the very interior of one's being.

Within one's very being is found a direct relationship with the ineffable Father, made possible by personal interiorization of the Father's speech or Word. This internal appropriation is made possible by the crucifixion of Word-as-Jesus. We have seen that the crucifixion enables Christians to "eat" the fruit (Jesus) and discover that they are actually in the Father, and the Father is simultaneously in them (*GTr* 18.27–31). The same salvific moment can also be understood as the Savior's reading of a book to Christians (whose names are already written in the book) who, upon hearing what is read, gain knowledge of themselves and simultaneously return to the Father (*GTr* 20.15ff.). Valentinus's reliance on the interior, personal authority of the visionary heart can be seen in the network of interrelated references to the "heart" of the Father and the "heart" of the Christian who has gained the mystical insight made available through the crucifixion of Jesus. Valentinus explicitly numbers himself among the saved Christians who "speak" of the "light" in the Father's "heart" (*GTr* 43.12–15). That "light" is clearly the Son or Word that has "come forward" out of the Father's heart and is therefore "in the heart of those that speak it" (*GTr* 26.5–6). The Word came forth from the heart of the "fullness that is in the father's thought and intellect" (*GTr* 16.35–36), entering the entirety as a "fruition {of} his heart" (*GTr* 23.35–24.1). It did so in order that it might also come forth as divine speech from the saved Christian's heart, for the Word (as the "living book of the living") forms an indissoluble link between the Father and all saved Christians: "In their hearts appeared the living book of the living, which is written in the father's thought and intellect" (*GTr* 19.34–20.1). The Word thus came forward, both from the "heart of those that speak it" (*GTr* 26.5–6) and from the Father, as his "bold speech" (frag. H). The manifestation of the

Word purifies the visionary's heart, enabling the Christian to "see God" (frag. H). As a result, the visionary possesses those insights from which the shared wisdom of classical and Christian literature is derived; he or she is enabled not merely to comment (like Philo or Clement), but to create (like Cornutus's mythologists, Heraclitus's Homer, Philo's Moses, or Clement's *logos*). Hippolytus reports that Valentinus claimed to have had the sort of foundational vision such a purified heart makes possible: "For Valentinus says he saw a newborn babe, and questioned it to find out who it was. And the babe answered him saying that it was the Word." Hippolytus adds that Valentinus used this visionary experience as the basis for his mythic system by adding to the experience "a certain pompous tale" (i.e., Gnostic myth) (frag. A).[47] Hippolytus perhaps grasped better than he knew the key to Valentinus's innovative rereading of prior Gnostic traditions.

Although Valentinus expresses his personal vision of lack being restored, his actual description of his own relation to "the place of repose" is no less ambiguous than is the Son's relation to the Father. As a writer, Valentinus—like Philo's Abraham—assumes a peculiar relation to the place "in" which, "about" which, or "from" which he speaks. The *Gospel of Truth* concludes with Valentinus extolling the place of repose—that place "from which they [the aeons] have emanated and the lot according to which they have received their establishment in the state of rest" (*GTr* 41.3–6). All the aeons "will hasten to return and to receive from that place in which they (once) stood at rest, tasting of it and being nourished and growing" (*GTr* 41.7–12). Each emanation, we are told, "has received its establishment" (*afji mpefteho*) in that place, yet "will hasten to return" (*fnapōt atsto arets nkesap*) to it. This statement of past and future modes of being leaves one curious about the present state of the emanations—and thus necessarily of Valentinus himself. He says a bit farther on that the emanations are "they who have possessions from above" (*peei pe prēte nneteounteu mmeu abal hn psa hre*) yet nevertheless are "straining toward the solitary and perfect" (*eousamt nsa piouei ouaeetf auō petjēk abal*) (*GTr* 42.12–16). The ambiguity of the present moment is unrelenting: the emanations repose "in the vicinity of truth" (*mpkōte mtmēe*) yet "it is precisely they who are the truth" (*alla ntau rō pe tmēe*) (*GTr* 42.24–26). They are in the Father, and the Father is in them—yet the aeons and the Father are not simply to be equated without further comment. The ambiguity remains as inescapable as the assurance of the author's tone:

> This is the place of the blessed [*peei pe ptopos nnimakarios*]. This is their place. As for the others, then, let them know in their own places that it is not right for me to say more, for *I have been* in the place of repose [*eahišōpe hm pma nmtan*]. No, it is there that *I shall dwell* [*ntaf petinašōpe nhētf*], continually

occupied with the father of the entirety and the true siblings, upon whom the father's love is poured out and in whose midst there is no lack of him. (*GTr* 42.37–43.8; my emphasis)

The rhetorical character of the *Gospel of Truth* suggests that Valentinus, as a writer if not as a visionary, has not quite closed the gap between self and deity or between language's words and language's meanings and referents or between time and eternity, despite his assertion that dispersal and death do not vitiate the emanations ("nor is death within them," *GTr* 42.20–21) inasmuch as they are "perfect" and "undivided" (*GTr* 42.28–29). Valentinus strives to validate his assertion of paradise regained by generating a rhetoric that through its ceaseless self-reflexivity seeks to deny the dispersal and death of a linear narrative in which successive elements appear only to die away. In the *Gospel of Truth*, we are in the midst of a rhetoric that strives to empty out present temporality into time past and time future. Assuming a stance at once retrospective and anticipatory, Valentinus declares: "I have been [*eahišōpe*] in the place of repose . . . there I shall be [*petinašōpe*]" (*GTr* 43.1, 3).

But where does Valentinus stand in the present—or rather, in what does Valentinus's present consist? Is it a state of lack or completion? Of ignorance or knowledge? Does he write about the place of repose from somewhere else, or from within it? Although he has been in the place of repose and will be there again, Valentinus seems to write from somewhere in between the present world and the place of his future hope:

For now their affairs are dispersed. But when unity makes the ways complete, it is in unity that all will gather themselves, and it is by acquaintance that all will purify themselves out of multiplicity into unity, consuming matter within themselves as fire, and darkness by light, and death by life. (*GTr* 25.7–19)

The condition of multiplicity seems to have ended: "So since these things have happened to each of us, it is fitting for us to meditate upon the entirety, so that this house might be holy and quietly intent on unity" (*GTr* 25.19–24). But "these things" is ambiguous—does it refer to the dispersion and multiplicity, darkness and death, or to gathering and unity, light and life? The holiness and unity of the house seem to be a goal rather than an achievement, even though its members are enjoined to "speak from (the perspective of) the superior day" (*GTr* 32.26–27). There is, then, unresolved tension between past and future, possession and straining.[48] The tension between past and future is evident even in a fragment that might be read as an exuberant profession of the achieved presence of repose, but which, as we have already observed, is in fact permeated with retrospective and prospective tension:

> From the beginning *you (plur.) have been immortal,* and you are children of
> eternal life. And you wanted death to be allocated to yourselves so that you
> might spend it and use it up, and *that death might die in you* and through you.
> For when you nullify the world and are not yourselves annihilated, you are
> lord over creation and all corruption. (Frag. F; my emphasis)

This fragment was preserved by Clement, who interpreted it against
the grain of its subtle tension between original immortality and the present need for active nullification. Clement appends to the fragment the
following comment:

> Now, like Basilides, he [Valentinus] supposes that there is a people that by its
> (very) nature is saved; that this race, indeed, has come down to us [non-
> Valentinians] for the destruction of death; and that the origination of death
> is the work of the creator of the world. Accordingly, he [Valentinus] under-
> stands the scriptural passage (Exod. 33.20) "no one shall see the face of god
> and live" as though god were the cause of death. (*Strom.* 4.23.89.4–5)[49]

Clement's interpretation of Valentinus's remarks relaxes the tension between original immortality and present striving for immortality in favor
of the present possession of repose as a state of salvation "by nature." But
the Valentinian fragment's exhortation to nullify the world without ultimate self-nullification denotes anxious struggle rather than confident
possession. On the other hand, the self-reflexive rhetoric of the *Gospel*
seeks to obliterate a temporality that might be marked out between past
and future, a temporality in which the author might be implicated and
from which he still might need to be rescued. Valentinus urges his readers
to realize that the realm of the lack, and specifically its temporality, is mere
illusion. Once they awaken, the nightmare is over. But the very passion of
Valentinus's rhetoric and the inability of his writing to efface temporal
distinctions altogether reveals an authentic allegorical anxiety that acknowledges death even as it unceasingly seeks to evade it by speaking of
something else.

CHRISTIAN INITIATION AND THE HISTORY WITHIN

Our examination of the *Gospel*'s reflections on the divine name has shown
that Valentinus's vision is essentially monistic. Consequently, we cannot
draw a sharp line between the spiritual realm of the aeons and emanations and the "created realm," for the two figures in Gnostic myth who
represented just such a division—Sophia and Ialdabaõth—have now
been conflated into "Error." Error personifies not two orders of reality
(spiritual and material, divine and created), but two epistemological possibilities (knowledge and ignorance), with their ontological equivalents
(existence and nonexistence). Thus we should think of Valentinian Chris-

tians taking their places among the rest of the aeons who have fallen from, or been constituted by, an original relation to the first principle and who receive their physicality and materiality—indeed, their individuality—as a result. This means that, strictly speaking, there can be no autonomous, nondivine, "secular" sphere of nature and history. What for other Christians might be natural or historical drama has now become for the Valentinians psychodrama—the patterns and sequences of nature and history now unfold simultaneously within the mind of God and the minds of the Valentinians.

To whom in early second-century Alexandria would such an extraordinary vision appeal? What practical ends might be served by reading or hearing a work like the *Gospel of Truth* or by joining a group for which such works were important? Does the *Gospel of Truth*, with its absence of specific allusions to any easily identifiable contemporary social and political realities, serve a real-life function for persons who, whatever their metaphysical speculations, must negotiate a thoroughly physical existence? Something of the emotional life of those Valentinians who are presumably the audience for the *Gospel of Truth* can be inferred from the images and analogies to which Valentinus appeals.[50] His audience consists of people who seem altogether recognizable—persons who yearn to be understood and loved by others and who have had their nights ruined by horrible nightmares. Like all those who live in a precarious society, they appreciate what it would mean to have possessions that others could not take from them, and they admire anyone who has that sort of possession (such as Jesus, whose "incorruptibility" is "a thing that no one can take from him," *GTr* 20.32–34). They must have seen in Error's agitation an emblem of their own fallenness, anxiety, and futility, their own perception that the world around them consistently failed to meet their needs or live up to their expectations.

Were there particular historical developments that might help account for the attractiveness of such a vision? It has been argued that Gnostic religions arose as a result of failed Jewish apocalyptic expectations.[51] Given the probable Jewish-Christian origins of Alexandrian Christianity, one ought to consider carefully whether Valentinian revision was linked to the fate of Judaism in Alexandria. Perhaps the connection lies not specifically in the failure of apocalyptic hopes but in a more generalized disenchantment with history and, in the case of Alexandria and Egypt, in the historical destruction of Judaism.

The early history of Christianity in Alexandria is shrouded in mystery. Scholars have sought to account for the silence in the record before the appearance of the bishop Demetrius at the end of the second or the beginning of the third century C.E. Perhaps, it is argued, "orthodox" authorities suppressed early voices because they deemed them to be

unacceptably heterodox; evidence of early deviant belief might have been systematically eradicated by later ecclesiastical authorities who themselves came to define the emerging, and ultimately victorious, Christian orthodoxy.[52] Early second-century Gnostic teachers such as Basilides and Valentinus may in fact have represented the true character of earliest Egyptian Christianity. Perhaps the traditions they represented were excised from the record by leaders like Demetrius, who then put in place an "official" list of the succession of Alexandrian bishops, beginning with the evangelist Mark (and deliberately excluding shadowy figures such as Theudas and Glaucias). The later church historian Eusebius of Caesarea, on whom we depend for much of our information about early Christianity, legitimated such a list by incorporating it uncritically into his account of Egyptian Christianity.[53] However, despite the plausibility of this widely accepted hypothesis, it actually rests more on inference from silence than on solid historical evidence. In fact, there are no more, or better, sources for first-century "heterodoxy" in Egypt (assuming the term itself has any meaning at all in such an early, pluralistic period) than for other sorts of Christianity. Scholars have therefore recently turned to other explanations; Palestinian Jewish Christianity now appears to be the key to both the origin and the character of early Egyptian Christianity.[54] It seems likely that Jewish Christian missionaries from Jerusalem first brought Christianity to Egypt.[55]

Until perhaps the end of the first century or the beginning of the second, Christians in Alexandria were almost certainly indistinguishable from Jews, having not yet emerged from Judaism as a group with sufficient distinctiveness to enable them to show up in the historical record as an independent community.[56] These early Jewish Christians would have lived in the Jewish areas of the city and participated in the life of the synagogues. At some point, they would have begun meeting additionally in house churches, which may have originally been house synagogues. The emergence of Christian groups distinct from the Jewish community must have occurred sometime early in the second century. Discernible Jewish and Gentile strains in Alexandrian Christianity seem evident from early references to (and papyrus fragments of) a *Gospel of the Hebrews* and a *Gospel of the Egyptians* (different from the Coptic Nag Hammadi text of the same name). The first may have been compiled for Jewish Christians living in the two "Jewish quarters" of the city, the second for Egyptian Gentile Christians who lived in the Rhakotis district.[57] However, it was probably not until the Jewish revolt of 115–17 c.e. that Jews and Christians in Alexandria finally went their separate ways.

The course of Jewish experience in Alexandria from Philo's day until Valentinus left the city sometime between 136 and 140 c.e., though poorly represented in the historical record, is best characterized as a series

of escalating disasters. We have already seen in the course of our discussion of Philo that Jewish life in Roman Alexandria was fraught with conflict, which became especially violent in the pogroms of 38 C.E. Precipitated by the visit of King Agrippa, endorsed by the Alexandrian prefect Flaccus, and tolerated by the emperor Gaius Caligula, this assault on the Alexandrian Jewish community involved considerable loss of life, desecration and destruction of synagogues, plundering of property, enforced ghettoization, and public humiliation. Upon Caligula's death by assassination in 41 C.E., the Jews counterattacked the Greeks, and although the Jews were fortified by clandestine shipments of arms and the influx of reinforcements from Palestine, loss of Jewish life was considerable.[58] After the rebellion, the emperor Claudius settled the Alexandrian "Jewish question" by protecting the Jews' ancestral rights and internal procedures as a *politeuma*, but he banned them from a gymnasium education and athletic contests, and consequently from Greek citizenship.[59]

Conflict between Jews and Greeks broke out again in 53 C.E. This time the Jews were led by a new, conservative, "nationalist" faction, which, unlike many Hellenized Jews, regarded Jerusalem, rather than the Greek *polis*, as their homeland, and the diaspora as a state of temporary exile. The Palestinian Jewish revolt of 66–70 C.E., which culminated in the destruction of the Jerusalem temple, also had a tremendous effect on Alexandria.[60] Jewish revolutionaries (*sicarii*) coming to Alexandria from Palestine once again fomented rebellion in Alexandria against the Romans, creating in the process sharp divisions and conflict within the Jewish community. At the request of the more orthodox Jewish leadership, the prefect Tiberius Julius Alexander (Philo's nephew) gave Roman soldiers authority to capture, torture, and execute the revolutionaries, as well as to burn down their homes and plunder their property.[61] Josephus's death toll of 50,000 probably exaggerates, but, in any case, the losses were far more devastating than those of 38 C.E. The lower classes suffered most, while the Jewish upper class escaped the brunt of the assault by professing loyalty to Rome.[62] When the war ended, the emperor Vespasian punished the Jews by requiring them to pay the half-shekel tax (formerly paid to the Jerusalem temple) to the Roman replacement for the Jewish God, Jupiter Capitolinus. The Jews seethed with resentment, regarding this tax as far more degrading than the *laographia*.[63] In the wake of the events of 66–70 C.E., Alexandrian Jews drew closer together, choosing ghettoization for protection. An increasingly nationalist feeling emerged, as Jews turned inward, seeking to preserve and protect Jewish traditions. This nationalist sentiment was probably fostered by the addition of Jewish revolutionaries captured by the Romans in Palestine and sold as slaves in Egypt.

From 70 to 115 C.E., violence between Jews and Greeks undoubtedly

continued; we know that Jews and Greeks clashed again in 110 C.E. But the most devastating conflict broke out in 115 C.E., when Egyptian Jews rose in solidarity with the revolutionary followers of the messianic "king" Loukuas-Andreus in Cyrene.[64] This revolt involved Jews not only in Alexandria and the Egyptian countryside, but also in Cyrene, Cyprus, Palestine, and Mesopotamia.[65] Fierce and brutal on all sides, the conflict resulted in tremendous loss of life in the Jewish communities, nearly annihilating Judaism in Egypt.[66] The synagogues were destroyed, the Jewish court ceased to function, and Jewish land was easily confiscated because the Jews themselves were gone. Indeed, Alexandrian Jews nearly vanished from the historical record.[67]

The virtual eradication of Alexandrian Judaism meant the end of the ideal of Hellenistic Judaism represented by Philo; indeed, his name would not be mentioned again in writing by a Jew until 1573.[68] The future of the Jewish world was increasingly being claimed by the emerging rabbinic orthodoxy of Jamnia. Opposed to the Philonic ideal, the Jamnian version of Judaism began early to make its influence felt in Alexandria.[69] The influence of Palestinian Judaism on Alexandrian Judaism had in fact been strong ever since the days of the first Hasmoneans, and there had always been a segment of the Jewish community in Alexandria that had never favored a "Philonic" rapprochement with the Greeks. 3 Maccabees even shows Jewish conservatives putting to death those who had abandoned the Jewish faith.[70]

Protorabbinic Judaism, from its center in Palestine, had already begun to send a message to diaspora Judaism before the end of the first century C.E. The Jamnian *Birkath-ha-Minim* (ca. 85 C.E.), inserted into the synagogue liturgy, prohibited Jewish Christians from attending the service; Palestinian letters sent to diaspora communities before 100 C.E. demanded the exclusion of all Christians from the synagogues; a third ruling from the period 90–120 C.E. banned the reading of Christian literature by Jews.[71] These anti-Jewish Christian (and anti-Christian) promulgations almost certainly reached Alexandria—the single largest diaspora community at the time. In the wake of the eradication of Hellenistic Judaism in Alexandria, the pressure from Jamnia left the remaining Jews and Christians in the city with a choice between emerging protorabbinic Judaism and non- (even anti-) Jewish Christianity. The halfway houses of Hellenistic Judaism and Jewish Christianity were now closed. The attacks on Alexandrian Judaism thus provide an explanation for the weakness and marginality of earliest Christianity in Egypt.

The final destruction of Alexandrian Judaism coincides with the emergence of a distinctively anti-Jewish Christianity, opposed to the Jewish Christianity that preceded it.[72] The *Epistle of Barnabas* may record one version of the anti-Jewish Christian reaction. The epistle was probably

written in Alexandria around 117–18 C.E., possibly by a converted rabbi from the Alexandrian synagogue. It provides evidence of a hard choice forced upon Jewish Christians at least in part by the de facto denial of the very possibility of a Jewish Christianity.[73] The Jewish mind-set of *Barnabas*, evident in its choice of images and examples, is unmistakable; the text refers, for example, to the land of milk and honey (*Barn.* 6.8), the ritual of the Day of Atonement (7.1–2), the 318 servants of Abraham (9.8), Jacob and Esau (13.1–7), and the Sabbath (15.1–9).[74] But the structure and exegetical method of the epistle provide the most striking evidence of its Jewish perspective. It is presented as a *talmud* or *didachē* ("teaching"), divided into *haggadah* and *halakhah*. It uses Philonic allegorical techniques to interpret fragments of Septuagint passages, in the manner of the *midrashim*. Finally, it applies biblical texts to its own contemporary historical situation in a manner reminiscent of the *pesher* technique found at Qumran.[75] The epistle as a whole thus seems to represent an overlap of traditions: the receding tradition of Hellenistic Jewish allegorization of the Philonic type and the emerging influence of rabbinic modes of thought and exegesis, already gaining an audience in the diaspora.[76] Although it emerges out of a decidedly rabbinic mind-set and reflects a distinctively Jewish version of Alexandrian Christianity, *Barnabas* positively bristles with anti-Jewish polemic. The author attacks the Jews and "their" law and even rejoices over the destruction of the Jerusalem temple. He has decided that God has taken the covenant away from the Jews and given it to the Christians (*Barn.* 4.7, 14.4). There is for him no such thing as Jewish Christianity, and he is bitter at having to reject his ancestral religion.[77]

But *Barnabas* does not represent the only possible Christian response to the failure of both Hellenistic Judaism and Jewish Christianity in Alexandria. Christians could also revive the model provided by Philo and seek to give expression to a non-Jewish, Hellenized Christianity (or Christianized Hellenism). Clement, as a conscious admirer, imitator, and plagiarizer of Philo, took a critical position against Judaism not altogether unlike that of *Barnabas*. But he moderates *Barnabas*'s anti-Judaism in a way that became normative for much subsequent Christianity, subordinating the precursor faith through typological allegory (as did *Barnabas*), but without the bitter rancor produced by proximity to the historical catastrophe. There were reasons why Clement would not be so bitter about the loss of Judaism, or even especially concerned with it. There simply was no significant Jewish presence for Clement to reckon with in late second-century Alexandria, and he himself had been converted to Christianity directly from paganism. A third option was also available: complete Hellenization and assimilation. Surely some Jews and Jewish Christians, in the wake of the destruction of Jewish aspirations and the

increasing marginality of Judaism in Alexandrian culture, went the way of Philo's notorious nephew Alexander and the "excessive" allegorists derided by Philo. Such Jews and Christians would have simply given up the distinctive traits of their religions and blended into the pluralism of the high culture of the city.

But Valentinus's response to the destruction of Alexandrian Judaism and Jewish Christianity was different. Valentinus disregards Judaism in its overt manifestations nearly altogether—but with a disregard that is distinctly different from the bitter repression of *Barnabas,* the subordinating superiority of Clement, the aggressive subversion of the Gnostics, or the implied polemic of Basilides. Yet Valentinus's disregard hides a subversion of Judaism more thoroughgoing than even the Gnostics': he offers a thoroughly Christianized version of what is taken to be Judaism's essential truths—the absolute transcendence of God (now represented by the divine name as the Son) and God's certain deliverance of God's people (now identified as the Valentinians) from suffering and evil. Valentinus offers a revisionary reading of a prior version of Gnosticism that had itself already gone a long way toward undermining Judaism, and the result is a thoroughgoing sublimation and transformation of Jewish covenantal monotheism. In Valentinus's writings, the historical and social world that has proved to be such a disappointment to both Jews and Christians (a collection of unfulfilled messianic hopes and unrealized apocalyptic dreams) has now been totally absorbed into a mythical world. The apocalypse now takes place, not in history, but in the mind; the Valentinian believer is urged to understand that all of apparent life has been but a nightmare that when the morning of *gnōsis* arrives, proves to have been unreal and insubstantial—yet all the more terrifying for that reason. In the end, the *Gospel of Truth* offers its readers a new theodicy: in contrast to the disappointment of history and its division, struggle, fear, and evil, the emanated Son brings the message that, despite appearances to the contrary, reality is good: "The father is without evil" (*GTr* 40.29).

Jewish Gnosticism, as represented by a work like *The Secret Book According to John* before its subsequent "Christianization," provides the link between earlier Judaism (and Jewish Christianity) and later Valentinian revisionism. Probably written by Jewish Gnostic intellectuals, this work subverts traditional Judaism, expressing a deep discontent with the Jewish creator God and Jewish law.[78] As Christianized, the text eliminates many Jewish components, a process that we have seen Valentinus take much farther. Other than the extended meditation on the name, only a few elements directly suggestive of Judaism remain in the *Gospel of Truth,* and these are quickly allegorized into spiritual truths. "What is the Sabbath?" asks Valentinus. The "children of interior understanding" or Val-

entinian Christians know that it is "that day on which salvation cannot be idle" (*GTr* 32.38–39). This allegorical reading generalizes the significance of Jesus' teaching that acts of mercy should be performed even on the Sabbath (Matt. 12.11), though Valentinus goes on to allegorize the day "on which salvation cannot be idle" into the spiritual state of the Valentinian children of "interior understanding," who are themselves the "day that is perfect" (*GTr* 32.32). There are a few other (possible) echoes of Judaism, but on the whole Valentinus's revision of Gnostic myth does not assume any overtly adversarial stance toward Jewish scripture and tradition—in contrast to the anti-Jewish aspects of the exegesis of his contemporary, Basilides.

The Valentinian rejection of earlier Gnostic parody and internal subversion of Judaism and its scripture reflects Valentinus's own monistic rejection of a dualistic, anticosmic version of Gnosticism.[79] We have already seen that it is simplistic and misleading to construe Valentinus's monism as anticosmic; the distinctions generated by the concept of a Jewish creator God (creator vs. creation) are not directly contradicted by Valentinus's vision; instead, division itself becomes the by-product of misperception. Consequently, Valentinus is more sympathetic to other aspects of the Jewish tradition (monotheism, covenant), and given the absence of a significant Alexandrian Jewish presence, he does not feel the need to struggle with it as did so many of his Gnostic predecessors. The Gnostics divided God into an unknown transcendent first principle and a subordinate world creator (identified as the God of the Jews)—such radical dualism constitutes the essence of the Gnostic rejection of normative Judaism.[80] Valentinus's monistic overcoming of that division reverses this anti-Jewish tendency.

There is a sociological correlate to Valentinus's visionary absorption of the world and history. Just as the Valentinian and his or her world have been completely absorbed by the divine fullness or entirety, so the early Valentinians seem to have remained within contemporary churches, as conventicles within larger Christian communities. Such has been the historically recurring strategy of groups that are concerned not so much to overturn or reject something completely as to penetrate into the as-yet-unexplored depths of what already exists, as well as to protest its shortcomings. The more recent and familiar examples of German pietist *collegia pietatis* or Wesleyan "class meetings" come readily to mind. Both Justin and Irenaeus accused Valentinians of being "wolves in sheep's clothing"—of hiding within non-Valentinian congregations and spreading their teachings secretly. Justin claims that the followers of Valentinus (among others) "style themselves Christians" but remain "confessors of Jesus in name only" (*Dial.* 35). Setting aside the obviously polemical cast

of such accounts, we can perhaps detect something of the truth about how Valentinian "missionaries" worked within the context of the established churches to persuade others of their distinctive point of view. Irenaeus charges them with "craftily constructed plausibilities" that draw away "the minds of the inexperienced," with "specious and plausible words" that "cunningly allure the simple-minded to inquire into their system," with error "craftily decked out in an attractive dress, so as, by its outward form, to make it appear to the inexperienced . . . more true than the truth itself" (*Haer.,* preface, 1.1–2).[81] What all of this probably means is that the Valentinians made extremely convincing and attractive appeals, perhaps putting their points in such direct and humanly relevant ways that even those innocent of high theology (i.e., most of the congregation) felt they were having revealed to them something of importance for their lives. One of the implications of Irenaeus's rhetoric is that the Valentinian appeals worked in large part because much of what they said was un-exceptional. "Their language resembles ours," writes Irenaeus—with the sarcastic stress on "resembles," of course (*Haer.,* preface, 1.2). We should remember that the very distinction between Valentinian and non-Valentinian was in fact being worked out in this period and should not be completely presupposed in our own reading of the sources.[82] In any case, the Valentinian mentality is not sectarian in the sense of desiring to construct a counterreality in the world in order to oppose what are judged to be reality-deficient churches. On the contrary, Valentinus's monistic vision cannot allow for such divisions—one cannot go somewhere else or join some other group. Rather, one is asked to understand the true character of one's place and one's self—only then can either become real.

We have relatively few clues about the relations between Valentinians and other Christians or between Valentinians and non-Christians, and what little evidence we do have generally comes from the deeply preju-diced reports of the heresiologists. The works of later Valentinians them-selves do offer, however, some glimpses into the communal life of Valen-tinian groups, especially their cultic and liturgical practices. It becomes clear that baptism, representing the moment of reorientation, awaken-ing, or reception of *gnōsis,* and tied closely to the metaphor of the divine name, is a rite of initiation absolutely central to the formation and self-identity of the Valentinian communities. Some remarks of one of Valen-tinus's students, Theodotus, as reported by Clement of Alexandria, sug-gest that we should connect our earlier literary and theological discussion of Valentinus's meditation on the divine name to the specific context of Valentinian baptismal practice.[83] Theodotus links the power of fate, death, dispersion—of existence without *gnōsis*—with Sophia's fall. Like Valentinus, Theodotus then connects this fall with the passion of Jesus:

And when the passion took place, the Whole shared in suffering in order to bring to correction the being which suffered. But if he who came down was the good-pleasure of the Whole—for "in him was the entire Pleroma in bodily form" (Col. 2.9)—and himself suffered, [then it is clear that the seed which was in him also shared in the suffering, and therefore it follows that the Whole and the All suffered (concludes Clement, who preserves this remark of Theodotus)]. But, as a result of the fall of the twelfth aeon [Sophia], the Whole in which it was trained, as they say, suffered. (*Ex. Theod.* 30.2–31.1–2)[84]

If we can rely on Clement's report, Theodotus has drawn striking parallels between the suffering of fallen Sophia, the divine Son, and the entire spiritual realm (Clement presents this excerpt as evidence that Valentinians are "forgetting the glory of God" by "impiously" saying that God "suffered," *Ex. Theod.* 30.1). It seems that Theodotus, like Valentinus, is working out a perspective on "sin and salvation" as understood within an essentially monistic system. His parallel between Sophia's fall, Jesus' passion, and the suffering of God is consistent with our earlier reading of the *Gospel of Truth,* in which the cause of ignorance and its remedy involved the same paradoxical moment of divine self-knowledge and self-negation. Like Valentinus, Theodotus finds in the divine name-as-Son the key to the interrelationship of the three "moments." He identifies God's (and a human being's) possession of the name with the possession of true "form"—true existence and knowledge. The lack or deficiency accompanying Sophia's fall is thus understood as our own deficient possession of the name—that is, our partial possession of only the name's "shadow"— and our attendant formlessness. In the midst of the sufferings of wisdom, which are the sufferings of the aeons, the aeons, says Theodotus,

> recognized that what they are, they are by the grace of the Father, an inexpressible name, form, and knowledge. The aeon [= Sophia] which desired to grasp that which is beyond knowledge fell into ignorance and formlessness. Therefore he [the Father] brought about a "void" of "knowledge" (that is, an emptiness for knowledge) which is a shadow of the name, which is the Son, the form of the aeons. Thus, the partial name of the aeons is the loss of the name. (*Ex. Theod.* 31.3–4)

The aeons (and thus all human beings) manifest a lack of knowledge, which is also a lack of that name (the Son) that constitutes their true form and existence. Their own names are at best "partial" because their names are no longer "echoes" of the name of the Son (and, hence, of the Father). Elsewhere, through an allegorical reading of a statement from the Gospel of John, Theodotus links this notion of the name-as-Son to the sort of distinction Valentinus makes in the *Gospel of Truth* between the invisible

name and the visible Jesus; for Theodotus, Jesus has both a visible aspect and bears an invisible name (his sonship):

> The visible part of Jesus was (the) Wisdom and the church of the superior seed, which he put on through the flesh, as Theodotus says: but the invisible part was the Name, which is the only-begotten Son. Therefore, when he says "I am the door" (John 10.7), he means "up to the *Horos* (Limit), where I am, you will come, you who belong to the superior seed." But when he himself enters (into the Pleroma), then the seed also enters with him, united and introduced through the "door." (*Ex. Theod.* 26.1–3)

Like Valentinus, Theodotus systematically overcomes dualistic perspectives. A limit (or "door") separates the divine realm from the fallen realm, but Jesus—as both visible flesh and invisible name—is able to lead the Valentinians (the church of the superior seed) into the highest realms: dualism is not finally a reality for any seed that he is able to escort through the "door." We have already been told by Clement that this "seed"—the community of Valentinians—has suffered in the passion of Jesus, an interpretation that makes sense in light of Theodotus's connection of that seed with Jesus' flesh.

How then is one as member of the suffering seed able to move beyond that "limit" that marks the transition from lack of knowledge and being to *gnōsis* and real existence? How does one (as a seed like that "seed of higher essence" deposited in Adam) unite with the Son in order to return to the Father? This union, with its promise of return, takes place through baptism. Theodotus clearly links baptism with saving *gnōsis:* "Until baptism, they [Valentinians] say, Fate is effective, but after it the astrologers no longer speak the truth." But the liturgical act is only an outward sign of an inward knowledge:

> It is not the bath (washing) alone that makes us free, but also the knowledge: who were we? what have we become? where were we? into what place have we been cast? whither are we hastening? from what are we delivered? what is birth? what is rebirth? (*Ex. Theod.* 78.1–2)

Baptism of individuals draws upon a prior baptism of angels, in which the original androgyny of the aeons, disrupted by Sophia's effort to know the Father without her consort, is restored. The restoration comes about as, first angels, then human beings, receive that invisible name (the only-begotten Son) with which even the earthly Jesus had to be baptized. Theodotus makes all of these connections through an innovative reading of a Pauline text:

> And when the apostle says, "What are they doing who are baptized for the dead?" (1 Cor. 15.29), what he is actually saying is that for us the angels of whom we are part were baptized. We are the dead, who have been put to

death through this condition. The living are the males who did not share in this condition [cf. frag. F]. "If the dead are not raised, why, then, are people baptized?" (1 Cor. 15.29). So then we are raised equal to angels, restored to the males, member to member, to form a unity. "Those who are baptized for the dead" (1 Cor. 15.29), they say, are the angels who are baptized for us, in order that we too, possessing the name, may not be held back and perverted by Horos (Limit) and the Cross from entering into the Pleroma. Hence also at the laying on of hands [after baptism] they say at the end, "for the angelic redemption," that is, the one which the angels also have, in order that he who has received the redemption may be baptized in the same name as that in which his angel was baptized before him. In the beginning the angels were baptized through the "redemption" of the name which came down upon Jesus in the dove and redeemed him. "Redemption" was necessary even for Jesus, in order that he might not be detained by the Ennoia of the deficiency in which he was placed, though conducted (thereto) through Sophia, as Theodotus says. (*Ex. Theod.* 22.1–7)

This passage suggests that Valentinian speculation on the divine name is much more than a tool for revisionary readings of Gnostic precursors; it is also directly connected with a theory and practice of baptism, as the cultic recovery (or celebration of the recovery) of the lost fullness of the divine realm. Baptism thus appears to be a central moment in Valentinian self-definition—literally a rebirth into genuine existence.

We can now return to the *Gospel of Truth* and reconsider some of its language with this baptismal context in mind. It is before baptism, one may surmise, that the aeons "know that they have emanated from him [the Father] like children who were within a mature man [as seeds?] but knew they had not yet received form nor been given name" (*GTr* 27.12–18). And so, after baptism "they receive the impulse toward acquaintance with the father," and he "gives birth to each" (*GTr* 27.20–21). The Valentinian *Gospel According to Philip* also testifies to the centrality of baptism as the locus of saving *gnōsis* and reception of the "name": "Anyone who goes down into the water and comes up without having received anything [i.e., an ordinary, non-Valentinian Christian, who receives only the "washing" without the *gnōsis;* cf. *Ex. Theod.* 78.2] and says, 'I am a Christian,' has borrowed the name" (*GPh* 64.22ff.).[85] That is, one has received the name not as "one's own" (*GTr* 22.12–13). The one who merely borrows the name is unlike Jesus, who received his name from the Father not as a loan, but as a direct expression of the divine essence. But the true believer should instead be like Jesus and receive the name "essentially"—not as a loan but as a gift: "But one who receives the holy spirit has the gift of the name" (*GPh* 64.25ff.). Like the Son in the *Gospel of Truth*, who goes down into the empty ways of fear to put on incorruptibility, "a thing that no one can take from him" (*GTr* 20.33–34), so "anyone who has received a gift [of

the baptismal name] will not have it taken away" (*GPh* 64.27ff.); after true baptism, it cannot be taken away, since, as the *Gospel of Truth* puts it, "one's name becomes one's own" (*GTr* 22.12–13). Those, on the other hand, who "borrowed" the name "will have it taken back" (*GPh* 64.28f.).

For Valentinians, initiation by baptism into the Christian life was thus a moment of personal and cultural revision because the self, society, and history were all absorbed into the inner life of God. Personal identity was sought not in the textual or historical worlds with their multiplicity of interpretations and behaviors, but in the process of self-recognition—of confrontation with one's essential nature—which was a personal interiorization and realization of the tripartite pattern of Christian existence. In the baptismal washing, one hoped to begin to discover answers to three questions that define a narrative—and a life—whose very temporality those answers would inevitably dissolve: Who was I? What have I become? Whither am I hastening? These are the questions of one who is not at home in the given world, one for whom society and culture do not define the self but instead, at best, provide the arena in which self-identity and human purpose might be achieved. Several generations later, Clement of Alexandria asked similar questions and read scripture and other cultural classics allegorically in order to answer them. He discovered that the answers had been, and continued to be, spoken by a divine voice or *logos*. This *logos* antedated society, culture, texts, and the self, standing over them all as the original source of meaning, truth, and personal identity.

FOUR

Clement: The New Song of the *Logos*

Like Valentinus, Clement (Titus Flavius Clemens) was an independent
Christian intellectual and teacher in second-century Alexandria. He was
born around 150 C.E. of pagan parents, probably in Athens. Following a
topos of Hellenistic intellectual autobiography, he tells us that after travels
to Italy, Syria, and Palestine in search of teachers, he finally discovered the
finest teacher of all in Egypt.[1] Upon arriving in Alexandria around 180
C.E., Clement began a vigorous teaching and writing career in the city that
lasted until 202/203 C.E., when the violent persecution of Christians by
the emperor Septimius Severus forced him to leave Egypt. He fled to
Cappadocia, where he joined a certain Alexander, who later became
bishop of Jerusalem. Clement died in Cappadocia before 215 C.E., without seeing Egypt again.[2]

Clement was a prolific author, and a good portion of his literary production has survived.[3] His major extant works are often referred to as a
trilogy, though only the first two treatises are clearly related to one another. There is first an appeal to pagans to embrace the new Christian
philosophy (*Exhortation to the Greeks; Protreptikos pros Hellēnas*), then a
handbook of social and personal ethics (*The Tutor; Paidagōgos*), and (apparently in place of a projected, but unwritten, third component of the
trilogy that would have been entitled *The Teacher*, or *Didaskalos*) a lengthy,
rambling series of obscurely arranged ruminations on Christianity as the
true *gnōsis* (*The Carpets* or *Miscellanies; Strōmateis*). The other complete
extant work is a homily on Mark 10.17–31 entitled *Who Is the Rich Man
Who Is Being Saved?* (*Quis dives salvetur; Tis ho sōzomenos plousios*). We also
have considerable portions of two collections of Clement's quotations
from other writings and notes: extracts from the work of Valentinus's
student Theodotus (*Excerpta ex Theodoto*) and comments on selected pas-

sages from Hebrew scripture (*Eclogae propheticae*). The rest of Clement's works have perished, except for a few fragments.[4]

We have now examined in some detail two strikingly different forms of allegorical reading for the sake of cultural revision. Philo read scripture allegorically on the assumption that Moses was an original author who had re-inscribed cultural and philosophical wisdom in the form of the Pentateuch. Valentinus read his precursors (especially Gnostic myth) allegorically, expressing his revision of culture in the form of his own creative allegorical composition. Clement illustrates yet a third mode of allegorical reading and cultural revision. He specialized in what he called the traditions of the "elders"—teachers who were thought to have transmitted by word of mouth the inner secrets of the Christian gospel, derived ultimately from Jesus himself. Following earlier Christian traditions, Clement identified Jesus as the divine Word or *logos*—a divine entity that, according to the Middle Platonic philosophy prevalent in Clement's day, mediated between the transcendent God and the material world. The first part of this chapter examines the distinctive hermeneutical application of this Middle Platonic concept of *logos* by Clement's immediate predecessor, Justin of Flavia Neapolis (Justin Martyr). Justin claimed that this *logos* or preexistent Christ was the voice of God, to be discovered in the pages of Hebrew scripture and certain works of pagan philosophy. With Justin as his model, Clement reads his precursor texts and traditions allegorically to discover beneath the surface of the words an original Word or divine voice.

In the second part of the chapter, I turn to a discussion of Clement's various applications of this voice-based hermeneutic. Prior in time and authority to all other sources of meaning and truth, this divine voice "speaks" wisdom through all sorts of writings, including, but not limited to, the texts that Christians call "scripture." Just as a ventriloquist "throws" his or her voice, making it appear as though any number of other objects are speaking, so Clement construes scripture and other texts as expressions of a single divine voice, the discourse of God's own speech. The *logos* speaks the allegorical "other" meanings of scripture and pagan classics, and the clarity and intensity of that voice determine the relative authority of those texts. Clement's mode of reading consequently relativizes all texts—whether classical literature, the Septuagint, or the New Testament—by subordinating them to an underlying divine discourse. Because he discovers the same speaker everywhere, he is able to relate very different texts to one another as he sees fit, avoiding when necessary or convenient their lexical details or historical interrelations. Clement's appeal to a divine voice allows him to relate diverse texts as "scripture" and "canon" in a bewildering variety of ways.

Although I have used the terms "scripture" and "New Testament"

throughout this study, we must always bear in mind that in the second century c.e. the boundaries of both were not clearly defined, but fluctuating and permeable. Unlike Valentinus, Clement holds a conception of the New Testament as a literary category, but that category does not match contemporary or later collections denoted by the same label. Furthermore, works such as the "prophetic and poetic" Sibylline oracles stand somewhere on the vague borderline between "scripture" and nonscriptural Greek literature. Rather than trying to decide on "independent" grounds which texts are part of Clement's "scripture" and which are not or—and this is a different question—which texts are "canonical" and which are not, I have taken a broadly pragmatic and functional approach that relates the revisionary capacity of "scripture" to existing texts that are treated as though canonical. When one text is subordinated to a second in an interpretative reading, the subordinated text may be said to have a certain functional "canonicity" because it has sufficient authority to attract commentary. The subordinating text may in turn be said to function as "scripture" in the sense that—at least for that moment—it exercises hermeneutical authority over the first, canonical text. Of course, this labeling does not decide whether the subordinated "canonical" text also functions as "scripture" in other interpretative contexts; on other occasions, it may indeed exercise authority over another "canonical" text, in which case it too "functions scripturally." "Canonicity," then, simply denotes the role of being the object of revisionary interpretation, while "scriptural" status denotes a measure of interpretative authority exercised over canonical texts. Neither category has any necessary relation to collections of texts later gathered together under the title New Testament. Only by broadening traditional categories in this way—which in fact is what Clement's *logos*-based allegorical revision demands—will we be able to appreciate the nature of the hermeneutical struggle in which Clement was engaged.

Finally, Clement's allegorical readings of classical, Jewish, and Christian texts also serve a number of social purposes. In the third part of the chapter, I examine Clement's hermeneutic as part of his social role as a theological teacher and ecclesiastical advocate in Alexandria. In particular, I analyze his use of allegorical interpretation to define the character and limits of his own Christian community in relation to a number of alternative Christian groups. This process of communal self-definition and social boundary maintenance grows directly out of Clement's own ambivalent sensibility; attentive to the authoritative claims of an emerging Christian "orthodoxy," he is equally responsive to the appeals of an esoteric and speculative Christian *gnōsis*. However, in the end, the desire for orthodoxy gains the upper hand, and Clement offers readers a domesticated version of the radical Christian *gnōsis* represented by Valentinus.

LOGOS THEOLOGY AS ALLEGORICAL HERMENEUTIC

Even though both Philo and Valentinus drew on current speculation about the divine *logos,* neither gave it the sort of thoroughgoing hermeneutical emphasis that Clement did. Clement's consistent emphasis on a theology of divine voice distinguishes his allegorical hermeneutic from both Philo's and Valentinus's. Because Clement understands scripture as a kind of tape recording of divine speech, he tends to characterize Moses as a divine spokesperson, rather than as Philo's divine scribe.[5] Through Moses and the rest of the prophets, the *logos* as the divine pedagogue speaks (*Paed.* 1.2.5.1; 3.11.75.3), and the varieties of that speech result in a wide range of rhetorical tones and modes of speech in the Septuagint. New Testament writings also display varied rhetorical modes. For example, Paul's declaration in 1 Corinthians 3.2 "I have given you milk to drink" is not simply a straightforward statement; the rhetorical scenario is more subtle—these words are spoken "mystically" by "the Holy Spirit in the apostle, using the voice of the Lord" (*Paed.* 1.6.49.2).

Just as scripture is the recorded speech of God, so faith—as both goal and presupposition of scripture reading—comes from hearing rather than reading:

> But as the proclamation [*kērygma*] [i.e., of the gospel] has come now at the fit time, so also at the fit time were the law and the prophets given to the barbarians, and philosophy to the Greeks, to fit their ears for the proclamation [*kērygma*]. (*Strom.* 6.6.44.1)

Thus Abraham at the oak of Mamre "through hearing believed the voice" (*Strom.* 5.1.4.1). "We ought not to surrender our ears to all who speak and write rashly," writes Clement,

> for cups also, which are taken hold of by many by the ears, are dirtied, and lose the ears; and besides, when they fall they are broken. In the same way also, those, who have polluted the pure hearing of faith by many trifles, at last becoming deaf to the truth, become useless and fall to the earth. (*Strom.* 5.1.12.4)

In a passage stressing the unity of a God who makes the same promises to Christians as to Hebrew patriarchs, Clement insists that Christians, as the seed of Abraham, are Israelites "convinced not by signs, but by hearing" (*Strom.* 2.6.28.4). He then quotes Isaiah 54.1 (= Gal. 4.27) as evidence for the application of Hebrew prophecy to Christians. However, Clement did not invent this notion of a divine voice speaking through the texts of both Christian and non-Christian literature. Before we turn to an examination of Clement's distinctive use of this voice-based hermeneutic, it will be helpful to consider his principal Christian hermeneutical model.

The notion of a divine voice speaking through scripture and other texts was the basis for the two "apologies" of Justin (ca. 100–ca. 165 c.e.), a Christian Platonist active in Rome in the middle of the second century c.e.[6] Justin combined a Christianized interpretation of the biblical concept of the "Word of God" with Middle Platonic speculation about the *logos* as an entity that "mediated" the relationship between the transcendent high God and the material world. This synthesis resulted in a conception of the *logos* as a divine voice that spoke through the mouths of Hebrew prophets like Moses and Greek philosophers like Socrates, and that through a paradoxical act of incarnation finally became physically embodied as the teacher Jesus of Nazareth. Upon the death, resurrection, and ascension of Jesus, the divine voice reappeared as the spirit of the risen Jesus in the preaching of the apostles. Justin's first apology, written about 156 c.e., was addressed to the Roman emperor Antoninus Pius and his adopted sons, Marcus Aurelius and Lucius Verus. The second apology (perhaps originally part of the first) was written about 161 c.e. and though addressed to the Roman Senate in the extant manuscript, was probably originally addressed to several emperors.[7] We have no indication that these works were read by any of the addressees, but they were widely read in Christian circles and became extremely influential in subsequent Christian theology.

Although Clement does not refer to Justin by name, it is virtually certain that he was familiar with Justin's writings.[8] Even in the unlikely event that Clement had not read Justin's works directly, he could have learned about Justin's ideas from the writings of Irenaeus, bishop of Lyons. In his work *Against Heresies* (ca. 180 c.e.), Irenaeus had adopted and transformed Justin's theology as it had been expressed in Justin's earlier work of the same title (now lost). Clement was familiar with Irenaeus's *Against Heresies,* which, as a papyrus fragment of the second century c.e. attests, was available in Alexandria soon after it was written.[9] He also had access to many of the same examples of early Christian biblical interpretation and Middle Platonic philosophy with which Justin was familiar. Indeed, if one were a philosophically literate person in the second century c.e. and lived in any of the major centers of the empire, such as Rome, Athens, or Alexandria, Middle Platonism would be virtually inescapable. It was especially easy for Clement to assimilate this philosophical tradition, for it was well represented both in Athens, where he grew up and was educated, and in Alexandria, where he later wrote and taught. The Middle Platonists Calvenus Taurus and Atticus were active in Athens, and the shadowy Eudorus as well as Philo (who was as much a Middle Platonist as he was an allegorical exegete) were based in Alexandria.[10] Clement also preserves a fragment from a work by the Middle Platonist Numenius of Apamea, a pagan contemporary of Justin

who will be important in our analysis of Justin's hermeneutic. Numenius flourished in the mid-second century and provides a very close philosophical parallel to Justin.

Clement set aside or minimized many of Justin's cruder formulations (in particular his demonology) and, unlike Justin, drew extensively on Aristotelian logic (especially in his discussions of the nature of faith). But he followed Justin's basic model of a hermeneutic of the divine voice.[11] Consequently, just as it proved useful to examine the works of Aristeas and Aristobulus as precursors of Philo's more far-reaching interpretation of scripture, so Justin's two brief apologies provide a helpful introduction to the sort of revisionary hermeneutical perspective that Clement was to extend to a much wider range of literature. We will begin our investigation of Justin's *logos* theology by commenting first on its biblical and philosophical roots. We will then examine his transformation of this essentially philosophical and theological formulation into a hermeneutical principle. In particular, we will want to observe in some detail how Justin turns a concept representing a divine being into one representing the meaning and interpretation of texts.

In the Hebrew Bible, the "Word of God" generally refers to divine agency in all its forms: speech, action, and other modes of self-revelation. For the most part, this "Word" does not become a distinct entity or hypostasis of its own but remains a metaphor for expressing the deity's self-extension into the nondivine realm. But in later Jewish speculation, the category "wisdom," functioning virtually as a synonym for "Word," did begin to assume a quasi-distinct status of its own. In the Book of Proverbs, for example, wisdom says of itself: "The Lord created me at the beginning of his work / the first of his acts of old. / Ages ago I was set up, / at the first, before the beginning of / the earth" (Prov. 8.22–23). In some circles of Jewish speculation, wisdom was even identified with the preexistent Torah itself, and both were understood to represent God's plan for, and instrument of, creation.[12] In early Christian literature, especially the Pauline epistles and the Gospel of John, the "Word" and/or "wisdom" was sometimes identified with the preexistent Son of God, who became incarnate, taking the form of Jesus of Nazareth (see, for example, 1 Cor. 1.18ff., 2.6ff.; Phil. 2; John 1.1–18).

Philo had already combined elements of Jewish speculation about the divine Word or wisdom with Middle Platonic ideas about the *logos*. In fact, he used Proverbs 8 as biblical support for his belief in an intermediary *logos* with quasi-independent status.[13] Providing a similar, but specifically Christian, variant of Philo's interpretation, Justin brought together reflection on the Word of God as Christ with aspects of Middle Platonic *logos* conceptions.[14] He too appealed to Proverbs 8, in this case to prove the preexistence of Christ (*Dial.* 61.3). This assimilation by Hellenistic Jews

and Christians of the biblical discussion of the divine "Word" with philosophical conceptions of the *logos* was facilitated by the Septuagint's translation of "Word of God" as *logos theou*.

Justin also drew extensively on prevailing philosophical ideas about a divine *logos*. By the second century C.E., Middle Platonism had largely displaced Stoicism as the dominant philosophical world view in the Greco-Roman world. Middle Platonism was a form of Platonic philosophy that drew upon other philosophical systems in order to address questions that Plato had left unanswered, to explore further ideas that he had suggested, and, in general, to make Platonism an attractive philosophy for the contemporary era. On the basis of an essentially Platonic philosophical framework and vocabulary, Middle Platonists embraced certain features of Stoic ethics and physics, Aristotelian logic, and Pythagorean metaphysics and number speculation as ways of giving fuller and more accurate expression to their understanding of Plato.[15] Middle Platonists were especially preoccupied with the nature and activity of the supreme principle or highest divine being. Despite having significant differences among themselves regarding the characterization of this being, most Middle Platonists emphasized its utter transcendence. They were convinced that the ultimate realm of true being could never come into direct contact with the ordinary realm of becoming. The realm of being was atemporal, immutable, and imperishable; the realm of becoming was subject to time, change, and decay. In order for such a transcendent God to have relevance for the world and human beings, the relationship between God and the world needed to be "mediated" by another entity. This entity would provide a "buffer zone," connecting God with, while protecting God from, the world. Various entities played this role, sometimes Plato's demiurge, sometimes his world soul; the principal mediator was often aided by a host of lesser intermediaries, including angels, demons, and disembodied souls.

Many Middle Platonists added to this mediating figure features characteristic of the Stoic *logos*. We have already seen that *logos* was the term used by Stoic philosophers to refer to God, that is, the divine, physical energy that permeated reality in the form of a fiery ether. By Philo's time, some Middle Platonists had taken up this Stoic notion of the *logos* and integrated it in their system. This integration naturally required the elimination of the materialistic features of the Stoic idea. The Middle Platonists reinterpreted the material energy of the Stoic *logos* as an immaterial force, which they then identified with the mediating entity, sometimes referred to as the "second" god. Meanwhile, they continued to speak of a first or high God, who remained uninvolved with the world and whose only act was the self-reflection that gave rise to the second, mediating god. The result, despite a variety of terminology, is essentially a two-tiered system: a

first God, completely transcendent and unknowable, and a second god (the *logos*), responsible for all divine contact with, and action upon, the material realm.[16] Sometimes the second god was further divided, producing a third divine entity. In such cases, the second god was characterized by closer association with the first God, while the third god (or "lower" dimension of the second god) concerned itself more directly with the material realm.

Both the Christian Middle Platonist Justin and the Pythagorizing Middle Platonist Numenius reflect many of these Middle Platonic ideas.[17] While a detailed comparative analysis of the two figures would exceed the scope of this book, a few observations of similarities and differences will give some idea of just how much these two Platonists share. Justin speaks of a first God who is eternal, immovable, unchanging, nameless and unbegotten, utterly detached from the material realm. As a result,

> you must not imagine that the unbegotten God himself came down or went up from any place. For the ineffable Father and Lord of all neither has come to any place, nor walks, nor sleeps, nor rises up, but remains in his own place, wherever that is. (*Dial.* 127; cf. *Dial.* 56)

There is also a second god or *logos*, who mediates between the high God and the world, and a "spirit" that occupies the third place.[18] Numenius also spoke of three divine entities: a first God, who exists in himself and is devoid of agency, a second god or demiurge responsible for all motion, and a third entity (which Proclus mistakenly identifies as creation—"what was fashioned"—but which almost certainly refers to a lower aspect of the second god).[19] There are, however, differences: Justin's high God is both Father and creator, while Numenius restricts creation to the second god or demiurge.[20] This difference probably reflects Justin's basic monotheism, as well as his identification of Plato's father and maker (Pl. *Tim.* 28C) with biblical descriptions of the creative action of God. Justin goes on to stress the close association between the first God and the second: the second god is emitted without any diminution in the being of the first God, as one fire is generated from another. Numenius uses the same analogy to stress the participation of the second god in the first.[21]

Both Justin and Numenius use a passage from an alleged Platonic epistle to endorse their views of multiple divine entities. In the *Second Epistle*, the author writes: "All things are about the King of all and exist for him, and he is the cause of all that is good. The second things are about the Second and the third about the Third."[22] Justin quotes the second sentence, interpreting Plato as referring to the Father, Son, and Holy Spirit (*Ap.* 1.60.7).[23] Numenius used the same passage as a warrant for the three gods of his system.[24] And just as Justin equated the Holy Spirit with the spirit hovering over the waters in Genesis 1.2 (*Ap.* 1.60.6), so

Numenius allegorized the same verse for his own purposes.[25] Thus we see that Justin and Numenius share much the same Middle Platonic theology, especially the distinction between a first God and a second.

The Middle Platonist first God had one further characteristic: it was "generative" or "productive" (*spermatikos*). This idea was taken from the Stoics. Although in borrowing this Stoic idea, Middle Platonists necessarily eliminated its materialistic aspects, they preserved its generative character. According to the Stoics, the divine *logos* had fragmented itself into the *logoi* that constituted human minds; the human mind was literally part of the divine ether that pervaded the cosmos. Like that cosmic fire, the *logos* of human reason was productive: it was able to generate "seeds," which were the principles and concepts of human thought. Hence, the Stoics called the *logos* the *logos spermatikos* or "generative *logos.*" Middle Platonists preserved this link between the second god (or *logos*) and human reason by thinking of the *logos* as a kind of cosmic mind in which human minds were now said to "participate." Through its illumination of the human mind, the Middle Platonic *logos* was thus the ultimate source of human thoughts.

This Middle Platonic notion of an immaterial, productive second god or *logos* was well in place by Justin's time; versions of it were prevalent in both Hellenistic Jewish and pagan metaphysical speculation. For example, in the preceding century, Philo had spoken of the *logos* as a divine hypostasis, separated from the divine intellect, and he had given it various names: Power, Second God, First Born of God, Son of God, Angel, and Apostle.[26] In two instances, Philo refers explicitly to the *logos spermatikos*— once as the transcendent creator of physical and spiritual life and once as human reason.[27] Justin may well have drawn on Philo's works and certainly drew on New Testament texts in formulating his own version of the *logos spermatikos*.[28] But it is also likely that he was familiar with Numenius's use of the conception. Numenius had described the relation of the first God to the second god or demiurge by drawing on an analogous relation between a farm owner and farm laborer. The farmer himself is responsible for the initial sowing of the crops, but the laborer then takes over the cultivation of the field. Numenius writes:

> Just as there is a relation between the farmer and the one that plants, so in just the same way is the first God related to the demiurge. The former, as farmer, sows [*speirein*] the seed [*sperma*] of every soul into all the things which partake of it; while the lawgiver plants and distributes and transplants what has been sown from that source into each one of us. (Frag. 13)[29]

As we shall see, Justin holds a similar view of a divine *logos* mediating the productive activity of God vis-à-vis individual human souls. Although Justin's notion of the *logos spermatikos* owes something to Philo and Nu-

menius, he goes his own way by following the Gospel of John and other Christian literature in identifying this *logos* with Christ alone.[30] For the Christian Middle Platonist Justin, the divine, generative *logos* was Christ or the preexistent Son of God, as well as the incarnate Son, Jesus of Nazareth. Such an assertion of the divine demiurge's direct association with matter would have been totally unacceptable, not to say repugnant, to Numenius.[31]

According to Justin, this divine *logos* was the single source of prophetic revelation (*Ap.* 1.12.7–10) and philosophical illumination (*Ap.* 1.5 and passim); it was also the essence of the words, and, finally, the person, of Jesus (*Ap.* 1.14ff.). Justin's hermeneutical application of the *logos* concept appears in three interrelated themes that dominate his writings: the *logos*'s spermatic or generative character, the battle between the *logos* and the demons, and the plagiarism of scripture by pagan philosophers. All three themes appear in Philo, and all three (especially the first and third) were developed by Clement as part of his own allegorical revision of pagan and Christian competitors.

Justin's basic claim is that Hebrew scripture is a transcription of divine speech. When scripture is properly read, one hears the voice of God: "When you hear the utterances of the prophets spoken as it were personally, you must not suppose that they are spoken by the inspired themselves, but by the divine *logos* who moves them" (*Ap.* 1.36.1). Understanding what the divine voice is saying requires a certain hermeneutical sophistication, however, for the voice adopts different points of view, depending on the character through which and the circumstance in which it speaks:

> For sometimes he [the divine *logos*] declares things that are to come to pass, in the manner of one who foretells the future; sometimes he speaks as from the person of God the Lord and Father of all; sometimes as from the person of Christ; sometimes as from the person of the people answering the Lord or his father, just as you can see even in your own writers, one person being the writer of the whole, but introducing the persons [*prosōpa*] who converse. (*Ap.* 1.36.2)

The prophetic voice of Hebrew scripture continues in the person of Jesus: when Jesus opens his mouth to teach, the divine *logos* speaks. This divine speech endures even after Jesus' death, in the preaching of the apostles: "by the power of God," the apostles "proclaimed to every race of human beings that they were sent by Christ to teach all the *logos* of God" (*Ap.* 1.39.3). The apostles are able to express the *logos* of God precisely because that *logos*, in the form of the risen spirit of Jesus, entered into them and enabled them to interpret Hebrew prophecy: through the

apostles, the *logos* has become the authoritative interpreter of its own message (*Ap.* 1.50.12).

It is interesting to note that Numenius seems to have held a similar view of the way literature could be designed to convey a message through various rhetorical modes of speech.[32] In a fragment from his lost work *On the Secrets in Plato,* he observes that Plato has intentionally conveyed certain points of view through the construction of the dramatic dialogue of the *Euthyphro.* In particular, Numenius notes that Plato dramatizes his criticism of Athenian religious orthodoxy by using Euthyphro as his spokesperson:

> Since speaking the truth was more important to him than life itself, he saw that there was a way he could both live *and* speak the truth without risk: he made Euthyphro play the part of the Athenians—an arrogant twit and a remarkably bad theologian—and set Socrates against him in his usual character, confronting everyone he met just as he was accustomed to do. (Frag. 23.12–18)[33]

It seems that Numenius, like Justin, was as much a hermeneutician as a philosopher. Like Justin, he seems to have been attentive to the way the basic message of a single author could be conveyed in various dramatic and rhetorical forms. And according to Origen, Numenius also did not refrain from "using in his own writings the words of the [Jewish] prophets and treating them allegorically [*tropologein*]" (Frag. 1b.6–8).[34] It seems likely, then, that Numenius, as a Platonist interpreter of literature, brought to his own work a hermeneutical sensibility similar to Justin's.

For Justin, the divine voice that speaks in Hebrew scripture, in the teaching of Jesus, and in the *kērygma* of the apostles also speaks in at least some pagan philosophy. He makes this clear when responding to the pagan challenge that Christian revelation had irresponsibly neglected the fates of those who lived before Jesus:

> We have been taught that Christ is the firstborn of God, and we have declared above that he is the *logos* of whom every race of human beings partook [*metechein*]; and those who lived with *logos* [*meta logou*] are Christians, even though they have been thought atheists; as, among the Greeks, Socrates and Heraclitus, and those like them; and among the barbarians, Abraham, and Ananias, and Azarias, and Misael, and Elias, and many others whose actions and names we now decline to recount, because we know it would be tedious. (*Ap.* 1.46.2–3)

Such persons who lived before Christ but who nevertheless shared in the *logos* (*meta logou*) are de facto Christians (*Ap.* 1.46.4).

By the same token, those who lived before Christ but who did not share in the *logos* (*aneu logou*) are de facto persecutors of Christ (*Ap.* 1.46.4). The

presence of the persecutors of the *logos*/Christ indicates that history was not a divine monologue; from the outset (i.e., from the fall of those angels who became demons), divine speech had to assert itself in the face of stringent opposition from demonic forces. According to Justin, the demons were originally angels, who subsequently turned against God. His account of this angelic fall assimilates Genesis 6, which describes the attack on the "daughters of men" by the "sons of God," to contemporary Middle Platonic speculation about demons:

> God, when he had made the whole world . . . committed the care of human beings and of all things under heaven to angels whom he appointed over them. But the angels transgressed this appointment, and were captivated by love of women, and begat children who are those that are called demons. (*Ap.* 2.4[5].2–3)

The demons, who coerced human beings into worshiping them, are responsible for "murders, wars, adulteries, intemperate deeds, and all wickedness" (*Ap.* 2.4[5].4). The mythmakers became the unwitting tools of demonic self-expression, and the poets became equally deluded accomplices of the mythmakers. Both attributed demonic activity to deities and their offspring:

> Whence also the poets and mythmakers, not knowing that it was the angels and those demons who had been begotten by them that did these things to men, and women, and cities, and nations, which they related, ascribed them to God himself, and to those who were accounted to be his very offspring, and to the offspring of those who were called his brothers, Neptune and Pluto, and to the children again of these their offspring. For whatever name each of the angels had given to himself and his children, by that name they called them. (*Ap.* 2.4[5].5–6)

Whether before or after the appearance of the *logos* in the person of Jesus, the demons constantly opposed its voice, wherever it appeared. This demonic opposition could take direct, violent forms, such as the persecution of Socrates, the crucifixion of Jesus, or the attacks on Justin and his Christian contemporaries. But the demons could also attack indirectly, through subversive literary representations and the willful misinterpretation of scripture. They were able to gain power over human minds through the images of themselves that they created; in effect, the demons personified themselves and generated mythical narratives in which they took leading roles. Those accounts frightened human beings into calling them "gods":

> Since of old these evil demons, effecting apparitions [*epiphaneiai*] of themselves, both defiled women and corrupted boys, and showed such fearful sights to men, that those who did not judge with *logos* [*logōi*] the actions that

were done, were struck with terror; and being carried away by fear, and not knowing that these were evil demons, they called them gods, and gave to each the name which each of the demons chose for himself. (*Ap.* 1.5.2)

But demonic mythology does not consist in wholly novel literary productions. On the contrary, demons are essentially parasitic—they create myths that distort or parody scripture in order to neutralize its effect:

> Before he [the *logos*] became a human being among human beings, some [mythmakers] under the influence of the evil demons just mentioned, told through the poets as having already occurred the myths they had invented, just as now they are responsible for the slanders and godless deeds alleged against us, of which there is neither witness nor demonstration. (*Ap.* 1.23.3)

Here Justin explains that the demons first corrupted the original makers of myths, and then the poets simply compounded the problem by incorporating those myths into their poetry. It is interesting to compare Justin with Cornutus. Both writers have a view of the corruption of original theological wisdom, but Cornutus holds a much more sanguine view of the mythmakers than Justin, for he has no theory of demonic corruption at the very origin. But for Justin, the demons corrupted truth and generated falsehood from the outset, and the poets who use pagan mythology only pass along the deceit.[35] Unlike Cornutus, Justin does not recommend the separation of pure original myth from contaminating additions: at their worst, the myths are entirely corrupt; at best, they are perversions of the true accounts of scripture that should entirely displace them.

When properly read, scripture prophesies the coming full appearance of the *logos* that will destroy the demons. But in a preemptive strike, the demons seek to erode the credibility of scripture and its proper interpretation by creating myths that look like scripture. The idea is that when the pagan myths are then criticized as fiction by Christians or other devotees of the *logos,* scripture itself will fall under the same critique of being fiction because of its similar mythical appearance:

> But those who hand down the myths which the poets have made adduce no proof to the youths who learn them; and we proceed to demonstrate that they have been uttered by the influence of wicked demons, to deceive and lead astray the human race. For having heard it proclaimed through the prophets that the Christ was to come, and that the ungodly among human beings were to be punished by fire, they put forward many to be called sons of Zeus, under the impression that they would be able to produce in human beings the idea that things which were said with regard to Christ were marvellous tales [*teratologiai*], like the things which were said by the poets. (*Ap.* 1.54.1–2)

Justin insists that the Jews, like the demons, also misread Hebrew scripture. Either they fail to recognize the messianic prophecies or, having

recognized them, fail to refer them to Jesus as the true Messiah. In particular, the Jews did not understand the theory of multiple speakers that Justin presents: consequently, "although the Jews possessed the books of the prophets," they "did not . . . recognize Christ even when he came" (*Ap.* 1.36.3). The Jews are not directly to blame, however; for like the Greek mythmakers and poets, they too were the unwitting instruments by which the demons continued their assault on the *logos.* Consequently, Justin can link Jewish hermeneutical failure (in this example, Jewish failure to see that the *logos,* not the ineffable high God, appears to Moses in the burning bush) and their persecution of Christ by associating both with the work of the demons:

> [Theophanies like the burning bush] are written for the sake of proving that Jesus the Christ is the Son of God and his apostle, being of old the *logos* [*proteron logos ōn*], and appearing sometimes in the form of fire, and sometimes in a bodiless image; but now, by the will of God, having become a human being for the human race, he endured all the sufferings which the demons instigated the senseless [*anoētoi*] Jews to inflict upon him; who, though they have it expressly [*rhētōs*] affirmed in the writings of Moses, "And an angel of God spoke to Moses in a flame of fire in a bush, and said, I am that I am, the God of Abraham, and the God of Isaac, and the God of Jacob," yet maintain that he who said this was the father and maker [*dēmiourgos*] of the universe. (*Ap.* 1.63.10–11)

For Justin, then, the proper interpretation of scripture and all other literature requires attending to the authentic divine speech in the text and resisting a variety of distorting interpretations and competing literary alternatives promulgated by the demons.

From time to time, those who lived with a share of the *logos* did seek to resist the mythology of the demons, but the demons were quick to fight back; this cosmic battle lies behind the career of Socrates. Socrates deserves the admiration of Christians because he

> cast out from the state both Homer and the rest of the poets, and taught human beings to reject the evil demons and those who did the things which the poets related; and he exhorted them to become acquainted with God who was to them unknown, by means of rational investigation [*dia logou zētēseōs*], saying "that it is neither easy to find the father and maker [*dēmiourgos*] of all, nor, having found him, is it safe to declare him to all." (Pl. *Tim.* 28C, altered, in *Ap.* 2.10.6)

But the demons quickly counterattacked:

> When Socrates skillfully endeavored, by true reason [*logōi alēthei*], to bring these things to light, and deliver human beings from the demons, then the demons themselves, by means of those who rejoiced in iniquity, brought

about his death, as an atheist and an impious person, on the charge that "he was introducing new divinities." (Pl. *Ap.* 24B in *Ap.* 1.5.3)

Justin argues that he and his Christian contemporaries are suffering the same attacks because they are simply carrying on the Socratic protest in a more intense form (more intense since, unlike Socrates, they enjoy the full presence of the *logos* in the form of Christ):

> For not only among the Greeks were these things condemned by *logos* [*hypo logou*] through Socrates [*dia Sōcratous*], but also among the barbarians by the *logos* himself [*hyp' autou tou logou*], who took shape, and became man, and was called Jesus Christ. (*Ap.* 1.5.4)

Whenever one detects similarity between pagan and biblical descriptions, there are, then, only a few possible explanations: we have already discussed two of them—either pagans who have been enlightened by their share of the *logos* have expressed an insight similar to scripture's or the evil demons have produced a distorted version of scripture. There is, however, a third possibility, which Justin probably took from Philo: that pagans have simply plagiarized the Bible directly. Justin argues, for example, that Plato takes his account of creation in the *Timaeus* from the opening verses of Moses' Genesis and that Hesiod derives his discussion of Erebus from Moses as well (*Ap.* 1.59.1–6). Similarly, Plato's idea in the *Timaeus* that the power of the high God was placed "crosswise" in the universe was in fact a misinterpretation of a biblical prophecy of Christ in Numbers 21 (*Ap.* 1.60). Like Philo, Justin is sure that Moses lived and wrote long before any of the Greek philosophers, but he is also sure that the *logos* existed before Moses. The key point, of course, is not that Christians "hold the same opinions as others," but that all others who share the *logos* "speak in imitation of ours" (*Ap.* 1.60.10)—or, as Justin more audaciously announces, "whatever things were rightly said among all persons, are the property of us Christians" (*Ap.* 2.13.4).[36]

Despite the fact that his use of *logos* theology as a hermeneutical principle enables him to bring together biblical revelation and philosophical illumination as a single act of divine self-manifestation and production of textual meaning, Justin firmly maintains the distinctiveness and superiority of the specifically Christian revelation. Even with his share of the *logos*, Socrates does not attain to the fullness of Christian insight. Justin tells his readers that he himself turned from Platonic philosophy to Christianity "not because the teachings of Plato are different from those of Christ, but because they are not in all respects similar, as neither are those of the others—Stoics, and poets, and historians" (*Ap.* 2.13.2).[37] It is true that "each one, by having portions of the divine generative *logos* [*apo merous tou spermatikou theiou logou*], spoke well, whenever he saw what was

congruent with it" (*Ap.* 2.13.3) and that "all the writers were able to see
realities [*ta onta*] dimly [*amydrōs*] through the spore of the implanted *logos*
that was in them [*dia tēs enousēs emphytou tou logou sporas*]" (*Ap.* 2.13.5). But
Justin immediately spells out the implication of his qualifications (i.e., "a
share" and "dimly"). There is, he insists, a vital distinction to be made
between "the seed and the ability to imitate it by one's own capacity"
(*sperma tinos kai mimēma kata dynamin dothen*) and "the thing itself, of which
there is participation and imitation by virtue of its own favor [*kata charin
tēn ap' ekeinou*]" (*Ap.* 2.13.6).

Justin thus makes it clear that Christians, not pagans, enjoy the full
presence, and, indeed, possession, of the *logos* itself. Socrates, we saw,
performed his critique "by rational investigation" (*dia logou zētēseōs*) (*Ap.*
2.10.6), but Christ performs the same critique "through his own power"
(*dia tēs heautou dynameōs*) (*Ap.* 2.10.7). Justin claims that this qualitative,
not quantitative, distinction was well recognized by persons from all walks
of life and of all degrees of education:

> For no one trusted in Socrates so as to die for this doctrine, but in Christ,
> who was partially known even by Socrates [*hypo Sōcratous apo merous gnōs-
> thenti*]—for he was and is the *logos* who is in every person, and who foretold
> the things that were to come to pass both through the prophets and in his
> own person [*di' heautou*] when he was made of like passions, and taught
> these things—not only philosophers and philologians believed, but also
> artisans and people entirely uneducated, despising both glory, and fear, and
> death: since he [or it—i.e., either Christ or his doctrine] is a power [*dynamis*]
> of the ineffable Father, and not the mere instrument of human reason
> [*anthrōpeiou logou kataskeuē*]. (*Ap.* 2.10.8)

In the end, Justin's voice of the *logos* drowns out the voices of all cultural
competitors by absorbing them into its own divine fullness. This voice is
the original voice of truth. As Justin points out, truth at its origin was one,
and religious sects developed only because human beings turned away
from the one truth to cultivate their own idiosyncratic opinions (*Dial.* 2.1–
2). Thus Justin provided a chronological account of heresy in his lost
work *Against Heresies,* in which heretical error was portrayed as a progressive deviation from original, single religious truth, handed down from
misguided teachers to misguided pupils. Justin's notion of heresy as deviance from original truth set the pattern not only for Irenaeus's *Against
Heresies,* but for most subsequent Christian heresiologists. Once again,
Numenius provides a parallel idea, in his work *On the Infidelity of the
Academy toward Plato.* Just as Justin insists that heretics corrupt the pure
divine truth, so Numenius contends that Plato's successors fell away from
the teaching of the master into sectarian division because they "did not
hold to the primitive heritage but rapidly divided, intentionally or not"

(frag. 24: cf. frags. 25–28).[38] Hence the pagan Middle Platonist, no less than his Christian contemporary, sought to recover an ancient and original wisdom, which was still spoken forth in the pages of ancient literature, despite the efforts of heretics and sectarians to corrupt it.

THE ANTECEDENT VOICE OF CULTURAL CLASSICS

Clement made much of Justin's perspective his own: he too argued that the meaning of Greek literature, when it has any valid or valuable meaning at all, is due to the voice of the divine *logos*. Even then, its meaning has already been anticipated by a previous discourse of the *logos* recorded in Hebrew scripture. And in the end, even this Hebraic discourse is but an echo or derivation of the Christian *logos*, for even though that *logos* achieved fullest literary expression in the pages of the New Testament, it preexists even Hebrew scripture. However, *logos* theology need not inevitably result in this particular hermeneutical emphasis on voice over writing. Philo was also a Middle Platonic *logos* theologian, yet we have already seen that he stressed the priority and authority of the scriptural text itself. But in his major treatises (*Protreptikos, Paidagōgos, Strōmateis*), Clement consistently valorizes voice over writing, as he records the results of his Christian revisionary readings of Hebrew scripture, classical literature, the New Testament, and other ancient texts.

We can begin to understand the particular ways Clement's revisionary reading works by considering the following typical instance of his reading of classical texts:

> Is it not absurd [*atopos*], my friends, that God always exhorts us to virtue, but we shun the benefit and delay salvation? For does not even John exhort to salvation and become altogether a hortative voice? Let us then ask him, "Who of men are you, and whence?" [Hom. *Od.* 1.170, 19.105]. He will not say "Elijah," and he will deny that he is the Christ; but he will confess: "A voice crying in [the] wilderness [*en erēmōi*]." Who then is John? In a word, one may say: "A hortative voice of the *logos* crying in [the] wilderness [*en erēmōi*]." "What do you cry, O Voice? Tell us also" [*Od.* 1.10]. "Make straight the ways of the Lord" [Isa. 40.3, quoted in Matt. 3.3; Mark 1.3; Luke 3.4; John 1.23]. (*Protr.* 1.9.1; with direct quotations underlined and identified)

To understand Clement's use of classical pagan texts in this selection we need first to recall the following passage in the Gospel of John, where Jewish priests and Levites are sent from Jerusalem to investigate the identity of John the Baptist:

> "Who are you?" He [John the Baptist] confessed, he did not deny, but confessed, "I am not the Christ." And they asked him, "What then? Are you Elijah?" He said, "I am not." "Are you the prophet?" And he answered,

"No." They said to him then, "Who are you? Let us have an answer for those who sent us. What do you say about yourself?" He said, "I am the voice of one crying in the wilderness, 'Make straight the way of the Lord,' as the prophet Isaiah said." (John 1.19–23)

Clement alters this Johannine passage in at least two ways. He replaces the query of the Jewish priests and Levites ("Who are you?") at two points with the words of Homer's Telemachus, who asks Athena, *tis pothen eis andrōn* ("Who among men are you, and whence?" *Od.* 1.170, 19.105). He also turns the evangelist's account of a past dialogue between the Jews and the Baptist into a contemporaneous interchange between Clement (along with his readers—"my friends") and the Baptist. Clement does not allude to Homer simply because of his apologetic desire to make Christianity appealing to his educated, urbane Alexandrian readership. He inserts these Homeric echoes into his reworking of a scriptural passage for the much-larger and far-reaching purpose of suggesting that the words of Homer belong with the language of scripture at least as an equal partner. In fact, by using Homeric diction in place of the Jews' questions put to the Baptist (who for Clement is the immediate precursor of Jesus, the incarnate divine *logos*), Clement illustrates his revisionary claim that the divine *logos* in the form of philosophy was a pedagogue leading the Greeks to Christ, just as the law led the Hebrews. Both pedagogues are ultimately the same *logos* that leads pupils to acknowledge its final and complete manifestation as Jesus of Nazareth (*Strom.* 1.5.28.3). Because the *logos* led the Greeks to recognize its impending self-manifestation, Clement can restate Jewish questions put to the Baptist as contemporary questions cast in the language of the Greeks' own cultural classic.

When Clement considers classical literature and philosophy on its own terms, rather than working it along with scripture into his interpretations, he is quick to point out that it only partially expresses the divine voice. He insists that even though the Greeks have received "certain sparks [*enausmata tina*] of the divine *logos*," they have not "arrived at the full flame [*telos*]" (*Protr.* 7.74.7). Clement reminds readers of the merely partial validity of classical sources by qualifying his general view that Greek thought is divinely inspired. Philosophy is a work of providence "somehow or other" (*hamē ge pē*) (*Strom.* 1.1.18.4), Plato speaks "as if" (*hoion*) inspired (*Strom.* 1.8.42.1), and Paul uses a verse from the Greek poet Epimenides because it expresses "something" (*ti*) of the truth (*Strom.* 1.14.59.3).[39] Most of the time, it seems, the Greeks possess the truth of the *logos* because they stole it from the Jews. Clement suggests that Jesus had just such plagiarizing Greeks in mind when he spoke allegorically concerning "thieves and robbers" (John 10.8). Yet even though Greek philosophers stole their insights from the Jews just as Prometheus stole fire

from Zeus, Clement thinks that they might also have had the "spirit of
perception" (Exod. 28.3, LXX)—"a trace of wisdom and an impulse from
God"—and thus arrived at some of their insights on their own (*Strom.*
1.17.87.1–2). He is also aware of another explanation for the echoes of
authentic non-Greek religious wisdom in Greek thought. Some simple
Christian fideists in Clement's own community believe that the devil
gave philosophy to the Greeks, and others, referring to Genesis 6, think
that certain angels came down from heaven and handed it over (*Strom.*
5.1.10.1–3). Clement sums up his ambivalent assessment of classical philosophy this way:

> But if the Hellenic philosophy comprehends not the whole extent of the
> truth, and besides is destitute of strength to perform the commandments of
> the Lord, yet it prepares the way for the truly royal teaching, training in
> some way or other [*hamē ge pē*], and molding the character, and fitting him
> who believes in providence for the reception of the truth. (*Strom.* 1.16.80.6)

Even if the Greeks came to knowledge of the divine *logos* on their own,
their wisdom is deficient because its authors have long since fallen from
original knowledge—"an innate original communion between men and
heaven"—into ignorance (*Protr.* 2.25.3). Human beings once knew the
one God, but postlapsarian humanity has succumbed to various forms of
idolatry.[40] Confident that this lost original knowledge of God has reappeared through the incarnation of the *logos*, Clement assesses pagan
idolatry from the perspective of one who possesses the newly recovered
original knowledge (*Protr.* 2.27.2). From this standpoint, Clement is able
to turn the classical heritage against itself. For example, classical art is fine
as long as it doesn't pretend to be a true representation of reality (*Protr.*
4.57.6); even the Greeks remember Pygmalion, who was conquered by an
image—"so powerful is art to delude" (*Protr.* 4.57.3). Or consider the
names of so-called deities. Once understood etymologically (though from
the perspective of the critique of etymology we saw in Cicero's dialogue),
they immediately reveal the nondivine status of their bearers. "Serapis"
obviously is derived from materials left over from the funerals of Osiris
and Apis (*Protr.* 4.48.6), and the so-called god Poseidon betrays his true
nature as mere water, the name being derived "from drink" (*ek tēs poseōs*)
(*Protr.* 5.64.3). Following the approach of Cicero's Velleius and Cotta,
Clement thus turns Stoic etymology to his own advantage; the "Adamic"
names of pagan deities reliably denote things, but these things are not
divine.[41]

When not attacking the false assumptions of pagan idolatry, Clement
criticizes classical accounts of divine behavior by repeating the common charge of "unfittingness." Clement knows the works of Alexandrian
scholars such as Dionysius Thrax (*Strom.* 5.8.45.4) and Didymus (*Strom.*

5.8.46.2), and he repeats the same criticisms of Homer that led such Alexandrian editors to athetize. In a list of deities who served as slaves of human beings, Clement includes a familiar example: "We read of Aphrodite, like a wanton serving-wench, taking and setting a seat for Helen opposite the adulterer, in order to entice him" (*Protr.* 2.35.2). Clement spells out the nuance of Homer's *bastazein* by adding the epithets "serving-wench" and "adulterer," embellishing a line that at least one Alexandrian editor deemed inauthentic.[42] He also highlights Aphrodite's intrigue with Ares behind the back of Hephaestus, a passage regularly allegorized by pagan critics. Clement begins with sarcasm: "Sing to us, O Homer, that beautiful song 'about the loves of Ares and Venus with the beautiful crown; how first they slept together in the place of Hephaestus secretly; and he gave many gifts, and dishonored the bed and chamber of King Hephaestus'" (*Od.* 8.266–70). Then, with a dramatic flourish, Clement breaks off: "Stop, O Homer, the song! It is not beautiful; it teaches adultery, and we are prohibited from polluting our ears with hearing about adultery" (*Protr.* 3.59.1–2). With nothing but contempt for the immoral myths of gods and goddesses, Clement offers a catalog of divine improprieties: "the incredible tales of their licentiousness, and their wounds, and their bonds, and their laughings, and their fights, their servitudes too, and their banquets; and furthermore, their embraces, and tears, and sufferings, and lewd delights" (*Protr.* 2.32.1). Elsewhere, after first paraphrasing and then citing a few Orphic lines about the immodest behavior of the goddess Demeter, Clement adds with thick sarcasm: "Fine sights truly, and becoming [*preponta*] a goddess" (*Protr.* 2.21.2). Clement begins another common charge against Homer with mock respect for the poet:

> And your poem, O Homer, fills me with admiration! "He said, and nodded with his shadowy brows; Waved on the immortal head the ambrosial locks, And all Olympus trembled at his nod" [*Il.* 1.528–30]. You make Zeus venerable, O Homer; and the nod which you ascribe to him is most reverend. (*Protr.* 2.33.1–2)

Heraclitus had written much the same near the beginning of his *Homeric Allegories:*

> Established as sacred through the verses [of Homer] is Zeus in heaven, shaking with an imperceptible nod, as [also] Poseidon, having set in motion suddenly "the high mountains and the woodland" [*Il.* 13.18]. The same things one might say about Hera: "She shook herself on her throne, and made high Olympus quake [*Il.* 8.199]." (*All.* 2.2–3)

But Clement has not finished, adding to his mock praise a final sarcastic dig: "But show him only . . . a woman's girdle, and Zeus is exposed, and his locks are dishonored. To what a pitch of licentiousness did that Zeus of

yours proceed, who spent so many nights in voluptuousness with Alcmene?" (*Protr.* 2.33.2–3). Note that what is "unfitting" or "monstrous" is never Clement's own favored texts (Hebrew scripture or New Testament writings) or even the Greek philosophical texts he wants to save, but rather those Greek mythical texts that depict "[idolatrous] images" (*Protr.* 6.67.2) or conjure up a "monstrous [*atopos*] imaginary scene" (*Protr.* 6.67.1). Elsewhere, Clement attacks a favorite target of those philosophically minded critics who had found Homer's poetry unfitting—his depiction of prayers (*Litai*) as the daughters of Zeus. Homer has the old charioteer Phoenix say to Achilles:

> Do you not know that prayers are daughters of almighty Zeus? They are wrinkled creatures, with a halting gait and downcast eyes, who make it their business to follow Sin about. But Sin is strong, and quick enough to leave them all behind. Stealing a march on them, she roams the world and brings mankind to grief. *They* come after and put the trouble right. (*Il.* 9.502ff.)

Homer probably intended the prayers as allegorical personifications of Zeus's response to penance; at least ancient readers like Archilochus and Alcaeus read the scene that way.[43] But Clement reads Homer's account literally, deriding the "halting, wrinkled, squinting" Prayers as "daughters of Thersites rather than of Zeus"[44] and asking sarcastically: "How in reason could men petition Zeus for a beautiful progeny—a thing he could not obtain for himself?" (*Protr.* 4.56.1). In contrast, Heraclitus reads the text allegorically, construing it as Homer's allegorical portrayal of suppliants—exactly the sort of defense one might make to the kind of damaging literal reading Clement insists on:

> Some are so ignorant as to have leveled the accusation that Homer, with respect to the Prayers, insulted the daughters of Zeus, having placed on them a distorted and deformed character. . . . But in these verses the character of suppliants is depicted. Consciousness of human failing comes slowly to everyone, and those who are supplicated are approached by the suppliants with difficulty, as they measure out, so to speak, the extent of their shame; neither do they look without trembling, but avert the glances of their eyes. And indeed, upon their faces the mind placed no joyful blush; but pale, with downcast eyes, [their faces] elicit pity at the first glance. Whence with good reason [Homer] shows not the daughters of Zeus, but the suppliants, "halting and wrinkled and squinting." (*All.* 37.1–4)

To Heraclitus, Homer is like "a painter of human passions" when he allegorizes the experience of suppliants as the daughters of Zeus (*All.* 37.6). But to Clement, Homer is at best a pornographer and at worst a blasphemer. Clement reads allegorically when he wishes, but he is also a shrewd literal reader when it serves his polemical purposes.

Even when Greek literature does express the discourse of the *logos,* it

does so in a doubly subordinate fashion. Subordinating acceptable classical texts first to Hebrew scripture, Clement then subordinates both classical and Hebraic texts to Christian scripture. Following Philo and his Hellenistic Jewish predecessors, as well as the chronological calculations of Justin's pupil Tatian (in his *Address to the Greeks*), Clement asserts the absolute priority of Hebrew scripture to classical literature, of Moses to Homer and Plato.[45] Moses turns out to be not only older than Greek poets and wise men, but even older than the Greek deities (*Strom.* 1.21.107.6). Having established the priority of Hebraic wisdom, Clement next shows that Greek wisdom is derived from it. The Greeks copied the miracles recorded in Hebrew scripture, and all their chief philosophical ideas are plagiarized from the same source (*Strom.* 2.1.1.1–2).[46] The Greeks were dependent on the Hebrews for more than just philosophical wisdom. Greek legislation followed the "model of Mosaic prophecy" (*Strom.* 1.26.170.4), and Greek generals even adapted Moses' military strategy (*Strom.* 1.24.160.3–5). When not imitating Moses, Greek writings borrow from the rest of Hebrew scripture, especially from the Sibyl (whom Clement treats as a Hebrew prophet and poet); for example, Xenophon learned his wisdom "from the prophetess of the Hebrews" (*Protr.* 6.71.4). Even the epitome of the classical ideal—the Delphic Oracle's injunction "Know thyself"—was "mystically" extrapolated by pagans from the text "You have seen your brother, you have seen your God" (*Strom.* 2.15.70.5). This sentence is obviously quoted as having the functional authority of scripture although its literary source is unknown. A few sentences later, Clement insists that "Know thyself" "is more clearly and often expressed by Moses, when scripture enjoins 'Take heed to thyself'" (e.g., Exod. 10.28, 34.12; Deut. 4.9) (*Strom.* 2.15.71.4). Elsewhere Clement more explicitly revises the Greek maxim, claiming that it actually means that one is to know for what one is born—namely, to obey the Mosaic commandments (*Strom.* 7.3.20.7). Clement's charge of plagiarism helps explain the discrepancies between Greek and Hebraic wisdom by suggesting that the Greeks misunderstood Hebrew scripture (*Strom.* 5.1.10.3). But even when the Greeks are right, they are right simply because they have managed to repeat a meaning that Moses or another Hebrew author expressed earlier and better. The famous rhetorical question of Numenius, quoted by Clement, signals the success of the revisionary readings of Greek philosophy initiated by Ptolemaic Jews, developed by Philo, Justin, and Tatian, and now exploited once again by Clement: "For what is Plato, but Moses speaking Attic Greek?" (*Strom.* 1.22.150.4).

Clement does not always subordinate pagan texts by reading them through lenses supplied by Hebrew scripture; he often reads them directly in light of his Christian assumptions (though, of course, the lenses of Hebrew scripture were already deeply tinted by those assumptions).

From the perspective of Christian assumptions alone, Plato is not a Moses speaking Attic Greek but the divine *logos* speaking Christian truth directly. Clement leaves no doubt that both the origin and goal of Greek philosophy is the divine *logos* (*Strom.* 1.13.57.6); for, he observes, "what is good proceeded from us to the Greeks" (*Strom.* 5.4.19.1).[47] When Jesus said "I am the truth," he was designating the locus of true philosophy (*Strom.* 1.5.32.4), a point obliquely indicated by philosophers like Pythagoras, who hinted at the church when referring to his common hall (*Strom.* 1.15.66.2), or by the Stoics, whose theories of world conflagration echo Christian beliefs concerning the resurrection (*Strom.* 5.1.9.4).[48] When Plato says that in the Greek mysteries there are "many bearers of the thyrsus, but few bacchanals," he means just what Jesus said regarding the true mystery of the kingdom—that "many are called but few chosen" (Matt. 22.14) (*Strom.* 1.19.92.3).[49]

It is clear that much of Clement's revisionary hermeneutic is made possible by the Middle Platonic *logos* theology that he borrowed from earlier Jewish and Christian apologists such as Philo, Justin Martyr, and Irenaeus. Given the fact that Clement and Philo share a common debt to this philosophical tradition and that Clement read Philo's works (often paraphrasing or directly quoting extensive portions), the principal differences between their revisionary hermeneutics are all the more striking.[50] Even at this early date, the Alexandrian tradition of allegorical interpretation is not as monolithic as is often supposed. Sometimes Clement expresses disagreement with a classical source and in the same breath approves of but subordinates another classical text to a scriptural source. When classical and Christian sentiments do agree, Clement often indicates both the agreement and the subordination of the classical source with great subtlety. Sometimes a classical source is taken over silently, as when Christians who quote Homer anonymously are said by Clement to "boast in the Lord" (*Paed.* 1.6.50.1) or when an unacknowledged quotation from Socrates is provided with a Christian introduction like "But our faith, being 'the light of the world' [Matt. 5.14] reproves unbelief" (*Strom.* 4.11.80.3). But while Clement does cite pagan literature anonymously (as in the passage we considered above concerning John the Baptist), he frequently cites it directly, with full attribution to specific authors and texts. Clement often indicates both the similar meaning and different authority of classical sources and Hebraic or Christian scripture simply by quoting a series of classical texts and then quietly giving scripture the last word.

In contrast, Philo seldom cites pagan literature directly, even though his readings of scripture are designed to demonstrate that the concepts of classical thought constitute the hidden meanings of scripture. This difference in approach toward classical texts is due to the different require-

ments imposed by Philo's revisionary appeal to a "first text" and Clement's appeal to a "first voice." If Moses is to turn pagan concepts into scriptural meanings, his classical precursors must be reduced to anonymity—Genesis cannot be written by Moses if it was written by Plato, and Genesis is scripture for Philo while the *Timaeus* is not, in part because Moses wrote the first and Plato the second. So Philo must take general ideas from the *Timaeus* (which he then abandons as a specifically identifiable text, along with its author) and present them as the "true meaning" of Genesis. Only when Philo has reduced the *Timaeus* and its author to a series of anonymous ideas and images can he make those ideas and images "scriptural" by proclaiming them to be scripture's underlying meaning. Quoting from the *Timaeus* with explicit attribution to Plato would only weaken Philo's revisionary strategy. In contrast, by using a divine voice rather than a specific text as the basis for revisionary reading, Clement can include direct quotations from competing literature, as well as titles of works and names of authors. He can do this precisely because the textual or authorial specificity of his precursors is irrelevant to the fact that when subjected to his revisionary reading, they express the same underlying voice or meaning. Because Clement, unlike Philo, does not make any single identifiable text the basis of his revisionary reading, all texts can keep their identities; their individual authors and their textual and historical specificity are quite secondary to their single divine author and that author's one consistent message. The difference, then, between a revisionary reading strategy based on a text and one based on a voice helps explain why Philo rarely quotes nonscriptural texts directly or cites them by title and author, while Clement fills his pages with direct quotations and explicit citations.

Clement's revisionary reading of Hebrew scripture is just as ambivalent as his reading of classical texts; once again, subordination of prior texts does not mean their complete replacement. The new song of the *logos* is the old song of the ancient psalmist. Yet the old song of the psalmist is ultimately the song of the even older *logos* who speaks through the younger psalmist (*Protr.* 1.5.2; cf. *Strom.* 6.6.49.2–3). When allegorically "discovered" in Hebrew scripture, the voice of the *logos* is thus both a unifying and a revisionary force; it brings together as a single entity the heterogeneous collection of texts that comprise Hebrew scripture, yet it subordinates those texts to its own deeper discourse and underlying logic. An especially rich example of this unification and revisionary subordination can be seen in the passage from the *Protreptikos* that follows immediately after the selection dealing with John the Baptist discussed above. Since Clement's reading of scripture is complex and often oblique, it will prove useful to have the passage before us in full, beginning with the paragraph we have already considered. Direct quotations are again underlined and identified:

Is it not absurd [*atopos*], my friends, that God always exhorts us to virtue, but we shun the benefit and delay salvation? For does not even John exhort to salvation and become altogether a hortative voice? Let us then ask him, "Who of men are you, and whence?" [Hom. *Od.* 1.170, 19.105]. He will not say "Elijah," and he will deny that he is the Christ; but he will confess: "A voice crying in [the] barren [*en erēmōi*]."[51] Who then is John? In a word, one may say: "A hortative voice of the *logos* crying in [the] barren [*en erēmōi*]." "What do you cry, O Voice? Tell us also" [*Od.* 1.10]. "Make straight the ways of the Lord" [Isa. 40.3, quoted in Matt. 3.3; Mark 1.3; Luke 3.4; John 1.23].

John is a precursor and the voice is a precursor of the *logos,* a hortative voice, preparing for salvation, a voice exhorting to the inheritance of the heavens, [a voice] through which the barren [*hē steira*][52] and [the] barren [*erēmos*] are no longer without fruit. This fecundity a voice of an angel foretold; this [voice] was a precursor of the Lord, preaching good news to [the] barren woman [*steira gynaika*] as John [preached] to the barren [*hē erēmos*].

Because of this voice of the *logos,* then, the barren [*hē steira*] has good children and the barren [*hē erēmos*] bears fruit; two voices were the precursors of the Lord, that of an angel and that of John, and they hint at the stored-up salvation, that, when this *logos* appears, we carry off, as fruit of productiveness, eternal life.

Scripture makes all this clear by referring both voices to the same thing: Let her who has not given birth listen, Let her who has not suffered birth-pangs utter a voice; for there are more children of the barren [*hē erēmos*] than of her who has a husband [*ho anēr*] [Isa. 54.1]. The angel preached to us good news {about a husband};[53] John exhorted us to recognize the cultivator [*ho geōrgos*], to seek the husband [*ho anēr*].

For one and the same is this one—the husband [*ho anēr*] of the barren [*hē steira*], the cultivator [*geōrgos*] of the barren [*hē erēmos*], the one who filled both the barren [*hē steira*] and the barren [*hē erēmos*] with divine power. For since many were the children of the woman of good race, but the Hebrew woman, once with many children, was childless because of unbelief, the barren [*hē steira*] receives the husband [*ho anēr*] and the barren [*hē erēmos*] the cultivator [*ho geōrgos*]. Then both are mothers because of the Word—one of fruits, the other of believers. But to those without belief, there yet remain both [the] barren [*steira*] and [the] barren [*erēmos*].

For this reason, John, the herald of the *logos,* exhorts [us] to become prepared for the coming of the Christ of God, and this was that which the silence of Zacharias hinted [Luke 1.20], which [silence] was awaiting fruit [in the form of a] precursor of the Christ, so that the *logos,* the light of truth, by becoming gospel, might destroy the mystic silence of the prophetic enigmas.

But if you truly desire to see God, take [to yourselves] God-worthy means of purification, not leaves of laurel and certain headbands embroidered with wool and purple, but binding [yourselves] around with righteousness, and

encircling [yourselves] with the leaves of temperance, be earnestly busy for Christ. "For I am the door," he says [John 10.9] which it is necessary for those who wish to understand God to search out and examine, that he might open the gates of the heavens for us.

For the gates of the *logos* are intellectual, to be opened by the key of faith: "No one knows God, except the Son and he to whom the Son should reveal [him]" [cf. Matt. 11.27]. And I know well that he who opened the door kept shut until now, afterwards will reveal what is within, and will show what we were not able to know before, if we had not come in through Christ, through whom alone God is beheld. (*Protr.* 1.9–10)

In this passage, Clement exploits two synonyms (*erēmos* and *steira*, which can both mean "a barren entity" but which are typically translated "wilderness" and "barren woman") to unify two scriptural verses—the Baptist's preaching in the barren wilderness (John 1.23) and the good news proclaimed by an angel to an infertile woman (Isa. 54.1). Clement claims that Isaiah refers "both voices [the Baptist's and the angel's] to the same thing" (*Protr.* 1.9.4), namely, to the single voice of the divine *logos*. However, the Septuagint version of Isaiah 54.1 does not seem to support this claim because it uses both *steira* and *erēmos* to characterize a single recipient of a single voice; it does not first speak of two different voices and then equate them, as Clement claims. Consequently, Clement restates the Septuagint version of Isaiah 54.1 in order to provide a scriptural warrant for his identification of the voice of the Baptist and the voice of the angel.[54] The two versions of Isaiah 54.1 are presented below with a summary of the basic contrast established by each.

The Septuagint Version of Isaiah 54.1

Rejoice, O barren [*steira*] who does not give birth; break forth and cry, O one who does not suffer birth-pangs: for more are the children of the barren [*erēmos*] than of her who has a husband [*hē echousa ton andra*].

Basic contrast:
1. *steira/erēmos* = "the barren," the "one who does not give birth" or "suffer birth-pangs"
2. *hē echousa ton andra* = "she who has a husband"

Clement's Version of Isaiah 54.1 (*Protr.* 1.9.4)

Let her who does not give birth listen [*akouein*]; let her who does not suffer birth-pangs break forth with a voice [*phōnē*]; for more are the children of the barren [*erēmos*] than of her who has a husband [*hē echousa ton andra*].

Basic contrast:
1. *erēmos* = "the barren," "she who does not give birth" or "suffer birth-pangs"
2. *hē echousa ton andra* = "she who has a husband"

The Septuagint version uses both *steira* and *erēmos* to denote an infertile woman, and it contrasts the promised fertility of this woman with the fertility of a married woman, of "her who has a husband." But Clement does not want Isaiah 54.1 to prove the identity of *steira* and *erēmos;* in his reading, the Baptist's preaching in the *erēmos* must remain different from the angel's message to the *steira* in order to establish the discontinuity between the old dispensation described in Hebrew scripture and the new dispensation described in the New Testament. But Clement also wants to claim that there is continuity between the two dispensations. He demonstrates this continuity not by following the Septuagint in its identification of *steira* and *erēmos* but instead by identifying the voices that speak to the *steira* and the *erēmos*. To do this, he drops *hē steira* from his paraphrase of Isaiah altogether, leaving simply "her who does not give birth." He also replaces "rejoice" with "listen" (*akouein*) and "cry out" with "break forth with a voice" (*phōnē*). The result is twofold: the first half of Clement's version of Isaiah now refers exclusively to *hē erēmos*, and the "voice" introduced in the Gospel of John's account of the Baptist is now retrojected into the Isaiah passage.

But Clement must in the end bring *hē steira* back into the passage because he has prefaced his version of Isaiah 54.1 with the claim that Isaiah refers both voices to the same thing (*Protr.* 1.9.4). He brings *hē steira* back into his reading of Isaiah by drawing on the Septuagint's contrast between "the barren" (*hē erēmos*) and "her who has a husband." In *Protreptikos* 1.9.5, Clement says that the one who will have a husband is *hē steira*, whose predicted childbearing will obviously require a husband. *Hē erēmos*, in contrast, lacks a husband but, says Clement, will receive a "cultivator" (*geōrgos*). In Clement's paraphrase of Isaiah 54.1, *hē steira* and *hē erēmos* are different (marking the discontinuity between old and new dispensations), but "the cultivator" (*ho geōrgos*) and "the husband" (*ho anēr*) are synonymous (highlighting the unity of divine revelation recorded by both testaments). He expresses their synonymy with a quick restatement: "The angel preached to us good news {about a husband}; John exhorted us to recognize the cultivator [*ho geōrgos*], *to seek the husband* [*ho anēr*]" (*Protr.* 1.9.5; my emphasis). The voice as "husband [*anēr*] filled the barren [woman] [*steira*] with divine power, and the same voice as cultivator [*geōrgos*] filled the barren [wilderness] [*erēmos*] with divine power" (*Protr.* 1.9.5). Thus, when the same voice [the *logos*] "became gospel," it broke the "mystic silence" of prophecy (*Protr.* 1.10.1)—prophecy presumably like that of Isaiah 54.1, which in Clement's reading speaks with the same voice heralded by the Baptist. The pattern of reading by which Clement unifies the texts in this selection from the *Protreptikos* thus relies on an appeal to an increasingly unmediated voice—a sequence ranging from the angel's

speech to the infertile woman, to the Baptist's speech to the infertile desert, to the final self-proclamation of the *logos* that "became gospel."

According to Clement's revisionary reading of Hebrew scripture, the voice of the *logos* expresses itself with increasing directness. The *logos* first spoke through "signs and wonders" such as the burning bush and the cloud in the wilderness because the perceptual limitations of the early Israelites demanded such a material mediation. Later on, however, the *logos* spoke more directly through Moses, Isaiah, and the rest of the "prophetic choir"—"a way of address more appealing to reason"; the last prophet, the Baptist, marks the end of this stage. Finally, the *logos* chose to speak without mediation, in the form of Jesus of Nazareth's direct address to his disciples (*Protr.* 1.8.1–3). In all three modes of expression, the same *logos* speaks to humanity the same message of exhortation and condemnation but does so in a way that clearly subordinates Hebrew scripture to the Christian dispensation. God promised to speak to Moses "mouth to mouth, and not in riddles" (Num. 12.8), but Clement announces that "it was really the Lord that was the instructor of the ancient people by Moses; but he is the instructor of the new people [the Christians] by himself, face to face" (*Paed.* 1.7.58.1).

The revisionary reading sequence of mediated/unmediated voice can also take the form of sequences that we can summarize according to their beginnings and ends: origin/goal, problem/solution, and law/gospel. Like the first pattern, these unifying patterns of reading also subordinate Hebrew scripture to Christian scripture and doctrine. Clement reads Hebrew scripture as part of a larger story of humanity's origin, its increasing spiritual perfection, and its final knowledge of God. The story begins with the creation of human beings in the divine "image and likeness" (Gen. 1.26), describes their sanctification through the incarnation and passion of the divine *logos,* and concludes with their final perfection, as the "likeness" in which they were created approaches its *telos*—the "image," that is, the *logos* (*Paed.* 1.20.98.3; cf. *Strom.* 7.10.57). Characters drawn from Hebrew scripture (e.g., Adam, Noah, Abraham, Isaac, Jacob) provide models or "types" for the increasing imitation of God that this pattern of reading enjoins (*Strom.* 2.19.98.3ff.). These characters can function as "types" for Christian perfection because they anticipate full Christian perfection by standing for Christ. Thus Isaac is a "type of Christ" (*Strom.* 1.5.31.3; cf. *Paed.* 1.5.23.1) because in his role as the intended sacrificial victim of Abraham, he is the figure God chose as "a type to us of the economy of salvation" (*Strom.* 2.5.20.2).[55] Clement uses "type" and synonymous terms to express both analogies and predictions. For example, the manna that "flowed down from heaven on the ancient Hebrews" is analogous to, and thus an apt illustration of, the spiritual nourishment provided by the *logos* (*Paed.* 1.6.41.2). This nourishment

required the *logos*'s suffering, which was earlier predicted by the analogous suffering of the innocent and righteous Abel, "the type [*typos*] of the new righteous one." When Abel was murdered, his blood reportedly cried out to God from the ground (Gen. 4.10), a remark read by Clement as a predictive type: "The blood that is the *logos* cries to God, since it intimated that the *logos* was to suffer" (*Paed.* 1.6.47.4). The figures of type, analogy, prediction, allusion, intimation, symbol, and shadow produce and reflect the origin/goal pattern according to which Clement allegorically reads Hebrew scripture. Constituting a common strategy of allegorical reading, these figures create continuity between the Hebrew text and Clement's Christian perspective while subordinating the Hebrew text by establishing the Christian perspective as Hebrew scripture's most profound meaning.

The origin/goal sequence contains within itself a subsequence marked out by problem and solution. The divine origin does not immediately lead to the divine goal because of a problem (the "fall") that must be redressed. The link between origin and goal, and the basis for the revisionary character of the origin/goal reading, was provided by the original "image and likeness" (the *logos*); the link between problem and solution is provided by the figure of the serpent—that "wicked reptile monster" (*Protr.* 1.7.4) whom the *logos* must overcome. Clement brings both sequences together, along with the mediated/unmediated voice sequence, in the following passage, which shows how the problem/solution reading strategy also subsumes Hebrew scripture within the Christian vision:

> The seducer is one and the same, he that at the beginning brought Eve down to death, now brings thither the rest of humanity. Our ally and helper, too, is one and the same—the Lord, who from the beginning gave revelations prophetically [*prophētikōs*], but now plainly [*enargōs*] calls to salvation. (*Protr.* 1.7.6)

Finally, by pointing to scripture's progression from law to gospel, Clement stresses the internal unity and consistency of revelation against the divisive hermeneutic of the Marcionites. While Marcion (d. ca. 160 c.e.) had argued in the generation before Clement that Jewish law and Christian gospel are antonyms, Clement insists that law and gospel are virtually synonymous. For Marcion, "law" denotes justice, and gospel "goodness," but Clement insists that while law and gospel are "two in name and time," they are "in power one," and are "dispensed through the Son by one God" (*Strom.* 2.6.29.2). Consequently, Clement argues that when Paul affirms that the law is "just and good" (Rom. 7.12), he uses both adjectives to characterize a single power (*Paed.* 1.8.73.3). As the creation of a single God (*Strom.* 1.27.174.3), law and gospel can never contradict one another (*Strom.* 2.23.147.2; cf. *Paed.* 3.12.87.4), and for the

same reason, the law and the prophets are in complete harmony (*Strom.* 6.15.125.3). Clement's reading of Hebrew scripture according to the law/gospel sequence thus escapes Marcionite theological dualism (justice vs. goodness) and textual dualism (the just God's "law" vs. the writings inspired by the good God, called "The Apostle" and "The Gospel"). But his reading still creates discontinuity by turning Marcionite dualism into a sequential progression and by drawing distinctions not between divine attributes (justice and goodness) or between texts (law and gospel) but between human responses (fear and love) and human communities (the old people and the new people):

> Formerly the older people had an old covenant, and the law disciplined the people with fear, and the *logos* was an angel; but to the fresh and new people has also been given a new covenant, and the *logos* has become flesh [or appeared], and fear has turned to love, and that mystic angel is born— Jesus. For this same instructor said then, "You shall fear the Lord God" [Deut. 6.2], but to us he addressed the exhortation, "You shall love the Lord your God" [Matt. 22.37]. (*Paed.* 1.7.59.1–2)

Yet this sequence of reading does not allow difference to become absolute discontinuity; although audience and time change, the voice and the work remain the same, fulfilled now by love rather than by fear (*Strom.* 4.18.113.5).

Like the evangelist John's revisionary reading of Genesis, Clement's reading has used the single discourse of the *logos,* in a variety of reading strategies, to capture the absolute origin for his own Christian hermeneutical foundation. Hebrew scripture is made to support, and defer to, the Christian claim to originality and spiritual authority, for the *logos* was at the very beginning "the teacher of all created beings" (*Strom.* 6.7.58.1). The laws of Moses are actually "the laws of the *logos*" (*hoi logikoi nomoi*) (*Paed.* 3.12.94.1). Consequently, Hebrew scripture must always yield to the hermeneutical key provided by its author, who is Christ: "The interpreter [*exēgētēs*] of the laws is the same one by whom 'the law is given'—the first interpreter of the divine commands, who unveiled [*exēgoumenos*] the bosom of the Father, the only-begotten Son" (*Strom.* 1.26.169.4). In the end, Athens must join Jerusalem in submitting to the (now Christianly specific) *logos:*

> Since the *logos* himself has come to us from heaven, we need not, I reckon, go any more in search of human learning to Athens and the rest of Greece, and to Ionia. For if we have as our teacher him that filled the universe with his holy energies in creation, salvation, beneficence, legislation, prophecy, teaching, we have the teacher from whom all instruction comes; and the whole world, with Athens and Greece, has already become the domain of the *logos.* (*Protr.* 11.112.1)

When all the world has become the Word's domain, Clement's allegorical reading has reached the limit of its revisionary extravagance.

The character of Clement's revisionary hermeneutic can be specified further by contrasting it with Philo's. Clement's and Philo's readings of Hebrew scripture share general features. Both use broad, sequential narrative patterns to unify the series of heterogeneous texts that make up the Hebrew Bible, and, in Clement's case, Christian scripture as well. For both, the sequential patterns represent a progressive divine education of humanity. But the differences between Clement's and Philo's broad patterns of reading are more striking than the similarities. Clement's Christian perspective on Hebrew scripture creates an antithetical element absent from Philo's reading. For Clement, the *logos*'s direct self-expression as Jesus of Nazareth and the texts that represent him as such provide an unassailable criterion for judging Hebrew scripture. For Philo, scripture and the one God that scripture represents stand in judgment over the world.

Yet the most telling differences between Clement's and Philo's readings of classical texts and Hebrew scripture lie not at the level of broad hermeneutical patterns, but at the more specific level of detailed readings of individual passages. Even though Clement, like Philo, reads intratextually—that is, making reference to various scriptural texts in the course of addressing one particular passage—his readings do not adhere as closely as Philo's to the lexical details of scriptural language. Indeed, the essential difference between the intratextual character of Clement's and Philo's allegorical readings can be summarized this way: Clement gives meaning control over lexical details, whereas Philo gives scripture's lexical expression control over its meaning. For example, at one point in his *Strōmateis*, Clement begins to link together three seemingly very different texts: passages from the Song of Miriam in Exodus, the *Phaedrus* allegory of the soul as a horse-drawn chariot, and the Genesis account of the attack on Joseph by his brothers. The three texts are loosely held together by a single image or metaphor of "falling," though, as we shall see, the connections become more intricate.

And when, again, it is said in the ode, For he has triumphed gloriously: the horse and his rider he has cast into the sea [Exod. 15.1, 21], the many-limbed and brutal passion, lust, with the rider mounted, who gives the reins to pleasures, he has cast into the sea, throwing them away [*apoballōn*] into the disorders of the world.

Thus also Plato, in his book on the soul [i.e., the *Phaedrus*], says that the charioteer and the horse that ran off fall down [*katapiptein*]; and so the myth hints that it was through the licentiousness of the steeds that Phaethon was thrown out [*ekpiptein*].[56]

> Indeed, it is the same with Joseph: the brothers having envied this young man, who by his knowledge was possessed of uncommon foresight, <u>stripped off the coat of many colors, and took and threw him into a pit. The pit was empty, it had no water</u> [Gen. 37.23–24], [either] rejecting the diverse knowledge stemming from the zealous man's love of learning, or, using the bare faith according to the law, they threw him into the pit which is empty of water, selling [him] into Egypt which is empty of the divine *logos*. The pit in which he was thrown was empty of knowledge, and the ingenuous young man, stripped of knowledge, naked of knowledge, seemed like his brothers. According to another meaning, the coat of many colors might be lust, moving toward a yawning gulf. (*Strom.* 5.10.52.5–53.4; with direct quotations underlined and identified)

Here Clement uses the conceptual or metaphorical notion of a falling horse and rider to link Exodus 15.1, 21 to Plato's myth of the charioteer (whom Clement identifies as Phaethon), and he reads into the Joseph story the Platonic criticism of the passions. The metaphor of falling allows Clement to move easily from Plato's myth to the story of Joseph and his coat in Genesis 37.23–24. The general metaphorical link of "falling" depends on a series of terms—*apoballein* ("to throw away"), *katapiptein* ("to throw down"), and *ekpiptein* ("to throw out"). But Clement does not take a Philonic interest in the lexical peculiarities of these words or draw specific lexical connections between them. Rather than drawing the reader's attention to the lexical expression (*lexis*) of these passages, he emphasizes the general image of "falling" that the words create. Clement next offers three possible allegorical readings of the Joseph story. The brothers may be rejecting their brother's wide-ranging knowledge; they may be putting Joseph in a state that lacks the divine *logos* because they themselves have only a bare Hebraic faith; or the coat may represent lust. None of these readings is lexically specific; Clement provides no lexical arguments to justify the identification of the coat as knowledge, beyond the implied analogy between "many colors" and "diverse" knowledge, or to characterize the faith of Joseph's brothers as "according to the law" or to describe Egypt as lacking the divine *logos*. To make this last description, Clement conflates Joseph's fall into the pit and his journey to Egypt. This conflation, suggesting the contrast of pits full of water and depths full of the *logos*, does anticipate Clement's next move, in which he will allude both to Jeremiah 2.13 (deep living springs) and to Romans 11.33 (depths of knowledge). But Clement never spells out these links, which are forged at the level of signified meaning or shared image rather than signifying expression or lexical details.

Clement then goes on to ponder the possibility of an uncovered pit as a metaphor for the depths of *gnōsis*, drawing on a legal text from Exodus, as well as on material from Isaiah, Jeremiah, and Romans:

And if one open up or hew out a pit [*lakkos*], it is said, and do not cover it, and a calf or ass should there fall in [*empiptein*], the owner of the pit shall pay the price in money, and give it to his neighbor; and the dead body shall be his [Exod. 21.33–34]. Here add that prophecy: The ox knows his owner [*kyrios*], and the ass [*onos*] his master's crib: but Israel has not understood me [Isa. 1.3]. In order, then, that none of these, who have fallen in with the knowledge [*gnōsis*] taught by you, and becoming incapable of the truth, should both disobey and fall away, it says, Be sure in the use of the *logos*, and shut up the living spring in the depth from those who approach irrationally, but offer a drink to those who have thirsted for truth [cf. Jer. 2.13]. Conceal it, then, from those who are unfit to receive the depth of knowledge [*gnōsis*] [Rom. 11.33], and so cover the pit. The owner of the pit, then, the gnostic, shall himself be punished, incurring the blame of the others' stumbling, and of being overwhelmed by the greatness of the *logos*, he himself having little share in the *logos* [*mikrologos*]; or transferring the worker into the region of contemplation, and on that account dislodging him from off-hand faith. And [he] will pay money [Exod. 21.34], rendering a reckoning, and submitting his accounts to the omnipotent will. (*Strom.* 5.10.53.5–54.4; with direct quotations underlined and identified)

With the words "pit" (*lakkos*) and "to fall in" (here *empiptein*), Exodus 21.33–34 furnishes Clement with two implicit links with what has preceded, as well as introducing the thematic notion of the necessity of covering up open pits, which Clement will interpret allegorically as a recommendation not to reveal deep *gnōsis* to those for whom it would be inappropriate. The "prophecy" of Isaiah 1.3, with its terms "ass" (*onos*) and "owner" (*kyrios*) also offers strong lexical links with the preceding Exodus quotation. Philo, we might imagine, would have made much of the lexical connections here; he would probably have gone out of his way to show readers that these different texts should be read together because of shared lexical details. But Clement says nothing of these lexical matters, instead moving directly to his allegorical reading; he is interested in theme, not linguistic distinctions. In referring to the "living spring," Clement alludes to Jeremiah 2.13—"For my people have committed two faults, and evil ones: they have forsaken me, the spring of water of life [*pēgē hydatos zōēs*], and hewn out for themselves broken cisterns [or pits] [*lakkoi*], which will not be able to hold water"—but he paraphrases rather than quotes the passage probably because he wants to anticipate the phrase from Romans 11.33 "the depth of knowledge" (*bathos tēs gnōsis*) by the phrase *en bathei*. Clement does not spell out (or even allude to) the specific lexical links that the Jeremiah text happens to afford by its use of *lakkos;* instead, he turns this text, which describes two deficient responses to God, into a characterization of how the Gnostic teacher should respond to two different sorts of learners: those who "approach irrationally" and those who "have thirsted for truth." He then turns to a phrase from

Romans 11.33: "Conceal it, then, from those who are unfit to receive 'the depth of knowledge,' and so cover the pit." Clement finally returns to the Exodus text, explicitly identifying the "owner of the pit" as the Gnostic teacher who will either be punished for failing to teach others or will help his disciple to exchange mere faith for higher *gnōsis*. This teacher will be judged on his teaching ability, which is what "paying money" means. Once again, Clement has the opportunity to make the lexical links explicit by emphasizing the repeated terms (*onos, kyrios, empiptein, bathos, lakkos*), but he does not comment on any of them. And in several cases, a text that could furnish explicit lexical links is not actually quoted but only paraphrased.

Clement finally moves to a grand summation of the essential message his reading of scripture has produced:

> This, then, is the type of the law and the prophets which were until John [Matt. 11.13; Luke 16.16]; while he, though speaking more perspicuously—as no longer prophesying, but pointing out as now present the one who was proclaimed symbolically from the beginning—nevertheless said, I am not worthy to loose the latchet of the Lord's shoe [Mark 1.7; Luke 3.16; John 1.27]. For he confesses that he is not worthy to baptize so great a power; for it behooves those who purify others to free the soul from the body and its sins, as the foot from the thong. Perhaps also this signified the final, the immediate, exercise of the Savior's power toward us by his presence, [formerly] concealed in the enigma of prophecy. For he [the Baptist], by pointing out to sight him that had been prophesied of and indicating the presence which had come walking forth into the light, loosed the latchet of the oracles of the [old] economy, by unveiling the meaning of the symbols. (*Strom.* 5.10.55.1–3; with direct quotations underlined and identified)

Clement has already laid the groundwork for this interpretation of the role of John the Baptist and the revisionary reading of Hebrew scripture that underlies it by inserting the term "*logos*" at various points in the preceding discussion: Egypt is "empty of the divine *logos*," and the Gnostic is both exhorted to "be sure in the use of the *logos*" and cautioned not to be "overwhelmed by the greatness of the *logos*" or to be found "having little share in the *logos*." Clement has also already subordinated Hebraic religion by labeling it a "bare faith according to the law." But his decisive revisionary move occurs when he announces that "this [*houtos*], then, is the type of law and prophets [*ho typos nomou kai prophētōn*] which were until John." The antecedent of *houtos* is vague—it appears to be not one particular text but the entire preceding cluster of texts and interpretations (although it does seem that Exodus 21.33–34 is the passage that unifies the texts and readings surrounding it). John himself occupies an ambiguous intermediate position: he is one of the prophets, yet he no longer

prophesies but instead points out the now-present *logos*, saying symbolically: "I am not worthy to loose the latchet of the Lord's shoe."
Clement offers two allegorical readings of this statement. On the one
hand, the Baptist may be explaining his inferior status and his incomplete
purification (he has not yet loosened his own foot from his own shoe, that
is, his soul from his body). On the other, by pointing out the now-present
logos, he in fact figuratively loosens the latchet of the Lord's shoe (he
unveils Hebrew prophecy—the "oracles of the [old] economy"), for the
underlying meaning of those oracles is now present, no longer "concealed
in prophecy."

The passage we have just examined reveals that Clement does not rely
on lexical details of scripture to formulate his revisionary readings. Instead, he quotes or alludes to texts that he then reads in light of the fully
present metatextual divine voice. Indeed, the entire selection we have
examined was the product of a reading of texts from the perspective of
this metatextual meaning. Consequently, general concepts and images,
rather than specific words and lexical particularities, provide the connections by which the logic of the passage proceeds. Although Clement
sometimes associates these linked concepts or images with shared or
repeated terms, he tends not to focus on the lexical details so much as on
the meanings they signify. For Clement, coherence at the allegorical level
of meaning is necessary, but there is no need to display explicit coherence
at the level of lexical expression. Consequently, Clement's intratextuality
is quite different from Philo's. When Philo uses the same scriptural texts
that Clement uses in this selection, he carefully distinguishes "rider"
(Exod. 15.21) from "horseman," thus demonstrating the kind of specific
concern for lexical detail absent from Clement's reading. Philo further
uses that distinction to resolve a potential conflict with another text (Gen.
49.17–18) (*Agr.* 94). Moreover, Philo's reading of Exodus 15.1, 21 occurs
in the midst of a lexically governed intratextual discussion leading to
readings of Deuteronomy 20.1 (*Agr.* 78) and 17.15f. (*Agr.* 84). As for the
Joseph episode, Philo is led to it in the course of an analysis of the Cain
and Abel story and focuses on the many-colored coat as a symbol of
Joseph's shifty political character (*Det.* 6ff.). Philo also uses Jeremiah 2.13
as a culmination of a series of texts dealing with "springs." He comments
on this text in connection with the concept of "depth of knowledge"
(*bathys epistēmas*), contrasting the wells of the wise Abraham and Isaac
(Gen. 21.30, 26.18) with the pits dug by the foolish (*Fug.* 200). Clement
almost certainly borrowed a great deal from Philo's discussion, for Philo
also uses Jeremiah 2.13 to characterize teachers and students. But though
Clement borrowed the general idea, he shows none of Philo's explicit
interest in the specific words of the text; he ignores, for example, the
noun "pit" and the adjective "broken."

The difference in the intratextual character of Philo's and Clement's allegorical reading not surprisingly reflects the principal difference in the very basis of their revisionary readings—the difference between a divine text and divine speech. Recourse to an original text imposes the demand for lexically specific correlations of hidden meaning and scriptural text. In contrast, reliance on divine speech relieves one from attending to specific lexical details, as long as the coherence of more general meaning can be established. This difference also accounts for the different literary forms of Clement's and Philo's interpretative writings. Their own genre choices reflect fundamental differences in their ways of reading texts as well as in the status of their own interpretative comments. Simply put, Philo clearly distinguishes text and commentary, whereas Clement often blurs text and commentary, though—unlike Valentinus—he does not erase the distinction between them altogether. Although Philo gives his treatises thematic titles, he follows a regular sequential path through the Pentateuch, quoting passages according to their scriptural sequence, commenting on them deliberately, and resolving interpretative problems. Such problems often demand intratextual solutions and lengthy digressions, but Philo usually returns to the sequential order of the Pentateuch and preserves the distinction between the sacred text and his comments on it. In contrast, Clement titles his own treatises for the divine speaker who speaks in both scripture and his own interpretations. His writings are consequently designed to augment scripture as further expressions of the ongoing educative speech of the *logos:*

> Eagerly desiring, then, to perfect us by a gradation conducive to salvation, suited for efficacious training [*paideusis*], a beautiful arrangement is observed by the philanthropic *logos,* who first exhorts [*protrepōn*] [in Clement's *Protreptikos*], then trains [*paidagōgōn*] [in the *Paedagōgos*], and finally teaches [*ekdidaskōn*] [or would have, had Clement written the projected *Didaskalos*]. (*Paed.* 1.3.3)

The major interpretative text that stands outside this scheme is given a common, uninformative genre category as title (*Strōmateis,* i.e., "Carpets" or "Miscellanies"). In all of these writings, Clement does not put scriptural quotations on display as specific lemmata that will be commented on; he quotes, paraphrases, or alludes to scripture and other texts, often without introductory formulas. By preserving such echoes of the Valentinian mode of allegorical interpretation through creative allegorical composition, Clement has taken a large step away from the Philonic text-commentary mode of reading. But his preservation of the Philonic respect for canonicity points toward his final domestication of radical Christian *gnōsis.*

SECTARIANISM AND DOMESTICATED *GNŌSIS*

Little is known of the details of Clement's teaching career. The standard account, drawn largely from remarks by Eusebius and by Clement himself, goes something like this. Out of the obscurity of late second-century Alexandrian Christianity emerged the figure of Pantaenus, a Sicilian Stoic philosopher and Christian convert. Pantaenus came to Alexandria, where by 180 c.e. he was directing the so-called Catechetical School—an ecclesiastically sponsored institution devoted to preparing candidates for Christian baptism by teaching them the basic tenets of the Christian faith. Pantaenus died around 200 c.e., but not before he had been discovered by Clement, who first became his student, later collaborated with him in the work of catechesis, and finally took over leadership of the school after his death. Clement ran the Catechetical School until persecution forced him to leave the city. After the persecution, the school was reopened under the leadership of the young Origen.[57]

If we are to arrive at an accurate understanding of the function of Clement's allegorical interpretation within his specific social and cultural context, we need to know whether the preceding account of his role as head of an official Alexandrian catechetical school is true. Although the standard account is routinely repeated by scholars, there are many reasons to doubt it. Indeed, it is not too much to say that the standard account may be systematically misleading. Much of it is based on remarks by the early fourth-century church historian and imperial propagandist Eusebius of Caesarea in his *Ecclesiastical History*.[58] But we must approach Eusebius's version of this matter (as indeed of all matters about which he writes) with considerable suspicion because the apologetic goal of his *History* is to demonstrate the continuity of "authentic," "orthodox" Christianity in all regions of the empire.[59] He consequently intended his lists of successions, whether of bishops or teachers, to prove that the deposit of faith delivered from Jesus to the apostles had in turn been transmitted in its purity by the apostles to subsequent, authorized teachers and leaders.[60] Precisely such a concern for the apostolic origin and pure transmission of tradition informs Eusebius's account of the Marcan founding of the Alexandrian church and his list of otherwise-unknown bishops stretching from the evangelist Mark to Demetrius. The benign, uncomplicated succession of directors of the Catechetical School from Pantaenus, to Clement, to Origen, and beyond serves a similar apologetic purpose.[61] Indeed, Eusebius clearly wishes to offer readers two complete and mutually supportive lines of Christian authority: an apostolic succession of Alexandrian bishops and a teaching succession of catechetical directors under episcopal sponsorship. How much of this should we believe?

It is clear from the hesitations, imprecisions, and frankly admitted

secondhand character of Eusebius's account that the archives at Caesarea provided the church historian with exceedingly little documentary evidence for the career of Pantaenus.[62] In fact, most of what Eusebius reports is rumor or is drawn from Clement's works. When all the available evidence, from Clement as well as from Eusebius, is taken together, further disconcerting features emerge. The accuracy of Eusebius's claim that Origen was Clement's pupil (*Hist. eccl.* 6.6.1) is called into question by the fact that Origen never refers in any of his writings to Clement, either as his own teacher or as head of the Catechetical School. In the letter of Origen that Eusebius quotes, in which Origen appeals to the precedent of Pantaenus to legitimate his own interest in pagan philosophy and heretical thought, Origen gives no indication that he knows of Pantaenus heading such a school.[63] While Eusebius claims explicitly that Clement succeeded Pantaenus, becoming a catechist in Alexandria (*Hist. eccl.* 6.6.1), elsewhere he simply says that Pantaenus "had charge of the life of the faithful" (*hēgeito . . . tēs tōn pistōn autothi diastribēs*), without explicitly mentioning catechumens (*Hist. eccl.* 5.10.1). Despite the conclusion drawn by most modern scholars, Clement does not identify the "Sicilian bee" he discovered in Egypt as Pantaenus, and elsewhere he makes it clear that there were many other teachers or "elders" from whom he received important esoteric Christian teachings.[64] Moreover, even a cursory reading reveals Clement's works not to be presentations of the rudiments of the faith for those seeking baptism, but speculative discussions of the inner, esoteric meaning of the faith for those seeking higher levels of spiritual perfection; the title of a lost work (*Exhortation to Endurance or To the Recently Baptized*) also suggests that postbaptismal training was Clement's concern.

Some scenario other than the standard account is needed if we are not simply to ignore the contradictions and inconsistencies in the historical record. The following account, though necessarily hypothetical, seems to accord better with the available evidence. Pantaenus, a Stoic philosopher, taught in Alexandria as a free-lance intellectual, gathering around him students—pagan, Christian, Jewish—who were attracted by the force of his ideas and interpretations. Although apparently a Christian, Pantaenus never received any official endorsement of his teaching from the Alexandrian bishop. Of course, the bishop's church must have had some sort of procedure for teaching inquirers the rudiments of the faith and inducting them into the community, but this task was performed by persons whose names have not been preserved. Despite Eusebius's wishful thinking, Pantaenus was never put in charge of such a catechetical institution. We know the name of only one of Pantaenus's disciples—Clement, who came to him not to be converted but to learn esoteric Christian philosophy and hermeneutics. Clement then followed in the

footsteps of his teacher (as Basilides had followed Glaucias, Valentinus had followed Theudas, and Justin Martyr had followed a series of teachers; see *Dial.* 2), "opening his own school"—that is to say, attracting students whom he instructed in the traditions of the "elder" Pantaenus.[65] Like Pantaenus, Clement received no institutional, ecclesiastical support for his teaching activity, and when persecution descended upon the city near the turn of the century, he left—and his "school" disappeared with him.

What relationship would such independent schools (i.e., informal clusters of disciples and teachers) have had to the formally constituted church of Alexandria? The relationship appears loose, flexible, and variable— ranging from the sort of *ecclesiola in ecclesia* of Valentinian Christians to the more marginalized, sectarian groups that followed shadowy figures like Carpocrates. Like the Valentinian Christians, Clement's followers were apparently members of the episcopally supervised church of Alexandria. At least Clement gives no indication that he taught and wrote for members of any church other than the one headed by Demetrius. But although Clement was fully aware and implicitly supportive of the emerging ecclesiastical establishment, he seems to have remained independent of that establishment in his teaching. He speaks of the orders of bishop, priest, and deacon but rarely mentions the bishops and their functionaries, and he makes no allusion at all to the bishop of Alexandria—despite the fact that Demetrius was becoming a powerful presence at the very moment when Clement was at the height of his Alexandrian career.[66]

Given this account of Pantaenus and Clement as independent, freelance Christian intellectuals formally unconnected with "official" Christianity as it was increasingly coming to be consolidated in Alexandria, what can be said of the Catechetical School that Origen made famous? If Clement's flight to Cappadocia can be taken as representative, the Severan persecutions had probably decimated the ad hoc groups attached to such teachers. Recognizing the need for a more vigorous, organized Christian indoctrination that would help fortify church members and insure institutional stability and continuity in perilous times, Demetrius commissioned the charismatic, heroic, near martyr Origen to take over catechetical instruction, which had previously been under the leadership of unknown Christian priests.[67] Later, Origen reorganized the modest Catechetical School into something much grander, giving it a "second stage" of higher Christian philosophy to which he devoted all his energies, having handed over the first stage of rudimentary instruction to Herakles. Subsequent developments revealed that Origen was unwilling to tailor both his personal behavior and his teaching to Demetrius's increasingly narrow and inflexible institutional requirements, and he was forced to move his school to Caesarea.

If, then, Clement and his teacher Pantaenus were not connected with the Catechetical School, even in its early stages, as Eusebius's tendentious historiography would have it, we should think of Clement in much the same way as we thought of Valentinus—as an independent teacher in loose relation to the Christian church in Alexandria, attracting students who sought to learn a higher Christian knowledge. The difference is that while Clement wanted to claim for himself the esoteric insights of Christian *gnōsis*, he also wanted to tie these insights to his own preferred version of Christianity, of which Demetrius was the official leader. The result is a domesticated *gnōsis* turned to institutional service.[68] While Clement was not the official teaching arm of Demetrius's church, he did not oppose the bishop and was undoubtedly a recognized and admired teacher of an especially philosophical version of the Christianity that Demetrius represented. There is no reason to think that Clement was not in Demetrius's church on Sundays, yet it is also likely that he taught in a variety of other contexts. We are left with the strong impression that his teaching took place on the margins of the Alexandrian church rather than at its center, where Eusebius would like us to see it. Clement carries out his interpretative activity precisely in the midst of a tension between the emerging church led by Demetrius and the attractions of a more speculative, meditative, spiritual *gnōsis*, possibly bequeathed to him by Pantaenus, but increasingly claimed by groups at odds with Demetrian Christianity.

Consequently, the tensions registered by Clement's revisionary reading of classical and Hebraic precursors were not solely literary. Clement's own Christian community confronted internal dissension from both orthodox fideists and speculative intellectuals, as well as external criticism from other Christian groups in Alexandria. Not surprisingly, Clement's revisionary readings preserve echoes of particular social struggles between Clement's own group and other Christian groups in Alexandria, as he sought to define and defend the distinctive boundaries and internal cohesiveness of his own religious group. We have already seen how Clement's revisionary reading seizes the high ground of absolute priority; this ground was social as well as literary. The priority of the *logos* that was "in the beginning" (*en archēi*, John 1.1) is matched by the priority of Clement's social group, the "original church" (*hē ex archēs ekklēsia*). Assuming "the high antiquity and perfect truth" of his church and following the precedent well established by Justin and Numenius, Clement declares that "the later sects, and those yet subsequent to them in time, were new inventions falsified [from the truth]" (*Strom.* 7.17.107.2). Clement thus extends his revisionary reading of classical and Hebraic literature to a "reading" of contemporary competing Christian groups, subordinating them to his own community. For example, Clement argues that just as Plato plagiarized from Moses, who in turn received all his wisdom from the (Chris-

tian) *logos,* so Marcion, leader of the Marcionite Christians, took his confused doctrines from Plato, whom he misunderstood (*Strom.* 3.3.21.2).

Clement is thus "reading" not so much texts as persons and groups in light of their authoritative texts. Just as he focuses on voice rather than text, so he emphasizes persons and groups rather than collections of sacred texts. Isaiah had written: "I have given thee for a covenant of the nations to establish the earth, and to cause to inherit the desert heritages; saying to them that are in bonds, Go forth; and bidding them that are in darkness, show themselves" (Isa. 49.8–9, LXX). Clement reads this oracle allegorically: those in bonds are the Jews, those in darkness the Greek idolaters (*Strom.* 6.6.44.3). These two groups are now displaced by a new group—the Christians. Yet the Christian group is not a different race of humanity; it is composed of former members of the other two groups (who were thus proto-Christians). But those groups have now been superseded:

> He made a new covenant with us; for what belongs to the Greeks and the Jews is old. But we, who worship him in a new way, in the third form, are Christians. For clearly, as I think, he showed that the one and only God was known by the Greeks in a Gentile way [*ethnikōs*], by the Jews in a Jewish way [*Ioudaikōs*], and in a new and spiritual way [*pneumatikōs*] by us. (*Strom.* 6.5.41.6–7)

This third group "is made [by the *logos*] out of the two [the Jew and the Greek] into a new person [cf. Eph. 2.15] in which he walks and dwells, in the church itself," and "the law, the prophets, and also the gospel were brought together in Christ's name into a single knowledge [*gnōsis*]" (*Strom.* 3.10.70.2–3).

As the source of Clement's revisionary reading of texts, the divine *logos* becomes for Clement a social matter because he is certain that the *logos* not only speaks through texts but entered the social order in definitive form as Jesus of Nazareth. As incarnate divine voice, Jesus uttered the message of God; some of his utterances were heard and recorded by the apostles in writings that comprise the New Testament, some were recorded in other writings, and some were so secret that the apostles transmitted them only by word of mouth. According to Clement, those who are able to read the written records of the living *logos* correctly are those who have access to this oral apostolic transmission of Jesus' authentic teaching. Clement argues that his opponents, "the sectarians," are cut off from this authentic apostolic tradition. Jesus, he observes, completed his teaching in the middle of the reign of Tiberius; the teaching of the apostles ended with Paul's ministry in the reign of Nero. It was only subsequently, beginning in the age of Hadrian, that Basilides, Valentinus, Marcion, and other "sectarians" arose. Thus Clement can conclude that "the human assem-

blies which [the sectarians] held were posterior to the catholic church" (*Strom.* 7.17.106.3). In response, the sectarians also sought to establish apostolic contact with the presence of the incarnate *logos*. We have already noted that the Basilideans claimed that Basilides was taught by Glaucias, the "interpreter of Peter"; and the Valentinians claimed that their leader was a "hearer of Theudas, a pupil of Paul" (*Strom.* 7.17.106.4). The struggle for apostolic foundation is one form assumed by the hermeneutical struggle for temporal priority and spiritual authority. But Clement insists that his opponents do not repeat ancient apostolic truths but fabricate their own "wisdom" out of their fertile imaginations. Denied any original access to truth, Christian sectarians are all condemned by Clement as perversely imaginative. At best, they distort insights plagiarized from Greek or Hebrew precursors or from Clement's "original" or "catholic" church.

Clement can use allegorical readings of scripture to gain leverage in this social struggle both with sectarians and those who, in rejecting them, unfairly reject philosophy. Clement is anxious to defend philosophy (and his own use of it) as an advantageous weapon to use against the sectarians. Fortunately, the divine *logos* anticipated the problem when it uttered verses from Proverbs, as Clement explains:

As if making comparison of those addicted to philosophy with those called sectarians, the *logos* most clearly says: Better is a friend that is near, than a brother that dwells afar off [Prov. 27.10]. And he who relies on falsehoods, feeds on the winds, and pursues winged birds [Prov. 9.12a]. I do not think that philosophy directly declares the *logos*, although in many instances philosophy attempts, and persuasively teaches us, probable arguments; but it assails the sects. Accordingly it is added: For he has forsaken the ways of his own vineyard, and wandered in the tracks of his own husbandry [Prov. 9.12b]. Such are the sects which deserted the original church. Now he who has fallen into a sect passes through an arid wilderness [Prov. 9.12c], abandoning the only true God, destitute of God, seeking waterless water, reaching an uninhabited and thirsty land, collecting sterility with his hands [Prov. 9.12c]. And those destitute of prudence [Prov. 9.16], that is, those involved in sects, I enjoin, remarks Wisdom, saying, Touch sweetly stolen bread and the sweet water of theft [Prov. 9.17]; the scripture manifestly applying the terms bread and water to nothing else but to those sects, which employ bread and water in the oblation, not according to the norm of the church. For there are those who celebrate the eucharist with mere water. But begone, stay not in her place [Prov. 9.18a]: "place" is the synagogue, not the church. He uses "place" homonymously. Then he subjoins: For so shall you pass through the water of another [Prov. 9.18b]; reckoning sectarian baptism not proper and true water. And you shall pass over another's river [Prov. 9.18b], that rushes along and sweeps down to the sea; into which he is cast who, having diverged from the stability which is according to truth,

rushes back into the heathenish and tumultuous waves of life. (*Strom.* 1.19.95.4–96.4; with direct quotations underlined and identified)

Clement argues that through the text of Proverbs the divine *logos* proclaims philosophy to be a "friend" who is "near" Clement's group, while noting that other groups, although "brothers," are "far away." Clement thus gives the words "friend" and "brother" allegorical meanings in order to turn the contemporary social struggle between his group and competing groups into the underlying meaning of the scriptural text. In Clement's reading, Proverbs uses the words "bread" and "water" to condemn the sectarian eucharist and the phrase "another water" to disparage their baptismal ceremonies. The centrality of liturgical behavior (the rituals of eucharist and baptism) in the passage quoted above shows that Clement is indeed contrasting different Christian social groups rather than merely different points of view. He contrasts the liturgical practices of these other groups with the practices of his own group, practices that he sums up under the invidious rubric of "the norm of the church" (*ho kanōn tēs ekklēsias*). Clement does not go into much detail about these alternative liturgical practices, though he clearly implies that the competing groups do not use wine in their eucharistic celebration (probably as a result of ascetic beliefs) and have their own baptismal ceremony (recall our discussion of Valentinian baptism at the end of the preceding chapter). He refers at one point to the sectarian "agape, falsely so called" (*Strom.* 7.16.98.2) and notes that "the followers of Basilides hold the day of his [Jesus'] baptism as a festival, spending the night before in reading" (*Strom.* 1.21.146.1).

Read allegorically, Proverbs is also relevant to the tensions within Clement's own community. Clement argues that the text distinguishes philosophy from heresy, condemning only the latter. He makes this point both to reassure "orthodox" fideists within his own group who are scornful of philosophy and to placate intellectuals within his group who are repelled by the obscurantist fideists and attracted to the competing groups who advocated a more enlightened Christianity.[69] The social conflict between these groups and Clement's group may have been fought out exegetically on the field of Proverbs 9.18a. Clement insists that the word "place" in "begone, stay not in her place" means the synagogue, not the church (i.e., his own group). He uses this reading against his opponents, who apparently read this text as a divine injunction to depart or keep away from Clement's group. In contrast, Clement argues that the text means that one should leave Judaism and join his own Christian community.

Of course, "place" is semantically indeterminate and is open to both readings, as well as to countless others. Although an allegorical reading

may help one reader overcome other interpretations by determining what the text will mean despite its lexical details or "customary" meaning, when the community of allegorical readers is itself multiple, as was the Christian community in late second-century Alexandria, allegorical readings may prove considerably less persuasive. With no commonly acknowledged "literal sense," the various competing communities of allegorical readers strive to sustain their own, true "literal" senses, namely, their own preferred allegorical readings. Indeed, in opposing his allegorically reading opponents (principally Valentinians and Basilideans), Clement is forced to appeal to something other than his own allegorical readings. The need to define and protect group boundaries forces Clement to read more "intratextually" than his essential appeal to an underlying voice might demand, and thus brings his hermeneutic closer to Philo's than to Valentinus's.

Clement's intratextual references generally serve the various patterns of reading discussed earlier. He attacks competing Christian groups for failing to read according to these patterns—for arbitrarily selecting texts from the prophets and combining them in inappropriate ways (*Strom.* 3.4.38.1).[70] Clement argues further that in treating scripture in such a cavalier manner, his opponents fail to acknowledge the variety of rhetorical modes employed by the divine *logos*. For example, adding the phrase "the shameful" before "God," they falsely understand the expression of the prophet Malachi ("They resisted God and were saved," Mal. 3.15) to be an injunction to avoid the malevolent creator God or craftsman. Clement argues first that even if the text did have the adjective "shameful" (it does not), it would refer to the devil, not to God (*Strom.* 3.4.38.3). The problem in this case, as Clement sees it, is that his opponents do not recognize that a prophetic statement is not always a direct message from God. A prophet may sometimes pick up an expression used by others and reply to it, as Malachi has done. Those who spoke the words quoted by Malachi were complaining because other nations were not punished for their transgressions, while they alone were punished (*Strom.* 3.4.38.4). Hence, they say indignantly that the others were saved even though they resisted God. To help make this reading stick, Clement adds that Jeremiah raised a similar complaint: "Why is it that the way of the ungodly prospers?" (Jer. 12.1) (*Strom.* 3.4.38.4). Using interpretation for social polemic has thus led Clement to bolster one passage of scripture with another, but this other reference is appropriate not because of the kind of shared lexical detail Philo might have discovered, but because the *logos* speaks a similar message through both prophets in the same rhetorical mode.

Clement often directs the results of his revisionary reading of Hebraic texts against the readings of his Christian competitors. For example, some of his opponents used Isaiah 40.6–8 to prove that the created order, and

especially the human body, is despicable: "All flesh is grass, and all the glory of man as the flower of grass; the grass is withered, and the flower has fallen; but the word of the Lord abides forever." In response, Clement invokes another text of Hebrew scripture (Jer. 13.24–27), which he interprets by two Pauline texts (2 Cor. 10.2 and 1 Cor. 3.3), arguing that the three texts provide the proper interpretation of the Isaiah passage, which contradicts the sectarian reading:

> And I scattered them like dry sticks, that are made to fly by the wind into the desert. This is the lot and portion of your disobedience, says the Lord. As you have forgotten me, and have trusted in lies, so will I discover your hinder parts to your face; and your disgrace shall be seen, your adultery, and your neighing and so on [Jer. 13.24–27]. For "the flower of grass" and "walking after the flesh" [2 Cor. 10.2] and "being carnal" [1 Cor. 3.3], according to the apostle, are those who are in their sins. The soul of man is confessedly the better part of man, and the body the inferior. But neither is the soul good by nature, nor, on the other hand, is the body bad by nature. (*Strom.* 4.26.163.5–164.3; with direct quotations underlined and identified)

The "withered grass" of Isaiah is echoed by the "dry sticks" of Jeremiah, which Jeremiah interprets as a penalty for disobedience. Then Clement uses Paul to give further moral import to the "flesh" of Isaiah (in "walking after the flesh"), and he links the disobedience of Jeremiah to the Pauline phrases, saying that the Pauline phrase (and the now-linked prophetic expressions of Isaiah and Jeremiah) refer to "those who are in their sins." Thus Clement uses Paul to interpret both texts of Hebrew scripture and to refute a sectarian reading of the Isaiah text. What Clement's opponents attribute to nature is, as a result of Clement's reading, attributed to human will. Clement's revisionary reading of Hebrew scripture thus functions socially to refute another Christian group's alternative reading.

Clement and his opponents also use scripture to debate the appropriateness of marriage. Clement's reading of a gospel saying shows how competing allegorical readings provided warrants for alternative social practices and also how allegorical readings that lack the sort of close links with lexical expression that Philo sought to establish must be sustained by the sheer will of their proponents. In Matthew's Gospel, Jesus says that he will be present wherever two or three are gathered in his name (Matt. 18.20). Clement argues that "three" refers to husband, wife, and child, making the point with the help of Proverbs 19.14 (*Strom.* 3.10.68.1).[71] Clement adds, however, that Paul's injunction in 1 Corinthians 7.8 for an unmarried man to remain unmarried is also valid (*Strom.* 3.10.68.2). He directs his reading of the gospel saying against those who believe the material world to be the product of an inferior deity and who conclude that marriage and childbearing ought to be avoided. They say that the

"two or three" of Matthew 18.20 indicates plurality, which is the domain of the inferior creator god who is linked with marriage; the Pauline text, indicating the unity of a single man, points to the Savior who is the Son of the good God (*Strom.* 3.10.68.3). Clement rejects this reading, insisting that the same God, through the Son, is with both the family and the single ascetic.

Analysis of specific lexical expressions plays almost no role in this dispute. In the absence of a commitment like Philo's to the authority of lexical expression, competing allegorical readings in the Alexandrian Christian communities cannot be adjudicated on textual grounds. Clement must simply assert that his reading is correct. Such an assertion governs his reading of an interchange in the *Gospel of the Egyptians* between Salome and Jesus. Salome asks Jesus: "How long shall death hold sway?" and Jesus responds: "As long as you women bear children." Clement's opponents read this interchange as a warrant for rejecting marriage and childbearing, but Clement insists that Salome's words "do not imply that this life is evil and the creation bad, and [Jesus'] reply only teaches the ordinary course of nature. For birth is invariably followed by death" (*Strom.* 3.6.45.3). But Clement offers no textual argument; he simply asserts the validity of his own reading.

The precariousness of Clement's allegorical strategy for confronting competing allegorical readings can be seen when Clement complains that the sectarians subvert the meaning of scripture by changing the tone of their voice and by relocating accents and marks of punctuation (*Strom.* 3.4.39.2). This charge looks like special pleading when we observe that Clement relies at one point on a debatable placement of a strong pause in order to make a passage from Paul (1 Cor. 3.2) agree with one in Exodus (Exod. 3.8) (*Paed.* 1.6.35.1–3). The more one refuses to acknowledge the lexical constraints of a text (its textuality), the more difficult it becomes to defend one's readings as authentic interpretations of the text rather than idiosyncratic exercises in personal imagination. However, Clement still maintains a tenuous distinction between text and commentary, despite blurring the lines between them, because he wants to convince readers that the interpretations he offers do in fact reveal scripture's authentic meaning. He thus attacks his competitors not for their false meanings as such, but for imposing those essentially alien meanings on the text, thus perverting the text's "true" meaning:

> [The sectarians] will not make use of all the scriptures, and then they will not quote them entire, nor as the body and texture [*to hyphos*] of prophecy prescribe. But selecting ambiguous expressions [*ta amphibolōs eirēmena*], they wrest them to their own opinions, gathering a few expressions here and there; not looking to the meaning [*to sēmainomenon*], but making use of the

mere expression [*psilēi . . . tēi lexei*]. For in almost all the quotations they make, you will find that they attend to the words alone [*ta onomata mona*], while they alter the meanings [*ta sēmainomena*]; neither having knowledge, as they claim, nor using the quotations they adduce according to their proper nature. (*Strom.* 7.16.96.1–3)

But this characterization fits Clement as well as his competitors; he is as selective in his use of the text of scripture as are his opponents. His reference to "the body and texture" of scripture is simply an implicit appeal to the various revisionary patterns of reading discussed above, not to the "neutral" lexical details of the text.

All of this is not to say that Clement and his opponents were unaware of the Alexandrian philological tradition, with its concern for the textual integrity of interpretation. Indeed, there is little doubt that by the second half of the second century c.e., the church of Alexandria possessed its own scriptorium dedicated to producing the best possible copies of scripture. This scriptorium would certainly have been aware of the long tradition of Alexandrian editorial techniques. When Origen became a church leader in the early third century, he brought with him a complete mastery of the Alexandrian philological tradition.[72] And Origen merely represented the culmination of a tradition of Christian appropriation of features of Alexandrian philology, a tradition stretching back well before Clement.[73] For example, Clement's teacher Pantaenus had used philological terms in his *Hypomnēmata* or commentaries on the prophets (as well as borrowing the genre of *hypomnēmata* itself from the Alexandrian grammarians).[74] Clement also thought of his *Strōmateis* as *hypomnēmata*—in the sense of a Platonic *pharmakon* or *aide-mémoire* rather than interpretative exegesis (he thinks of his work as "memoranda [*hypomnēmata*] . . . stored up against old age, as a remedy against forgetfulness [*lēthēs pharmakon*]" (*Strom.* 1.1.11.1). Indeed, the full title of his work is *Tōn kata tēn alēthē philosophian gnōstikōn hypomnēmatōn strōmateis*, "Patchwork of the Gnostic Memoranda According to the True Philosophy." Clement's opponents also adopted the genres of the Alexandrian editorial and interpretative tradition. Basilides wrote many volumes of *Exēgētika* on scripture, and several generations later, the Valentinian Herakleon compiled his own scriptural *Hypomnēmata*.[75] In Rome, Marcion also apparently presented himself in the guise of a Greek literary critic (*kritikos*), and Alexandrian editorial techniques provided the models for the Marcionite prologue and chapter headings.[76]

Naturally, all this critical display provided opportunity for criticism. Clement and other church leaders ridiculed their opponents for philological pretensions and interpretative distortions. Clement pours general scorn upon all who are more interested in dividing words than divining the truth of God:

Inflated with this art of theirs, the wretched sophists, babbling away in their own jargon; toiling their whole life about the division of names and the nature of the composition and conjunction of sentences, show themselves greater chatterers than turtle-doves; scratching and tickling, not in a manly way, in my opinion, the ears of those who wish to be tickled . . . just as in old shoes, when all the rest is worn and is falling to pieces, and the tongue alone remains. (*Strom.* 1.3.22.4–5)

Clement's polemic against "sophists" applies not simply to pagan linguistic philosophers or philologists, but also to Christian sectarians: the biblical reference to "vain talkers and deceivers" (Titus 1.10) applies to all "wranglers, whether they follow the sects, or practice miserable dialectic arts" (*Strom.* 1.8.41.2). Similarly, the Roman bishop Hippolytus derides the Gnostic biblical interpreters as "those who have discovered a new grammatical technique [*kainē technē grammatikē*]" (*Haer.* 5.8.1), and both the North African Tertullian and Irenaeus of Lyons sarcastically label Marcion an *emendator* (Tert. *Adv. Marc.* 4.3.4; Iren. *Haer.* 3.1.1).[77]

But this dispute as to who is a proper philologist, grammarian, editor, or interpreter is ultimately irresolvable and little more than a polemical strategy because the participants are committed more to meaning than to textuality. What is important is the correct meaning, not whether the correct meaning is textual—although clearly there is sufficient expectation that correct meanings can be textually defended to give such polemics strategic value, and Clement's commitment to a pre-textual voice goes hand in hand with a belief that the voice does in fact speak in a scriptural idiom. But these Christian interpreters simply do not really have the true spirit of disinterested criticism that seeks to establish authentic textual meaning on its own terms—a scholarly ideal that was Alexandrian philology's noble legacy, whatever its other hermeneutical shortcomings. Clement's own allegorical readings rely as much on "ambiguous expressions" as those of his opponents, as his use of the homonym "place" makes clear. In the end, Clement acknowledges the revisionary freedom of all allegorical reading (except his own): by using a reading that attends to expression only in order to alter meanings, "people subvert [*anatrepein*] all true teaching" (*Strom.* 7.16.96.4). In the midst of these allegorical battles, the adjective "true" (or its functional equivalent) provides the last defense against, or mask for, the will to hermeneutical power. Clement believes that "truth" resides in the meaning of a text, and that his opponents "subvert true teaching" by "changing the meanings." The "true" meanings consist of "what perfectly belongs to [*oikeion*] and becomes [*prepon*] the sovereign God" (*Strom.* 7.16.96.4). Clement thus appears to reject competing readings (or, sociologically speaking, perhaps to exclude competing readers from his own community) not

because those readings are false to the text, but because they are false to the true nature of God.

A profound acquaintance (*gnōsis*) with God seems at first glance to be Clement's final criterion for a correct reading of scripture—and such would be the sort of pure Gnostic hermeneutic we saw in Valentinus, justifying Clement's claim that the contents of his *Strōmateis* are in accord with the "true Gnostic philosophy." But Clement's "true" Gnosticism is not the unfettered, imaginative, mythopoetic Gnosticism of Valentinus, but a domesticated Gnosticism, for he qualifies the only norm a true Gnostic of the Valentinian stamp can acknowledge—a profound acquaintance with God. For Clement, such knowledge, if it is not simply to be the misguided musings of one's imagination, must be an acquaintance that is scriptural and intratextual. Here is the real commitment that lies behind Clement's polemical use of the charges of unprofessional editorial and philological techniques on the part of his adversaries. It is not enough to know what befits God; one must also establish such fitting knowledge from scripture and then show how "each one of the points demonstrated in the scriptures" can be demonstrated "again from similar scriptures" (*Strom.* 7.16.96.4). Clement's various unifying and subordinating patterns of reading Hebrew scripture define what that genuine knowledge will look like—only by reading scripture according to certain rules can one reliably identify authentic divine knowledge. A direct, experiential acquaintance with God, unmediated by writing, would provide the capacity and audacity to judge and overturn scripture, as Clement charges the sectarians with doing. But for Clement, true knowledge of God remains constrained by scripture as read according to patterns that embrace Hebraic as well as Christian texts and equate the Hebrew God with the "Father" of Jesus.

Clement insists that this sort of intratextual knowledge of God differs from the knowledge espoused by Valentinians and Basilideans. He argues that his opponents have flaunted the normative textual constraints that his own patterns of reading respect, "plainly fighting against almost the whole scriptures" (*Strom.* 7.16.96.5). Instead of attending to all that has been "spoken by the Lord through the prophets and by the Gospel, and, besides, attested and confirmed by the apostles," the sectarians "invariably choose," says Clement, "the opinion that seems to them to be more splendid" (*Strom.* 7.16.97.2). Clement's polemic stems from what he takes to be a fundamental difference between a hermeneutic based on an essentially nonlinguistic, pre-textual experience and one that remains grounded in certain ways of reading certain texts:

If one by nature [*physei*] knows God, as Basilides thinks . . . [and if] faith is not the rational assent of the soul exercising free will, but an undefined

> beauty, belonging immediately to the creature;—the commandments both
> of the old and of the new covenant are, then, superfluous, [as they are also]
> if one is saved by nature, as Valentinus would have it, and is a believer and
> an elect man by nature, as Basilides thinks. (*Strom.* 5.1.3.2–3)

Clement has no use for this sort of Gnostic hermeneutic, and he castigates
its adherents in a rhetoric that despite its overwrought character still
manages to express indirectly the true basis of his criticism:

> In consequence of not learning the mysteries of ecclesiastical knowledge [*ta
> tēs gnōseōs tēs ekklēsiastikēs mystēria*], and not having capacity for the grandeur
> of the truth, too indolent to descend to the depth of things, reading super-
> ficially, [the sectarians] have dismissed the scriptures. (*Strom.* 7.16.97.4)

Clement uses the terms "mystery," "truth," and "depth" ironically—such
terms were especially favored by the radical Gnostic groups he opposes.
When Clement says that his opponents reject "the mysteries of ecclesiastical knowledge," he means that they do not read scripture according to his
own revisionary patterns (which are, he maintains, the normative patterns of the "original" church) and that they read it with false anthropo-
logical assumptions based on an unacceptable theology. In sum, they lack
the "true" *gnōsis* that is "ecclesiastical." As for "reading superficially," a
cursory glance at our own contemporary literary polemics will suggest the
perennial usefulness of the charge.

Clement's allegorical reading, like Philo's, is intimately related to his
theological affirmation of an absolute distinction between a creator God
and the created order. Clement believes that his opponents reject this
theological distinction and as a result judge the text on the basis on a false
anthropology—one that identifies the essential self with God. He declares
in opposition:

> But God has no natural relation to us, as the creators of the sects will have
> it; neither on the supposition of his having made us out of nothing, nor on
> that of having formed us from matter; since the former did not exist at all,
> and the latter is totally distinct from God, unless we shall dare to say that we
> are a part of him and of the same essence [*homoousios*] as God. (*Strom.*
> 2.16.74.1)

Interestingly enough, Clement, like Valentinus, recognizes that theodicy
lies behind the issue: "And I know not how anyone who knows God can
bear to hear this [that we share God's essence] when he looks to our life
and sees in what evils we are involved" (*Strom.* 2.16.74.2). Clement thus
charges his opponents with elevating personal insight over sacred text
and with taking the admirable ideal of spiritual experience of the unwritten gospel to an unacceptable point that denies the essential principle of
negative theology and flies in the face of an acceptable theodicy.

In order to claim the epithet "Gnostic" for his own circle, Clement brought the human soul as close to God as his apophatic theology allowed. The true (i.e., Clementine) Gnostic, he announces, reaches "places [*topoi*] better than the better places, embracing the divine vision [*theōria*] not in mirrors or by means of mirrors" (*Strom.* 7.3.13.1). Yet despite Clement's rhetorical appeal to a vision bordering on identification of the self with God ("not in mirrors"), he qualifies that vision by saying that the true Gnostic will be only as near to God "as possible." Philo's Abraham came as near as possible to the place of God, only to discover that God was in no place at all. Similarly, although Clement's true Gnostic has in some sense grasped his ultimate spiritual reward, he also realizes that this reward is "not yet true as to time and place" (*Strom.* 6.9.75.2). In very precise formulations of his spiritual ideal, Clement carefully maintains this tension between divine presence and divine absence. On the one hand, "through love," the true Gnostic "is already in the midst of that in which he is destined to be"; "through *gnōsis*," he has "anticipated hope" and no longer desires anything, having, "as far as possible [*hōs hoion te*], the very thing desired" (*Strom.* 6.9.73.4). But Clement's qualifications ("anticipated," "as far as possible") and Philonic paradoxes ("in the midst of that in which he is destined to be") suggest that his true Gnostic, like Philo's Abraham, has come to the place of fulfillment, yet paradoxically still sees it from afar. While it is in some sense true that "through love, the future is for him already present" (*Strom.* 6.9.77.1), the true Gnostic nevertheless "by love goes to meet the future" (*Strom.* 6.9.77.2); the true Gnostic does not enjoy unmediated divine presence, only a divine promise (*Strom.* 6.9.77.1). In the end, Clement's true Gnostic remains bound by the constraints of apophasis: the first cause cannot be "in a place, but [remains] above both place, and time, and name, and conception" (*Strom.* 5.11.71.5), while the true Gnostic, caused rather than causal, created rather than creative, remains limited by space and time.

Philo's Abraham was a sojourner on earth, living somewhere between Ur of the Chaldeans and an ineffable, unlocalizable deity; Clement's true Gnostic is likewise a sojourner. Drawing on the parallelism of Hebrew scripture's statement "I am a stranger in the earth, and a sojourner with you" (e.g., Gen. 23.4), Clement seeks to distinguish strangers (his opponents) and sojourners (true Gnostics):

> Basilides says that he apprehends that the elect are strangers to the world [*kosmos*], being supramundane [*hyperkosmion*] by nature. But this is not the case. For all things are of one God. And no one is a stranger to the world by nature, their essence being one, and God one. But the elect man dwells as a sojourner, knowing all things to be possessed and disposed of. (*Strom.* 4.26.165.3–4)

Like Philo, Clement is moved to comment on Abraham's near sacrifice of Isaac, especially on Genesis 22.3–4; "Abraham, when he came to the place which God told him of on the third day, looking up, saw the place from afar" (*Strom.* 5.11.73.1). Unlike Philo, Clement remains seemingly untroubled by the lexical peculiarities of this sentence and confidently interprets it according to one possible reading. Like his predecessor, Clement finds in the verse an indication of Abraham's spiritual progress: the first day yields the sight of good things, the second day the soul's best desire. On the third day, the mind perceives spiritual realities—and here Clement adds his Christian revision, finding in the three days a "type" of the resurrection ("the eyes of the understanding being opened by the teacher who rose on the third day") and a "type" of baptism ("the three days may be the mystery of the seal, in which God is really believed") (*Strom.* 5.11.73.2). But Clement's Christian revision of this text does not transgress Philo's apophatic reservation:

> It is consequently "afar off" (*makrothen*) that he "sees the place." For the region of God is hard to attain. . . . It is seen by Abraham from a distance, rightly, because of his being in [the realms of] generation. . . . Thence says the apostle: "Now we see as through a glass, but then face to face." (*Strom.* 5.11.73.3–74.1)

Clement does go on to look past this moment of reserve: Abraham is "forthwith initiated by the angel," presumably ultimately enjoying that "face-to-face" encounter that Plato describes philosophically in *Republic* 7.532AB, which Clement paraphrases (*Strom.* 5.11.73.2). But the "gnostic Moses" makes the essential point regarding earthly life in the "realms of generation": Moses "does not circumscribe within space that which cannot be circumscribed" (*Strom.* 5.11.74.4). He is the place of the world, but the world is not his place. Insofar as they are spiritually mature and have discovered those "places" of the self that constitute their very identities, Clement and his fellow Alexandrian allegorical readers find themselves in a place—in a culture—that is not yet their own.

Afterword

The Bible's claim to truth is not only far more urgent than Homer's, it is tyranni-cal—it excludes all other claims. The world of the Scripture stories is not satisfied with claiming to be a historically true reality—it insists that it is the only real world, is destined for autocracy. . . . Far from seeking, like Homer, merely to make us forget our own reality for a few hours, it seeks to overcome our reality: we are to fit our own life into its world, feel ourselves to be elements in its structure of universal history.
 —Erich Auerbach, *Mimesis*

Build therefore your own world. As fast as you conform your life to the pure idea in your mind, that will unfold its great proportions. A correspondent revolution in things will attend the influx of the spirit. . . . The kingdom of man over nature, which cometh not with observation,—a dominion such as now is beyond his dream of God,—he shall enter without more wonder than the blind man feels who is gradually restored to perfect sight.
 —Ralph Waldo Emerson, *Nature*

It may well be that the forgetting of the question of God will be the nub of cultures now nascent. It may be that the verticalities of reference to "higher things," to the impalpable and mythical which are still incised in our grammars, which are still the ontological guarantors of the arcs of metaphor, will drain from speech (con-sider the "languages" of the computer and the codes in artificial intelligence). Should these mutations of consciousness and expression come into force, the forms of aesthetic making as we have known them will no longer be productive. They will be relegated to historicity. Correspondingly, the modes of response, of hermeneu-tical encounter as I have outlined them, will become archeologies. Philology will no longer know a Logos *for its love.*
 —George Steiner, *Real Presences*

Although allegorical readers of scripture in ancient Alexandria sought to convince their audiences that they were interpreting the text itself, they were actually seeking to revise their culture through their allegorical readings. Modern commentary on allegory, however, has tended to follow the misleading self-interpretations of the ancient writers by focusing on the text being read: allegorical reading is then said either to violate the integrity of that text, to unveil its deeper meaning, or to demonstrate that it has no meaning at all. But these approaches overlook the revisionary

function performed by allegorical reading in its historical, social, and cultural contexts. Allegory is not so much about the meaning or lack of meaning in texts as it is a way of using texts and their meanings to situate oneself and one's community with respect to society and culture. We have seen that ancient allegorical readers used their readings of scripture to reinterpret the world and the other cultural classics that helped sustain and legitimate that world. Their texts thus come to us as records of a world already interpreted, witnesses to interpretative acts of cultural critique and revision performed on the world precisely through an allegorical reading of scripture and other culturally significant texts.

Understanding the dynamic acts of interpretation that these texts represent has required us to relocate them within the forces that defined their limits and possibilities. Literary and sociopolitical "Hellenicity" constituted one such force. The concern for "Hellenicity" centered on perhaps the most burning cultural question in the educated Hellenistic world: What does it mean to speak Greek and to "be Greek"? As a literary phenomenon, Hellenicity was marked by philosophical and aesthetic controversies concerning the origin, nature, and functions of language. In its social and political dimensions, it was characterized by tensions between cultural and religious particularity and accommodation, usually discussed by modern scholars under the rubric of "Hellenization." The visible concerns of Hellenicity and Hellenization received formative impulses from the deeper, and more elusive, force of "common sense." In the case of ancient Alexandria (as in the Hellenistic world at large, and perhaps in most times and places), such common sense was defined by a spectrum of often hidden and largely unexamined assumptions about "the given," marked by the polar extremes of *to prepon* and *to atopon:* that which was "appropriate" or "fitting," or "in place," and that which was "inappropriate," "unfitting," literally or figuratively "in no place at all." Literary Hellenicity and sociopolitical Hellenization were determined by largely inflexible ancient assumptions concerning what was given and obvious or unthinkable and unacceptable in thought, writing, speech, and action. Cultural innovation required an assault on these assumptions, but assumptions so deeply embedded in the psyche hardly ever succumb to direct attack. The strategies of revision we have examined were more oblique, seeking to absorb these assumptions into new interpretative schemes. In some cases, and to some extent, these strategies were successful. Yet, on the whole, they appear more as testimonies of a certain discontent and aspiration than as altogether successful efforts at cultural transformation and innovation.

Cultural revision through an allegorical reading of scripture demands that one relate scripture and the world while refusing to identify them. If "the given" and "the obvious" function as the sole criteria for textual

meaning and reference, scripture will depict and reinforce the everyday assumptions of its readers and consequently offer no revision of the readers' world. On the other hand, if such a text were read in a way that bore no relation at all to the "given" and "obvious," it would have no relevance for the reader, at least insofar as he or she desired to retain and endorse some elements of the given world. The readers of scripture examined in this study did not situate themselves at these extremes, where textual meaning becomes either identical with or alien to their own world. Instead, their apophatic theological sensibility led them to discover between absolutely representational and absolutely nonrepresentational modes of reading sacred texts the possibility of allegorical readings that contained within themselves the element of negation essential for any revisionary hermeneutic. If a text is to depict any recognizable world at all, it must be susceptible to a reading determined in part by the "given" and "obvious"—a "literal" reading. But if that text is to enable readers to challenge or escape the given world, it must also be susceptible of another reading, which denies the hegemony of the first reading—and perhaps as a consequence the hegemony of the given order of things. Consequently, readers committed to the revisionary capacity of a sacred text cannot allow its meaning to be captured by a "literal sense." The allegorical potential ensures that meaning does not so exclusively become a function of one sort of reading (or one group of readers) that it seems to become an attribute—a "sense"—of the text itself. The ever-present semantic and referential indeterminacy in allegorically construed texts always provides the possibility for one "self-evident" reading to be overturned by another.

Reading allegorically does not, however, automatically ensure that common sense will not reign; by itself, allegorical reading does not necessarily lead to a revisionary interpretation of the world. An allegorical reader may reject one reading as mere cultural mime only to embrace another culturally determined reading defined by the allegorical reader's own common sense (however uncommon it may appear to those whom the allegorist labels "literalists"). But as long as readers believe that scripture ought to describe their world in some respect, the allegorical potential is a necessary, if not sufficient, condition for a reading of scripture that revises, rather than endorses, the status quo. In allegorical reading, the meaning one provisionally discovers or imposes, no matter how many other readings one must surpass in order to generate it, reflects the judgment and will of the text's readers, not the nature of the text. Yet the literary character of the text—the peculiarities of its syntax, diction, metaphors, and so forth—provides textual constraints that are inevitably acknowledged by allegorical readings even as they are transcended or subverted. Such transcendence or subversion is never absolute; allegorical "other" readings are parasitic with regard to at least logically prior

readings, and the irreducible textuality of the text being read is the Archimedean point on which this opposition is poised.

Making productive use of the opposition between exclusively representational and exclusively nonrepresentational readings, allegorical reading of scripture in ancient Alexandria functioned in three different ways. Allegorical readers such as Aristeas, Aristobulus, and Philo absorbed other meaning systems into scripture itself; they gave scripture other meanings so that other meanings might become scriptural. In this mode, initial nonrepresentational readings of scripture gave way to new representational claims, as scripture was offered as the only true representation of reality. In some respects, this ancient model may seem especially recognizable to us today. Contemporary thought in the humanities has taken a "linguistic turn," in which attempts to secure firm epistemological foundations for knowledge have given way to a recognition of the way notions of meaning and truth are functions of the linguistic worlds in which we live. Philo's attempt to reconstrue his world according to a scriptural paradigm that privileges a certain "literal" reading of the text proved to have a long career in Western culture. The Philonic paradigm was taken up by Augustine, whose works can together be understood as a massive Christian effort to absorb all of late antiquity into a "biblical" world. The attempt culminated in the *City of God*, in which Augustine reinterprets all of human history, from its beginnings down to his own day, according to a biblical typology of Cain and Abel. This tradition of biblical reinscription of reality came to North America with the Puritans, who attempted to reconstrue their culture according to yet another version of the Philonic paradigm. We are now living among the ruins of the tradition whose Alexandrian origins can be found in Philo's attempts at cultural revision through cultural reinscription. Deconstruction and the rabbinic tendencies of some versions of contemporary critical theory also belong to the tradition that includes Philonic textuality, though of course in a version that seeks to eradicate all traces of Philonic Platonism.

We have seen other Alexandrian allegorical readers such as Valentinus create for themselves a new version of culture not by textualizing reality through scriptural commentary but by producing their own creative compositions. Reading in this mode generated allegorical compositions that rendered an alternative world as the expression of a personal religious vision. This mode also occupies both ends of the representational/nonrepresentational spectrum. Valentinus underscores scripture's failure at representation in the allegorical freedom with which he reads and alters texts, but his confidence in the representational capacity of his own new allegorical composition is extravagant—even if what is finally represented is an essentially unrepresentable *gnōsis*. Like Philo, Valentinus is an early exemplar of a Western interpretative tradition of enor-

mous cultural significance. Readers will surely have identified him as a precursor of Hegel, and, indeed, Valentinus stands near the beginning of the influential Western Gnostic-Romantic-idealist tradition of insight, imagination, and visionary experience. If the Puritans represent the Philonic outpost in early American culture, Emerson and the Transcendentalists provide an American version of the Valentinian visionary perspective. Here is a tradition of interpretation that is self-consciously antitraditional, finding the sources of cultural revision in a principled struggle to escape the chains forged by time and tradition. Currently, this interpretative perspective, with its privileging of the self or subject over language and texts, is enduring something of a cultural eclipse; we are no longer sure what it would mean to talk about "the self" or "the subject" except as the construction of various discursive formations. But there are increasing signs of discontent with a notion of the self or subjectivity that is little more than a linguistic or sociocultural version of Hume's bundle of arbitrarily associated sense impressions. In some form or other, the Valentinian-Emersonian tradition will, I think, have its day once again.

Finally, we have seen Clement subordinate all texts, including scripture, to another criterion of meaning as the product of a divine voice or *logos*. This sort of reading was designed to evade the constraints produced by the textuality of various writings in favor of a discovered or imposed metatextual meaning. Much more than the Philonic mode (though somewhat less than the Valentinian), this mode calls into question the representational capacity of scripture by appealing to a nontextual norm for interpretation, yet that norm, in the form of the *logos*, provides fully adequate representations of reality. Ever since Clement quoted extensively from Philo, this interpretative tradition has historically accompanied the Philonic tradition: the nontextual, experiential "Word" has, in the Western religious tradition, generally been viewed as the other side of the revelatory text of scripture. Thus, the "Word of God" has been understood as both written text and spiritual illumination, and each was generally felt to validate the other, though in the Lutheran and Calvinist traditions, the written word has been given a certain interpretative priority over the experiences of spiritual illumination. But various mystical traditions and the dissenting Protestant sects (e.g., the Lutheran and Wesleyan pietist traditions and the Anabaptist traditions), when they have not gone as far as Valentinus, have endorsed some version of Clement's metatextual *logos*, in the sense of a source of meaning and truth to which scripture or other texts bear witness, but which cannot be captured, contained, or exhaustively defined by them. The Clementine interpretative perspective has had its most significant modern appearance in Schleiermacher's hermeneutical theory and has been restated in various related forms by Heidegger, Gadamer, and Ricoeur. Among religious

interpreters today, it is probably still the hermeneutic of choice. Its presence in contemporary secular literary criticism and literary theory is considerably less significant, though the Clementine-Schleiermacher position is defended in some form by all those who still like to talk about the human meaning of cultural classics and who favor the word "interpretation" rather than "reading" for what they do with them.

However transformed, then, these three Alexandrian allegorical traditions remain with us, their broad outlines recognizable whenever we ask about the sources of interpretative authority: Is it a canonical text and communal practice, a personal mystical vision, or some notion of meta-textual and communally invariant meaning? We are still either seeking answers to such questions of hermeneutical authority or—in the wake of various postmodernisms—seeking to change or otherwise reconceive the questions themselves. Despite their differences, all three modes of allegorical reading of scripture in ancient Alexandria were fueled by a fundamental tension created by mimetic and antimimetic attitudes toward representation, not unlike those marked out by our premodern and postmodern tendencies—with our modernism, in the guise of someone like Wallace Stevens, offering us the uneasy *via media* of representations self-consciously entertained as inescapable, supreme fictions. The texts we have considered express the mimetic/antimimetic tension in various kinds of languages about creation and fall, reality and appearance, presence and absence, identity and difference, *via essentia* and *via negativa*. The interpreters we have examined are always of two minds: God (or meaning) is sufficiently present to, or represented by, scripture (or literature) to make reading necessary, yet God (or meaning) is sufficiently absent from, and thus unrepresented by, scripture (or literature) to make it necessary always to read another way. They argue that the same ambiguous theological and semantic presence and absence characterizes culture as well. But for allegorical readers of scripture engaged in cultural revision, this ambiguity can never be true of both scripture and culture in the same way at the same time, for revisionists reject both nihilistic despair and Constantinian triumphalism. Only when God or meaning is present to the text but less so to the world or present to the world and less so to the text does the allegorical imagination emerge. In that imagination's founding discontinuity lies both its discontent and its hope.

NOTES

1. These three categories are, at best, rough generalizations for the sake of an initial orientation; they certainly do not summarize all of the historically important views of allegory. Later in this introduction, I will offer several further distinctions. For a survey of diverse critical views of allegory within the history of English literature alone, see Edward A. Bloom, "The Allegorical Principle," *ELH: A Journal of English Literary History* 18 (September 1951): 163–90. Although I am focusing here on scholarly interpreters of allegory, these three general views characterize many composers of allegory as well. For example, one might call Prudentius (*Psychomachia*) a traditional allegorist and Thomas Pynchon (*The Crying of Lot 49*) a late modern allegorist.

2. The priority of the religious appeal to a divine *logos* for subsequent secular confidence in the ability to uncover hidden meaning in texts is analyzed by Jacques Derrida, *Of Grammatology,* trans. Gayatri Chakravorty Spivak (Baltimore and London: Johns Hopkins Univ. Press, 1974). Derrida contends that "the sign and divinity have the same place and time of birth. The age of the sign is essentially theological" (14). He goes on to argue that appeals to the sign, the *logos,* or "the idea of the book" are essentially theological efforts at withstanding the disseminating forces of "writing" (*écriture*):

> The idea of the book is the idea of a totality, finite or infinite, of the signifier; this totality of the signifier cannot be a totality, unless a totality constituted by the signified [e.g., by the *logos*] preexists it, supervises its inscriptions and its signs, and is independent of it in its ideality. The idea of the book, which always refers to a natural totality, is profoundly alien to the sense of writing. It is the encyclopedic protection of theology and of logocentrism against the disruption of writing, against its aphoristic energy, and . . . against difference in general. (18)

3. The importance of this traditional view for contemporary theology has recently been defended by Andrew Louth, "Return to Allegory," chapter 5 in *Discerning the Mystery: An Essay on the Nature of Theology* (Oxford: Clarendon Press, 1983), 96–131.

4. See Robert Hollander, *Allegory in Dante's* Commedia (Princeton: Princeton Univ. Press, 1969); Jean Pépin, *Dante et la tradition de l'allégorie,* Conférence Albert-le-Grand, 1969 (Montreal: Institut d'études médievales, 1970); E. Ann Matter, *The Voice of My Beloved: The Song of Songs in Western Medieval Christianity* (Philadelphia: Univ. of Pennsylvania Press, 1990).

5. Especially in his "Notes Toward a Supreme Fiction," in *The Palm at the End of the Mind: Selected Poems and a Play,* ed. Holly Stevens (New York: Knopf, 1971), 207–34, Wallace Stevens represents the general sensibility that informs one of the earliest and one of the most recent modern books on allegory: Edwin Honig's *Dark Conceit: The Making of Allegory* (1959; reprint, Hanover, N. H.: Univ. Press of New England, 1982) and Jon Whitman's *Allegory: The Dynamics of an Ancient and Medieval Technique* (Cambridge, Mass.: Harvard Univ. Press, 1987). Several chapters of Honig's analysis and defense of the creative processes that produce allegory begin with epigraphs taken from Stevens's poetry, and the author concludes his book by invoking Stevens directly:

> The sun can be looked at steadily only through smoked glass. As Wallace Stevens has remarked, "how clean the sun when seen in its idea." And so the idea of allegory may only be—to invoke Stevens again—a "name for something that never could be named" and actually should "bear no name" other than "inconceivable idea," existing "in the difficulty of what it is to be." (183)

While not referring to Stevens directly, Whitman expresses a point of view quite similar to Honig's when he contends that the "fall from our pristine state of language has not been a total loss," because we have consequently "constructed a most beautiful consolation for our exile, the solace of fiction," which "tries to express a truth by departing from it in some way" (1). For Whitman, allegory turns out to be "the extreme case" of fiction's "dislocation of words from their objects." He argues that "allegorical writing thus exposes in an extreme way the foundation of fiction in general" (2). A similar Stevensonian perspective, though cast in somewhat darker tones through the addition of certain motifs drawn from Kafka's parables (especially "Before the Law"), pervades Frank Kermode's eloquent and provocative study of nonliteral or symbolic interpretation of biblical narrative, *The Genesis of Secrecy: On the Interpretation of Narrative* (Cambridge, Mass.: Harvard Univ. Press, 1979). Kermode concludes with the following remark:

> World and book, it may be, are hopelessly plural, endlessly disappointing; we stand alone before them, aware of their arbitrariness and impenetrability, knowing that they may be narratives only because of our hermetic tricks. Hot for secrets, our only conversation may be with guardians who know less and see less than we can; and our sole hope and pleasure is in the perception of a momentary radiance, before the door of disappointment is finally shut on us. (145)

With its exquisite ambiguity created by the juxtaposition of the subjunctive (three "mays") and the decisive "finally shut," this passage (in which even the Kafkaesque "radiance" is not only "momentary" but also at best a "perception") marks the borderline between the perspectives I have called late modern and postmodern. The ambivalence of Kermode's general point of view has been noted by Frank Lentricchia in his foreword to Kermode's *Forms of Attention* (Chicago and London: Univ. of Chicago Press, 1985). Lentricchia points to the oscillation in that work "between the theory that the text is a readerly function and product, and the traditional opposition to that theory, which insists that values . . . can inhere objectively in texts" (x). Not surprisingly, the epigraph to *Forms of Attention* is Wallace Stevens's lament "The imperfect is our paradise."

6. For a canonical statement, see Paul de Man, "The Rhetoric of Temporality," chapter 10 in *Blindness and Insight: Essays in the Rhetoric of Contemporary Criticism*, 2d ed., rev. (Minneapolis, Minn.: Univ. of Minnesota Press, 1983), 187–228. The deconstructionist view of allegory thus completely inverts its traditional meaning. Northrop Frye, "Levels of Meaning in Literature," *Kenyon Review* 12 (Spring 1950): 250, claims that "the purpose of allegory is to emphasize the connection of poetry with affirmative truth; the purpose of irony is to emphasize its withdrawal from it." Given these definitions, contemporary deconstructionists now use the term "allegory" for what Frye calls irony. Not surprisingly, then, the second half of de Man's essay, following his analysis of symbol and allegory in Romantic literature and theory, is a discussion of irony.

7. See Jesse M. Gellrich, *The Idea of the Book in the Middle Ages: Language Theory, Mythology, and Fiction* (Ithaca, N. Y.: Cornell Univ. Press, 1985). Gellrich observes that in the medieval period

> signs and signification, as they were explored in *grammatica* (the first discipline of the seven liberal arts) and in the hermeneutics of Scripture, remained committed to a larger intellectual preoccupation with stabilizing the sign, moving it out of the realm of potential arbitrariness, and tracing utterance back to a fixed origin, such as the primal Word spoken by God the Father. (21)

8. J. Hillis Miller, "The Critic as Host," in *Deconstruction and Criticism: Harold Bloom, Paul de Man, Jacques Derrida, Geoffrey Hartman, J. Hillis Miller* (New York: Seabury Press, 1979), 253, refers to the "uneasy joy of interpretation" made available by deconstructionist reading.

9. The following two examples of ancient rhetorical definitions of allegory are typical. (1) "*Allēgoria* is speech (*logos*) which makes precisely clear some one thing but which presents the conception of another according to likeness to the greatest extent. For example, 'The straw of which [referring to the "battle-cry" of the preceding verse] the bronze spreads on the ground in greatest numbers'" (*Il.* 19. 222) (from Trypho [first century B.C.E.], *On Tropes*, in L. Spengel, ed., *Rhetores graeci*, vol. 3 [Frankfurt: Minerva, 1966], 193.8–12). In this passage, Homer compares wartime slaughter to harvesting with a sickle, with "the bronze" functioning as the controlling metaphor. (2) "*Allēgoria*, then, is speech (*lexis*) which says one thing, but which presents a conception of another, as that which is said to the

serpent: 'Thou art accursed above every beast of the field' [cf. Gen 3.14]. It being understood allegorically in reference to the mental serpent, the Devil." (XXIX Anonymous [date unknown], *On Poetic Tropes,* in Spengel, *Rhetores graeci,* vol. 3, 207. 18–23). Both examples are taken from Patricia Matsen's very useful compilation and translation of ancient rhetorical definitions of allegory and related tropes and figures, "Appendix II: From Spengel's *Rhetores Graeci,*" in *Classical Theories of Allegory and Christian Culture,* by Phillip Rollinson and Patricia Matsen (Pittsburgh: Duquesne Univ. Press, 1981), 112–13. For an excellent overview of ancient uses of the term "allegory," see Whitman, *Allegory,* appendix I, 263–68. Northrop Frye offers a brief but comprehensive theoretical and historical overview in his article "Allegory," in *The Princeton Encyclopedia of Poetry and Poetics,* ed. Alex Preminger, enl. ed. (Princeton: Princeton Univ. Press, 1974), 12–15.

10. The literature on narrative is now enormous, and there is considerable disagreement about its character and function. I have found the following works useful: Wayne C. Boothe, *The Rhetoric of Fiction,* 2d ed. (1961; Chicago: Univ. of Chicago Press, 1983); Robert Scholes and Robert Kellogg, *The Nature of Narrative* (London: Oxford Univ. Press, 1965); Frank Kermode, *The Sense of an Ending: Studies in the Theory of Fiction* (New York: Oxford Univ. Press, 1967); J. Hillis Miller, ed., *Aspects of Narrative: Selected Papers from the English Institute* (New York: Columbia Univ. Press, 1971); W. J. T. Mitchell, ed., *On Narrative* (Chicago: Univ. of Chicago Press, 1980–81), especially Hayden White, "The Value of Narrativity in the Representation of Reality," 1–23; Frederic R. Jameson, *The Political Unconscious: Narrative as a Socially Symbolic Act* (Ithaca, N. Y.: Cornell Univ. Press, 1982). For theological reflections on narrative, see George W. Stroup, "A Bibliographic Critique," *Theology Today* 32 (1975): 133–43; Michael Goldberg, *Theology and Narrative: A Critical Introduction* (Nashville, Tenn.: Abingdon, 1982); Frank McConnell, ed., *The Bible and the Narrative Tradition* (New York: Oxford Univ. Press, 1986); Garrett Green, ed., *Scriptural Authority and Narrative Interpretation* (Philadelphia: Fortress, 1987); Stanley Hauerwas and L. Gregory Jones, eds., *Why Narrative? Readings in Narrative Theology* (Grand Rapids, Mich.: Eerdmans, 1989). For the interaction of biblical exegesis and literary theory, see Susan A. Handelman, *The Slayers of Moses: The Emergence of Rabbinic Interpretation in Modern Literary Theory,* SUNY Series on Modern Jewish Literature and Culture, ed. Sarah Blacher Cohen (Albany: State Univ. of New York Press, 1982); Northrop Frye, *The Great Code: The Bible and Literature* (New York: Harcourt Brace Jovanovich, 1983). For recent discussions of the character of biblical narrative itself, see Herbert N. Schneidau, *Sacred Discontent: The Bible and Western Tradition* (Berkeley and Los Angeles: Univ. of California Press, 1976); Robert Alter, *The Art of Biblical Narrative* (New York: Basic Books, 1981); Meier Sternberg, *The Poetics of Biblical Narrative: Ideological Literature and the Drama of Reading* (Bloomington, Ind.: Indiana Univ. Press, 1985); Geoffrey H. Hartman and Sanford Budick, eds., *Midrash and Literature* (New Haven: Yale Univ. Press, 1986); Robert Alter and Frank Kermode, eds., *The Literary Guide to the Bible* (Cambridge, Mass.: Harvard Univ. Press, 1987). For a philosophical discussion of narrative, see Paul Ricoeur, *Time and Narrative,* 3 vols.: vols. 1 and 2 trans. Kathleen McLaughlin and David Pellauer; vol. 3 trans. Kathleen Blamey and David Pellauer (Chicago: Univ. of Chicago Press, 1983–88).

11. Modern writers use various terms to refer to allegorical interpretation as

distinct from allegorical composition, including *allegoresis* (e.g., Maureen Quilligan, *The Language of Allegory: Defining the Genre* [Ithaca, N. Y.: Cornell Univ. Press, 1979], 25–26) and "imposed allegory" (e.g., Rosemond Tuve, *Allegorical Imagery: Some Medieval Books and Their Posterity* [Princeton: Princeton Univ. Press, 1966], 219–333).

12. Whitman's study of allegory from Homer to Bernard Silvestris, *Allegory: The Dynamics of an Ancient and Medieval Technique* (see note 5 above), emphasizes the interrelationship of composition and interpretation; see especially chapter 1, "The Allegorical Problem." See also Robert Lamberton, *Homer the Theologian: Neoplatonist Allegorical Reading and the Growth of the Epic Tradition*, The Transformation of the Classical Heritage 9, ed. Peter Brown (Berkeley and Los Angeles: Univ. of California Press, 1986), 144–61 (especially chapter 4, "The Interaction of Allegorical Interpretation and Deliberate Allegory"). Much recent literary theory has been devoted to eradicating or at least calling into question traditional text/commentary distinctions. A foundational text is Oscar Wilde, "The Critic as Artist," in *The Artist as Critic: Critical Writings of Oscar Wilde*, ed. Richard Ellmann (New York: Random House, 1968), 340–408. Geoffrey H. Hartman echoes Wilde in "Literary Commentary as Literature," chapter 8 in *Criticism in the Wilderness: The Study of Literature Today* (New Haven: Yale Univ. Press, 1980), 201:

> Literary commentary may cross the line and become as demanding as literature: it is an unpredictable or unstable genre that cannot be subordinated, a priori, to its referential or commenting function. Commentary certainly remains one of the defining features, for it is hardly useful to describe as "criticism" an essay that does not review in some way an existing book or other work. But the perspectival power of criticism, its strength of recontextualization, must be such that the critical essay should not be considered a supplement to something else. . . . A reversal must be possible whereby this "secondary" piece of writing turns out to be "primary."

Jacques Derrida provides a concrete illustration of the breakdown of text/commentary distinctions in *Glas,* trans. John P. Leavey, Jr., with Richard Rand (Lincoln, Neb.: Univ. of Nebraska Press, 1986). For an analogous discussion regarding a contrast between "proper" history (which preserves a fact/interpretation distinction) and "metahistory" (which blurs this distinction), see Hayden White, "Interpretation in History," chapter 2 in *Tropics of Discourse: Essays in Cultural Criticism* (Baltimore: Johns Hopkins Univ. Press, 1978), 52ff., and also his *Metahistory: The Historical Imagination in Nineteenth-Century Europe* (Baltimore: Johns Hopkins Univ. Press, 1973). Frank Kermode's *The Genesis of Secrecy* (see note 5 above) analyzes the particular compositional form taken by some Christian nonliteral readings of Hebrew scripture: the "realistic" canonical gospels.

13. Consider E. D. Hirsch, Jr.'s insistence in *Validity in Interpretation* (New Haven: Yale Univ. Press, 1967) versus Hans-Georg Gadamer's *Horizontverschmelzung* ("fusion of horizons") in *Wahrheit und Methode*, 2d ed. (Tübingen: J. C. B. Mohr [Paul Siebeck], 1965), translated into English as *Truth and Method*, ed. Garrett Barden and John C. Cumming (New York: Crossroad, 1975), on an absolute distinction between a text's own inherent meaning (*Sinn*) and the reader's assessment of its significance (*Bedeutung*); cf. the definition offered by Morton W.

Bloomfield, "Allegory as Interpretation," *New Literary History* 3 (Winter 1972): 301: "Allegory . . . is the seeing of the significance of a literary work beyond its meaning."

14. For a striking example in modern literature, see Vladimir Nabokov's *Pale Fire,* in which Kinbote's commentary on Shade's poem soon engulfs the precursor text with its own fantastic narrative; see also Miller's discussion of the text/commentary relationship in terms of host and parasite in "Critic as Host" in *Deconstruction and Criticism* and Whitman's basic claim concerning the distinctive character of Bernard Silvestris's allegory: "Bernard *interprets* the story of creation by *creating* allegorical agents to act out the story; he thus radically integrates the act of interpretation with the act of personification" (*Allegory,* 10).

15. On canon and canon formation, see James Sanders, *Torah and Canon* (Philadelphia: Fortress, 1972); Brevard S. Childs, *Introduction to the Old Testament as Scripture* (Philadelphia: Fortress, 1979), especially parts 1 and 6; Jonathan Z. Smith, "Sacred Persistence: Towards a Redescription of Canon," chapter 3 in *Imagining Religion: From Babylon to Jonestown* (Chicago: Univ. of Chicago Press, 1982), 36–52; Kermode, *Forms of Attention.*

16. Jameson, *Political Unconscious,* 58, links "interpretation" to what I have called the "traditional" view of allegory:

> A criticism which asks the question "What does it mean?" constitutes something like an allegorical operation in which a text is systematically *rewritten* in terms of some fundamental master code or "ultimately determining instance." On this view, then, all "interpretation" in the narrower sense demands the forcible or imperceptible transformation of a given text into an allegory of its particular master code or "transcendental signified": the discredit into which interpretation has fallen is thus at one with the disrepute visited on allegory itself.

For Jameson, this perspective nevertheless holds out the opportunity for the investigator to push beyond questions of meaning to those of ideology and power (which are the sorts of questions I am also trying to raise). He thus adds:

> Yet to see interpretation this way is to acquire the instruments by which we can force a given interpretive practice to stand and yield up its name, to blurt out its master code and thereby reveal its metaphysical and ideological underpinnings.

17. My inquiry into ancient allegory is based on a nominalist understanding of definitions. I do not assume that allegory actually exists as a self-identical entity or process that, despite local variations, endures throughout history in some essentially invariant form. Global proposals about allegory based on such "Platonic" assumptions tend to be either reductive or so inclusive as to be analytically useless. Local, inductive studies (which is what I try to offer in this book) are preferable; whether they converge on a single phenomenon deserving a single name should be the question, rather than the presupposition, of investigation.

18. I. A. Richards, *The Philosophy of Rhetoric* (New York: Oxford Univ. Press, 1936), 89–112. In addition to Aristotle's well-known discussion of metaphor in the *Poetics,* other important treatments of the subject include Max Black, *Models*

and Metaphor: Studies in Language and Philosophy (Ithaca, N. Y.: Cornell Univ. Press, 1962); id., "More About Metaphor," in *Metaphor and Thought,* ed. Andrew Ortney (Cambridge: Cambridge Univ. Press, 1979), 19–43 (with a large bibliography on metaphor); John Searle, *Expression and Meaning: Studies in the Theory of Speech Acts* (Cambridge: Cambridge Univ. Press, 1979); Sheldon Sacks, ed., *On Metaphor* (Chicago: Univ. of Chicago Press, 1979); Warren A. Shibles, *Metaphor: An Annotated Bibliography and History* (Whitewater, Wis.: The Language Press, 1971) (containing a useful index of general terms and names, as well as an analytical index); Mark Johnson, ed., *Philosophical Perspectives on Metaphor* (Minneapolis, Minn.: Univ. of Minnesota Press, 1981); Paul Ricoeur, *The Rule of Metaphor: Multidisciplinary Studies of the Creation of Meaning in Language,* trans. Robert Czerny, with Kathleen McLaughlin and John Costello, S. J. (Toronto: Univ. of Toronto Press, 1977); Terence Hawkes, *Metaphor,* The Critical Idiom 25, ed. John D. Jump (London: Methuen, 1972); Christine Brooke-Rose, *A Grammar of Metaphor* (London: Secker & Warburg, 1958); Janet Martin Soskice, *Metaphor and Religious Language* (Oxford: Clarendon Press, 1985).

19. Cf. Quint. *Inst.* 9.2.46, following Cicero, "a continuous metaphor makes an allegory" (*allēgorian* facit continua *metaphora*), in *The* Institutio Oratoria *of Quintilian,* 4 vols., trans. H. E. Butler, Loeb Classical Library (1920–22; reprint, Cambridge, Mass.: Harvard Univ. Press, 1966–69).

20. For a survey of some ancient uses of the term "personification," see Whitman, *Allegory,* appendix II, 269–72. See also Morton W. Bloomfield, "A Grammatical Approach to Personification Allegory," *Modern Philology* 60 (1962–63): 161–71; Steven Knapp, *Personification and the Sublime: Milton to Coleridge* (Cambridge, Mass.: Harvard Univ. Press, 1985). Stephen A. Barney, *Allegories of History, Allegories of Love* (Hamden, Conn.: Archon Books, 1979), locates the origin of allegory in personification. For the relation between personification and Roman religion, see L. R. Lind, "Roman Religion and Ethical Thought: Abstraction and Personification," *Classical Journal* 69 (December 1973–January 1974): 108–19; Charles Forster Smith gives examples of personification in ancient Greek history writing in "Personification in Thucydides," *Classical Philology* 13 (July 1918): 241–50. See further L. R. Lind, "Primitivity and Roman Ideas: Survivals," *Latomus* 35 (April–June 1976): 245–68; Harold L. Axtell, *The Deification of Abstract Ideas in Roman Literature and Inscriptions* (1907; reprint, New Rochelle, N. Y.: Aristide D. Caratzas, 1987).

21. The Latin text and an English translation of Prudentius's *Psychomachia* may be found in *Prudentius,* vol. 1, trans. H. J. Thomson, Loeb Classical Library (Cambridge, Mass.: Harvard Univ. Press, 1949), 274–343. For an examination of the *Psychomachia* that analyzes the way its allegory functions as a biblical revision of Virgilian epic motifs, see Macklin Smith, *Prudentius' "Psychomachia": A Reexamination* (Princeton: Princeton Univ. Press, 1976).

22. Scholars thus sometimes speak of "personification allegory." For example, Whitman, *Allegory,* 4, views personification as a form of "compositional allegory" when it "personifies abstract concepts *and fashions a narrative around them*" (my emphasis). But see Michael Murrin's review of Whitman's book in the *Journal of Religion* 69 (April 1989): 296–97, for the criticism that Whitman fails to distinguish personification and allegory sufficiently. Murrin argues that "at best the

presence of personifications in a fiction says *nothing* about its allegorical status" (297).

23. See William Dudley Woodhead, *Etymologizing in Greek Literature from Homer to Philo Judaeus* (Montreal: Univ. of Toronto Press, 1928); Ernst Robert Curtius, "Etymology as a Category of Thought," excursus 14 in *European Literature and the Latin Middle Ages*, trans. Willard R. Trask (Princeton: Princeton Univ. Press, 1953), 495–500.

24. See Barney, *Allegories of History*, 61–81; Smith, *Prudentius' "Psychomachia,"* 23–26, 168–233.

25. Hans W. Frei, "The 'Literal Reading' of Biblical Narrative in the Christian Tradition: Does It Stretch or Will It Break?" in *Bible and Narrative Tradition*, ed. McConnell, 36–77.

26. See Hans von Campenhausen, *The Formation of the Christian Bible*, trans. J. A. Baker (Philadelphia: Fortress, 1972), 302ff.

27. Whitman makes this tendency of allegory to "be at odds with itself" the central principle of his study; in his own words, "the more allegory exploits the divergence between corresponding levels of meaning, the less tenable the correspondence becomes. Alternatively, the more it closes ranks and emphasizes the correspondence, the less oblique, and thus the less allegorical, the divergence becomes" (*Allegory*, 2).

28. This crucial point has been made in different ways by a number of critics and theorists. Northrop Frye, *Anatomy of Criticism: Four Essays* (Princeton: Princeton Univ. Press, 1957), 89, observes that all interpretation, insofar as it goes beyond mere recitation of the text and thus necessarily adds to the text a degree of abstract meaning, is "allegorical" (cf. Bloomfield, "Allegory as Interpretation," 301: "Allegory is . . . the interpretative process itself"). Such a view underscores the highly interpretative dimension of all "meanings," including "literal meaning." The implication of Frye's view is that "literal meaning," insofar as it really is a "meaning," is simply one allegorical reading preferred over others for strategic reasons. As Frye observes in "Levels of Meaning," 248, literality in any sense more basic than the discovery of "meaning" could only refer to "the preliminary effort to unite the symbols in a verbal structure, and the *Gestalt* perception of the unity of the structure which results." Such a process "is the incommunicable act of total apprehension which precedes criticism." Much the same point is implicit in Frank Kermode's "The Plain Sense of Things," in *Midrash and Literature*, ed. Hartman and Budick, 179–94, where he underscores the essential "metaphoricity" of literal meaning. Similarly, Miller, in "Critic as Host," in *Deconstruction and Criticism*, 218, asks:

> Is the "obvious" reading, though, so "obvious" or even so "univocal"? May it not itself be the uncanny alien which is so close that it cannot be seen as strange, host in the sense of enemy rather than host in the sense of open-handed dispenser of hospitality? Is not the obvious reading perhaps equivocal rather than univocal, most equivocal in its intimate familiarity and in its ability to have got itself taken for granted as "obvious" and single-voiced?

Finally, Frank Lentricchia, commenting in *Criticism and Social Change* (Chicago: Univ. of Chicago Press, 1983), 103, on some ideas of Kenneth Burke, observes

that a formalist critic's claim for the formal self-sufficiency of literature (which notions of literal sense often endorse) is true only to the extent that it is empty:

> Form qua form . . . is unto itself because it is ideologically empty and untouched by power. Purity of form exists only as an abstraction in the mind of the formalist. . . . Form is always a thing to be appropriated (always on the way to appropriation) by the political process conceived in its broad hegemonic sense.

29. See Kathryn E. Tanner, "Theology and the Plain Sense," in *Scriptural Authority and Narrative Interpretation*, ed. Green, 59–78. In addition to this work by Tanner and the essay by Frei, " 'Literal Reading' of Biblical Narrative," in *Bible and Narrative Tradition*, ed. McConnell, the following theoretical discussions of literal meaning are useful: Searle, "Literal Meaning," chapter 5 in *Expression and Meaning*, 117–36; Bloomfield, "Allegory as Interpretation"; Michel Foucault, *The Order of Things: An Archeology of the Human Sciences* (New York: Random House, 1970) (a translation of *Les mots et les choses*); id., *The Archeology of Knowledge*, trans. A. M. Sheridan (New York: Pantheon, 1972); Clifford Geertz, "Common Sense as a Cultural System," chapter 4 in *Local Knowledge: Further Essays in Interpretive Anthropology* (New York: Basic Books, 1983), 73–93; Roman Jakobson, "Two Aspects of Language and Two Types of Aphasic Disturbances," in *Fundamentals of Language*, ed. Roman Jakobson and Morris Halle, 2d ed. (Paris: Mouton, 1975); W. J. T. Mitchell, *Iconology: Image, Text, Ideology* (Chicago: Univ. of Chicago Press, 1986).

For historical treatments of "literality," in addition to Kermode's essay, "The Plain Sense of Things," in *Midrash and Literature*, ed. Hartman and Budick, see Max Pohlenz, "Tὸ πρέπον: Ein Beitrag zur Geschichte des griechischen Geistes," in *Kleine Schriften*, vol. 1 (Hildesheim: Georg Olms, 1965), 100–39; Brevard S. Childs, "The Sensus Literalis of Scripture: An Ancient and Modern Problem," in *Beiträge zur alttestamentlichen Theologie: Festschrift für Walther Zimmerli zum 70. Geburtstag*, ed. Herbert Donner, Robert Hanhart, and Rudolf Smend (Göttingen: Vandenhoeck & Ruprecht, 1977), 80–93; Hans W. Frei, *The Eclipse of Biblical Narrative: A Study in Eighteenth and Nineteenth Century Hermeneutics* (New Haven: Yale Univ. Press, 1974); Raphael Loewe, "The 'Plain' Meaning of Scripture in Early Jewish Exegesis," in *Papers of the Institute of Jewish Studies, London*, vol. 1, ed. J. G. Weiss, Brown Classics in Judaica Series (Lanham, Md.: Univ. Press of America, 1989), 140–85.

30. Cf. Jameson, *Political Unconscious*, 38:

> Is the text a free-floating object in its own right, or does it "reflect" some context or ground, and in that case does it simply replicate the latter ideologically, or does it possess some autonomous force in which it could also be seen as negating that context?

In addition to the works by Jameson, Lentricchia, and Hartman already cited, the following studies have informed my reflections on "culture" and cultural criticism: Giles Gunn, *The Culture of Criticism and the Criticism of Culture* (New York: Oxford Univ. Press, 1987); George A. Lindbeck, *The Nature of Doctrine: Religion and Theology in a Postliberal Age* (Philadelphia: Westminster, 1984); Richard Rorty, *Contingency, Irony, and Solidarity* (Cambridge: Cambridge Univ. Press, 1989);

James Clifford, *The Predicament of Culture: Twentieth Century Ethnography, Literature, and Art* (Cambridge, Mass.: Harvard Univ. Press, 1988); Raymond Williams, *Marxism and Literature* (New York: Oxford Univ. Press, 1977); Clifford Geertz, *The Interpretation of Cultures* (New York: Basic Books, 1973); Barbara Herrnstein Smith, *On the Margins of Discourse* (Chicago: Univ. of Chicago Press, 1978); Frederic R. Jameson, "The Symbolic Inference; or, Kenneth Burke and Ideological Analysis," in *The Ideologies of Theory: Essays 1971–1986*, vol. 1: *Situations of Theory*, Theory and the History of Literature 48, ed. Wlad Godzich and Jochen Schulte-Sasse (Minneapolis, Minn.: Univ. of Minnesota Press, 1988), 137–52; M. M. Bakhtin, *The Dialogic Imagination*, ed. Michael Holquist and trans. Caryl Emerson and Michael Holquist (Austin: Univ. of Texas Press, 1981); Edward W. Said, *The World, the Text, and the Critic* (Cambridge, Mass.: Harvard Univ. Press, 1983).

31. For religion as a tool of social and cultural legitimation, see Peter L. Berger, *The Sacred Canopy: Elements of a Sociological Theory of Religion* (Garden City, N. Y.: Doubleday, 1969); Peter L. Berger and Thomas Luckmann, *The Social Construction of Reality: A Treatise in the Sociology of Knowledge* (Garden City, N. Y.: Doubleday, 1966). See also Said, *World, Text, and Critic*, especially his introduction and conclusion.

32. See Lentricchia, *Criticism and Social Change*, 79–80, on Kenneth Burke; Lentricchia notes that the dominant forces of sociopolitical hegemony are

> internally divided, different from themselves in their very "substance."
> ... No hegemonic condition is fatally fixed because no hegemonic condition
> rests on natural or God-given authority, though it is one of the key strategies
> of hegemonic education to inculcate those very claims.

33. Frank Kermode, *The Classic: Literary Images of Permanence and Change* (Cambridge, Mass.: Harvard Univ. Press, 1983), 40, discusses how allegorical readings functioned to "accommodate" old classics to the demands of a modern culture for "relevance."

34. Herbert Hunger, "Allegorische Mythendeutung in der antike und bei Johannes Tzetzes," *Jahrbuch der Österreichischen Byzantinischen Gesellschaft* 3 (1954): 35–54; see especially 37–38 for a rejection of Tate's insistence (see note 35 below) on the nonapologetic function of allegory:

> J. Tate goes too far when he effectively dismisses altogether the apologetic
> root of the allegorical interpretation of myth . . . and, in its place, thrusts
> into the foreground the exegesis of Homer as allegory's positive starting
> point. Even if apology does not represent the single root of the allegorical
> interpretation of myth, it undoubtedly gives it a strong impulse and motive.
> (37)

Eduard Zeller, *Die Philosophie der Griechen in ihrer geschichtlichen Entwicklung*, 3.1, 4th ed., ed. Eduard Wellmann (Leipzig: O. R. Reisland, 1909), 345, also emphasizes allegory's apologetic function:

> For so much in it [Stoic allegory] must appear to us as a manifest and utterly
> worthless frivolity: but the Stoics themselves were in bitter earnest with their
> explanations. For them, such explanations served as the sole method of

rescuing popular belief and countering the most severe reproaches of the traditions and poetic works with which the Greeks had nourished themselves from earliest childhood.

Recent scholarship has challenged the view that Stoics read texts allegorically and that they did so for apologetic reasons (see note 1 to chapter 1). Moreover, the work that Zeller has in mind here is the *Homeric Allegories* of Heraclitus, who is no longer considered a Stoic (see my discussion in "Reading Homer as an Allegorical Poet" in chapter 1). But Zeller's remark nevertheless represents a long-held and still-influential view of the purpose of much ancient allegorical interpretation.

35. J. Tate is the principal representative of this view. See his "The Beginnings of Greek Allegory," *Classical Review* 41 (1927): 214–15; "Plato and Allegorical Interpretation," *Classical Quarterly* 23 (1929): 142–54; *Classical Quarterly* 24 (1930): 1–10; "On the History of Allegorism," *Classical Quarterly* 28 (1934): 105–14. Tate, "History of Allegorism," 107, argues that early writers such as Pherecydes, Heraclitus, and Parmenides were competing with Homer as a mythmaking philosopher. As they studied Homer and Hesiod, "the clearer it seemed to them that those early poets had wielded the myths for the purpose of teaching philosophic doctrines, however inadequate or mistaken those doctrines frequently appeared to them to be." Hence, Tate concludes that ancient allegorical interpretation "was in its very first germs positive, not defensive, in its aim; that is to say, it was practiced in order to make more explicit the doctrines which the students of the poets believed to be actually contained in the poets' words, and not simply to defend the poets against censure."

36. Cf. the positions of Zeller and Tate as characterized by Glenn W. Most, "Cornutus and Stoic Allegoresis: A Preliminary Report," *ANRW* II.36.3 (1989): 2019–20.

37. In his analysis of the ways in which ancient allegorical interpretation served Neoplatonist metaphysics, Lamberton, *Homer the Theologian*, makes reference to the hermeneutical theories of Hans-Georg Gadamer in *Truth and Method*. Peter Steinmetz, "Allegorische Deutung und allegorische Dichtung in der alten Stoa," *Rheinische Museum* 129 (1986): 18–19, argues that Stoic allegorical interpretation is not only an action performed upon a literary text but actually defines a text's very "literariness." See Most's critique of Steinmetz's notion of "allegorische Deutung von Dichtung als Dichtung" ("Cornutus and Stoic Allegoresis," 2023ff.). Steinmetz's approach is similar in some ways to the efforts of some deconstructionists to use "allegory" as a synonym for the "literariness" of literature (see de Man, "Rhetoric of Temporality," chapter 10 in *Blindness and Insight*).

38. The remark is made by Velleius, an Epicurean spokesperson in Cicero's dialogue *On the Nature of the Gods* (1.41). (See my discussion in "Opposition to Etymology and Allegory" in chapter 1.)

39. For a combination of Nietzsche and Freud that emphasizes the weakness of most traditional nonliteral readings and valorizes the positive readings attained (rarely) by the "strongest" readers, see Harold Bloom, *The Anxiety of Influence: A Theory of Poetry* (New York: Oxford Univ. Press, 1973); id., *A Map of Misreading* (New York: Oxford Univ. Press, 1975); id., *Kabbala and Criticism* (New York: Continuum, 1984).

40. See Herbert Marks, "Pauline Typology and Revisionary Criticism," in *Modern Critical Views: The Bible*, ed. Harold Bloom (New York: Chelsea House, 1987), 305–21.

41. Angus Fletcher draws on Freudian theories of obsessive-compulsive neurosis in *Allegory: The Theory of a Symbolic Mode* (Ithaca, N. Y.: Cornell Univ. Press, 1964); Bloom, *Kabbala and Criticism*, combines Freud, Nietzsche, and the Kabbala; Kermode, *Genesis of Secrecy*, combines Kafka and Stevens.

42. Frank Lentricchia criticizes Kermode, Bloom, and de Man for failing to attend adequately to the sociocultural dimension of interpretation in *After the New Criticism* (Chicago: Univ. of Chicago Press, 1980); see especially chapter 2 ("Versions of Existentialism") and chapter 9 ("Harold Bloom: The Spirit of Revenge"). Lentricchia extends his critique of de Man's formalist theory by contrasting it with the perspective of Marxist theorist Kenneth Burke, in *Criticism and Social Change*. My own view is that Kermode is considerably more sensitive to historical and cultural dimensions of interpretation than is Bloom and that the insights of both theorists can fruitfully be extended into areas on which they themselves have not chosen to concentrate.

43. Along with German critics such as Goethe and Schelling, Coleridge offered a series of influential formulations of the contrast between symbol and allegory. For an overview, see John Gatta, Jr., "Coleridge and Allegory," *Modern Language Quarterly* 38 (1977): 62–77; see also Honig, *Dark Conceit*, 39–50. References to important studies of the distinction made by Coleridge may be found in Knapp, *Personification and the Sublime*, 149–50 n. 8. At least since its denigration at the hands of Romantic theorists (if not even earlier at the hands of the Protestant Reformers), allegory has often been the trope with which thinkers in many different fields have invidiously compared whatever literary form they liked better. For example, modern New Testament scholarship on the parables of Jesus since the work of Adolph Jülicher (*Die Gleichnisreden Jesu*, 2 vols. [Tübingen: J. C. B. Mohr (Paul Siebeck), 1888–89]) consistently treats the parables as symbolic rather than allegorical. For a survey of parable research up through the mid-1970s, see Norman Perrin, *Jesus and the Language of the Kingdom: Symbol and Metaphor in New Testament Interpretation* (Philadelphia: Fortress, 1976); see especially 92–93 and 156–59 for Perrin's discussion of the way distinctions between parable and allegory in biblical scholarship are rooted in the nineteenth-century contrast of symbol and allegory. See also Stephen L. Wailes, *Medieval Allegories of Jesus' Parables*, UCLA Center for Medieval and Renaissance Studies Series 23 (Berkeley and Los Angeles: Univ. of California Press, 1987).

44. Honig's ground-breaking *Dark Conceit* marks the beginning of the contemporary rehabilitation of allegory in the face of the Romantic critique. But in some ways, Honig's defense remains implicitly determined by the terms of the Romantic comparison. The following remark, for example, seems to defend allegory by attributing to it the sort of integration of idea and image that Coleridge insisted only symbols could provide: "A good allegory, like a good poem, does not exhibit devices or hammer away at intentions. It beguiles the reader with a continuous interplay between subject and sense in the storytelling, and the narrative, the story itself, means everything" (5).

45. In addition to the foundational text by de Man already cited (see note 6

above), see J. Hillis Miller, "The Two Allegories," in *Allegory, Myth, and Symbol,* ed. Morton W. Bloomfield, Harvard English Studies 9 (Cambridge, Mass.: Harvard Univ. Press, 1981), 355–70. The de Manian deconstructionist approach to the distinction between allegory and symbol applauds the allegorical demystification of the symbol's false assertion of a synecdochic presence of meaning in images. The influence of this perspective can be seen in the following studies: Jonathan Culler, "Literary History, Allegory, and Semiology," *New Literary History* 7 (1975–76): 259–70, especially 262–64; Jerome C. Christensen, "The Symbol's Errant Allegory: Coleridge and His Critics," *ELH* 45 (1978): 640–59; John A. Hodgson, "Transcendental Tropes: Coleridge's Rhetoric of Allegory and Symbol," in *Allegory, Myth, and Symbol,* ed. Bloomfield, 273–92. For criticism and modifications of the de Manian reading, see Knapp, *Personification and the Sublime,* 10–23, and David Dawson, "Against the Divine Ventriloquist: Coleridge and de Man on Symbol, Allegory, and Scripture," *Literature and Theology* (October 1990): 293–310. Carolynn Van Dyke discusses allegory in light of deconstructionist theory in *The Fiction of Truth: Structures of Meaning in Narrative and Dramatic Allegory* (Ithaca, N. Y.: Cornell Univ. Press, 1985).

46. See Michael Sells, "Apophasis in Plotinus: A Critical Approach," *Harvard Theological Review* 78 (1985): 47–65. The connection between negative or apophatic theology and the poetics of absence has been noted by deconstructionists themselves; see Jacques Derrida, "Des Tours de Babel," in *Difference in Translation,* ed. Joseph F. Graham (Ithaca, N. Y.: Cornell Univ. Press, 1985), 209–48 (Graham offers an English translation of Derrida's essay in the same volume, pp. 165–207). Derrida maintains that "translation, as holy growth of language, announces the messianic end, surely, but the sign of that end and of that growth is 'present' (*gegenwärtig*) only in the 'knowledge of that distance,' in the Entfernung, *the remoteness* that relates us to it. One can know this remoteness, have knowledge or a presentiment of it, but we cannot overcome it" (202–3). In this essay, Derrida is translating and commenting on Walter Benjamin's "Die Aufgabe des Übersetzers," in *Gesammelte Schriften* 4.1, ed. Tillman Rexroth, Werkausgabe vol. 10 (Frankfurt: Suhrkamp, 1972), 9–21. An English translation of this essay by Harry Zohn is available as "The Task of the Translator," in Walter Benjamin, *Illuminations,* ed. Hannah Arendt (New York: Schocken, 1969), 69–82.

47. See Paul Ricoeur, *Essays on Biblical Hermeneutics,* ed. Lewis S. Mudge (Philadelphia: Fortress, 1980); David Tracy, *Blessed Rage for Order: The New Pluralism in Theology* (New York: Seabury, 1978); id., *The Analogical Imagination: Christian Theology and the Culture of Pluralism* (New York: Crossroad, 1981).

48. For the theoretical foundations of Romantic biblical hermeneutics, see F. D. E. Schleiermacher, *Hermeneutics: The Handwritten Manuscripts,* ed. Heinz Kimmerle and trans. James Duke and Jack Forstman, American Academy of Religion Texts and Translation Series 1 (Missoula, Mont.: Scholars Press, 1977).

49. Erich Auerbach's characterization of typology, which follows, remains the most influential.

Figural interpretation establishes a connection between two events or persons, the first of which signifies not only itself but also the second, while the second encompasses or fulfills the first. The two poles of the figure are

separate in time, but both, being real events or figures, are within time, within the stream of historical life. Only the understanding of the two persons or events is a spiritual act, but this spiritual act deals with concrete events whether past, present, or future, and not with concepts or abstractions; these are quite secondary, since promise and fulfillment are real historical events, which have either happened in the incarnation of the Word, or will happen in the second coming. ("'Figura,'" in *Scenes from the Drama of European Literature,* Theory and the History of Literature 9, ed. Wlad Godzich and Jochen Schulte-Sasse [Minneapolis, Minn.: Univ. of Minnesota Press, 1984], 53)

Following Auerbach, A. C. Charity offers two definitions, one general and one specific to Christian usage, in *Events and Their Afterlife: The Dialectics of Christian Typology in the Bible and Dante* (Cambridge: Cambridge Univ. Press, 1966), 1. According to Charity, typology is

[1] the broad study, or any particular presentation, of the quasi-symbolic relations which one event may appear to bear to another—especially, but not exclusively, when these relations are the analogical ones existing between events which are taken to be one another's "prefiguration" and "fulfillment." . . . [2] the science of history's relations to its fulfillment in Christ.

For representative attacks on ancient allegory for neglecting the "literal, historical sense" of scripture, see K. J. Woollcombe, "The Biblical Origins and Patristic Development of Typology," in *Essays on Typology,* ed. G. H. W. Lampe and K. J. Woollcombe (Naperville, Ill.: A. R. Allenson, 1957), 39–75; Joseph A. Galdon, *Typology and Seventeenth-Century Literature* (Paris: Mouton, 1975), especially 32–38. For a recent challenge to Auerbach's typology vs. allegory distinction, see Sanford Budick, "Milton and the Scene of Interpretation: From Typology toward Midrash," in *Midrash and Literature,* ed. Hartman and Budick, 195–212. In particular, Budick challenges Auerbach's characterization of early Alexandrian allegory as antitypological, arguing for a definition of typology in which the procedure is not subject to teleology and closure, as Auerbach claims.

50. For a classic analysis of this theory of levels, see Henri de Lubac, *Exégèse médiéval: Les quatre sens de l'écriture,* vol. 1, pts. 1 and 2, vol. 2, pts. 1 and 2 (Paris: Aubier, 1959–64); see Charity, *Events and Their Afterlife,* 172–78, for a summary discussion of the four levels of exegesis. Northrop Frye restates the classical fourfold scheme as the basis for his own view of literature and literary criticism in "Levels of Meaning," 247–62.

51. According to Charity, *Events and Their Afterlife,* 171 n. 2, the first formal definitions distinguishing allegory from typology date from the period of Protestant scholasticism. J. Gerhard (1582–1637) provides one of the earliest definitions in his *Loci theologici:*

A type [*typus*] exists when the Old Testament puts forward some fact in order to foresignify or adumbrate something done or to be done in the New Testament. An allegory exists, when either the Old or the New Testament expounds something in a new sense and accommodates it to a spiritual

doctrine or new institution. A type consists in the collation of facts. An allegory is concerned not so much with facts as with the conceptions themselves, from which it extracts useful and recondite doctrine. (My translation of the Latin text, which Charity quotes from Gerhard von Rad, "Typologische Auslegung des Alten Testament," *Evangelische Theologie* 12 [1952]: 20 n. 7.)

Charity notes further that the first use of the word *typologia* occurs in the middle of the nineteenth century (in Latin—as *typologia*—around 1840, and in English—as "typology"—in 1844).

52. For a standard critique of allegory by a proponent of typology as the form of the Bible's own hermeneutical activity, as it applies itself to the religious life of its readers, consider the following from Charity, *Events and Their Afterlife,* 162:

It would be hard to deny that the allegorical methods deriving from Philo and Hellenism carry, even among the Christians, a tendency to transpire in propositions of stable and general truth which may be quite unconnected with revelation. For the allegorical method in exegesis represents fundamentally a desire to sophisticate a mythological view of life about which one has become self-conscious, a wish to make a revered and traditional myth or *cultus* respectable intellectually; and as such, therefore, when the Christians or Philo apply it to a history whose very historicity is of the utmost significance, it tends by its very nature to conflict with or even to dissipate this significance, to bring about a "devaluation of history."

See also p. 251, where Charity states that allegory is "in the normal sense of the word—an abstracting and generalizing psychological system . . . substituted for life and history." Interestingly, on p. 58 Charity levels a similar critique against modern defenders of typology, contending that they have failed to acknowledge the demand for existential application placed by biblical typology upon its readers and have instead defended typology by appeals to archetypal or formal characterizations that, in effect, move toward the allegorical method as Charity describes it.

53. Charity, *Events and Their Afterlife,* 175, alludes to the Hellenic/Hebraic division that lies at the heart of the allegory/typology contrast. Regarding the usefulness of the medieval fourfold sense, he remarks:

Though the methods most commonly associated with the doctrine [of a fourfold sense] are only attached to it accidentally by the historical circumstances of the Hellenistic milieu in which Christianity grew up in the early centuries, the essential *schema* of the doctrine is still recognizably Hebraic. . . . [In certain instances] it is obviously possible to replace the *schema*'s usual concomitants, the Hellenistic-allegorical methods of late antiquity, with the more dialectical methods which might realize its typological potential.

Jean Daniélou defends allegorical procedures under the name of typology in *From Shadows to Reality: Studies in the Biblical Typology of the Fathers,* trans. Wulstan Hibberd (London: Burns & Oates, 1960). James Samuel Preus brings Augustine and Luther together as typological exegetes in *From Shadow to Promise: Old Testament Interpretation from Augustine to the Young Luther* (Cambridge, Mass.: Harvard

Univ. Press, Belknap Press, 1969). Just as the literary contrast between allegory and symbol, derived from Christian incarnational and sacramental theology, eventually reentered the theological debate, so the theological distinction between allegory and typology eventually affected literary discussions; see, for example, C. S. Lewis's analysis of the medieval *psychomachia* in *The Allegory of Love: A Study in Medieval Tradition* (1936; reprint, New York: Oxford Univ. Press, 1967).

54. For characterizations of the debate by leading representatives of both sides, see George Lindbeck, *Nature of Doctrine;* id., "Barth and Textuality," *Theology Today* 43 (October 1986): 361–76; David Tracy, "Lindbeck's New Program for Theology: A Reflection," *The Thomist* 49 (1985): 460–72. See further William C. Placher, "Revisionist and Postliberal Theologies and the Public Character of Theology," *The Thomist* 49 (1985): 392–416 (Placher's "postliberals" are the same as "intratextualists"); Gary Comstock, "Truth or Meaning: Ricoeur versus Frei on Biblical Narrative," *The Journal of Religion* 66 (1986): 117–40. For a recent defense of the intratextualist position and a comprehensive survey of its principal advocates and opponents, see William C. Placher, *Unapologetic Theology: A Christian Voice in a Pluralistic Conversation* (Louisville, Ky.: Westminster/John Knox, 1989). For a view of the debate from the opposing perspective, see Mark I. Wallace, *The Second Naiveté: Barth, Ricoeur, and the New Yale Theology,* Studies in American Biblical Hermeneutics 6 (Macon, Ga.: Mercer Univ. Press, 1990).

55. Intratextual theologians argue that only this sort of reading of scripture can preserve the identity of that community's founder, of its deity, and hence of the community itself. Consequently, they typically condemn allegorical readings of scripture for replacing the distinctive typological meaning with ideas and images supplied by the nonscriptural cultural context. Intratextualist resistance to allegorical "extratextuality" thus reiterates in literary, rather than philosophical, terms Adolph Harnack's indictment of the "Hellenization" of early Christianity. Consequently, it is not surprising that these theologians find Harnack's representative of "acute Hellenization"—Gnosticism—to be an especially distressing instance of "heretical" extratextuality (see Hans W. Frei, "Redeemed Redeemer in Myth and Gospel," chapter 6 in *The Identity of Jesus Christ: The Hermeneutical Bases of Dogmatic Theology* [Philadelphia: Fortress, 1975]; Lindbeck, *Nature of Doctrine,* 118).

56. For example, one historically influential rule for typology insists that the second meaning may not call into question the historical credibility of the first: the "spiritual rock" in the wilderness that was Christ remains a geologically real rock in a geographically real wilderness. Thus while Auerbach, " 'Figura,' " in *Drama of European Literature,* 54, admitted that typology was essentially a mode of allegory, he quickly separated the two hermeneutical procedures on the basis of historicity:

> Since in figural interpretation one thing stands for another, since one thing represents and signifies the other, figural interpretation is "allegorical" in the widest sense. But it differs from most of the allegorical forms known to us by the historicity both of the sign and what it signifies.

Other scholars have also recognized that allegory is the more comprehensive category—Karlfried Froehlich, " 'Always to Keep the Literal Sense in Holy Scripture Means to Kill One's Soul': The State of Biblical Hermeneutics at the Begin-

ning of the Fifteenth Century," in *Literary Uses of Typology from the Late Middle Ages to the Present,* ed. Earl Miner (Princeton: Princeton Univ. Press, 1977), 20, calls typology "the specifically Christian form of allegory." There have been efforts to break down the absolute separation of the two modes; see, for example, Rudolph Bultmann, "Ursprung und Sinn der Typologie als hermeneutischer Methode," *Theologische Literaturzeitung* 75–76 (1950–51): 205–12; H. Crouzel, "La distinction de la 'typologie' et 'allegorie,'" *Bulletin de littérature ecclésiastique* 65 (1964): 161–74; James Barr, "Typology and Allegory," chapter 4 in *Old and New in Interpretation: A Study of the Two Testaments* (New York: Harper & Row, 1966), 103–48; Harry Austryn Wolfson, *Faith, Trinity, Incarnation: The Philosophy of the Church Fathers,* vol. 1, 3d ed. (Cambridge, Mass.: Harvard Univ. Press, 1970), 24ff., especially 39ff.

57. See David Dawson, "Allegorical Intratextuality in Bunyan and Winstanley," *The Journal of Religion* 70 (April 1990): 189–212.

58. Cf. Jameson, "Symbolic Inference," in *Ideologies of Theory,* ed. Godzich and Schulte-Sasse, 141:

> The literary or aesthetic gesture thus always stands in some active relationship with the real, even where its activity has been deliberately restricted to the rather sophisticated operation of "reflecting" it. Yet in order to act on the real, the text cannot simply allow reality to persevere in its being outside of itself, inertly, at a distance; it must draw the real into its own texture.

59. Thus my approach differs from Whitman's, for although he denies that the theoretical developments he charts "constitute a deliberate or steady 'evolution' toward a goal," he nevertheless argues that "while this interaction [between interpretative and compositional allegory from their ancient origins to the twelfth century] develops over the broad course of allegorical writing, it reaches a critical stage . . . in the twelfth century. The decisive turning point in this movement is the *Cosmographia* of Bernard Silvestris, written near the midpoint of the century. In this text, the coordinating tendencies of earlier movements in antiquity and the Middle Ages begin to coalesce in a comprehensive, far-reaching design." Thus Whitman speaks of "the kinds of interactions necessary to produce the rich strategies of personification which culminate in the *Cosmographia*" (*Allegory,* 10, 9–10, 12, respectively). Murrin, 295–97, criticizes Whitman for allowing Bernard to "control" his study "teleologically."

60. R. P. C. Hanson, *Allegory and Event: A Study of the Sources and Significance of Origen's Interpretation of Scripture* (Richmond, Va.: John Knox, 1959), 63, gives the standard "Alexandrian" application of the typology/allegory contrast:

> But Alexandrian allegory has in all its forms one feature in common with Hellenistic allegory; it is unhistorical. It does not use typology. Its ultimate aim is to empty the text of any particular connection with historical events. Even in the matter of allegorizing the Torah we can safely conclude that the Alexandrian allegorists saw no profound significance in its literal meaning, however cautiously they may have expressed their conviction. Philo can see no point in history as history; to him it is simply so much material to be allegorized into philosophy, just as Heraclitus can see no point in the literal

meaning of Homer's description of the quarrels of gods and goddesses, and Plutarch discourages belief in the literal meaning of the legends about Isis and Osiris.

Similar perspectives inform Charles Bigg's *The Christian Platonists of Alexandria: The 1886 Bampton Lectures* (1913; reprint, Oxford: Clarendon Press, 1968) and Robert M. Grant's *The Letter and the Spirit* (London: S. P. C. K., 1957).

CHAPTER 1: PAGAN ETYMOLOGY AND ALLEGORY

1. I have used the Greek text of Cornutus edited by Carolus Lang, *Cornuti theologiae graecae compendium* (Leipzig: Teubner, 1881) (hereafter designated *Epidr.* and cited by chapter, page, and line). Lang's text is reproduced in Robert Stephen Hays, "Lucius Annaeus Cornutus' *Epidrome (Introduction to the Traditions of Greek Theology):* Introduction, Translation, and Notes," Ph.D. diss., University of Texas, 1983. I have used Hays's translation, with occasional alterations. The most likely title of Cornutus's work is *Epidromē tōn kata tēn hellēnikēn theologian paradedomenōn* (see Hays, 122 n. 1). My understanding of Cornutus's etymologizing and its distinction from the allegorizing interpretations of Heraclitus has been greatly informed by A. A. Long's paper "Stoic Readings of Homer," delivered at the symposium "Homer's Ancient Readers," which was held at Princeton University 6–7 October 1989 (references to this paper are to a prepublication version generously provided by Professor Long). Long makes important distinctions between different kinds of Stoic etymologists, and more generally, between the Stoic practice of etymological analysis of myth and the non-Stoic effort to read poets like Homer as intentional composers of allegory. In the process, he convincingly challenges Rudolf Pfeiffer's influential assertion that the Stoics were necessarily allegorical readers of poetry. For an excellent recent examination of the Stoics and allegory, including an overview of scholarly research on the topic, see Most, "Cornutus and Stoic Allegoresis," 2014–65. Unlike Long, Most generally conflates etymology and allegory (though he also implies a distinction: "The prime method Cornutus makes use of in the 'Epidrome' is etymology" [2027]). Like Most, Hays also tends to conflate etymology and allegory (though he too seems to imply some sort of distinction, referring at one point to "allegory which proceeded by the method of etymology of divine names" [5]). In addition to the *Compendium*, Cornutus wrote the following works, now lost: (1) at least one work on Aristotle's *Categories*, (2) *On Figures of Speech (De figuris sententiarum)*, (3) *Rhetorical Skills (Rhetorikai technai)*, (4) *On Proper Pronunciation (De enuntiatione)* or *On Proper Spelling (De orthographia)*, (5) one or more commentaries on Virgil's *Aeneid* (see Hays, 32–33).

2. As my division of the following passage from Cornutus's *Epidrome* makes clear, there are at least three groups involved: (1) the ancient mythmakers, (2) the poets who have handed down the myths, and (3) contemporary interpreters, such as Cornutus (who provides the final interpretation in this passage):

1. The myths hold [*mythologeisthai*] that he [*Dionysos*] was torn apart by the Titans and put back together by Rhea.
2. Those who passed on the myth [*hoi paradontes ton mython*] hinted indi-

rectly [*ainittomenoi*] that farmers, who are sucklings of the earth, smashed the clusters together and separated from one another the parts of "Dionysos" which was in them. But the confluence [*syrrysis;* cf. Rhea] of the sweet new wine gathered them into the same place again and produced one body from them. Homer's myth of how the god as he once fled Lycurgus' plot, submerged himself under the sea [*kata thalattēs*] and was rescued by Thetis [*Thetis*], manifestly contains this understanding.

3. For vines are the nurses [*tithēnai*] of Dionysos. Lycurgus despoiled the "nurses," i.e., took off their grapes. Then the vine was mixed with water [*thalattēi*] and safely stored away. Such is Dionysos. (*Epidr.* 30.62.10–22)

3. J. Tate, "Cornutus and the Poets," *Classical Quarterly* 23 (1929): 43–44, suggests that Cornutus found precedent for this approach in Aristotle's account of the truth hidden behind mythology (*Metaph.* 11.8.19–22).

4. See Tate, "Cornutus and Poets," 41 with n. 3. Consider the "later fabrication" added to myths of Hades and Demeter (*Epidr.* 28.54.14), as well as the reference to a "more recent story" (*hē neōtera historia*) (*Epidr.* 31.63.8).

5. For an etymologist, there is nothing accidental about names, as Cornutus indicates when he observes that the name of Asclepius's wife (*Ēpionē*) "is not taken into the myth idly, for it demonstrates the possibility of assuaging disturbance through gentle [*ēpios*] use of drugs" (*Epidr.* 33.71.3–5).

6. Cornutus was a practicing textual critic. For discussion of his emendations of the text of Virgil, see James E. G. Zetzel, *Latin Textual Criticism in Antiquity,* Monographs in Classical Studies (Salem, N. H.: The Ayer Company, 1981), 38–41.

7. See Most, "Cornutus and Stoic Allegoresis," 2025–26.

8. Stoic philosophy constitutes the bridge between ancients and moderns, as the following references to the *hēgemonikon* indicate:

Athena is the intelligence [*synesis*] of Zeus and is identical with his providence [*pronoia*], just as there are temples of Athena Pronoia. She is said to have been born from the head of Zeus: perhaps because the ancients [*hoi archaioi*] assumed that the ruling faculty [*to hēgemonikon*] of our soul was located there, just as other men of later times [i.e., Stoics] also decided. (*Epidr.* 20.35.6–12)

The closing remarks of Cornutus also suggest that the entire treatise is intended to enable students to detect for themselves the same correlations between ancient truths and modern Stoic physics:

And so, my child, it is my hope that you may be able in this way to take the other things which have been handed down to us in mythical form, ostensibly about the gods, and may bring them into conformity with the elementary models I have taught you. (*Epidr.* 35.75.18–35.76.2)

9. Cf. *Epidr.* 9.9.14: ancient mythmakers gave epithets "according to their different intentions" (*kata diaphorous epinoias*).

10. Unless otherwise noted, Stoic texts are from A. A. Long and D. N. Sedley, *The Hellenistic Philosophers,* vol. 1: *Translations of the Principal Sources, with Philosophical Commentary;* vol. 2: *Greek and Latin Texts with Notes and Bibliography* (Cam-

bridge: Cambridge Univ. Press, 1987). In the area of Stoic linguistics I have been guided by Michael Frede, "Principles of Stoic Grammar," in *The Stoics*, ed. J. M. Rist (Berkeley and Los Angeles: Univ. of California Press, 1978), 38–39. For an excellent introduction to ancient grammar and linguistics as a whole, see Jan Pinborg, "Classical Antiquity: Greece," in *Current Trends in Linguistics*, vol. 13, ed. Thomas A. Sebeok (The Hague: Mouton, 1975), 69–126.

11. See Origen *c. Cels.* 1.24; Philo *Op.* 148, *QuGen.* 1.20; Varro *Ling.* 5.89. See also Max Pohlenz, *Die Stoa: Geschichte einer geistigen Bewegung*, vol. 1 (Göttingen: Vandenhoeck & Ruprecht, 1948), 41ff.

12. Hays, "Cornutus' *Epidrome*," 13; Long and Sedley, *Hellenistic Philosophers*, vol. 1, 241.

13. Cf. *Epidr.* 32.65.20–32.66.2:

Apollo has received his name because they considered him to be one who "delivers" [*apolyōn*] us from diseases; or, because he is one who "drives them from us" [*apelaunōn*]. By this same conception [*ennoia*] he was also called "Healer" [*Paiēōn*] and thought to be a physician.

14. Cf. Cic. *Fin.* 3.33 (*SVF* 3.72); Sen. *Ep. mor.* 120.4ff.

15. Hays, "Cornutus' *Epidrome*," 15.

16. Pinborg, "Classical Antiquity: Greece," in *Current Trends*, vol. 13, ed. Sebeok, 95.

17. Although Cornutus relies heavily on the etymological precedent set by the Old Stoa, he can take an independent position on occasion. Thus he notes that even though it is possible to refer the twelve labors of the hero Herakles to the god, "as Cleanthes did," "it is not necessary for us always to give priority to that inventor of ingenious arguments" (*Epidr.* 31.64.16–17).

18. Etymology was also a useful method of ensuring the Hellenicity of an expression, for the original name-givers were, of course, speakers of perfect Greek (Frede, "Principles of Stoic Grammar," in *Stoics*, ed. Rist, 68–69; see Sext. Emp. *Math.* 1.241ff.).

19. Frede, "Principles of Stoic Grammar," in *Stoics*, ed. Rist, 70; cf. Varro *Ling.* 6.2.

20. Most, "Cornutus and Stoic Allegoresis," 2027–28, points out that Cornutus's etymologies rarely seem to go back to what could be called fundamental units and that he does not seem to worry about offering many different etymological alternatives. But Cornutus may not go "all the way back" either because his treatise is merely introductory or because the system was felt to be teachable even when the most primordial mimetic elements remained implicit. In addition, see *Compendium* 7 for an effort to coordinate different etymologies. The significant passage begins "But the nature of the world when it had gained its full strength, which we were saying is called Zeus . . ." (*Epidr.* 7.8.3–4).

21. D.L. 7.56. Stoic dialectic (the science of the real nature of things) studied both verbal expression (*lexis*—how voice is articulated to say something) and verbal expression as meaningful (the "meaning"—*to sēmainomenon* or *to lekton*—what is or could in fact be said) (D.L. 7.43, 62). While expression itself is corporeal (since spoken *phōnē* consists of vibrations of air and written *phōnē* of marks on paper), meanings are not. Moreover, because "existence" for the materialist Stoics

denotes the capacity to act or to be acted upon, a capacity that "meanings" do not have, the Stoics thought that "meanings" did not exist. However, they did think that they were "real." "Centaur," they contended, has a perfectly real meaning, even though neither centaurs nor the meaning of "centaur" exists. For the Stoics, then, language consisted of corporeal expressions (combinations of phonemes and graphemes), which, if they issued from a rational being, could "mean" something real and incorporeal.

22. *Ep. mor.* 117.13, quoted and discussed by A. A. Long, *Hellenistic Philosophy: Stoics, Epicureans, Sceptics,* 2d ed. (Berkeley and Los Angeles: Univ. of California Press, 1986), 136. In my exegetical comments, I have drawn heavily on Long's discussion of this passage.

23. Seneca suggests that by itself the personal name "Cato" is like the noun "wisdom" in denoting the nature of a body—in this case, the disposition of the material that is Cato as he is walking. The material nature of ethical and intellectual qualities like "wisdom" is orthodox Stoicism.

24. The Stoics argue that complete meanings require the combination of predicates with "cases." It is tempting to identify the Stoic "case" with lexical inflection since the formation of a case generally requires one to change the ending of a noun. But the Stoics distinguish cases from inflections; oddly enough, for them case is a matter of meaning, while inflection is a matter of mere expression. This peculiar Stoic view can be clarified by contrasting it with the Aristotelian position. For Aristotle, the cases of a noun are the lexical forms that the noun assumes in its genitive, dative, and accusative forms (the so-called oblique cases, inflected on the basis of the nominative). Aristotelian cases are simply the lexical forms produced by inflections, and both cases and inflections are features of verbal expression. But for the Stoics, there can be no purely lexical relationship between cases and inflections because while inflection is a feature of words, Stoic cases are neither features of words nor words themselves; instead, cases "subsist" (not "exist") on the level of what is signified or meant. Cases are semantic, rather than lexical, entities, constituents of what is meant rather than of the expressions themselves.

25. See Jakobson, "Two Aspects of Language," in *Fundamentals of Language,* ed. Jakobson and Halle.

26. The components of conceptions, expressions, and meanings are then combined in various ways according to complex, shared principles of syntactical composition. The Stoics apparently believed, for instance, that there existed a syntax of incorporeal meanings directly corresponding to the syntax of the corporeal verbal expressions themselves (the titles of several of Chrysippus's lost treatises indicate that meanings, like expressions, have syntax: *On the Syntax of Meanings (lekta); On the Syntax and the Elements of Meanings, to Philippus*—D.L. 7.193). Some Stoics even tried to show that proper names differed from common nouns in declension, in order to indicate that there was a corresponding difference represented by the declensions at the level of meanings (Frede, "Principles of Stoic Grammar," in *Stoics,* ed. Rist, 73). They further insisted that even conjunctions and articles, like nouns and verbs, are parts of meaningful speech rather than simply parts of expression. It is tempting to speculate that the Stoics might have drawn on this theory of a "syntax of *lekta*" corresponding to lexical syntax in

order to justify continuous allegorical readings of texts, in which every lexical element was given a corresponding nonliteral meaning. Such a view would lead to the possibility of treating every element of a text as potentially meaningful on another mysterious level of *"lekta."* But we have no evidence that Stoics ever applied such a theory to the general reading of texts or used it to endorse the allegorical reading of literature.

27. *SVF* 2.151.

28. *SVF* 2.152.

29. Sext. Emp. *Math.* 1.154 (Athens), 1.150–53 (gender); Simpl. *In cael.* 396.5ff., especially 396.19ff. ("immortal"); cited by Frede, "Principles of Stoic Grammar," in *Stoics,* ed. Rist, 72.

30. See Claude Imbert, "Stoic Logic and Alexandrian Poetics," in *Doubt and Dogmatism: Studies in Hellenistic Epistemology,* ed. M. Schofield, M. Burnyeat, and J. Barnes (Oxford: Clarendon Press, 1980), 182–216.

31. Cf. *Epidr.* 20.36.20–20.37.1: Athena "quite appropriately [*pany eikotōs*] . . . shares the aegis with Zeus. For she is identical with that thing in respect to which Zeus excels and is superior to everything."

32. Most, "Cornutus and Stoic Allegoresis," 2030–31.

33. Most, "Cornutus and Stoic Allegoresis," 2038–39, points to *Epidr.* 32.67.17–68.8 (Apollo and music), 32.65.1–2 (Apollo as sun and archer), 32.66.19–67.2 (Apollo as "unshorn" and "golden-tressed"). See also Mark Morford, "Nero's Patronage and Participation in Literature and the Arts," *ANRW* II.32.3 (1985): 2012. Morford points out that Cornutus was probably a freedman of Seneca's family and that as a well-known and highly respected scholar he provided patronage for poets. Such literary patronage was often absorbed by Nero's own personal patronage.

34. Hays, "Cornutus' *Epidrome,*" 32. In his edition of the posthumous poems of his pupil Persius, Cornutus removed or toned down passages critical of Nero.

35. Ramsay MacMullen, *Enemies of the Roman Order: Treason, Unrest, and Alienation in the Empire* (Cambridge, Mass.: Harvard Univ. Press, 1966), 54. See also Ursula Vogel-Weidemann, "The Opposition Under the Early Caesars: Some Remarks on Its Nature and Aims," *Acta Classica* 22 (1979): 91–107, especially 98–100 on "philosophical opposition" to the principate. J. P. Sullivan, *Literature and Politics in the Age of Nero* (Ithaca, N. Y.: Cornell Univ. Press, 1985), 106, suggests that Cornutus was probably exiled not for criticizing Nero's plan to write a poem on Rome's founding but rather because of his presence in the circle around Thrasea Paetus and his general association with the Annaean family, which was involved in opposition to Nero.

36. MacMullen, *Enemies of Roman Order,* 57. Vogel-Weidemann, "Opposition Under the Early Caesars," 98–99, discusses the escalating attempts to crush the Stoic resistance to the emperor.

37. Most, "Cornutus and Stoic Allegoresis," 2041.

38. Vogel-Weidemann, "Opposition Under the Early Caesars," 99.

39. Most, "Cornutus and Stoic Allegoresis," 2040. He points to *Epidr.* 10.11.9–12, 11.12.2–5, 13.13.20–14.2, 16.21.15–18 (2033 n. 149).

40. *Epidr.* 9.10.10–16 (see Most, "Cornutus and Stoic Allegoresis," 2040).

41. Vogel-Weidemann, "Opposition Under the Early Caesars," 100.

42. Cornutus displays an uncharacteristic hint of embarrassment when criticizing the ancients in the following passage:

> It may be that Priapus [*Priapos*] is the same—that by which all things "enter into the light" [*proeisin eis phōs*]—and that the ancients represented their ideas about the nature of the cosmos in their superstitious and exaggerated fashion. At any rate, the magnitude of his genitals suggests the superabundant fecundity which God contains. (*Epidr.* 27.50.15–18)

More customary is Cornutus's disregard of propriety, as in this passage:

> The satyrs are introduced [in depictions of Dionysos] having intercourse with the nymphs and trying to seduce them and jovially raping some of them because the mixing of wine into water was seen to be useful. (*Epidr.* 30.60.12–15)

43. For an overview of philosophical criticism of religion in the period under discussion, see Harold W. Attridge, "The Philosophical Critique of Religion under the Early Empire," *ANRW* II.16.1 (1978): 45–78. For Heraclitus, I have used the critical edition of Félix Buffière, *Héraclite, Allégories d'Homère* (Paris: Société d'édition "Les Belles Lettres," 1962), which includes the Greek text, a French translation, and an introduction. Translations from the Greek are my own, though I have been aided at various points by Buffière's French version. Citations follow Buffière's chapter and sentence divisions. This Hellenistic writer should not be confused with the pre-Socratic philosopher by the same name; I will always refer to the latter as the "pre-Socratic" Heraclitus. A helpful study, which includes a useful summary of scholarship and bibliography, is Cynthia Louise Thompson, "Stoic Allegory of Homer: A Critical Analysis of Heraclitus' 'Homeric Allegories,'" (Ph.D. diss., Yale University, 1973). Among the most important accounts of ancient allegory are Félix Buffière, *Les mythes d'Homère et la pensée grecque* (Paris: Société d'édition "Les Belles Lettres," 1956); and Jean Pépin, *Mythe et allégorie: Les origines grecques et les contestations judéo-chrétiennes,* new ed. (Paris: Études Augustiniennes, 1976). For a brief account of early classical allegorical interpretation by a literary historian, see Michael Murrin, *The Allegorical Epic: Essays in Its Rise and Decline* (Chicago: Univ. of Chicago Press, 1980), 3–25. The most likely title of Heraclitus's work is *Hērakleitou Homērikōn problēmatōn eis ha peri theōn Homēros ēllēgorēsen* (see Buffière, *Héraclite,* vii–viii, viii n. 1). Although he makes use of Stoic concepts, Heraclitus is not an orthodox Stoic like Cornutus (Buffière, *Héraclite,* xxii–xxxix). In *Mythes d'Homère,* 70, Buffière notes that Heraclitus is not a Stoic seeking to harmonize Homer with the theories of that school, but rather a rhetorician "preoccupied with the triumph of Homer over all the schools." By the first century C. E., Stoic ideas had joined a mixture of other philosophical concepts that had accompanied a long-standing tradition of eclectic exegesis of Homer. To draw on this tradition was not to identify oneself with any particular philosophical school, even when one used school jargon. Note that at *All.* 33.1, Heraclitus refers to "the most eminent Stoics" as a group in which he appears not to include himself. For discussion of another important example of ancient allegorical reading of Greek myth, Pseudo-Plutarch's *De vita et poesi Homeri (Life and Poetry of*

Homer), see Thompson, "Stoic Allegory of Homer," 93–105, and Buffière, *Mythes d'Homère*, 71–77.

44. In contrast to Cornutus's focus on names rather than narratives. Long, "Stoic Readings of Homer," 8, notes that Cornutus "is interested in what we might call proto-myth, myth detached from narrative context in a poem."

45. Heraclitus also knows of more recent myths that were composed after the poet's time (see *All*. 7.10).

46. According to George Kennedy, *The Art of Persuasion in Greece* (Princeton: Princeton Univ. Press, 1963), 298, *metalēpsis*, along with onomatopoeia, *katachrēsis*, and metaphor, is a trope of similarity. It consists in the substitution of a partial synonym, such as "chant" for "say." Kennedy observes further that the rhetorical theory of tropes originated in Stoic theories about the origin of words.

47. See the Introduction, note 9.

48. Heraclitus relies on a standard ancient rhetorical definition of allegory as a trope that expresses one thing by means of something else (*All*. 5.2), and he thinks of it as a specific art or skill (*All*. 5.1). He also offers some stock examples of ancient allegory (*All*. 5).

49. Throughout the treatise, the verbs "to allegorize," "to philosophize," and "to theologize" are used synonymously.

50. See *All*. 13.5, 15.2, 23.2, 24.5, 41.12, 61.3.

51. See *All*. 22.1, 41.5, 68.2.

52. Compared with Cornutus, Heraclitus's use of etymology is relatively infrequent. Whereas for Cornutus, etymological analysis is the end result of his interpretation, it is only one means to Heraclitus's end.

53. Is this why Heraclitus says at one point that though he will be following the interpretations of Apollodorus, he will not offer an inappropriately lengthy discussion (by reproducing all that Apollodorus says?) but will limit himself to what is necessary given his own "conjecture" (*All*. 7.1–3)?

54. While cosmic harmony is ultimately indestructible, the alternation of elements can take place, for Heraclitus's narrative sensibility requires him to allow for Hera's later escape.

55. Cornutus gives virtually the same etymology (*ōkeanos*, from "the one who swims swiftly," *ho ōkeōs neomenos*) but does not attribute it to Homer (*Epidr*. 8.8.13).

56. Heraclitus (*All*. 23.1–2) points out that his later discussion of Hera's chains (*All*. 40) also makes the same point—another instance of his concern to preserve narrative consistency.

57. Cf. *Epidr*. 5.5.2–4.

58. Other instances of claims for Homer's originality and the derivative nature of other thinkers include the following: (1) Plato's theory of the soul (*All*. 17.4ff.); as Heraclitus explains, "Plato . . . diverted [*metardeuein*] these things, as if from a spring, from the Homeric verses to his own dialogues" (*All*. 18.1); (2) Homer's intimation of the three parts of philosophy, when he writes that Hercules struck Hera "with a three-barbed arrow" (*Il*. 5.393; *All*. 34.4); (3) Empedocles' notion of cosmic strife, derived from the depiction of the two cities of peace and war on Achilles' shield (*All*. 49); (4) Eratosthenes' idea of four geographical and climatic zones, also derived from Achilles' shield (*All*. 50).

59. Quotations are taken from Cicero, *De natura deorum, Academica*, trans.

H. Rackham, Loeb Classical Library (New York: G. P. Putnam's Sons, 1933). References are to book and marginal numbering. I have also made use of Arthur Stanley Pease, ed., *M. Tulli Ciceronis De natura deorum*, 2 vols. (Cambridge, Mass.: Harvard Univ. Press, 1955, 1958).

60. Balbus has several explanations for the origin and nature of the gods and goddesses of popular worship. They may be personifications of virtues or passions (such as Faith, Mind, Virtue, Honor, Wealth, Safety, Concord, Liberty, Fortune, Desire, Pleasure) or of natural forces. Or they may be either gifts of the gods elevated to divine status (thus "we speak of corn as Ceres, wine as Liber") or dead heroes also divinized (such as Hercules, Castor, Pollux, Romulus) (*Nat. d.* 2.60–64).

61. Chrysippus himself wrote two works on etymology, *Peri tōn etymologikōn pros Dioklea* (seven books) and *Etymologikōn pros Dioklea* (four books) (D.L. 7.200).

62. Two different schools of etymological thought existed at Rome; one sought the origin of words in Latin, the other in Greek (Pease, *Ciceronis De natura deorum*, vol. 2, 709–10, with note).

63. Note that this analysis of Saturn occurs as part of a larger explication of how the elements of fire, air, earth, and water are represented as mythological deities (*Nat. d.* 2.63–69).

64. I have translated *per quandam significationem* literally as "by means of a certain kind of interpretation" rather than as "allegorically" (as does the Loeb translator Rackham) in order to make a distinction between the practice of etymological analysis (which is what Cicero is describing here) and the practice of reading or composing narratives as allegories (as in Heraclitus). Pease, *Ciceronis De natura deorum*, vol. 1, 256 note, suggests that the *quandam* may indicate that the description being offered is only approximate, or it may represent an apology for a translation from the Greek. His view is that " 'a sort of allegorical interpretation' is perhaps what Cicero here intends to say."

65. Chrysippus probably treated the poets much the same way as did Cornutus—as preservers of portions of ancient myth—and not the way Heraclitus did—as composers of allegories. However, Tate, "Cornutus and Poets," 42, disagrees, arguing that Chrysippus, like other early Stoics, "believed Homer and Hesiod to have been original thinkers, who expressed sound doctrine in the mythical style proper to the primitive times in which they lived." In contrast, Cornutus, in preserving mythical fragments and holding a "low estimate of the poets," "was diverging from the orthodox Stoic position," as Cicero makes clear in *De natura deorum* 1.41 when he has Velleius say that Chrysippus read the ancient poets as proto-Stoic philosophers. Cicero would not have said this, argues Tate, "if Chrysippus (like Cornutus) had treated the poets as having transmitted scraps and shreds of an ancient philosophy which they themselves did not understand." But Tate does not give sufficient weight to the polemical dialogue in which Cicero presents Velleius's attack (see Long, "Stoic Readings of Homer," 2). Moreover, when Velleius speaks of the "myths" of the poets, he does not make it clear whether he believes that Chrysippus thinks that the poets themselves composed the myths or merely transmitted them. Tate's appeal to Heraclitus overlooks the fact that while Heraclitus adopts some Stoic etymological readings (which were the common property of all Homer exegetes by his time), he offers no endorsement of Stoic hermeneutics as such.

66. *Praenotiones* is a translation of the Greek *prolēpseis*.

67. Note that Cicero seems to make a distinction between a nonliteral exposition of names (etymology) and a nonliteral interpretation of myth or narrative.

68. Quotations are from *Seneca*, vol. 3, trans. John W. Basore, Loeb Classical Library (1935; reprint, Cambridge, Mass.: Harvard Univ. Press, 1975).

69. Despite Seneca's disclaimer, his comment is motivated by the correspondence between the Latin *gratiae* ("graces") and *gratus* ("benefit").

70. Tate, "Cornutus and Poets," 43, points out that Cornutus also implicitly criticizes Chrysippus for oversubtle etymologies, such as the derivation of Tritogeneia from the three divisions (*tria genē*) of philosophy (*Epidr.* 20.37.14–16).

71. The Loeb editor Basore notes that "as the daughter of Ocean, she was the 'Wide-spreading One' "—from *eurynein*, "to make wide or broad."

72. Tate, "Cornutus and Poets," 41 n. 2, notes that Seneca (in *Ep. mor.* 88.5) "rejects the view that there is Stoic or any other philosophy contained in Homer."

73. Quotations are from the following editions: J. Gwyn Griffiths, ed., *Plutarch's De Iside et Osiride* (Cambridge: Univ. of Wales Press, 1970), with introduction, translation, and commentary; *How the Young Man Should Study Poetry*, in *Plutarch's Moralia*, vol. 1, trans. Frank Cole Babbitt, Loeb Classical Library (New York: G. P. Putnam's Sons, 1927).

74. D. A. Russell, *Plutarch*, Classical Life and Letters, ed. Hugh Lloyd-Jones (New York: Scribners, 1973), 81, points out that Plutarch was certainly aware of, and made use of, works like those of Cornutus and Heraclitus.

75. See Russell, *Plutarch*, 84–99, on Plutarch's application of Aristotle's ideal of the "mean."

76. Cornutus (*Epidr.* 31) also criticizes Cleanthes for unrestrained etymologizing (Tate, "Cornutus and Poets," 43).

77. This myth was developed into a full-blown allegorical composition by Apuleius in his *Metamorphoses or The Golden Ass*.

78. As Plutarch explains further, "it is not the same thing at all to imitate something beautiful and something beautifully, since 'beautifully' means 'fittingly and properly' [*to prepontōs kai oikeiōs*] and ugly things are 'fitting and proper' for the ugly" (*De aud. poet.* 18D); "if . . . we remind our sons that authors write them, not because they commend or approve them, but with the idea of investing mean and unnatural [*atopa*] characters and persons with unnatural [*atopa*] and mean sentiments, they could not be harmed by the opinions of poets" (*De aud. poet.* 18E–F).

79. Note Plutarch's impatience with the study of technical "glosses" (collections of the meanings of strange or obsolete words). Instead, he calls for greater moral sensitivity to poetic usage.

80. See Russell, *Plutarch*, 51–53, for further discussion of these techniques.

81. Plato uses the term *hyponoia* to refer to the nonliteral meanings of Greek myths.

82. See his specific examples of instances where poets simply repeat the original insights of philosophers (*De aud. poet.* 35Fff.).

83. Plutarch commends the emended versions (*hai paradiorthōseis*) of Cleanthes and Antisthenes (*De aud. poet.* 33Cff.).

84. I have used the following editions: Hartmut Erbse, ed., *Scholia graeca in Homeri Iliadem* (*Scholia vetera*), 6 vols. (Berlin: Walter de Gruyter, 1969–83), cited

as E, by volume, page, and lemma; G. Dindorf, ed., *Scholia graeca in Homeri Odysseam*, 2 vols. (1855; reprint, Amsterdam: Adolf M. Hakkert, 1962), cited as D, by page and lemma; William G. Rutherford, ed. and trans., *Scholia Aristophanica*, 3 vols. (London: Macmillan, 1896–1905), cited as R, by volume, page, and lemma; John Williams White, ed., *The Scholia on the* Aves *of Aristophanes* (Boston: Ginn & Company, 1915). Translations from the Homeric scholia are my own; those from the scholia on Aristophanes are by Rutherford. Translations from the *Iliad* and *Odyssey* are by E. V. Rieu, *The Iliad* (Baltimore: Penguin, 1950) and *The Odyssey* (Baltimore: Penguin, 1946), which I have occasionally altered to bring them into clearer relation to the Greek of the scholia. All references to Homer have been standardized and are to book and line. Translations from Aristophanes are from *Aristophanes*, 3 vols., trans. Benjamin Bickley Rogers, Loeb Classical Library (1924; reprint, Cambridge, Mass.: Harvard Univ. Press, 1967–72), also modified when appropriate. The fundamental survey of Alexandrian scholarship in the context of Hellenistic scholarship as a whole is Rudolf Pfeiffer, *History of Classical Scholarship: From the Beginnings to the End of the Hellenistic Age* (Oxford: Clarendon Press, 1968). An older, but still useful, study (if read in light of Pfeiffer's corrections and revisions) is John Edwin Sandys, *A History of Classical Scholarship*, 3 vols. (1958; reprint, New York: Hafner, 1964). I have also benefited from E. G. Turner, *Greek Papyri: An Introduction* (Oxford: Clarendon Press, 1968), especially chapter 7, "Papyri and Greek Literature." For general surveys of the period in question, see the following: F. E. Peters, *The Harvest of Hellenism: A History of the Near East from Alexander the Great to the Triumph of Christianity* (New York: Simon and Schuster, 1970); H[arold] Idris Bell, *Egypt from Alexander the Great to the Arab Conquest: A Study in the Diffusion and Decay of Hellenism*, The Gregynog Lectures 1946 (1948; reprint, Westport, Conn.: Greenwood Press, 1977).

85. Sandys, *History of Classical Scholarship*, vol. 1, 127. Scholion D on *Iliad* 5.385 offers a typical expression of Alexandrian distaste for allegorical reading. The Alexandrian scholar Aristarchus (217 B.C.E.–145 B.C.E.) recommends that interpreters take the myth of Otus and Ephialtes as a bit of legend "due to poetic license [*kata tēn poiētikēn exousian*] and not waste time on things not said by the poet [*mēden exō tōn phrazomenōn hypo tou poiētou periergazomenoi*]" (Pfeiffer, *History of Classical Scholarship*, 226–27). In another version of this statement, a scholiast makes the antiallegorical sensibility of Aristarchus even more explicit by inserting *allēgorikōs* after *periergazomenoi* (Pfeiffer, 227 n. 1).

86. See Sext. Emp. *Math.* 1.176–79; Arist. *Rh.* 1404b1; D.L. 7.59. On Alexandrian grammar and linguistics, see Pinborg, "Classical Antiquity: Greece," in *Current Trends*, vol. 13, ed. Sebeok, 106–10. Alexandrian grammarians assessed the degree of Hellenicity according to criteria furnished by their analysis of etymology, analogy, customary usage, and historical authority (Pinborg, 108 n. 35).

87. For a thorough analysis of the Alexandrian philological practice of analogy, see Detlev Fehling, "Varro und die grammatische Lehre von der Analogie und der Flexion," *Glotta* 35 (1956): 214–70, discussed in Pinborg, "Classical Antiquity: Greece," in *Current Trends*, vol. 13, ed. Sebeok, 108. Following a distinction made famous by the Roman linguist and literary historian Varro, scholars have traditionally called the Alexandrians who created paradigms of inflectional regularity Analogists, contrasting them with Pergamene interpreters known as Anomalists,

who were preoccupied with the ambiguous relations between words and their meanings. In terms defined by this traditional scheme, the Alexandrian philologists were concerned with the "analogy" between word forms and inflections, the Stoics with the "anomaly" between word forms and meanings (Frede, "Principles of Stoic Grammar," in *Stoics*, ed. Rist, 72). It seems clear, however, that the two parties were not addressing the same issue, and even Varro himself thought that the opposition between them was due to a misunderstanding (see Varro *Ling.* 9.1). Furthermore, Varro's own systematization of the confused controversy has been discredited in recent scholarship (see Pinborg, 107, for a summary of Fehling's conclusions). For these reasons, and also because the traditional labels for this controversy do little to clarify the hermeneutical issues I am exploring, I have abandoned the categories of "anomaly" and "analogy" altogether.

88. Presumably, a modern editor of e. e. cummings's poetry might consider morphological irregularities evidence of original creative deviation rather than scribal corruption.

89. Assuming, then, that formally similar words should have similar inflections, Aristarchus identified patterns of declensional and conjugational regularity in the language of Homer and other Greek writers. He next isolated word forms deviating from the principles underlying such patterns. Finally, he emended those deviant word forms to fit the appropriate inflectional rules or athetized them as either hopeless corruptions or interpolations. To "athetize" (*athetein*) means to designate a line or lines as spurious by means of a critical sign; it does not mean to delete the lines altogether from the text. For example, for reasons that remain unknown (but which probably reflected editorial skepticism about authenticity), all of the *Iliad*'s account of the making of the shield of Achilles by Hephaestus (*Il.* 18.478–608) was athetized by Aristarchus's predecessor Zenodotus (b. ca. 325 B.C.E.).

90. Pl. *Rep.* 2.377C–392C. For Xenophanes, see G. S. Kirk and J. E. Raven, *The Presocratic Philosophers: A Critical History with a Selection of Texts* (Cambridge: Cambridge Univ. Press, 1957), 168, frag. 169 (= Sext. Emp. *Math.* 9.193).

91. See M. van der Valk, *Researches on the Text and Scholia of the* Iliad, vol. 2 (Leiden: Brill, 1963–64), 11–13, 35.

92. Modern textual critics seeking to determine authenticity follow much the same procedure, though, unlike their Alexandrian predecessors, they recognize that great poets can produce surprisingly idiosyncratic originalities. Moreover, although modern critics expect a certain degree of morphological regularity within a single author's usage, they do not expect such regularity within the language as a whole. For a classic and concise statement of modern principles of textual criticism, see Paul Maas, *Textual Criticism*, trans. Barbara Flower (Oxford: Clarendon Press, 1958).

93. This textual editing was generally done in a careful, tentative fashion; Alexandrian editors did not claim to have the last word on the text and its authenticity. Noting the denigration of the "revised" (i.e., critically edited) text of Homer by Timon of Phlius (ca. 320 B.C.E.–230 B.C.E.), Pfeiffer, *History of Classical Scholarship*, 173, observes that "a characteristic attitude of the Greek spirit" was a "distrust of a hypothetical 'genuine' text, and an inclination to save the 'old text' hallowed by tradition." He points both to the reluctance shown by Aristarchus's

predecessor Aristophanes (ca. 257 B.C.E.–180 B.C.E.) to athetize or to make conjectural emendations and to the general Alexandrian practice of putting signs in the margins or writing separate commentaries rather than deleting questionable texts (173–74).

94. E.1.433.423a.

95. D.518–19.525.

96. E.5.543.130–32(a).

97. E.5.543.130–32(b).

98. E.5.520.23. Cornutus handles the problem of Hermes as thief this way:

> Some, desiring to suggest his function by employing incongruities, passed on the story of him as a thief and set up an altar of "Guileful Hermes" [*Dolios Hermēs*]. For unnoticed, he slips men's previous assumptions away from them. There are even times when he steals away the truth by persuasiveness. That is why they say of certain people that they use "a con-man's words." In fact, sophistry is the unique privilege of those who know how to use rational speech. (*Epidr.* 16.25.11–18)

For a case where Homeric lines were felt to be unfitting because they conflicted with other parts of the narrative, see E.5.520–21.23 on Paris's hut (*Il.* 24.29). For a similar case of internal narrative contradictions, see E.5.521.23.

99. E.1.432.423(a).

100. Alexandrian editors had other techniques for establishing consistency, such as appealing to the attributes of a general class to which a character belongs (see D.345.238 on Queen Arete) or paying close attention to the characteristics of specific individuals (see E.2.204.433 on Andromache). Alexandrian editors could also counter charges of impropriety by pointing out the underlying motivation of characters (see E.4.180.83–96 on Achilles' admonition to Patroclus).

101. R.1.72.685.

102. R.1.114.1153.

103. For further details, see P. M. Fraser, *Ptolemaic Alexandria*, vol. 1 (Oxford: Clarendon Press, 1972), 305–12.

104. Van der Valk, *Researches on the* Iliad, vol. 2, 13.

105. For parallels between Zenodotus's editorial techniques and those of Jewish interpreters, see Saul Lieberman, *Hellenism in Jewish Palestine*, 2d ed. (New York: Jewish Theological Seminary, 1962), 36–37. See also David Daube, "Alexandrian Methods of Interpretation and the Rabbis," in *Essays in Greco-Roman and Related Talmudic Literature*, selected with a prolegomena by Henry A. Fischel, The Library of Biblical Studies, ed. Harry M. Orlinsky (New York: KTAV, 1977), 165–82, and, in the same volume, Saul Lieberman, "Rabbinic Interpretation of Scripture," 289–324.

CHAPTER 2: PHILO: THE REINSCRIPTION OF REALITY

1. D. A. Russell, *Criticism in Antiquity* (London: Duckworth, 1981), 112.

2. One should not overstate this basic contrast, however. Jewish scribes (*soferim*) in Palestine sought to establish the text actually revealed to Moses. They intro-

duced certain critical signs into manuscripts and occasionally emended texts for various reasons (Lieberman, *Hellenism in Jewish Palestine*, 20ff.).

3. For a convenient anthology of examples of these and other genres, see James H. Charlesworth, ed., *The Old Testament Pseudepigrapha*, 2 vols. (Garden City, N. Y.: Doubleday, 1983, 1985), which includes introductions and basic bibliographies. See also Carl R. Holladay, comp. and trans., *Fragments from Hellenistic Jewish Authors*, vol. 1: *Historians* (Chico, Calif.: Scholars Press, 1983), which includes texts, apparatus, translations, and commentary.

4. For Aristobulus, I have used the following Greek texts and English translations (occasionally modified): fragment 1 (= Euseb. *Hist. eccl.* 7.32.16–18) in Eduard Schwartz, ed., *Eusebius Werke*, 2: *Kirchengeschichte, zweiter Teil*, GCS 9.2 (Leipzig: Hinrich's, 1908), 722, 724; fragments 2–5 (= Euseb. *Praep. evang.* 8.10, 13.12, 7.14): frag. 2 in Karl Mras, ed., *Eusebius Werke*, 8: *Die Praeparatio evangelica*, GCS 43.1 (Berlin: Akademie-Verlag, 1982), 451–54; frags. 3–5 in GCS 43.2 (Berlin: Akademie-Verlag, 1983), 190–97. English translation by A. Yarbro Collins, "Aristobulus: A New Translation and Introduction," in *Old Testament Pseudepigrapha*, vol. 2, ed. Charlesworth, 831–42. The basic study is Nikolaus Walter, *Der Thoraausleger Aristobulos: Untersuchungen zu seinen Fragmenten und zu pseudepigraphischen Resten der jüdisch-hellenistischen Literatur* (Berlin: Akademie-Verlag, 1964). For Pseudo-Aristeas, I have used Moses Hadas, ed. and trans., *Aristeas to Philocrates (Letter of Aristeas)* (New York: Harper & Brothers, 1951). Hereafter I will refer to the author simply as Aristeas.

5. The details of my discussion of this point come largely from Russell, *Criticism in Antiquity*, 96–97. For a careful analysis of allegory as defined by ancient rhetoricians, see Reinhart Hahn, "Die Allegorie in der antiken Rhetorik" (Inaug. diss., Tübingen, 1967).

6. See Fulgentius, "The Exposition of the Content of Virgil According to Moral Philosophy," in *Classical and Medieval Literary Criticism: Translations and Interpretations*, ed. Alex Preminger, O. B. Hardison, and Kevin Kerrane (New York: Frederick Ungar, 1974), 329–40.

7. C. Jenson, ed., *Philodemos über die Gedichte: Fünftes Buch* (Berlin, 1923), 7.

8. Russell, *Criticism in Antiquity*, 97. Lamberton, *Homer the Theologian*, 20, echoes Russell's point, noting that in ancient allegorical interpretation "there is never any suggestion that the goal of the commentator is anything but the elucidation of the intention or meaning (*dianoia*) of the author." The ancient rhetorical perspective thus bears little resemblance to modern notions of "rhetoricity," which generally refer to the instability and self-subverting character of textual signifiers, "the vertiginous possibilities of referential aberration." For this latter notion, see Paul de Man, "Semiology and Rhetoric," chapter 1 in *Allegories of Reading: Figural Language in Rousseau, Nietzsche, Rilke, and Proust* (New Haven: Yale Univ. Press, 1979), 3–19. One important point of similarity between the ancient and the modern notions, however, is that both exploit the figurative character of language. As an art of persuasive communication, ancient rhetoric demanded that figures have an understandable literal, as well as an interesting nonliteral, meaning (i.e., they should be both clear and out of the ordinary). It also required that the use of tropes be governed by the overall persuasive goals of rhetorical discourse. These goals are not shared by many postmodern theorists of allegory, for

whom allegorical discourse is not a means of communication and persuasion but a kind of self-critical reading that reflects on the character of its own semantic indeterminacy.

9. Martin Hengel, *Judaism and Hellenism: Studies in Their Encounter in Palestine during the Early Hellenistic Period*, vol. 1, trans. John Bowden (1974; reprint, Philadelphia: Fortress, 1981), 164, suggests that for Aristobulus such inappropriate readings came from two sources: Greeks who criticized literal Jewish law or anthropomorphisms, and conservative Jews who criticized nonliteral readings.

10. An important Stoic hermeneutical criterion. See also *Praep. evang.* 13.12.9 (*physikōs*), 8.10.3 (*physikē diathesis*); *Aris. to Phil.* 171 (*physikē dianoia tou nomou*), on which, see Hengel, *Judaism and Hellenism*, vol. 2, 107 n. 380.

11. This depiction of Demetrius as librarian is almost certainly false. Demetrius opposed Philadelphus's accession to the throne and was consequently exiled by the king. Although connected with the founding of the Library, he was not a librarian (Fraser, *Ptolemaic Alexandria*, vol. 1, 689–90).

12. On the uncertain date of Aristobulus, see Hengel, *Judaism and Hellenism*, vol. 2, 106–107 n. 378; for Aristeas, see Collins, in *Old Testament Pseudepigrapha*, vol. 2, ed. Charlesworth, 81–84. The dating of Ptolemaic Jewish literature is very uncertain.

13. Fraser, *Ptolemaic Alexandria*, vol. 1, 84. Aristeas says that the corporate body (*politeuma*) of Jews approved the translation of scripture (*Aris. to Phil.* 310). In this early period, special quarters for the Jews constituted a mark of honor.

14. Fraser, *Ptolemaic Alexandria*, vol. 1, 694.

15. Indicated in part by the assurance with which the Jewish author adopts the persona of a high Greek official and assesses Judaism favorably from that perspective (Hadas, *Aristeas to Philocrates*, 61).

16. See Hadas, *Aristeas to Philocrates*, 5–6, and Fraser, *Ptolemaic Alexandria*, vol. 1, 698–99.

17. Fraser, *Ptolemaic Alexandria*, vol. 1, 699.

18. Ibid., 695. Because of the fragmentary evidence of Jewish interpretation in the Ptolemaic age, lines of influence and tradition stretching from these early figures to the later Philo are speculative and have the status of tentative suggestions.

19. Fraser, *Ptolemaic Alexandria*, vol. 1, 695.

20. Hadas, *Aristeas to Philocrates*, 102 n. 16.

21. V. Tcherikover, "The Ideology of the Letter of Aristeas," *Harvard Theological Review* 51 (1958): 70–71, points to the "perplexing anonymity" of the translators at the symposium, who refrain from emphasizing their nationality, but he suggests that even so, "it is clear that the dialogues with the Elders of Jerusalem were supposed to reveal to the King (and in fact to the reader) the very essence of Judaism. If they do not fulfill this purpose, what else were they meant for?" Tcherikover, 71, argues further that this essence is that "Judaism is a combination of a universal philosophy with the idea of monotheism"—such is Judaism in "its ideal purity." But the point of the symposium may instead be to show that Jewish wise men and translators of Jewish law respond to Greek questions with "Greek" answers while referring all the answers to God, that is, *their* God. The oddity of Tcherikover's conclusion is matched by Hengel's remarks on Aristobulus's discussion of wisdom:

We do not even find here the unique connection with Israel, which was achieved in Ben Sira through the identification of wisdom *with the law*. Its place is taken by the identification of wisdom with the cosmic principle of seven, *which had been revealed to Israel in a special way through the Sabbath commandment.* (*Judaism and Hellenism*, vol. 1, 168; my emphasis)

Hengel disregards the fact that the special revelation to Israel identifies wisdom and the cosmic principle of seven with the law (i.e., the Sabbath *commandment*); despite Hengel's conclusion, this identification seems to constitute a "unique connection with Israel."

22. For a recent instance of this widely held view, see John J. Collins, *Between Athens and Jerusalem: Jewish Identity in the Hellenistic Diaspora* (New York: Crossroad, 1983). With respect to the claim made by philosophically minded Jews like Aristeas that the God of the Jews is the same as the God of non-Jews, Collins, 180, quotes with approval a remark by Hadas, *Aristeas to Philocrates,* 62:

The theology premised is applicable to all mankind, not to the Jews alone, and God's providence is universal. . . . The Jews follow their own traditional usage to attain a religious end; the same end may be attained by others by a different path.

23. Historically, it was certainly a Jewish desire that prompted the translation. However, the reversal of the facts supports the subordination of Greeks to Jews that the work seeks to achieve. Hadas, *Aristeas to Philocrates,* 101 n. 15, accounts for the linkage of the Septuagint translation and the liberation of Jewish slaves by accepting Aristeas's rhetorical use of the incident as the real motive for its inclusion: "Courtesies could . . . not be logically extended to one portion of the Jewish people and requests made of them while the king himself was responsible for holding another portion in bondage." This is plausible as a rationale offered to the king by the Greek persona assumed by Aristeas, but it is not the only or best explanation of the Jewish author's rationale, which is to demonstrate the power that the Jewish God exercises over the Greeks. Fraser, *Ptolemaic Alexandria,* vol. 1, 700, believes that the royal decree freeing the Jewish slaves is genuine; the highly placed author of the narrative probably consulted it in the appropriate archive.

24. Thus Hadas's conclusion, *Aristeas to Philocrates,* 61, that "on both sides the respect is earned, not bestowed as a bounty or extorted by *force majeure* or the sheer weight of tradition" must be qualified. There is a clear indication that Greek respect can be coerced if necessary—though of course Ptolemy is presented as agreeing immediately out of his sheer benevolence to the suggestion to release Jewish slaves.

25. My point, of course, directly contradicts the intention behind Hadas's insistence on Aristeas's "universalization" of Judaism. Aristeas's idealized description of contemporary Palestine and the Temple, derived from scriptural details and expressed in scriptural idiom, has led to the recognition that Alexandrian Jewish reading of scripture begins to create a new, scripturally defined world. Hadas observes: "It is the Bible which is now the central factor in Jewish survival, and Palestine is of interest as comprising, as it were, a part of the Bible" (*Aristeas to Philocrates,* 64). Hadas adds that for the diaspora Jews of Alexandria "the Bible

had become their sole bond with Judaism, to which, with proper universalization, they were determined to cling" (68). I would argue, however, that one should say about Greek culture as the underlying meaning of scripture what is here said of Palestine—as a result of reading scripture allegorically, Greek culture too is now "part of the Bible" to which Alexandrian Jews are "determined to cling." One might observe further that the "proper universalization" of Jewish scripture results from Jewish insistence that all truth was originally written there. Arnaldo Momigliano, *Alien Wisdom: The Limits of Hellenization* (Cambridge: Cambridge Univ. Press, 1975), 149, points to what he calls "the dilemma of Hellenistic civilization": "It has all the instruments for knowing other civilizations—except command of languages. It has all the marks of a conquering and ruling upper class—except faith in its own wisdom." In a way, we see Aristobulus and Aristeas exploiting these weaknesses, by proving their own "command of language" (in the form of a privileging of Jewish scripture) and their own "wisdom" (in the claim that scripture flowed from the original source of all authentic wisdom, namely, from God, through Moses). Momigliano concludes his account of the "limits of Hellenization" with Augustus, and notes that, for his purposes, "we are not supposed to know what happened, to Greeks as well as to Romans, when a new barbarian sect decided to preach in Greek to the Gentiles" (149). The following chapters on Valentinus and Clement will suggest something of what happened when the revisionary strategies of Hellenistic Jews were taken up by Christian interpreters.

26. *Som.* 1.64. I have used the following critical editions of Philo's works, making minor alterations in the translation when necessary: *Philo*, 10 vols., ed. and trans. F. H. Colson and G. H. Whitaker, Loeb Classical Library (Cambridge, Mass.: Harvard Univ. Press, 1929–62); *Questions and Answers on Genesis and Exodus*, 2 vols., trans. Ralph Marcus, Loeb Classical Library (Cambridge, Mass.: Harvard Univ. Press, 1953). For an excellent overview of recent research, see Peder Borgen, "Philo of Alexandria: A Critical and Synthetical Survey of Research since World War II," *ANRW* II.21.1 (1984): 98–154. See also Burton L. Mack, "Philo Judaeus and Exegetical Traditions in Alexandria," *ANRW* II.21.2 (1984): 227–71.

27. Cf. *Fug.* 75–77.

28. For a stimulating reflection on the notion of Adamic language and its relation to the theory and practice of translation, see George Steiner, *After Babel: Aspects of Language and Translation* (New York: Oxford Univ. Press, 1975). Noting the difference between "separation" and "confusion," Philo prefers to read the account of the Tower of Babel not as a description of the origin of diverse human languages, but as an allegory of the destruction of vice (*Conf.* 189–95).

29. See also *QuGen.* 1.20, 22, 32; also *L.A.* 1.30, 100; 3.95, 108–109.

30. See *Deus* 43–44; *QuGen.* 1.38; *D.L.* 7.45–46.

31. See also *QuGen.* 2.77 for Noah's accurate naming of his sons Ham and Canaan.

32. Philo may have another reason for stressing continuity of form besides defending the accuracy of the Septuagint translation. He may wish to justify the awkward Greek syntax and obscurity of portions of the Septuagint. Such features do in fact stem from ancient efforts to translate the Hebrew into Greek as literally

as possible, even when the Hebrew idiom was not understood and a literal translation produced virtual nonsense.

33. Cf. *Mos.* 2.38:

> Yet who does not know that every language [*dialektos*], and Greek especially,
> abounds in names [*onomata*], and that the same thought [*enthymēma*] can be
> put in many shapes by paraphrasing more or less freely [*metaphrazonta kai
> paraphrazonta*] and suiting the expression [*lexis*] to the occasion?

34. Cf. *Post.* 23.

35. See Jaap Mansfeld, "Philosophy in the Service of Scripture: Philo's Exegetical Strategies," in *The Question of "Eclecticism": Studies in Later Greek Philosophy*, ed.
John M. Dillon and A. A. Long, Hellenistic Culture and Society 3 (Berkeley and
Los Angeles: Univ. of California Press, 1988), 70–102, especially 81–82, 87–89,
on the two Adams and their relation to Philo's notions of literal and nonliteral
interpretation.

36. Cf. *Mut.* 15.

37. See Pl. *Cra.* 440A.

38. Cf. *Mig.* 12.

39. Catachresis was one of eight basic tropes discussed in ancient grammatical
treatises. See Kennedy, *Art of Persuasion*, 297.

40. See Quint. *Inst.* 8.6.34.

41. Cf. *L.A.* 3.86; *Cong.* 161–62; *QuEx.* 2.4.

42. See also *Her.* 237; *Conf.* 64; *Gig.* 56.

43. See *Abr.* 52; *Plant.* 120ff.; *L.A.* 1.16, 2.5; *Fug.* 108.

44. Philo connects the celebration not with the passing by of the Angel of Death
but with the crossing of the Red Sea.

45. The suspension is only momentary because while Philo's nonliteral reading
is a perspective from which he reads the literal account of historical and contemporary events, that reading does not replace the literal-historical account. In this
instance, Philo has inserted his nonliteral reading (*Spec.* 2.147) between the literal-
historical reading (*Spec.* 2.146) and a literal description of the present-day festival
(*Spec.* 2.148–49).

46. For a similar example, see *Post.* 49ff., where every impious person is said to
become an architect of Cain's city "in his own miserable soul" (*Post.* 53).

47. For a discussion of this sort of Alexandrian practice and its influence on
protorabbinic interpretation in Philo's time and later, see Daube, "Alexandrian
Interpretation," in *Greco-Roman and Talmudic Literature*, selected by Fischel.

48. E.g., *QuGen.* 2.12; *Cher.* 84.

49. On Philo's enhancement of Moses' status, see Mansfeld, "Philosophy in
Service of Scripture," in *Question of "Eclecticism*," ed. Dillon and Long, 94ff.

50. See *Mos.* 1.162; *Dec.* 1; *Virt.* 194.

51. Philo's sense of the text as written is most commonly conveyed with the
introductory formula "it is written" (*gegraptai* or *anagegraptai*) (e.g., *Post.* 179; *Spec.*
1.56, 2.3), as well as by direct references to writing (*Conf.* 23; see also *Sob.* 12, 69;
Som. 1.47; *Mut.* 12; *Dec.* 121). There is generally an implied identity between

something "written by Moses" and something "in accordance with the most holy writing" (*kata to hierōtaton gramma*) (*Mig.* 139).

52. Thus the injunctions not to hear but to "read the Law" (*legein ton nomon*) (e.g., *Som.* 1.92).

53. Cf. *Her.* 167; *Dec.* 50.

54. Cf. *Det.* 75.

55. Victor A. Tcherikover and Alexander Fuks, eds., *Corpus Papyrorum Judicarum*, vol. 1 (Cambridge, Mass.: Harvard Univ. Press, 1957), 77–78 (hereafter *CPJ*).

56. For this description of Alexandrian society and politics, I have relied principally on E. Mary Smallwood, ed. and trans., *Philonis Alexandrini Legatio ad Gaium* (Leiden: Brill, 1961), supplemented by Tcherikover and Fuks, *CPJ*.

57. Smallwood, *Philonis Legatio ad Gaium*, 227–28.

58. Ibid., 225.

59. There were two other Greek *poleis* in Egypt: Ptolemais and Naukratis.

60. Tcherikover and Fuks, *CPJ*, vol. 1, 53.

61. Ibid., 68.

62. Smallwood, *Philonis Legatio ad Gaium*, 235.

63. See Montgomery J. Shroyer, "Alexandrian Jewish Literalists," *Journal of Biblical Literature* 55 (1936): 261–84.

64. Tcherikover and Fuks, *CPJ*, vol. 1, 69.

65. Ibid., 74.

66. Ibid., 49.

67. Ibid., 54.

68. Joseph. *Ap.* 1.288–92; cf. 228–51.

69. Joseph. *Ap.* 1.305–11; cf. Tac. *Hist.* 5.3.

70. The degree to which such works might be labeled anti-Semitic as well as, or instead of, anti-Jewish depends on the definitions one employs. My reading of this material suggests the presence of a strong racial and ethnic dimension to this prejudice, but little understanding of the religious issues involved. For discussions of the topic from various points of view, see the following: Rosemary Radford Ruether, *Faith and Fratricide* (New York: Seabury, 1974); John G. Gager, *The Origins of Anti-Semitism: Attitudes toward Judaism in Pagan and Christian Antiquity* (New York: Oxford Univ. Press, 1983); for later periods, Heiko A. Oberman, *The Roots of AntiSemitism in the Age of Renaissance and Reformation*, trans. James Porter (Philadelphia: Fortress, 1983).

71. See Alan Wardman, *Religion and Statecraft Among the Romans* (Baltimore: Johns Hopkins Univ. Press, 1982).

72. We have already seen that, for Philo, the Greeks were indebted to Moses for philosophy. Here we see that they were indebted to him for their political thought as well (see *Spec.* 4.61).

73. Colson's translation of *tines hoi tous rhētous nomous . . . hypolambanontes* as "some regarding laws in their literal sense" is misleading. A more accurate rendering (which Colson adopts in *Mig.* 93) would be "some regarding the specific, written [or spoken] laws" since elsewhere Philo does not seem to use *rhētos* at-

tributively to mean "literal sense." Removing "sense" from the opening phrase makes it more consistent with the rest of the text, which clearly concerns obedience to "the customs [*ēthē*] fixed by divinely empowered men" (*Mig.* 90). What Philo says must be followed is not the "literal sense" but quite specifically "the letter of the laws" or perhaps "the specific laws" (*hoi rhētoi nomoi*) (*Mig.* 93).

74. See David M. Hay, "Philo's References to Other Allegorists," *Studia Philonica* 6 (1979–80): 41–75.

75. Tcherikover and Fuks, *CPJ*, vol. 1, 77 and n. 59.

76. Tcherikover has himself modified this view. See V. Tcherikover, "Jewish Apologetic Literature Reconsidered," *Eos* 48 (1956): 169–93.

77. Tcherikover and Fuks, *CPJ*, vol. 1, 77–78.

78. See *Mos.* 2.14.

79. Erwin R. Goodenough, "Philo's Exposition of the Law and his De Vita Mosis," *Harvard Theological Review* 26 (1933): 112.

80. Goodenough, "Philo's Exposition of Law," 124, tries to show that like the *Life of Moses* (which he believes is clearly directed to the Greeks), the *Exposition* must also be viewed as an apologetic to the Greeks (a difficult task, given its insistent concern for the law). Goodenough's project also involves trying to show how the treatise *On Curses and Blessings* did not belong originally with the treatise *On Rewards and Punishments*—and hence did not form part of the *Exposition*. Goodenough has to remove *On Curses and Blessings* to maintain that what Philo had in mind throughout the *Exposition* is "a philosophic and mystical Judaism" in which "specific laws . . . have no essential place."

81. Goodenough's translation, "Philo's Exposition of Law," 118.

82. Goodenough, "Philo's Exposition of Law," 118.

83. Goodenough points out a parallel to this passage in *Mos.* 2.216 as evidence for his argument, but again, a counterreading seems possible. Philo here stresses that the Sabbath observance is retained "even now" (cf. the description of the Pharos festival—"even to the present day"—*Mos.* 2.41): "The Jews every seventh day occupy themselves with the philosophy of their fathers, dedicating that time to the acquiring of knowledge and the study of the truths of nature." So far this description does sound like the sort of detached observation that could be designed for Gentile consumption. But Philo's deeper purpose may appear in the next line, a rhetorical question seemingly directed at his fellow Jews: "For what are our places of prayer throughout the cities but schools of prudence and courage and temperance and justice and also of piety, holiness and every virtue by which duties to God and men are discerned and rightly performed?" (*Mos.* 2.216).

84. See Wayne A. Meeks, "The Divine Agent and His Counterfeit in Philo and the Fourth Gospel," in *Aspects of Religious Propaganda in Judaism and Early Christianity*, ed. Elizabeth Schüssler Fiorenza (Notre Dame, Ind.: Univ. of Notre Dame Press, 1976), 43–67.

85. Erwin R. Goodenough, *Introduction to Philo Judaeus* (New Haven: Yale Univ. Press, 1940), 31. For a more detailed discussion, see Erwin R. Goodenough, *The Politics of Philo Judaeus: Practice and Theory* (New Haven: Yale Univ. Press, 1938), 90ff., especially 101–3.

86. Quotations from the *Legatio ad Gaium* are from the Loeb edition. See also the edition, translation, and commentary provided by Smallwood (see note 56

above) and the related treatise *In Flaccum* in Herbert Box, ed. and trans., *Philonis Alexandrini In Flaccum* (London: Oxford Univ. Press, 1939).

87. Smallwood, *Philonis Legatio ad Gaium*, 236.

88. Ibid., 240.

CHAPTER 3: VALENTINUS: THE APOCALYPSE OF THE MIND

1. See the careful assessment of the evidence by Anne Marie McGuire, "Valentinus and the *Gnōstikē Hairesis:* An Investigation of Valentinus's Position in the History of Gnosticism" (Ph.D. diss., Yale University, 1983), 77. Clement (*Strom.* 7.17.106.4–107.1) says that Valentinus, along with Basilides and Marcion, was active as a Christian teacher during Hadrian's reign (117–38 C.E.) (for the system of references to Clement, see chapter 4, note 3). Irenaeus reports that Valentinus arrived in Rome at the time of Hyginus (136–40 C.E.), "flourished under Pius, and remained until Anicetus" (155–66 C.E.) (*Haer.* 3.4.3). Since most of Hadrian's reign was over by the time Valentinus moved to Rome, he was a Christian in Alexandria. He may have lived and taught in Rome for over twenty years.

2. For Valentinus's birthplace and Greek education, see Epiphanius's report of an oral tradition in *Adv. haeres.* 31.2; on Basilides and Valentinus teaching in Alexandria in the same period, see Clem. *Strom.* 7.17.106.4.

3. Clem. *Strom.* 7.17.106.4. For an introduction to Basilides, see Bentley Layton, "The Significance of Basilides in Ancient Christian Thought," *Representations* 28 (Fall 1989): 135–51.

4. Valentinus's authorship of the *Gospel of Truth* is disputed in modern scholarship. For a brief review of the current spectrum of opinion, see Harold W. Attridge, "The Gospel of Truth as an Exoteric Text," in *Nag Hammadi, Gnosticism, and Early Christianity*, ed. Charles W. Hedrick and Robert Hodgson, Jr. (Peabody, Mass.: Hendrickson, 1986), 240–41. I am persuaded that Valentinus is the author of this text both by my own synthesis of Valentinus's revisionary hermeneutic and by Benoit Standaert's stylistic comparison of portions of the *Gospel* with the unquestionably genuine fragments in his "'L'évangile de vérité': Critique et lecture," *NTS* 22 (1976): 243–75 (see especially 259–65).

5. Quoted by Harold Bloom in "Lying Against Time: Gnosis, Poetry, Criticism," in *The Rediscovery of Gnosticism*, vol. 1: *The School of Valentinus*, ed. Bentley Layton, Studies in the History of Religions 41 (Leiden: Brill, 1980), 71.

6. The relation between these Gnostic texts and the group called "Sethians" in some reports of ancient heresiologists is debated. See Hans-Martin Schenke, "Das sethianische System nach Nag-Hammadi-Handschriften," in *Studia coptica*, ed. Peter Nagel, Berliner byzantinistischer Arbeiten 45 (Berlin: Akademie, 1974), 165–73; id., "The Phenomenon and Significance of Gnostic Sethianism," in *Rediscovery of Gnosticism*, vol. 2, ed. Layton, 588–616. The relationship between Sethianism and revisionary Valentinianism was the organizing principle of the International Conference on Gnosticism held at Yale University in 1981. In addition to the preceding volume of papers from that conference, see also volume 1: *The School of Valentinus*, ed. Bentley Layton, Studies in the History of Religions 41 (Leiden: Brill, 1980). See McGuire, "Valentinus and *Gnōstikē Hairesis*," for a thorough analysis of the features of Sethian mythology in relation to Valentinian

texts. For an interpretative anthology of translations of Sethian and Valentinian works that explores further the relationships between these two bodies of ancient Gnostic thought and literature, see Bentley Layton, *The Gnostic Scriptures: A New Translation with Annotations and Introductions* (Garden City, N. Y.: Doubleday, 1987). I have used Layton's translations of Gnostic texts and the *Gospel of Truth*, occasionally altering them in light of the original texts. For a detailed examination of the literary dependencies and redactional history of Sethian texts, see John D. Turner, "Sethian Gnosticism: A Literary History," in *Nag Hammadi*, ed. Hedrick and Hodgson, 55–87.

7. The preceding summary is drawn largely from *The Secret Book According to John* (*Apocryphon of John*), in Layton, *Gnostic Scriptures*, 28–51. For the representative character of the basic myth recounted in this text, see Birger A. Pearson, "The Problem of 'Jewish Gnostic' Literature," in *Nag Hammadi*, ed. Hedrick and Hodgson, 19ff. Pearson agrees that this myth probably forms the basis of Valentinus's own composition.

8. The translation of the passage is from *Plato*, vol. 7, trans. R. G. Bury, Loeb Classical Library (New York: G. P. Putnam's Sons, 1929).

9. I have used Layton's translation of the fragments in *The Gnostic Scriptures*, with significant modifications in light of the Greek originals. The critical Greek text is provided by Walther Völker, ed., *Quellen zur Geschichte der christlichen Gnosis* (Tübingen: J. C. B. Mohr [Paul Siebeck], 1932). Layton, frag. C = Völker, frag. 1.

10. Layton, frag. D = Völker, frag. 5. The translation of the last sentence of the fragment was originally suggested to me by my colleague Anne McGuire. Layton translates the final sentence, *synergei de kai to tou theou aoraton eis pistin tou peplasmenou*, as "And also god's invisible cooperates with what has been modeled to lend it credence." But *synergein* in the sense of "cooperate with" generally takes the dative, not the genitive; when it governs the accusative, as in Aristotle's *synergein eis tas eutuchias* (*Eth. Nic.* 1171b23), it means "contributes towards" (see LSJ, 9th ed., S.V. *synergeō*). Valentinus thus seems to say: "The invisible of god contributes toward the faith of the one who has been modeled."

11. The viability of this translation was suggested to me by Anne McGuire. It represents one of two possibilities, depending on whether one takes the genitive relative pronoun *hou* to refer to "manifestation" or to "act of speaking." The pronoun *hou* functions to designate God the Father as the possessor of either manifestation or bold speech. McGuire's suggested translation does not limit *parrhēsia* to the Father, but simply identifies the Father's specific form of *parrhēsia*. The implication, then, is that other beings might also exercise *parrhēsia*, perhaps in other ways. As the fragments under discussion already hint, and as my later discussion of the *Gospel of Truth* will further demonstrate, Father, Son, and human being all exercise *parrhēsia* and exercise it precisely in the same fashion: through the manifestation of the Son. Hence, the most convincing reason to adopt the translation I have offered must await that fuller discussion. The justification for the alternative translation adopted by Layton is clear: the clause in question is introduced by a quotation of Matthew 19.17, in which Jesus insists that the "one who is good" is his Father, and this identification is repeated later in the fragment ("But when the father, who alone is good, visits the heart"). Yet Layton, *Gnostic Scriptures*, 244, also points out that "the saving action of the son is also spoken of as

a visitation of the father, so that the distinction of father and son is deemphasized." Hence one might easily adopt Layton's more restrictive translation as the best guess about what Valentinus seems to have written, while at the same time remaining aware that the apparent restriction of *parrhēsia* to the Father's manifestation of the Son is undercut and transformed. Such a procedure would be thoroughly typical of Valentinus's "dialectical" style, which frustrates all efforts at univocal translation. Seeking to avoid vagueness and indecision, translators choose one meaning when Valentinus's rhetoric, while perhaps offering one meaning, at the same time deliberately keeps open other possibilities. My own preference in translating is to make a choice and then point out the alternative possibilities, rather than taking the edge off competing meanings by translating vaguely and speaking generally of the "polysemous" or "indeterminate" character of Valentinus's prose.

12. In doing so, Valentinus has conflated traditional Christian Middle Platonic language about the generative or "spermatic" divine *logos* (derived from Stoic ideas) with his own metaphor of the divine name. I will discuss this Middle Platonic tradition in some detail in "*Logos* Theology as Allegorical Hermeneutic" in chapter 4.

13. From Clem. *Strom.* 4.13.89.2–3 (Layton, frag. F; Völker, frag. 4), in Layton, *Gnostic Scriptures,* 241.

14. A caravansary is "a rural inn of the East, with large enclosed courtyard for pack animals, where caravans may stop overnight" (Layton, *Gnostic Scriptures,* 245, note c).

15. From Clem. *Strom.* 2.20.114.3–6 (Layton, frag. H; Völker, frag. 2), in Layton, *Gnostic Scriptures,* 245.

16. From Clem. *Strom.* 3.7.59.3 (Layton, frag. E; Völker, frag. 3), in Layton, *Gnostic Scriptures,* 239.

17. I have used the critical Coptic text of the *Gospel of Truth* in Harold W. Attridge, ed., *Nag Hammadi Codex I (The Jung Codex),* vol. 1: *Introduction, Texts, Translations, Indices,* The Coptic Gnostic Library (Leiden: Brill, 1985). Quotations are from the English translation by Bentley Layton in *Gnostic Scriptures,* 253–64, which I have occasionally modified in light of the Coptic, usually for the sake of greater literalness.

18. *Plasma* ("model") can also mean "fiction" or "fabrication."

19. See Pearson, "'Jewish Gnostic' Literature," in *Nag Hammadi,* ed. Hedrick and Hodgson, 19–25, on *The Secret Book According to John* as a Jewish Gnostic text with secondary Christian revisions.

20. Standaert, "'L'évangile de vérité,'" 254, argues for two organizational patterns in the *Gospel:* a formal, nonlinear "schéma concentrique," sometimes reinforced by, and sometimes in tension with, a thematic, linear "succession des thèmes" marked by progression from lack and deficiency to possession and plenitude. He reinforces his claim for a linear, thematic progression by noting an overall shift in verb tenses: past tenses predominate in the first half of the *Gospel,* present and future tenses in the second half (254 n. 1).

21. Standaert, "'L'évangile de vérité,'" 247ff., discusses some of the same tensions.

22. See Standaert, "'L'évangile de vérité,'" 255ff., for a discussion of these and other stylistic oddities of the *Gospel.* On this passage in particular, see 258 with n. 3.

23. Colin H. Roberts, *Manuscript, Society and Belief in Early Christian Egypt,* The Schweich Lectures of the British Academy (London: Oxford Univ. Press, 1979). See also H[arold] Idris Bell, "Evidences of Christianity in Egypt during the Roman Period," *Harvard Theological Review* 37 (July 1944): 185–208.

24. *Sōtēr* appears to be a late addition to the list; it is absent from the earliest texts. Roberts, *Early Christian Egypt,* 39–40, observes that this term appears in the New Testament only in the Pauline and Lucan writings, except for one passage in John and several in 2 Peter. He suggests that Jewish Christians would have disliked its pagan associations and that other Christian groups may have been suspicious of its use by Gnostic sects.

25. Roberts, *Early Christian Egypt,* 28.

26. Ibid., 28–29.

27. Ibid., 30–33.

28. Quoted with alterations from *The Apostolic Fathers,* vol. 1, trans. Kirsopp Lake, Loeb Classical Library (Cambridge, Mass.: Harvard Univ. Press, 1977), 340–409.

29. Roberts, *Early Christian Egypt,* 35–37. See also Clem. *Strom.* 6.11.84.3: "They say, then, that the character representing 300 is, as to shape, the type of the Lord's sign, and that the *iōta* and the *ēta* signify the savior's name." Roberts, 37 n. 2, notes that Clement's statement suggests the precedence of *Iēsous* over other *nomina sacra* and of the suspended over the contracted form. He also notes that Clement's "they say" suggests that $\overline{ie}$ was "no longer current in Clement's day." Since Clement quotes elsewhere from the *Epistle of Barnabas,* he may well have discovered the symbolism in that text.

30. Eucharistic words include *haima* ("blood"), *artos* ("bread"), *oinos* ("wine"), *sarx* ("flesh"), *sōma* ("body"), and *logos.*

31. Roberts, *Early Christian Egypt,* 40. This early Jewish Christian title may have been dropped precisely because it was favored by Gnostics. Irenaeus writes that the basic claim of Valentinianism is that "the Power which is above all others, and contains all in his embrace, is termed Anthropos; hence does the Savior style himself the 'Son of Man'" (*Haer.* 1.12.4). See further Richard N. Longenecker, *The Christology of Early Jewish Christianity,* Studies in Biblical Theology, 2d ser. (Naperville, Ill.: Alec R. Allenson, 1970), 82–93. We know that the *nomina sacra* played a role in later Valentinian revisionary readings of Christian writings. According to Irenaeus, Ptolemy (reportedly Valentinus's first student) exploited the suspended form of the name "Jesus" in order to discover hints of a system of aeons:

But the eighteen aeons are even supposed to be clearly disclosed by the two initial letters of his name in Greek (*Iēsous,* "Jesus"), that is, the letters *I* (iota) and *ē* (eta). Similarly, they say that the ten aeons are signified by the initial letter *I* (iota) of his name, and this is why the savior said, "Not an iota, not a dot, will pass until the entirety comes into being" [*heōs an panta genētai*—this phrase from Matthew 5.18 is usually translated "until all is accomplished"]. (Iren. *Haer.* 1.3.2, in Layton, *Gnostic Scriptures,* 286)

According to Roberts, 46 n. 1, iota was considered a perfect letter (because 10 = 1 + 2 + 3 + 4).

32. Roberts, *Early Christian Egypt*, 44–45 n. 4. Roberts, 45–46, points especially to the tradition of synagogue *lector* and to the traditional care in writing and preserving the rolls of the Torah. See Roberts, 42ff., for arguments that support Jerusalem, rather than Alexandria or Rome, as the probable source of the *nomina sacra.*

33. See the discussion by L. Cerfaux, "La première communauté chrétienne à Jérusalem (Act., II, 41–V, 42)," *Ephemerides theologiae Lovanienses* 16 (1939): 5–31.

34. See Gilles Quispel, "Qumran, John and Jewish Christianity," in *John and Qumran*, ed. James H. Charlesworth (London: Geoffrey Chapman, 1972), 137–55, especially 154.

35. Cerfaux, "La première communauté chrétienne," 148–49; see also Longenecker, *Christology of Early Jewish Christianity*, 43–46, on identification of the divine name with Jesus. Longenecker, 42–43, points to the messianic use of the name by the Qumran community, as, for example, in "O Lord, we await your name" (1QIsa26.8); he also notes, 43 and n. 78, that Philo uses *to onoma* as one designation for the *logos:*

> And many names are his; for he is called the Beginning [*archē*], and the Name of God [*onoma theou*], and His Word [*logos*], and the Man after His Image [*ho kat' eikona anthrōpos*], and he that sees [*ho horōn*], that is Israel. (*Conf.* 146)

36. For more examples, see Daniélou, *Shadows to Reality*, 149ff.

37. Roberts, *Early Christian Egypt*, 41–42.

38. See Quispel, "Qumran, John and Jewish Christianity," in *John and Qumran*, ed. Charlesworth, 154, for a discussion of some of these passages.

39. See Roberts, *Early Christian Egypt*, 41–42.

40. See William Schoedel, "Gnostic Monism and the Gospel of Truth," in *Rediscovery of Gnosticism*, vol. 1, ed. Layton, 379–90. See also Standaert, " 'L'évangile de vérité,' " 258, who notes that the *Gospel's* free manner of moving from the worlds of personality and morality to cosmology seems odd only to those approaching the text from a post-Kantian dualistic perspective.

41. "Ways" are the same as emanations, places, aeons, and selves.

42. The name "Barbelo" (the first emanation of Sethian myth whose function is here taken over by the Son) may be a wordplay on the Tetragrammaton: *barba' 'elo,* "in four, God." This etymology was first proposed by W. Wigan Harvey, ed., *Sancti Irenaei episcopi lugdunensis libros quinque adversus haereses*, vol. 1 (Cambridge: Typis Academicis, 1857), 221 n. 2. Not widely accepted for some time, the etymology has recently been defended by M. Scopello, "Youel et Barbelo dans le traité de l'Allogene," in *Colloque international sur les textes de Nag Hammadi*, ed. B. Barc (Quebec: Université Laval, 1981), especially 378–79, cited by Pearson, " 'Jewish Gnostic' Literature," in *Nag Hammadi*, ed. Hedrick and Hodgson, 23 and n. 36. The word might also suggest to speakers of Egyptian the terms for "emission," "projection," and "great," perhaps even "the great emission" (see Layton, *Gnostic Scriptures*, 15 and n. 3).

43. Jacques-É. Ménard, *L'évangile de vérité,* Nag Hammadi Studies 2 (Leiden: Brill, 1972), 183 nn. 8 and 9, 184 n. 10.

44. Here I disagree with some of the conclusions of Joel Fineman in his "Gnosis and the Piety of Metaphor: The Gospel of Truth," in *Rediscovery of Gnosticism,* vol. 1, ed. Layton, 289–312. Fineman insists that

> both the Son and the Name of the Father are metonymies of the Father himself (i.e., contiguously related figures of the Father that represent him whole). As such, as metonymies of the Father, they testify to the absence of the Father in that they continually refer to Him whom they replace. (301)

Fineman finds in this metonymy a movement of desire motivated by a sense of lack that pervades the *Gospel* (302). Thus when Fineman later asks with regard to Valentinian fragment D, "What does it mean to say that the Name filled up what was lacking in the image save that what the image lacked was the Name?" he answers, "But the Name is itself also an image" (305). But this is not what Valentinus claims about the name-as-Son. On the contrary, the name of the Father as Son is precisely not a mere name, image, or metaphor, but a *kyrion onoma*—an "Adamic name" that makes present precisely the reality that it denotes. Thus Fineman's conclusion that "Gnosticism is a singular theology because it continually speaks of God as a phenomenon present precisely by virtue of His absence, as a trace which witnesses to what is no longer there" (306), though it adequately captures the second "moment" in the basic tripartite oscillation of fullness, lack, and fulfillment, is finally more persuasive as a reading of Lacan than it is of the *Gospel of Truth.* Fineman insists that Gnosticism avoided the Christian "fantasy of identification, the equating of word with thing" because it realized that "language is always metaphoric, figurative, substitutive" (307). But as we have seen, the Stoics held both notions long before Christianity, and the Stoic ambience of the *Gospel of Truth* is evident not only in its monism but in its insistence on the qualitatively different character of the name of the Father. Referring to the *Gospel's* use of a parable of Jesus, Fineman, 307–8, puts Valentinianism in suspension between "the present partiality of the ninety-nine sheep and the missing fullness of the One, between the left hand as figure of loss and the right hand as figure of plenitude (*GTr* 31.35–32.16)," but that is not where the *Gospel* itself ends the parable: the Savior rejoices upon the discovery of the one hundredth sheep— and "when 1 is found, the sum total transfers to the right hand" (*GTr* 32.7–9). Fineman concludes:

> Gnosticism proposes to link these oppositions [of lack and fullness, absence and presence] each to the other without quite collapsing the opposition into an identity. It thus problematizes its oppositions without erasing them, and then proceeds to make that problem into its piety. (308)

Gnosticism is thus "the troubled difference *between*" monism and dualism (308). However, Fineman comes close to my argument that the *Gospel* depicts a monism achieved through self-knowledge and knowledge of God when he adds that this troubled difference "permits both these transcendentalisms [monism and dualism] to be thought in their own purity, *so that, once thought, they can retrospectively efface and disavow the very difference that is their possibility*" (308; my emphasis).

Fineman seems to describe this effacement through correct thought as something of an eschatological possibility (in contrast to the achieved recuperation of divine presence celebrated by the orthodoxy that succeeded Gnosticism), where I would see it as the very essence of the achieved piety that the *Gospel* celebrates. For a recent analysis of the *Gospel of Truth* that builds on Fineman's reading with the help of Edmund Jabès, Roland Barthes, and Michel Foucault, see Patricia Cox Miller, "'Words With An Alien Voice': Gnostics, Scripture, and Canon," *Journal of the American Academy of Religion* 57 (Fall 1989): 459–83.

45. Harold Bloom's conclusion in "Lying Against Time," in *Rediscovery of Gnosticism*, vol. 1, ed. Layton, that Valentinus's vision is finally supermimetic reflects an accurate recognition of the way Valentinus's final vision transcends a seemingly proto-postmodern deconstructive antimimesis (cf. my comments on Fineman in the preceding note). Bloom claims that Valentinian *gnōsis* begins in

> a liberating knowledge that excludes all aesthetic irony, precisely because the inaugurating realization in such knowledge makes of all Creation and all Fall one unified event, and sees that event as belonging altogether to the inner life of God, and not to the life of man, except insofar as man is Anthropos or pre-existent Adam, that is, not part of Creation. (60)

But although Bloom seems to begin with a rejection of dualism (and consequently irony, which demands a double vision) by claiming that creation and fall are a single event, he still distinguishes creation from a divine realm that Anthropos might occupy. I have argued that this distinction between divine and created realms, while true of some versions of Gnosticism, is not true of Valentinus's own thought, which is unrelentingly monistic. For Valentinus, the first principle "surrounds every way, while nothing surrounds him" (*GTr* 22.25–27). This insistence on God's transcendence was widely shared in the ancient Hellenistic world by pagans, Jews, and Christians. In the *Shepherd,* for instance, Hermas insists that God "contains all" while remaining "uncontained" (*Man.* 1.1), and we have seen in the last chapter that Philo offers his own version of the traditional rabbinic insistence that "God is the place of the world, but the world is not his place." Bloom argues that Gnostics accept the second half of this aphorism, but not the first. Like his Gnostic precursors, Valentinus does seem at first glance to accept the second, antimimetic or apophatic, half of the aphorism, while rejecting the first, mimetic or representational, half. But actually he accepts both halves. His monism leads him to agree that God is "the place of the world" insofar as the world is real. Yet "the world is not his place" insofar as the world has a deficient or ultimately nonexistent status. Bloom's division of the aphorism applies to Valentinus's Gnostic predecessors, but it does not apply to Valentinus himself. Bloom's dualistic reading carries through to his view of the "place" about which Valentinus speaks near the end of the *Gospel.* Bloom insists that such a place or name "empties out a previous place *in the same spot*" and that "into this emptiness, a new fullness is placed, but a revisionary fullness, one that postpones or defers the future. . . . Gnosticism would go further and banish the future altogether, until that acosmic, atemporal restoration to the Pleroma takes place of all pneumatics simultaneously" (72). But in Valentinus's monistic vision, the categories "acosmic" and "atemporal" (and hence Bloom's "until") are not relevant because there is no

independently existing cosmos that is not subsumed by the deity (and no deity or divine realm that is not subsumed by the cosmos). Bloom's reading of the Valentinian place of repose as a deferred or unrealized fullness or merely fictionalized presence (a "lie against time") does indeed seem to me to be the heart of Bloom's own self-acknowledged, necessary misreading of Valentinianism—a reading that is in the end more consistent with the antimimetic strain in Hebraic thought than with the *Gospel*'s claims for achieved presence via a series of christological tropes. Standaert, "'L'évangile de vérité,'" 250, observes how explicit references to the Word-Savior in the prologue are later replaced in the *Gospel* by the terms "life," "light," "seed," or "name," suggesting that the mediatorial role of the Son has been successful and that in speaking of the "place of repose" Valentinus speaks of an achieved mediation as the absorption of the aeons into the fullness and presence of God. Standaert concludes:

> The Son is the Father insofar as the Father is revealed, and the Father is the Son insofar as the Son was unknowable. The entire conclusion of *The Gospel* thus points toward knowledge of the Father, which is communion in identification without any more mediation. (250 n. 1)

Standaert points to *Gospel of Truth*, 42.25–30 as the decisive text: "They are themselves the truth, and the Father is in them, and they are in the Father, being perfect, not able to be separated from that authentically good Being" (ibid.). The Son, like the believers, is also present with the Father. We have seen that the *Gospel* underscores this presence by stressing that the Son is the most "lordly name" of the Father, "lordly" being the precise opposite of "catachrestic." Thus the Son remains the crucial exception to Bloom's claim that "in a Gnostic metaphor, the 'inside' term or *pneuma* and the 'outside' cosmic term are so separated that every such figuration becomes a catachresis, an extension or abuse of metaphor" (65). Once again, Bloom's insistent dualism (here pneuma vs. cosmos) leads him to overlook the specific claim that the name of the Son is not a metaphor at all but the essence of the Father. Bloom's strong misreading of the *Gospel of Truth* thus resists what I take to be Valentinus's thoroughgoing christological subversion of Jewish monotheism and antimimesis.

46. From Clem. *Strom.* 6.6.52.4 (Layton, frag. G; Völker, frag. 6), in Layton, *Gnostic Scriptures*, 243.

47. From Hippol. *Haer.* 6.42.2 (Layton, frag. A; Völker, frag. 7), in Layton, *Gnostic Scriptures*, 231.

48. See Joel Fineman, "The Structure of Allegorical Desire," in *Allegory and Representation*, ed. Stephen J. Greenblatt (Baltimore: Johns Hopkins Univ. Press, 1981), 30, who observes that allegory typically avoids the extremes of simple literalism and "the exegesis of the free-floating signifier," becoming instead "for literature as for theology, a vivifying archaeology of occulted origins and a promissory eschatology of postponed ends." The tension evident in Valentinus's writing thus calls in question his proclamation of a realized eschatology.

49. Layton, *Gnostic Scriptures*, 241.

50. See Attridge, "Gospel of Truth," in *Nag Hammadi*, ed. Hedrick and Hodgson, 239–55, for a speculative counterproposal that the *Gospel* presupposes a

developed Valentinian mythology that it largely hides from its non-Valentinian audience.

51. Robert M. Grant, *Gnosticism and Early Christianity*, rev. ed. (New York: Harper & Row, 1966).

52. This famous hypothesis was proposed in 1934 by Walter Bauer, *Rechtgläubigkeit und Ketzerei im ältesten Christentum* (Tübingen, 1934); the second edition of Bauer's work appeared in English as *Orthodoxy and Heresy in Earliest Christianity*, trans. Paul J. Achtemeier et al. and ed. Robert A. Kraft and Gerhard Krodel (Philadelphia: Fortress, 1971). Bauer's hypothesis has become the orthodox view of Christian origins in Egypt—see, for example, Robert M. Grant, "The New Testament Canon," in *The Cambridge History of the Bible*, vol. 1: *From the Beginnings to Jerome*, ed. P. R. Ackroyd and C. F. Evans (Cambridge: Cambridge Univ. Press, 1970), 298: "In the second century, as far as our knowledge goes, Christianity in Egypt was exclusively 'heterodox.'"

53. The first part of Eusebius's succession list runs as follows: Mark (the evangelist), Anianos, Abilios, Cerdon, Primos, Iustos, Eumenos, Markos, Celadion, Agrippinos, Julianos, Demetrius, Herakles—continuing down to Eusebius's own day. He does not say where he obtained the list. Such lists or doxographies, a frequent feature of the struggles between Hellenistic philosophical schools, were used regularly by Christians like Eusebius to prove that the "true, apostolic" teaching had been delivered intact down through the ages despite the presence of Gnostics and other heretics. Demetrius is the first name on the list (aside from the evangelist Mark) that is historically known from other sources.

54. Scholars who significantly qualify or reject the Bauer hypothesis, proposing instead various theories of Jewish Christian origins of Egyptian Christianity include the following: Jean Daniélou, *The Theology of Jewish Christianity*, trans. John A. Baker (London: Longwood & Todd, 1964); Manfred Hornschuh, "Die Anfänge des Christentums in Aegypten," *Patristische Texte und Studien*, 5 (Bonn: Friedrich-Wilhelms-Universität, 1965); Roberts, *Early Christian Egypt*, especially 49ff.; Helmut Koester, *Introduction to the New Testament*, vol. 2: *History and Literature of Early Christianity* (Philadelphia: Fortress, 1982).

55. W. D. Davies, "Paul and Jewish Christianity According to Cardinal Daniélou: A Suggestion," in *Judéo-christianisme: Recherches historiques et théologiques offertes en hommage au Cardinal Jean Daniélou* (Paris: Recherches de science religieuse, 1972), 69–79, agrees with Daniélou that a Jewish Christian mission from Palestine (probably a group under the authority of James) brought Christianity to Alexandria; see also Birger A. Pearson, "Earliest Christianity in Egypt: Some Observations," in *The Roots of Egyptian Christianity*, Studies in Antiquity and Christianity, ed. Birger A. Pearson and James E. Goehring (Philadelphia: Fortress, 1986), 132–59.

56. Pearson, "Earliest Christianity," in *Roots of Egyptian Christianity*, ed. Pearson and Goehring, 145. Roberts, *Early Christian Egypt*, 58, notes that because Judaism was a *religio licita* and Jews paid a poll tax after 70 c.e., their presence (unlike that of non-Jewish Christians) would be registered by Roman law.

57. For the *Gospel of the Egyptians*, see Clem. *Strom.* 3.6.45.3, 3.9.63.1–2, 3.9.64.1, 3.9.66.1–2, 3.13.92.1–93.1; *Ex. Theod.* 67.2. The *Gospel of the Hebrews* was known as an authoritative text by both Clement and Origen. Clement, for

example, cites a passage from the *Gospel of the Egyptians* that is shared by the *Gospel of Thomas* (= *Strom.* 3.6.45.3). Convenient English translations of the extant fragments of these and other noncanonical gospels are collected in Ron Cameron, ed., *The Other Gospels: Non-Canonical Gospel Texts* (Philadelphia: Westminster, 1982).

58. Joseph. *AJ* 19.278. Cited by Tcherikover and Fuks, *CPJ*, vol. 1, 68.

59. Tcherikover and Fuks, *CPJ*, vol. 1, 73–74.

60. See Joseph. *BJ* 2.487ff.

61. Ibid., 7.409–19.

62. Tcherikover and Fuks, *CPJ*, vol. 1, 79.

63. Ibid., 82. For the *laographia*, see my earlier discussion, chapter 2, 115–16.

64. Dio Cass. 68.32; Euseb. *Hist. eccl.* 4.2; Tcherikover and Fuks, *CPJ*, vol. 1, 89–90.

65. Tcherikover and Fuks, *CPJ*, vol. 1, 87.

66. Ibid., 92 n. 86.

67. There are only forty-four documents alluding to Egyptian Jews from the period 117–337 c.e.; in contrast, there are nearly three hundred for the preceding period of Roman rule (Roberts, *Early Christian Egypt*, 58).

68. L. W. Barnard, *Studies in the Apostolic Fathers and Their Background* (New York: Schocken, 1966), 45 n. 2.

69. Ibid., 46; Tcherikover and Fuks, *CPJ*, vol. 1, 83–85.

70. Cf. 3 Macc. 7.10ff., in Tcherikover and Fuks, *CPJ*, vol. 1, 67–68.

71. Barnard, *Apostolic Fathers*, 52–53.

72. See Roberts, *Early Christian Egypt*, 58, and Barnard, *Apostolic Fathers*, especially 44ff. My discussion of Egyptian Judaism in this period draws heavily on Barnard's discussion. Surveying the clashes between Greeks and Jews in Alexandria, Roberts concludes that "the internecine feuds between Jews and Greeks would have constituted a barrier difficult if not impossible for the Christian mission to surmount" (56). Indeed, Christianity may have been nearly eradicated in the anti-Jewish pogroms as well (56 n. 2).

73. See Barnard, *Apostolic Fathers*, for the arguments for authorship.

74. Barnard, *Apostolic Fathers*, 47, with some rabbinic parallels in the notes.

75. Barnard, *Apostolic Fathers*, 47–50.

76. Ibid., 51.

77. Ibid., 54.

78. Pearson, "'Jewish Gnostic' Literature," 16–19.

79. For the link between the Gnostic spirit and anticosmic, anti-Jewish stances, see Pearson, "'Jewish Gnostic' Literature," 17.

80. Pearson, "'Jewish Gnostic' Literature," 22.

81. Quoted from the text in Alexander Roberts and James Donaldson, eds., *The Ante-Nicene Fathers*, vol. 1: *The Apostolic Fathers with Justin Martyr and Irenaeus* (1884; reprint, Grand Rapids, Mich.: Eerdmans, 1977).

82. McGuire, "Valentinus and *Gnōstikē Hairesis*," 80–81.

83. For a discussion of baptismal practices among various groups contemporary with the Valentinians, see Turner, "Sethian Gnosticism," in *Nag Hammadi*, ed. Hedrick and Hodgson, 69 n. 6.

84. The best critical text of the *Excerpta ex Theodoto* is *Extraits de Théodote: Texte*

grec, introduction, traduction et notes, ed. François Sagnard, Sources chrétiennes (1948; reprint, Paris: Éditions du Cerf, 1970). English translations from Sagnard's text are by David Hill in *Gnosis: A Selection of Gnostic Texts,* vol. 1, ed. Werner Foerster (Oxford: Clarendon Press, 1972), 222–33.

85. *The Gospel According to Philip,* in Layton, *Gnostic Scriptures,* 329–53.

CHAPTER 4: CLEMENT: THE NEW SONG OF THE *LOGOS*

1. Cf. Justin *Dialogue with Trypho, a Jew* 2 (in *Ante-Nicene Fathers,* vol. 1, ed. Roberts and Donaldson).

2. Johannes Quasten, *Patrology,* vol. 2: *The Ante-Nicene Literature after Irenaeus* (1953; reprint, Utrecht-Antwerp: Spectrum, 1975), 5–6.

3. I have used the standard critical Greek text, Otto Stählin, ed., *Die griechischen christlichen Schriftsteller der ersten drei Jahrhunderte,* 4 vols. (Berlin: Akademie-Verlag, 1905–36). In general, English translations are from Roberts and Donaldson, *Ante-Nicene Fathers,* vol. 2: *Fathers of the Second Century* (1884; reprint, Grand Rapids, Mich.: Eerdmans, 1979). When necessary, however, I have modified this translation or simply retranslated the text. I quote also from Henry Chadwick's translation of *Strōmateis* 3 and 7 in John Ernest Leonard Oulton and Henry Chadwick, *Alexandrian Christianity: Selected Translations of Clement and Origen with Introductions and Notes* (Philadelphia: Westminster, 1955) and from Clement of Alexandria, *Christ the Educator,* trans. Simon P. Wood (New York: Fathers of the Church, 1954). Quotations from the *Eclogae propheticae* are based on an unpublished translation by Alan Scott. References to Clement's works will be to treatise, book (when applicable), and chapter. Paragraph and sentence numbers as given in Stählin's right-hand margin are included as well, thus *Strom.* 1.10.22.4–5. This system of reference has been used instead of the more customary volume, page, and line of the Stählin edition in order to provide easy access to the English translations as well as to the standard Greek text.

4. The lost works include a lengthy commentary on Hebrew and Christian scripture (*The Outlines* or *Sketches; Hypotypōseis*) as well as the following titles: *On the Pasch, Ecclesiastical Canon or Against the Judaizers, On Providence* (Clementine authorship uncertain), *Exhortation to Endurance or To the Recently Baptized, Discourse on Fasting, On Slander, On the Prophet Amos* (Clementine authorship uncertain) (from Quasten, *Patrology,* vol. 2, 6–19).

5. Moses, writes Clement, "who was after the law . . . foretold that it was necessary to hear in order that we might, according to the apostle, receive Christ, the fullness of the law" (*Strom.* 4.21.130.3). Clement takes the proclamation of Deuteronomy 18.18, "I will put my words in his mouth, and he shall speak to them all that I will command him," as a clear indication of Moses' prophetic (and decidedly oral) role.

6. I have used the Greek texts in A. W. F. Blunt, ed., *The Apologies of Justin Martyr,* Cambridge Patristic Texts, ed. A. J. Mason (Cambridge: Cambridge Univ. Press, 1911). I have largely followed the English translation in Roberts and Donaldson, *Ante-Nicene Fathers,* vol. 1, though I have also made modifications, especially in light of Edward Rochie Hardy's translation, "The First Apology of

Justin, the Martyr," in *Early Christian Fathers*, ed. Cyril C. Richardson, The Library of Christian Classics 1 (New York: Macmillan, 1970), 242–89, as well as Blunt's suggestions. I will designate the first apology by *Ap.* 1 and the second by *Ap.* 2. References to the second apology will give both the chapter numbers of the original manuscript (preserved by Blunt) and, in brackets, the chapter numbers according to the reordering adopted by the *Ante-Nicene Fathers* translators.

7. Robert M. Grant, *Greek Apologists of the Second Century* (Philadelphia: Westminster, 1988), 55.

8. Henry Chadwick, *Early Christian Thought and the Classical Tradition: Studies in Justin, Clement, and Origen* (New York: Oxford Univ. Press, 1966), 40; also "Clement of Alexandria," in *The Cambridge History of Later Greek and Early Medieval Philosophy*, ed. A. H. Armstrong (Cambridge: Cambridge Univ. Press, 1967), 170–71. Clement does refer to Justin's pupil Tatian: see *Strom.* 1.21.101.1–2 for Clement's appeal to Tatian to prove the antiquity of Moses and *Strom.* 3.12.81 for his rejection of Tatian's encratism.

9. *POxy.* iii. 405, cited by Roberts, *Early Christian Egypt*, 14.

10. The standard discussion of Middle Platonism, which has the virtue of resisting generalizations and describing the specific systems of individual philosophers, is John Dillon, *The Middle Platonists: 80 B.C. to A.D. 220* (Ithaca, N. Y.: Cornell Univ. Press, 1977). I have also made use of the summary discussions in R. A. Norris, Jr., *God and World in Early Christian Theology: A Study in Justin Martyr, Irenaeus, Tertullian, and Origen* (New York: Seabury, 1965), 41–68, especially 52–53. Clement draws upon Philo's exegetical works frequently, often in the form of direct quotation and without attribution. My discussion of Justin's apologies in the context of Middle Platonism draws on the detailed studies of Carl Andresen, "Justin und der mittlere Platonismus," *Zeitschrift für die Neutestamentliche Wissenschaft und die Kunde der Älternen Kirche* 44 (1952–53): 157–95; Ragnar Holte, "Logos Spermatikos: Christianity and Ancient Philosophy According to St. Justin's Apologies," *Studia Theologica* 12 (1958): 109–68.

11. Chadwick, *Early Christian Thought*, 40–41.

12. Holte, "Logos Spermatikos," 122–23.

13. Ibid., 123.

14. Justin himself reports that he studied with Epicurean, Stoic, Aristotelian, and Platonic teachers, though this autobiographical account may be shaped according to his general claim for the absorption of all useful pagan philosophy by Christianity (see *Dial.* 1–9).

15. Dillon, *Middle Platonists*, xiv–xv, points out that what is commonly, but misleadingly, referred to as Middle Platonism's "eclecticism" is an anachronism. These philosophers saw themselves not as eclectics, but as drawing on the insights of competing philosophical systems to help give coherent expression to their own unified and systematic vision of Plato's "authentic" philosophy.

16. Dillon, *Middle Platonists*, 367, notes that this distinction between the supreme God and the demiurge may be found in Numenius and all other Pythagoreans, as well as in Albinus. He adds that Platonists who do not make a complete separation between the two gods nevertheless make a very strong distinction, which is functionally equivalent.

17. I have used Numenius, *Fragments*, ed. and trans. Édouard Des Places (Paris:

"Les Belles Lettres" [Budé], 1973). See the discussion of the relevant fragments of Numenius in Dillon, *Middle Platonists*, 367ff.

18. Cf. *Ap.* 1.13.3:

> Our teacher of these things is Jesus Christ, who also was born for this purpose, and was crucified under Pontius Pilate, procurator of Judea, in the time of Tiberius Caesar; and that we reasonably worship him, having learned that he is the Son of the true God himself, and holding him in the second place, and the prophetic spirit in the third, we will prove.

19. Cf. frags. 11, 12, 15, 21. At one point, Justin also conflates the second god or *logos* with the third entity, the spirit: "It is wrong, therefore, to understand the spirit and the power of God as anything else than the Word, who is also the first-born of God" (*Ap.* 1.33.6).

20. See Dillon, *Middle Platonists*, 367–69.

21. *Dial.* 61:

> For he [the *logos*] can be called by all those names [Holy Spirit, Glory of the Lord, Son, Wisdom, Angel, God, Lord, *Logos*, Captain] since he ministers to the Father's will, and since he was begotten of the Father by an act of will; just as we see happening among ourselves: for when we give out some word, we beget the word; yet not by abscission, so as to lessen the word [which remains] in us, when we give it out: and just as we see also happening in the case of a fire, which is not lessened when it has kindled [another], but remains the same; and that which has been kindled by it likewise appears to exist by itself, not diminishing that from which it was kindled.

Compare the same analogy used by Justin's pupil, Tatian (*Oration* 5) and by Numenius (frag. 14).

22. Pl. *Ep.* 2.312E (quoted by Grant, *Greek Apologists*, 62).

23. Grant, *Greek Apologists*, 215 n. 46, records other early uses of the Plato passage: Athenagoras *Leg. pro Christ.* 23.7; Clement *Strom.* 5.14.103.1; Celsus in Origen *c. Cels.* 6.18. Hippolytus charged that Valentinus used the passage in his invention of the *plērōma* (*Haer.* 6.37.5–6).

24. Frag. 15.

25. Frag. 30.

26. Holte, "Logos Spermatikos," 123.

27. Cf. *Her.* 119: *aoratos kai spermatikos kai technikos logos; L.A.* 3.150: *ho spermatikos kai gennētikos tōn kalōn logos orthos* (cited by Holte, "Logos Spermatikos," 124 n. 54).

28. Holte, "Logos Spermatikos," 128, suggests that he may have been especially influenced by Matthew 13.3ff., Jesus' parable of the sower who sows the word of God.

29. See Dillon, *Middle Platonists*, 368, for discussion of this passage. He observes that this notion of a divine sowing is similar to Nicomachus's description of the Monad being "seminally (*spermatikos*) all things in Nature" and is reminiscent of Plato *Timaeus* 41E, where the demiurge sows souls into the various "organs of Time," as well as of *Republic* 10.597D, which describes God as a "planter" (*phytourgos*) of physical objects. Dillon discusses the transformation of Stoic *spermatikoi*

logoi into the generative, but immaterial, "ideas of God" in Antiochus, Seneca (*Ep.* 58, which preserves a Platonic source), Philo, and Albinus (95, 137, 159, and 285, respectively).

30. Holte, "Logos Spermatikos," 127.

31. Cf. *Ap.* 1.13.4:

> For they proclaim our madness to consist in this, that we give to a crucified man a place second to the unchangeable and eternal God, the creator of all; for they do not discern the mystery that is herein, to which, as we make it plain to you, we pray you to give heed.

See Dillon, *Middle Platonists,* 369, 373ff., on Numenius's negative evaluation of matter.

32. The following discussion of Numenius as literary interpreter is drawn entirely from Lamberton's discussion in *Homer the Theologian,* 64–70.

33. Lamberton's translation, *Homer the Theologian,* 63.

34. Lamberton, *Homer the Theologian,* 62, concludes that Numenius almost certainly used allegorically interpreted passages from the Christian New Testament as well as the Hebrew Bible.

35. Little can be said about Numenius's views on demons. Dillon, *Middle Platonists,* 378, points to Numenius's allegorical interpretation of the battle between the Athenians and the Atlantians in the *Timaeus* as a conflict between "more noble souls who are nurslings of Athena, and others who are agents of generation (*genesiourgoi*), who are in the service of the god who presides over generation (Poseidon)" (frag. 37). Dillon speculates further that the category "servants of Poseidon" might represent material demons who were "engaged in snaring souls into incarnation."

36. Cf. *Ap.* 1.23.1:

> Whatever we assert in conformity with what has been taught us by Christ, and by the prophets who preceded him, are alone true, and are older than all the writers who have existed . . . ; we claim to be acknowledged, not because we say the same things as these writers said, but because we say true things.

37. Cf. *Ap.* 1.20.1–3:

> And the Sibyl and Hystaspes said that there should be a dissolution through fire by God of things corruptible. And the philosophers called Stoics teach that even God himself shall be resolved into fire, and they say that the world is to be formed anew by this revolution; but we understand that God, the creator of all things, is superior to the things that are changed. If, therefore, on some points we teach the same things as the poets and philosophers whom you honor, and on other points are fuller and more divine in our teaching, and if we alone afford proof of what we assert, why are we unjustly hated more than all others?

38. See Lamberton's discussion in *Homer the Theologian,* 54–59.

39. Cf. *Paed.* 1.6.36.1: Paul says in 1 Corinthians 3.2, "I have given you milk to drink [*gala hymas epotisa*]"—speaking allegorically of the Word—and Clement

claims that "Homer oracularly declares involuntarily something like this" (*toiouton ti kai Homēros akōn manteuetai*) when he calls righteous men "milk-fed" (*galaktophagoi*) (*Il.* 13.6).

40. See *Protr.* 2.26.

41. Clement also turns the shared meanings of synonyms against the Greeks. By "showing the similarity of names" (*synōnymiai*) for gods, Clement is able to argue that they cannot all be real—and hence, not one of them is (*Protr.* 2.27.5).

42. See chapter 1, 67–68.

43. Pfeiffer, *History of Classical Scholarship,* 5.

44. Thersites was a bowlegged misfit among the Greeks at Troy, despised by Achilles and Odysseus.

45. See *Strom.* 1.21.101.2ff. for Clement's extensive borrowing from Tatian. Clement may have been a pupil of Tatian, as suggested by his reference to a teacher in Syria (*Strom.* 1.1.11.2). He explicitly mentions Philo (*Strom.* 1.15.72.4) and Aristobulus (*Strom.* 5.14.97.7) as witnesses to the antiquity of the Jewish philosophy. He "proves" the antiquity of that philosophy (*Strom.* 1.21.101ff.), using chronologies established by Alexandrian scholar-critics like Apollodorus and Eratosthenes (*Strom.* 1.16.79.3). Cf. *Strom.* 5.14.140.2: "The whole of Greek wisdom was derived from the barbarian philosophy"; *Strom.* 6.7.55.3–4: "Philosophy, then, consists of dogmas found in each sect . . . [which have been] stolen from the barbarian God-given grace [and] have been adorned by Greek speech."

46. Cf. *Strom.* 6.3.28. The roll call of Greek plagiarists includes Heraclitus, Plato, Antisthenes, Orpheus, Aristotle, the Stoics, and Pythagoras. Some typical examples are Heraclitus (*Strom.* 5.1.9.3), Plato (*Strom.* 2.19.100.3, 5.11.67.3ff., 1.1.10.2; *Paed.* 1.8.67.1, 3.11.54.2), Antisthenes (*Strom.* 5.14.108.4), Orpheus (*Strom.* 5.14.123.1), Aristotle (*Strom.* 1.17.87.3), the Stoics (*Strom.* 5.1.9.4, 5.3.17.6), Pythagoras (*Strom.* 2.18.92.1, 5.5.27.7), and philosophers in general (*Strom.* 5.5.29.3).

47. Cf. *Strom.* 1.18.90.1: "The true philosophy has been communicated by the Son." Cf. *Strom.* 1.5.28.3 and 1.19.91.5: "By the unknown god, God the creator was in a roundabout way worshipped by the Greeks; but . . . it was necessary by positive knowledge to apprehend and learn him by the Son"; see also *Protr.* 10.98.3–4 for a comparison of the true image of the Son and the false image of Jove; cf. *Strom.* 1.11.53.2: "Philosophers, then, are children, unless they have been made men by Christ"; *Strom.* 1.20.97.2,4: "While truth is one, many things contribute to its investigation. But its discovery is by the Son . . . that is the only authentic truth, unassailable, in which we are instructed by the Son of God"; *Strom.* 5.13.87.1: "Human beings must then be saved by learning the truth through Christ, even if they should attain Greek philosophy by practicing philosophy."

48. Justin had made the same point earlier (*Ap.* 1.20.2). Pythagoras also "spoke mystically" of Christians (*Strom.* 4.23.151.3).

49. See *Strom.* 5.14.93.2 for another "apostolic sentiment" from Plato; *Strom.* 3.3.18.1–2 for the agreement of Plato and Paul; *Strom.* 1.29.181.5 for God's direct speech through the poet Pindar. Clement's endorsement of the proleptic "Christian" sentiments of pagan authors is never automatic, however. The Greek ideal of continence (not to be subservient to desire) is not the same as the Christian refusal

to experience desire at all (*Strom.* 3.7.57.1). The Greeks are wrong to think that mercy is an evil, for the prophets insist that it is something good (*Strom.* 4.6.38.1).

50. See Annewies van den Hock, *Clement of Alexandria and His Use of Philo in the "Stromateis": An Early Christian Reshaping of a Jewish Model* (Leiden: Brill, 1988).

51. *Erēmos*, without the article here (although constructed with an article as grammatically feminine elsewhere in this selection), is, of course, normally rendered "the wilderness" in the biblical passage (as I translated it on p. 199).

52. *Hē steira* ("the barren," here constructed as grammatically feminine) is, of course, normally rendered "the barren woman" in this passage.

53. I have translated and placed in brackets the variant reading of P* *andra*, which Stählin omits from his edition.

54. It is possible that Clement had a version of the Septuagint before him that differed from the standard text (and which happened to make the point he is advancing). It is also possible that he is quoting from memory and simply remembers the passage incorrectly. Finally, given his frequent paraphrases of scripture, it is also possible that he is offering his own preferred version of the text. Since the text of the Septuagint was not standardized in Clement's time, alterations would be hard to identify. In any case, the contrast with the standard text of the Septuagint serves to highlight the distinctive goals of Clement's exegesis.

55. For other "types" or "signs," see *Paed.* 1.5.22.2; *Strom.* 6.16.145.7, 5.6.35.1, 5.6.37.5, 5.6.38.1, 5.6.40.3.

56. Later commentators on Plato identified this horse as lust, one of two irrational parts of the soul (see *Rep.* 439D–E). Plato does not identify the charioteer as Phaethon.

57. See Quasten, *Patrology*, vol. 2, 4–6 for the standard account.

58. My discussion of this evidence and the hypothetical counterproposal I derive from it is drawn principally from the arguments of Gustave Bardy, "Aux origines de l'école d'Alexandrie," *Recherches de science religieuse* 27 (1937): 65–90. Bardy extends his reinterpretation of the Catechetical School to include its post-Origen history in "Pour l'histoire de l'école d'Alexandrie," *Vivre et penser*, 2d ser. (1942): 80–109. For criticism of Bardy's argument, see Martiniano Pellegrino Roncaglia, "Pantene et le didascalé d'Alexandrie: Du Judéo-christianisme au christianisme hellénistique," in *A Tribute to Arthur Vööbus: Studies in Early Christian Literature and Its Environment, Primarily in the Syrian East*, ed. Robert H. Fischer (Chicago: The Lutheran School of Theology at Chicago, 1977), 212–33.

59. For a host of reasons why one should be suspicious of Eusebius's historiography, see Robert M. Grant, *Eusebius as Church Historian* (Oxford: Clarendon Press, 1980). See also Timothy D. Barnes, *Constantine and Eusebius* (Cambridge, Mass.: Harvard Univ. Press, 1981); Robert L. Wilkin, *The Myth of Christian Beginnings* (Notre Dame, Ind.: Univ. of Notre Dame Press, 1980).

60. See Layton, "Significance of Basilides," 135–36, for a brief description of heresiological doxography. See also Gérard Vallée, *A Study in Anti-Gnostic Polemics: Irenaeus, Hippolytus, and Epiphanius*, Studies in Christianity and Judaism 1 (n.p.: Canadian Corporation for Studies in Religion, 1981).

61. *Hist. eccl.* 6.6.1: "Pantaenus was succeeded by Clement, who guided catechesis at Alexandria up to such a date that Origen also was one of his pupils"; *Hist. eccl.* 6.13.1–2: "But of Clement the *Strōmateis*, all the eight books, are preserved to

us . . . and of equal number with these are his books entitled the *Hypotypōseis*, in which he mentions Pantaenus by name as his teacher, and has set forth his interpretation of the scriptures and his traditions." References to Eusebius are from *Ecclesiastical History,* 2 vols., trans. Kirsopp Lake, Loeb Classical Library (Cambridge, Mass.: Harvard Univ. Press, 1975).

62. *Hist. eccl.* 5.10.1–5.11.2 (italics are used to emphasize the problematic passages):

> At that time a man very famous for his learning named Pantaenus had charge of the life of the faithful in Alexandria, for from ancient custom a school of sacred learning existed among them. This school has lasted on to our time, and *we have heard* that it is managed by men powerful in their learning and zeal for divine things, but *tradition says* that *at that time* Pantaenus was especially eminent, and that he had been influenced by the philosophic system of those called Stoics. *They say* that he showed such zeal in his warm disposition for the divine word that he was appointed as a herald for the gospel of Christ *to the heathen in the East,* and was sent as far as India. For indeed there were until then many evangelists of the word who had forethought to use inspired zeal on the apostolic model for the increase and the building up of the divine word. One of these was Pantaenus, and *it is said* that he went to the Indians, and *the tradition* is that he found there that among some of those there who had known Christ the Gospel according to Matthew had preceded his coming; for Bartholomew, one of the apostles, had preached to them and had left them the writing of Matthew in Hebrew letters, which was preserved until the time mentioned. Pantaenus, after many achievements, was at the head of the school in Alexandria until his death, and orally and in writing expounded the treasures of the divine doctrine. In his time Clement, the namesake of the pupil of the apostles who had once ruled the church of Rome, was famous in Alexandria for his study of the Holy Scriptures with Pantaenus. In the *Hypotypōses* which he composed he mentioned Pantaenus by name as his teacher, and *he seems to me* to allude to him in the first book of the *Strōmateis,* when he speaks thus in reference to the more distinguished members of the apostolic succession which he had received [an altered quotation from Clement follows].

63. *Hist. eccl.* 6.19.12–14:

> But as I was devoted to the word, and the fame of our proficiency was spreading abroad, there approached me sometimes heretics, sometimes those conversant with Greek learning, and especially philosophy, and I thought it right to examine both the opinions of the heretics, and also the claim that the philosophers make to speak concerning truth. And in doing this we followed the example of Pantaenus, who, before us, was of assistance to many, and had acquired no small attainments in these matters, and also Heraclas, who now has a seat in the presbytery of the Alexandrians, whom I found with the teacher of philosophy, and who had remained five years with him before I began to attend his lectures. And though he formerly wore ordinary dress, on his teacher's account he put it off and assumed a philo-

sophic garb, which he keeps to this day, all the while studying Greek books as much as possible.

Cf. *Hist. eccl.* 6.14.8–9 (a letter of Alexander to Origen):

> For this also has proved to be the will of God, as you know, that the friendship that comes to us from our forefathers should remain unshaken, nay rather grow warmer and more steadfast. For we know as fathers those blessed ones who went before us, with whom we shall be ere long: Pantaenus, truly blessed and my master, and the holy Clement, who was my master and profited me, and all others like them. Through these I came to know you, who are the best in all things, and my master and my brother.

64. *Strom.* 1.1.11.1–2:

> Now this work of mine in writing is not artfully constructed for display; but my memoranda are stored up against old age, as a remedy against forgetfulness, truly an image and outline of those vigorous and animated discourses which I was privileged to hear, and of blessed and truly remarkable men. Of these the one, in Greece, an Ionian; the other in Magna Graecia: the first of these from Coele-Syria, the second from Egypt, and others in the East. The one was born in the land of Assyria, and the other a Hebrew in Palestine. When I came upon the last (he was the first in power), having tracked him out concealed in Egypt, I found rest. He, the true, the Sicilian bee, gathering the spoil of the flowers of the prophetic and apostolic meadow, engendered in the souls of his hearers a deathless element of knowledge.

Clement's only other remark about his teacher Pantaenus comes in the course of fragmentary exegetical comments on Psalm 19.4 ("And he placed his tent in the sun"):

> Some, such as Hermogenes, say the body of the lord is to be put in the sun, and some say the body is "his tent," which others say is the church of the faithful, but Pantaenus told us that "prophecy, as usual, delivers the phrases indefinitely, using the present for the future tense, and again the present for the past tense," which is also apparent here. (*Ecl. proph.* xxviii.56.2–3)

Cf. Justin *Ap.* 1.42.1–2:

> But when the prophetic spirit speaks of things that are about to come to pass as if they had already taken place—as may be observed even in the passages already cited by me—that this circumstance may afford no excuse to readers (for misinterpreting them), we will make even this also quite plain. The things which he absolutely knows will take place, he predicts as if already they had taken place.

65. Roberts, *Early Christian Egypt,* 54, offers a provocative proposal regarding the role of Basilides and Valentinus in the early "Catechetical School." He wonders whether Pantaenus might have been given leadership of such a school because it had been taken over by Basilides and Valentinus, thus making their names stand out in early second-century Egyptian Christianity. Pantaenus's monistic

Stoicism might have been viewed as just the necessary antidote to Gnostic dualism. But this proposal is unlikely, not only given the uncertain existence of any ecclesiastical school at this early date at all, but also in light of Basilides' unquestioned Stoicism (see Layton, "Significance of Basilides") and Valentinus's own monism.

66. Bardy, "Aux origines de l'école d'Alexandrie," 82 n. 58.

67. Ibid., 86ff.

68. For general discussion of late second-century efforts by an emerging anti-Gnostic orthodoxy to domesticate Gnosticism in Alexandria, see Roberts, *Early Christian Egypt*, 51 n. 3, and Koester, *Introduction to New Testament*, vol. 2, 54.

69. This group viewed philosophy as a tool of the devil designed to promote heresy. See *Strom.* 1.9.45.6 for "those who are called orthodox" (*hoi orthodoxastai kaloumenoi*) and *Strom.* 5.11.68.3 for criticism of their anthropomorphic, non-allegorical scripture reading. See *Strom.* 1.5.28–30 for a reading of scripture that, following Philo's allegorical reading of Sarah and Hagar, defends the use of philosophy by Christians. I am drawing on Henry Chadwick's analysis of this basic division within Clement's own community, outlined in his *Early Christian Thought and the Classical Tradition.*

70. Other readers (Marcionites?) read literally "sayings intended to be understood allegorically" (*Strom.* 3.4.38.1).

71. "House and wealth are inherited from fathers, but a prudent wife is from the lord" (Prov. 19.14).

72. Günther Zuntz, *The Text of the Epistles: A Disquisition Upon the Corpus Paulinum*, The Schweich Lectures of the British Academy, 1946 (London: Oxford Univ. Press, 1953), 272–73.

73. Zuntz, *Text of the Epistles*, 275.

74. See Clem. *Ecl. proph.* 56.2; Euseb. *Hist. eccl.* 5.10.4 ("Pantaenus . . . orally and in writing expounded [*hypomnēmatizomenos*] the treasures of the divine doctrine"), cited by Zuntz, *Text of the Epistles*, 273 n. 2.

75. Zuntz, *Text of the Epistles*, 275. The second-century Christian Papias also wrote something called *Exēgēseis* (Zuntz, 276).

76. Zuntz, *Text of the Epistles*, 275.

77. Iren. *Haer.* 3.1.1: *emendatores apostolorum* (cited by Zuntz, *Text of the Epistles*, 241 n. 2). Zuntz adds that Tertullian and Irenaeus are criticizing Marcion's misinterpretation of the meaning of scripture, not his misconstruction of its wording. There is no evidence that Marcion really acted as a true editor making critical comparisons of various recensions of the biblical texts; on the contrary, he makes numerous textual blunders.

SELECT BIBLIOGRAPHY
OF WORKS CONSULTED

I. PRIMARY SOURCES: INDIVIDUAL AUTHORS

Aristeas. *Aristeas to Philocrates (Letter of Aristeas)*. Edited and translated by Moses Hadas. New York: Harper & Brothers, 1951.

Aristobulus. *Fragments*. In *Eusebius Werke, 2: Kirchengeschichte, zweiter Teil, Die griechischen christlichen Schriftsteller der ersten drei Jahrhunderte* 9.2., edited by Eduard Schwartz. Leipzig, 1908; *Eusebius Werke, 8: Die Praeparatio evangelica, Die griechischen christlichen Schriftsteller der ersten drei Jahrhunderte* 43.1 and 43.2, edited by K. Mras. Berlin, 1982–83.

———. "Aristobulus: A New Translation and Introduction." Translated by A. Yarbro Collins. In *The Old Testament Pseudepigrapha*, vol. 2, edited by James H. Charlesworth. Garden City, N. Y.: Doubleday, 1985.

Aristophanes. *Aristophanes*. 3 vols. Translated by Benjamin Bickley Rogers. Loeb Classical Library. 1924. Reprint. Cambridge, Mass.: Harvard Univ. Press, 1967–72.

Aristotle. *The Basic Works of Aristotle*. Edited by Richard McKeon. New York: Random House, 1941.

Aulus Gellius. *The Attic Nights of Aulus Gellius*. 3 vols. Translated by John C. Rolfe. Loeb Classical Library. 1927. Reprint. Cambridge, Mass.: Harvard Univ. Press, 1967–70.

Barnabas. *The Epistle of Barnabas*. In *The Apostolic Fathers*, vol. 1, translated by Kirsopp Lake. Loeb Classical Library. Cambridge, Mass.: Harvard Univ. Press, 1977.

Cicero. *De natura deorum, Academica*. Translated by H. Rackham. Loeb Classical Library. New York: G. P. Putnam's Sons, 1933.

———. *M. Tulli Ciceronis De natura deorum*. 2 vols. Edited by Arthur Stanley Pease. Cambridge, Mass.: Harvard Univ. Press, 1955, 1958.

Clement. *Clement of Alexandria. Miscellanies. Book VII. The Greek Text with Introduction, Translation, Notes, Dissertations and Indices*. Edited and translated by Fenton John Anthony Hort and Joseph B. Mayor. New York: Macmillan, 1902.

———. *Clemens Alexandrinus.* 4 vols. In *Die griechischen christlichen Schriftsteller der ersten drei Jahrhunderte,* edited by Otto Stählin. Berlin: Akademie-Verlag, 1905–36.

———. *The* Excerpta ex Theodoto *of Clement of Alexandria.* Edited by Robert Pierce Casey. London: Christophers, 1934.

———. *Le Protreptique.* Translated by Claude Mondésert. 2d ed. Sources chrétiennes. Paris: Éditions du Cerf, 1949.

———. *Les Stromates.* Vols. 1 and 2 translated by Claude Mondésert, vol. 5 by Pierre Voulet. Sources chrétiennes. Paris: Éditions du Cerf, 1951–81.

———. *Clement of Alexandria. Christ the Educator.* Translated by Simon P. Wood. New York: Fathers of the Church, 1954.

———. *Stromates 3.* In *Alexandrian Christianity: Selected Translations of Clement and Origen with Introductions and Notes,* edited and translated by John Ernest Leonard Oulton and Henry Chadwick. Philadelphia: Westminster, 1955.

———. *Le Pédagogue.* 3 vols. Vol. 1 translated by Marguerite Harl, vol. 2 by Claude Mondésert, vol. 3 by Claude Mondésert and Chantal Matray. Sources chrétiennes. Paris: Éditions du Cerf, 1960–70.

———. *Extraits de Théodote: Texte grec, introduction, traduction et notes.* Edited and translated by François Sagnard. Sources chrétiennes. 1948. Reprint. Paris: Éditions du Cerf, 1970.

———. *The Ante-Nicene Fathers.* Vol. 2: *Fathers of the Second Century,* edited by Alexander Roberts and James Donaldson. 1884. Reprint. Grand Rapids, Mich.: Eerdmans, 1979.

———. *Eclogae propheticae.* Translated by Alan Scott. Unpublished manuscript.

Cornutus. *Cornuti theologiae graecae compendium.* Edited by Carolus Lang. Leipzig: Teubner, 1881.

———. Robert Stephen Hays, "Lucius Annaeus Cornutus' *Epidrome (Introduction to the Traditions of Greek Theology):* Introduction, Translation, and Notes." Ph.D. diss., University of Texas, 1983.

Diogenes Laertius. *Lives of the Eminent Philosophers.* 2 vols. Translated by R. D. Hicks. Loeb Classical Library. 1925. Reprint. Cambridge, Mass.: Harvard Univ. Press, 1966–70.

Eusebius. *Eusebius Werke,* 2: *Kirchengeschichte, zweiter Teil. GCS* 9.2. Edited by Eduard Schwartz. Leipzig: Hinrich's, 1908.

———. *Ecclesiastical History.* 2 vols. Translated by Kirsopp Lake. Loeb Classical Library. Cambridge, Mass.: Harvard Univ. Press, 1975.

———. *Eusebius Werke,* 8.1 and 8.2: *Die Praeparatio evangelica. GCS* 43.1 and 43.2. Edited by Karl Mras. Berlin: Akademie-Verlag, 1982–83.

Fulgentius. "The Exposition of the Content of Virgil According to Moral Philosophy." In *Classical and Medieval Literary Criticism: Translations and Interpretations,* edited by Alex Preminger, O. B. Hardison, and Kevin Kerrane, 329–40. New York: Frederick Ungar, 1974.

Heraclitus (the pre-Socratic). *The Art and Thought of Heraclitus: An Edition of the Fragments with Translation and Commentary.* Edited and translated by Charles H. Kahn. Cambridge: Cambridge Univ. Press, 1979.

Heraclitus. *Héraclite: Allégories d'Homère.* Edited and translated by Félix Buffière. Paris: Société d'édition "Les Belles Lettres," 1962.

Hesiod. *Theogony.* Translated by Norman O. Brown. 1953. Reprint. Bobbs-Merrill, 1976.

Homer. *The Odyssey.* Translated by E. V. Rieu. Baltimore: Penguin, 1946.

———. *The Iliad.* Translated by E. V. Rieu. Baltimore: Penguin, 1950.

———. *The Iliad.* 2 vols. Translated by A. T. Murray. Loeb Classical Library. 1924–25. Reprint. Cambridge, Mass.: Harvard Univ. Press, 1971–76.

———. *The Odyssey.* 2 vols. Translated by A. T. Murray. Loeb Classical Library. 1919. Reprint. Cambridge, Mass.: Harvard Univ. Press, 1974–75.

Irenaeus of Lyons. *Sancti Irenaei episcopi lugdunensis libros quinque adversus haereses.* 2 vols. Edited by W. Wigan Harvey. Cambridge: Typis Academicis, 1857.

Justin Martyr. *The* Apologies *of Justin Martyr.* Edited by A. W. F. Blunt. Cambridge Patristic Texts, edited by A. J. Mason. Cambridge: Cambridge Univ. Press, 1911.

———. "The First Apology of Justin, the Martyr." Translated by Edward Rochie Hardy. In *Early Christian Fathers,* edited by Cyril C. Richardson, 242–89. The Library of Christian Classics 1. New York: Macmillan, 1970.

———. *Dialogue with Trypho, a Jew.* In *The Ante-Nicene Fathers.* Vol. 1: *The Apostolic Fathers with Justin Martyr and Irenaeus,* edited by Alexander Roberts and James Donaldson. 1884. Reprint. Grand Rapids, Mich.: Eerdmans, 1977.

Longinus. *'Longinus' On the Sublime.* Edited and translated by D. A. Russell. Oxford: Clarendon Press, 1964.

Numenius. *Fragments.* Edited and translated by Édouard Des Places. Paris: "Les Belles Lettres" (Budé), 1973.

Origen. *Origen: Contra Celsum.* Translated by Henry Chadwick. 1953. Reprint. Cambridge: Cambridge Univ. Press, 1965.

Philo. *Opera.* 6 vols. Edited by Leopold Cohn and Paul Wendland. Berlin: Georgii Reimeri, 1896–1915.

———. *Philo.* 10 vols. Edited and translated by F. H. Colson and G. H. Whitaker. Loeb Classical Library. Cambridge, Mass.: Harvard Univ. Press, 1929–62.

———. *Philonis Alexandrini In Flaccum.* Edited and translated by Herbert Box. London: Oxford Univ. Press, 1939.

———. *Questions and Answers on Genesis and Exodus.* 2 vols. Translated by Ralph Marcus. Loeb Classical Library. Cambridge, Mass.: Harvard Univ. Press, 1953.

———. *Philonis Alexandrini Legatio ad Gaium.* Edited and translated by E. Mary Smallwood. Leiden: Brill, 1961.

———. *De providentia I et II.* Edited and translated by Mireille Hadas-Lebel. Paris: Éditions du Cerf, 1973.

———. *Philo of Alexandria: The Contemplative Life, the Giants, and Selections.* Edited and translated by David Winston. New York: Paulist, 1981.

Philodemus. *Philodemus über die Gedichte: Fünftes Buch.* Edited by C. Jensen. Berlin, 1923.

Plato. *Opera.* 5 vols. in 6. Edited by J. Burnet. Oxford: Clarendon Press, 1905–10.

———. *Timaeus.* In *Plato,* vol. 7, translated by R. G. Bury. Loeb Classical Library. New York: G. P. Putnam's Sons, 1929.

———. *Plato's* Phaedrus. Translated by R. Hackforth. Cambridge: Cambridge Univ. Press, 1952.

Plutarch. *De Audiendis Poetis.* In *Moralia* 1, edited by W. R. Paton and I. Wege-haupt. Leipzig: Teubner, 1925.

———. *How the Young Man Should Study Poetry.* In *Plutarch's* Moralia. Vol. 1, translated by Frank Cole Babbitt. Loeb Classical Library. New York: G. P. Putnam's Sons, 1927.

———. *Plutarch's* De Iside et Osiride. Edited with introduction, translation, and commentary by J. Gwyn Griffiths. Cambridge: Univ. of Wales Press, 1970.

Prudentius. *Prudentius.* 2 vols. Translated by H. J. Thomson. Loeb Classical Library. Cambridge, Mass.: Harvard Univ. Press, 1949.

Pseudo-Plutarch. *De vita et poesi Homeri.* In *Moralia* 7, edited by G. N. Bernardakis. Leipzig: Teubner, 1896.

Quintilian. *The* Institutio Oratoria *of Quintilian.* 4 vols. Translated by H. E. Butler. Loeb Classical Library. 1920–22. Reprint. Cambridge, Mass.: Harvard Univ. Press, 1966–69.

Seneca. *Seneca.* 10 vols. Translated by John W. Basore. Loeb Classical Library. 1935. Reprint. Cambridge, Mass.: Harvard Univ. Press, 1975.

Sextus Empiricus. *Sextus Empiricus.* 4 vols. Translated by R. G. Bury. Loeb Classical Library. 1933–49. Reprint. Cambridge, Mass.: Harvard Univ. Press, 1961–68.

Valentinus. *Fragments.* In *Quellen zur Geschichte der christlichen Gnosis,* edited by Walther Völker. Tübingen: J. C. B. Mohr (Paul Siebeck), 1932.

———. *Evangelium veritatis: Codex Jung f. VIIIv–XVIv (p. 16–32), f. XIXr–XXIIr (p. 37–43).* Edited and translated by Michel Maline, Henri-Charles Puech, and Gilles Quispel. Zurich: Rascher, 1956.

———. *The Gospel of Truth: A Valentinian Meditation on the Gospel. Translation from the Coptic and Commentary.* Edited and translated by Kendrick Grobel. New York: Abingdon, 1960.

———. *Evangelium veritatis: Codex Jung f. XVIIr–XVIIIv (p. 33–36).* Edited and translated by Michel Maline, Henri-Charles Puech, Gilles Quispel, and Walter Till. Zurich: Rascher, 1961.

———. *L'évangile de vérité: Rétrouversion grecque et commentaire.* Edited and trans-lated by Jacques E. Ménard. Paris: Letouzey and Ané, 1962.

———. *The Gospel of Truth.* In *Nag Hammadi Codex I (The Jung Codex).* Vol. 1: *Introduction, Texts, Translations, Indices,* edited by Harold W. Attridge. The Coptic Gnostic Library. Leiden: Brill, 1985.

Varro. *On the Latin Language.* 2 vols. Translated by Roland G. Kent. Loeb Classical Library. 1938. Reprint. Cambridge, Mass.: Harvard Univ. Press, 1967–79.

II. PRIMARY SOURCES: COLLECTIONS

Arnim, Hans von, ed. *Stoicorum veterum fragmenta.* 4 vols. 1905–24. Reprint. Stuttgart: Teubner, 1964.

Bate, Walter Jackson, ed. *Criticism: The Major Texts.* Enl. ed. New York: Harcourt Brace Jovanovich, 1970.

Cameron, Ron, ed. *The Other Gospels: Non-Canonical Gospel Texts.* Philadelphia: Westminster, 1982.

Charlesworth, James H., ed. *The Old Testament Pseudepigrapha.* 2 vols. Garden City, N. Y.: Doubleday, 1983, 1985.

Dindorf, G., ed. *Scholia graeca in Homeri Odysseam.* 2 vols. 1855. Reprint. Amsterdam: Adolf M. Hakkert, 1962.

Erbse, Hartmut, ed. *Scholia graeca in Homeri Iliadem (Scholia vetera).* 6 vols. Berlin: Walter de Gruyter, 1969–83.

Foerster, Werner, ed. Gnosis: *A Selection of Gnostic Texts.* 2 vols. Translated by R. McL. Wilson. Oxford: Clarendon Press, 1972, 1974.

Holladay, Carl R., comp. and trans. *Fragments from Hellenistic Jewish Authors.* Vol. 1: *Historians.* Chico, Calif.: Scholars Press, 1983.

Institute for Antiquity and Christianity. *The Nag Hammadi Library in English.* Translated by the Coptic Gnostic Library Project, Institute for Antiquity and Christianity, James M. Robinson, Director. 1977. Reprint. New York: Harper & Row, 1981.

Keil, Heinrich, ed. *Grammatici latini.* 1857–70. Reprint. Hildesheim: Olms, 1961.

Kirk, G. S., and J. E. Raven. *The Presocratic Philosophers: A Critical History with a Selection of Texts.* Cambridge: Cambridge Univ. Press, 1957.

Layton, Bentley. *The Gnostic Scriptures: A New Translation with Annotations and Introductions.* Garden City, N. Y.: Doubleday, 1987.

Long, A. A., and N. Sedley. *The Hellenistic Philosophers.* Vol. 1: *Translations of the Principal Sources with Philosophical Commentary;* vol. 2: *Greek and Latin Texts with Notes and Bibliography.* Cambridge: Cambridge Univ. Press, 1987.

Matsen, Patricia. "Appendix II: From Spengel's *Rhetores Graeci.*" In *Classical Theories of Allegory and Christian Culture* by Phillip Rollinson and Patricia Matsen. Pittsburgh: Duquesne Univ. Press, 1981.

Novum Testamentum Graece. Edited by Eberhard Nestle and Kurt Aland. 26th ed. Stuttgart: Deutsche Bibelstiftung, 1979.

Oates, Whitney J., ed. *The Stoic and Epicurean Philosophers: The Complete Extant Writings of Epicurus, Epictetus, Lucretius, Marcus Aurelius.* New York: Random House, 1940.

Oates, Whitney J., and Eugene O'Neill, Jr., eds. *The Complete Greek Drama.* 2 vols. New York: Random House, 1938.

Russell, D. A., and M. Winterbottom, eds. *Ancient Literary Criticism: The Principal Texts in New Translations.* Oxford: Clarendon Press, 1972.

Rutherford, William G., ed. and trans. *Scholia Aristophanica.* 3 vols. London: Macmillan, 1896–1905.

Septuaginta. Edited by Alfred Rahlfs. 1935. Reprint. Stuttgart: Deutsche Bibelgesellschaft, 1979.

Spengel, Leonard, ed. *Rhetores graeci.* 3 vols. 1853–56. Reprint. Frankfurt: Minerva, 1966.

Stern, Menahem, ed. and trans. *Greek and Latin Authors on Jews and Judaism.* 2 vols. Jerusalem: The Israel Academy of Sciences and Humanities, 1974–80.

Tcherikover, Victor A., and Alexander Fuks, eds. *Corpus Papyrorum Judicarum.* 3 vols. Cambridge, Mass.: Harvard Univ. Press, 1957–64.

White, John Williams, ed. *The Scholia on the Aves of Aristophanes.* Boston: Ginn & Company, 1915.

III. SECONDARY SOURCES

Allen, Don Cameron. *Mysteriously Meant: The Rediscovery of Pagan Symbolism and Allegorical Interpretation in the Renaissance.* Baltimore: Johns Hopkins Univ. Press, 1970.

Alter, Robert. *The Art of Biblical Narrative.* New York: Basic Books, 1981.

Alter, Robert, and Frank Kermode, eds. *The Literary Guide to the Bible.* Cambridge, Mass.: Harvard Univ. Press, 1987.

Andresen, Carl. "Justin und der mittlere Platonismus." *Zeitschrift für die Neutestamentliche Wissenschaft und die Kunde der Älternen Kirche* 44 (1952–53): 157–95.

Arnold, E. V. *Roman Stoicism: Being Lectures on the History of the Stoic Philosophy, with Special Reference to Its Development within the Roman Empire.* Cambridge: Cambridge Univ. Press, 1911.

Atkins, J. W. H. *Literary Criticism in Antiquity: A Sketch of Its Development.* 2 vols. Cambridge: Cambridge Univ. Press, 1961.

Attridge, Harold W. "The Philosophical Critique of Religion under the Early Empire." *ANRW* II.16.1 (1978): 45–78.

———. "The Gospel of Truth as an Exoteric Text." In *Nag Hammadi, Gnosticism, and Early Christianity,* edited by Charles W. Hedrick and Robert Hodgson, Jr., 239–55. Peabody, Mass.: Hendrickson, 1986.

Auerbach, Erich. "'Figura.'" Translated by Ralph Manheim from the original German text in *Neue Dantestudien* (Istanbul, 1944) and reprinted in *Scenes from the Drama of European Literature,* Theory and the History of Literature 9, edited by Wlad Godzich and Jochen Schulte-Sasse, 11–71. Minneapolis, Minn.: Univ. of Minnesota Press, 1984.

———. *Mimesis: The Representation of Reality in Western Literature.* Translated by Willard R. Trask. Princeton: Princeton Univ. Press, 1953.

Axtell, Harold L. *The Deification of Abstract Ideas in Roman Literature and Inscriptions.* 1907. Reprint. New Rochelle, N. Y.: Aristide D. Caratzas, 1987.

Bakhtin, M. M. *The Dialogic Imagination.* Edited by Michael Holquist and translated by Caryl Emerson and Michael Holquist. Austin: Univ. of Texas Press, 1981.

Baldwin, Charles Sears. *Medieval Rhetoric and Poetic (to 1400) Interpreted from Representative Works.* New York: Macmillan, 1928.

Bardy, Gustave. "Aux origines de l'école d'Alexandrie." *Recherches de science religieuse* 27 (1937): 65–90.

———. "Pour l'histoire de l'école d'Alexandrie." *Vivre et penser* 2d ser. (1942): 80–109.

Barnard, L. W. *Studies in the Apostolic Fathers and Their Background.* New York: Schocken, 1966.

Barnard, P. Mordaunt, ed. *The Biblical Text of Clement of Alexandria in the Four Gospels and the Acts of the Apostles.* Cambridge: Cambridge Univ. Press, 1899.

Barnes, Timothy D. *Constantine and Eusebius.* Cambridge, Mass.: Harvard Univ. Press, 1981.

Barney, Stephen A. *Allegories of History, Allegories of Love.* Hamden, Conn.: Archon Books, 1979.

Barr, James. "Typology and Allegory." Chapter 4 in *Old and New in Interpretation: A Study of the Two Testaments.* New York: Harper & Row, 1966.

Bate, H. N. "Some Technical Terms of Greek Exegesis." *The Journal of Theological Studies* 24 (1922): 59–66.

Bauer, Walter. *Orthodoxy and Heresy in Earliest Christianity.* Translated from the second German edition by Paul J. Achtemeier et al. and edited by Robert A. Kraft and Gerhard Krodel. Philadelphia: Fortress, 1971.

Bell, H[arold] Idris. "Evidences of Christianity in Egypt during the Roman Period." *Harvard Theological Review* 37 (July 1944): 185–208.

———. *Egypt from Alexander the Great to the Arab Conquest: A Study in the Diffusion and Decay of Hellenism.* The Gregynog Lectures 1946. 1948. Reprint. Westport, Conn.: Greenwood Press, 1977.

Benjamin, Walter. *Illuminations.* Edited by Hannah Arendt. New York: Schocken, 1969.

———. "Die Aufgabe des Übersetzers." In *Gesammelte Schriften* 4.1, edited by Tillman Rexroth, 9–21. Werkausgabe vol. 10. Frankfurt: Suhrkamp, 1972.

Berger, Peter L. *The Sacred Canopy: Elements of a Sociological Theory of Religion.* Garden City, N. Y.: Doubleday, 1969.

Berger, Peter L., and Thomas Luckmann. *The Social Construction of Reality: A Treatise in the Sociology of Knowledge.* Garden City, N. Y.: Doubleday, 1966.

Bevan, Edwyn. *Stoics and Sceptics.* Oxford: Clarendon Press, 1913.

———. *Sibyls and Seers: A Survey of Some Ancient Theories of Revelation and Inspiration.* London: George Allen & Unwin, 1928.

Bezanker, Abraham. *An Introduction to the Problem of Allegory in Literary Criticism.* Ann Arbor, Mich: University Microfilms, 1955.

Bigg, Charles. *The Christian Platonists of Alexandria: The 1886 Bampton Lectures.* 1913. Reprint. Oxford: Clarendon Press, 1968.

Black, Max. *Models and Metaphor: Studies in Language and Philosophy.* Ithaca, N. Y.: Cornell Univ. Press, 1962.

———. "More About Metaphor." In *Metaphor and Thought,* edited by Andrew Ortney, 19–43. Cambridge: Cambridge Univ. Press, 1979.

Bloom, Edward A. "The Allegorical Principle." *ELH: A Journal of English Literary History* 18 (September 1951): 163–90.

Bloom, Harold. *The Anxiety of Influence: A Theory of Poetry.* New York: Oxford Univ. Press, 1973.

———. *A Map of Misreading.* New York: Oxford Univ. Press, 1975.

———. "Lying Against Time: Gnosis, Poetry, Criticism." In *The Rediscovery of Gnosticism,* edited by Bentley Layton. Vol. 1: *The School of Valentinus,* 57–72. Studies in the History of Religions 41. Leiden: Brill, 1980.

———. *Kabbala and Criticism.* New York: Continuum, 1984.

Bloomfield, Morton W. "A Grammatical Approach to Personification Allegory." *Modern Philology* 60 (1962–63): 161–71.

———. "Allegory as Interpretation." *New Literary History* 3 (Winter 1972): 301–17.

———, ed. *Allegory, Myth, and Symbol.* Harvard English Studies 9. Cambridge, Mass.: Harvard Univ. Press, 1981.

Boer, Willem den. *De allegorese in het werk van Clemens Alexandrinus* (summary in French). Leiden: Brill, 1940.

Bonner, Stanley F. *Education in Ancient Rome: From the Elder Cato to the Younger Pliny.* Berkeley and Los Angeles: Univ. of California Press, 1977.

Boothe, Wayne C. *The Rhetoric of Fiction.* 1961. 2d ed. Chicago: Univ. of Chicago Press, 1983.

Borgen, Peder. "Philo of Alexandria: A Critical and Synthetical Survey of Research since World War II." *ANRW* II.21.1 (1984): 98–154.

Borgen, Peder, and Ronald Skarsten. "Quaestiones et Solutiones: Some Observations on the Form of Philo's Exegesis." *Studia Philonica* 4 (1976–77): 1–15.

Bousset, Wilhelm. *Jüdisch-christlicher Schulbetrieb in Alexandria und Rom: Literarische Untersuchungen zu Philo und Clemens von Alexandria, Justin und Irenäus.* Göttingen: Vandenhoeck & Ruprecht, 1915.

Bréhier, Émile. *Les idées philosophiques et religieuses de Philon d'Alexandrie.* 3d ed. Paris: Vrin, 1950.

Brooke-Rose, Christine. *A Grammar of Metaphor.* London: Secker & Warburg, 1958.

Budick, Sanford. "Milton and the Scene of Interpretation: From Typology toward Midrash." In *Midrash and Literature,* edited by Geoffrey H. Hartman and Sanford Budick, 195–212. New Haven: Yale Univ. Press, 1986.

Buffière, Félix. *Les mythes d'Homère et la pensée grecque.* Paris: Société d'édition "Les Belles Lettres," 1956.

Bultmann, Rudolph. "Ursprung und Sinn der Typologie als hermeneutischer Methode." *Theologische Literaturzeitung* 75–76 (1950–51): 205–12.

Campenhausen, Hans von. *The Formation of the Christian Bible.* Translated by J. A. Baker. Philadelphia: Fortress, 1972.

Centre national de la recherche scientifique. *Biblia patristica: Index des citations et allusions bibliques dans la littérature patristique.* Vol. 1: *Des origines à Clément d'Alexandrie et Tertullien.* Paris: Éditions du Centre national de la recherche scientifique, 1975.

Cerfaux, L. "La première communauté chrétienne à Jérusalem (Act., II, 41–V, 42)." *Ephemerides theologiae Lovanienses* 16 (1939): 5–31.

Chadwick, Henry. *Early Christian Thought and the Classical Tradition: Studies in Justin, Clement, and Origen.* New York: Oxford Univ. Press, 1966.

———. "Clement of Alexandria." In *The Cambridge History of Later Greek and Early Medieval Philosophy,* edited by A. H. Armstrong, 168–81. Cambridge: Cambridge Univ. Press, 1967.

———. "Philo and the Beginnings of Christian Thought." In *The Cambridge History of Later Greek and Early Medieval Philosophy,* edited by A. H. Armstrong, 133–57. Cambridge: Cambridge Univ. Press, 1967.

Charity, A. C. *Events and Their Afterlife: The Dialectics of Christian Typology in the Bible and Dante.* Cambridge: Cambridge Univ. Press, 1966.

Childs, Brevard S. "The Sensus Literalis of Scripture: An Ancient and Modern Problem." In *Beiträge zur alttestamentlichen Theologie: Festschrift für Walther Zimmerli zum 70. Geburtstag,* edited by Herbert Donner, Robert Hanhart, and Rudolf Smend, 80–93. Göttingen: Vandenhoeck & Ruprecht, 1977.

———. *Introduction to the Old Testament as Scripture.* Philadelphia: Fortress, 1979.

Christensen, Jerome C. "The Symbol's Errant Allegory: Coleridge and His Critics." *ELH* 45 (1978): 640–59.

Christiansen, Irmgard. *Die Technik der allegorischen Auslegungswissenschaft bei Philon von Alexandrien.* Tübingen: J. C. B. Mohr, 1969.

Clark, Donald Lemen. *Rhetoric in Greco-Roman Education.* New York: Columbia Univ. Press, 1957.

Clifford, Gay. *The Transformations of Allegory.* London: Routledge & Kegan Paul, 1974.

Clifford, James. *The Predicament of Culture: Twentieth Century Ethnography, Literature, and Art.* Cambridge, Mass.: Harvard Univ. Press, 1988.

Collins, John J. *Between Athens and Jerusalem: Jewish Identity in the Hellenistic Diaspora.* New York: Crossroad, 1983.

Comstock, Gary. "Truth or Meaning: Ricoeur versus Frei on Biblical Narrative." *The Journal of Religion* 66 (1986): 117–40.

Crouzel, H. "La distinction de la 'typologie' et 'allegorie.'" *Bulletin de littérature ecclésiastique* 65 (1964): 161–74.

Culler, Jonathan. "Literary History, Allegory, and Semiology." *New Literary History* 7 (1975–76): 259–70.

Curtius, Ernst Robert. "Etymology as a Category of Thought." Excursus 14 in *European Literature and the Latin Middle Ages,* translated by Willard R. Trask. Princeton: Princeton Univ. Press, 1953.

Dahl, Nils A., and Alan F. Segal. "Philo and the Rabbis on the Names of God." *Journal for the Study of Judaism* 9 (1978): 1–20.

Daniélou, Jean. *Philon d'Alexandrie.* Paris: Fayard, 1958.

———. *From Shadows to Reality: Studies in the Biblical Typology of the Fathers.* Translated by Wulstan Hibberd. London: Burns & Oates, 1960.

———. *The Theology of Jewish Christianity.* Translated by John A. Baker. London: Longwood & Todd, 1964.

———. *Gospel Message and Hellenistic Culture.* Translated and edited by John A. Baker. Philadelphia: Westminster, 1973.

Daube, David. "Alexandrian Methods of Interpretation and the Rabbis." In *Essays in Greco-Roman and Related Talmudic Literature,* selected with a prolegomena by Henry A. Fischel, 165–82. The Library of Biblical Studies, edited by Harry M. Orlinsky. New York: KTAV, 1977.

Davies, W. D. "Paul and Jewish Christianity According to Cardinal Daniélou: A Suggestion." In *Judéo-christianisme: Recherches historiques et théologiques offertes en hommage au Cardinal Jean Daniélou,* 69–79. Paris: Recherches de science religieuse, 1972.

Davison, James E. "Structural Similarities and Dissimilarities in the Thought of Clement of Alexandria and the Valentinians." *Second Century* 3 (1983): 201–17.

Dawson, David. "Allegorical Intratextuality in Bunyan and Winstanley." *The Journal of Religion* 70 (April 1990): 189–212.

———. "Against the Divine Ventriloquist: Coleridge and de Man on Symbol, Allegory, and Scripture." *Literature and Theology* (October 1990): 293–310.

Derrida, Jacques. *Of Grammatology.* Translated by Gayatri Chakravorty Spivak. Baltimore and London: Johns Hopkins Univ. Press, 1974.

———. "Des Tours de Babel." In *Difference in Translation,* edited by Joseph F. Graham, 209–48. Translated in the same volume by Joseph F. Graham, 165–207. Ithaca, N. Y.: Cornell Univ. Press, 1985.

———. *Glas.* Translated by John P. Leavey, Jr., with Richard Rand. Lincoln, Neb.: Univ. of Nebraska Press, 1986.

Devitt, Michael, and Kim Sterelny. *Language and Reality: An Introduction to the Philosophy of Language.* Cambridge, Mass.: MIT Press, 1987.

Dillon, John. *The Middle Platonists: 80 B.C. to A.D. 220.* Ithaca, N. Y.: Cornell Univ. Press, 1977.

Dodds, E. R. *The Greeks and the Irrational.* Berkeley and Los Angeles: Univ. of California Press, 1951.

Edelstein, Ludwig. *The Meaning of Stoicism.* Cambridge, Mass.: Harvard Univ. Press, 1966.

Elias, Julius A. *Plato's Defence of Poetry.* Albany: State Univ. Press of New York, 1984.

Empson, William. *Seven Types of Ambiguity.* 3d ed. London: Chatto and Windus, 1956.

Fehling, Detlev. "Varro und die grammatische Lehre von der Analogie und der Flexion." *Glotta* 35 (1956): 214–70.

Feldman, Louis H. *Scholarship on Philo and Josephus (1937–1962).* New York: Yeshiva Univ. Press, 1963.

Festugière, A. J. *La révélation d'Hermès Trismégiste.* 4 vols. Paris: Gabalda, 1949–54.

Fineman, Joel. "Gnosis and the Piety of Metaphor: The Gospel of Truth." In *The Rediscovery of Gnosticism,* edited by Bentley Layton. Vol. 1: *The School of Valentinus,* 289–312. Leiden: Brill, 1980.

———. "The Structure of Allegorical Desire." In *Allegory and Representation,* edited by Stephen J. Greenblatt, 26–60. Baltimore: Johns Hopkins Univ. Press, 1981.

Fletcher, Angus. *Allegory: The Theory of a Symbolic Mode.* Ithaca, N. Y.: Cornell Univ. Press, 1964.

Foucault, Michel. *The Order of Things: An Archeology of the Human Sciences.* New York: Random House, 1970. Translation of *Les mots et les choses.*

———. *The Archeology of Knowledge.* Translated by A. M. Sheridan. New York: Pantheon, 1972.

Fraser, P. M. *Ptolemaic Alexandria.* 3 vols. Oxford: Clarendon Press, 1972.

Frede, Michael. "Principles of Stoic Grammar." In *The Stoics,* edited by J. M. Rist, 27–75. Berkeley and Los Angeles: Univ. of California Press, 1978.

Frei, Hans W. *The Eclipse of Biblical Narrative: A Study in Eighteenth and Nineteenth Century Hermeneutics.* New Haven: Yale Univ. Press, 1974.

———. "Redeemed Redeemer in Myth and Gospel. Chapter 6 in *The Identity of Jesus Christ: The Hermeneutical Bases of Dogmatic Theology.* Philadelphia: Fortress, 1975.

———. "The 'Literal Reading' of Biblical Narrative in the Christian Tradition: Does It Stretch or Will It Break?" In *The Bible and the Narrative Tradition,* edited by Frank McConnell, 36–77. New York: Oxford Univ. Press, 1986.

Froehlich, Karlfried. " 'Always to Keep the Literal Sense in Holy Scripture Means to Kill One's Soul': The State of Biblical Hermeneutics at the Beginning of the Fifteenth Century." In *Literary Uses of Typology from the Late Middle Ages to the Present,* edited by Earl Miner, 20–48. Princeton: Princeton Univ. Press, 1977.

Frye, Northrop. "Levels of Meaning in Literature." *Kenyon Review* 12 (Spring 1950): 246–62.

——. *Anatomy of Criticism: Four Essays*. Princeton: Princeton Univ. Press, 1957.

——. "Allegory." In *The Princeton Encyclopedia of Poetry and Poetics*, edited by Alex Preminger, 12–15. Enl. ed. Princeton: Princeton Univ. Press, 1974.

——. *The Great Code: The Bible and Literature*. New York: Harcourt Brace Jovanovich, 1983.

Gadamer, Hans-Georg. *Truth and Method*. Edited by Garrett Barden and John C. Cumming. New York: Crossroad, 1975. Translation of *Wahrheit und Methode*. 2d ed. Tübingen: J. C. B. Mohr (Paul Siebeck), 1965.

Gager, John G. *The Origins of Anti-Semitism: Attitudes toward Judaism in Pagan and Christian Antiquity*. New York: Oxford Univ. Press, 1983.

Galdon, S. J., Joseph A. *Typology and Seventeenth-Century Literature*. Paris: Mouton, 1975.

Gatta, John, Jr. "Coleridge and Allegory." *Modern Language Quarterly* 38 (1977): 62–77.

Geertz, Clifford. *The Interpretation of Cultures*. New York: Basic Books, 1973.

——. "Common Sense as a Cultural System." Chapter 4 in *Local Knowledge: Further Essays in Interpretive Anthropology*, 73–93. New York: Basic Books, 1983.

Gellrich, Jesse M. *The Idea of the Book in the Middle Ages: Language Theory, Mythology, and Fiction*. Ithaca, N. Y.: Cornell Univ. Press, 1985.

Goldberg, Michael. *Theology and Narrative: A Critical Introduction*. Nashville, Tenn.: Abingdon, 1982.

Goodenough, Erwin R. "Philo's Exposition of the Law and His De Vita Mosis." *Harvard Theological Review* 26 (1933): 109–25.

——. *The Politics of Philo Judaeus: Practice and Theory*. New Haven: Yale Univ. Press, 1938.

——. *Introduction to Philo Judaeus*. New Haven: Yale Univ. Press, 1940.

Graeser, Andreas. "The Stoic Theory of Meaning." In *The Stoics*, edited by J. M. Rist, 77–100. Berkeley and Los Angeles: Univ. of California Press, 1978.

Grant, Robert M. *The Letter and the Spirit*. London: S. P. C. K., 1957.

——. *Gnosticism and Early Christianity*. Rev. ed. New York: Harper & Row, 1966.

——. "The New Testament Canon." In *The Cambridge History of the Bible*. Vol. 1: *From the Beginnings to Jerome*, edited by P. R. Ackroyd and C. F. Evans, 284–308. Cambridge: Cambridge Univ. Press, 1970.

——. "Early Alexandrian Christianity." *Church History* 40 (1971): 133–44.

——. *Eusebius as Church Historian*. Oxford: Clarendon Press, 1980.

——. *Greek Apologists of the Second Century*. Philadelphia: Westminster, 1988.

Green, Garrett, ed. *Scriptural Authority and Narrative Interpretation*. Philadelphia: Fortress, 1987.

Greenblatt, Stephen J., ed. *Allegory and Representation*. Baltimore: Johns Hopkins Univ. Press, 1981.

Grube, G. M. A. *The Greek and Roman Critics*. London: Methuen, 1965.

Gunn, Giles. *The Culture of Criticism and the Criticism of Culture*. New York: Oxford Univ. Press, 1987.

Hahn, Reinhart. "Die Allegorie in der antiken Rhetorik." Inaug. diss., Tübingen, 1967.

Hamerton-Kelly, Robert G. "Sources and Traditions in Philo Judaeus: Prolegomena to an Analysis of His Writings." *Studia Philonica* 1 (1972): 3–26.

Handelman, Susan A. *The Slayers of Moses: The Emergence of Rabbinic Interpretation in Modern Literary Theory.* SUNY Series on Modern Jewish Literature and Culture, edited by Sarah Blacher Cohen. Albany: State Univ. Press of New York, 1982.

Hanson, R. P. C. *Allegory and Event: A Study of the Sources and Significance of Origen's Interpretation of Scripture.* Richmond, Va.: John Knox, 1959.

———. "Biblical Exegesis in the Early Church." In *The Cambridge History of the Bible.* Vol. 1: *From the Beginnings to Jerome,* edited by P. R. Ackroyd and C. F. Evans, 412–53. Cambridge: Cambridge Univ. Press, 1970.

Hartman, Geoffrey H. *Criticism in the Wilderness: The Study of Literature Today.* New Haven: Yale Univ. Press, 1980.

Hartman, Geoffrey H., and Sanford Budick, eds. *Midrash and Literature.* New Haven: Yale Univ. Press, 1986.

Hauerwas, Stanley, and L. Gregory Jones, eds. *Why Narrative? Readings in Narrative Theology.* Grand Rapids, Mich.: Eerdmans, 1989.

Havelock, Eric A. *Preface to Plato.* Cambridge, Mass.: Harvard Univ. Press, 1963.

Hawkes, Terence. *Metaphor.* The Critical Idiom 25, edited by John D. Jump. London: Methuen, 1972.

Hay, David M. "Philo's References to Other Allegorists." *Studia Philonica* 6 (1979–80): 41–75.

Heinemann, Isaak. *Philons griechische und jüdische Bildung: Kulturvergleichende Untersuchungen zu Philons Darstellung der jüdischen Gesetz.* Breslau: Marcus, 1932.

———. *Altjüdische Allegoristik.* Breslau: Marcus, 1936.

Heinisch, Paul. *Der Einfluss Philos auf die älteste christliche Exegese (Barnabas, Justin und Clemens von Alexandria): Ein Beitrag zur Geschichte der allegorisch-mystischen Schriftauslegung im christlichen Altertum.* Münster: Aschendorff, 1908.

Hengel, Martin. *Judaism and Hellenism: Studies in Their Encounter in Palestine during the Early Hellenistic Period.* 2 vols. Translated by John Bowden. 1974. Reprint (2 vols. in 1). Philadelphia: Fortress, 1981.

Hersman, Anne Bates. *Studies in Greek Allegorical Interpretation: I. Sketch of Allegorical Interpretation before Plutarch. II. Plutarch.* Chicago: Blue Sky, 1906.

Hinks, Roger Packman. *Myth and Allegory in Ancient Art.* London: The Warburg Institute, 1939.

Hirsch, E. D., Jr. *Validity in Interpretation.* New Haven: Yale Univ. Press, 1967.

Hock, Annewies van den. *Clement of Alexandria and His Use of Philo in the "Stromateis": An Early Christian Reshaping of a Jewish Model.* Leiden: Brill, 1988.

Hodgson, John A. "Transcendental Tropes: Coleridge's Rhetoric of Allegory and Symbol." In *Allegory, Myth, and Symbol,* edited by Morton W. Bloomfield, 273–92. Harvard English Studies 9. Cambridge, Mass.: Harvard Univ. Press, 1981.

Hollander, Robert. *Allegory in Dante's Commedia.* Princeton: Princeton Univ. Press, 1969.

Holte, Ragnar. "Logos Spermatikos: Christianity and Ancient Philosophy According to St. Justin's Apologies." *Studia Theologica* 12 (1958): 109–68.

Honig, Edwin. *Dark Conceit: The Making of Allegory.* 1959. Reprint. Hanover, N. H.: Univ. Press of New England, 1982.

Hornschuh, Manfred. "Die Anfänge des Christentums in Aegypten." *Patristische Texte und Studien* 5. Bonn: Friedrich-Wilhelms-Universität, 1965.

Hunger, Herbert. "Allegorische Mythendeutung in der antike und bei Johannes Tzetzes." *Jahrbuch der Österreichischen Byzantinischen Gesellschaft* 3 (1954): 35–54.

Imbert, Claude. "Stoic Logic and Alexandrian Poetics." In *Doubt and Dogmatism: Studies in Hellenistic Epistemology,* edited by M. Schofield, M. Burnyeat and J. Barnes, 182–216. Oxford: Clarendon Press, 1980.

Jaeger, Werner. *The Theology of the Early Greek Philosophers.* Translated by Edward S. Robinson. Oxford: Clarendon Press, 1947.

———. *Early Christianity and Greek Paideia.* 1961. Reprint. New York: Oxford Univ. Press, 1977.

Jakobson, Roman. "Two Aspects of Language and Two Types of Aphasic Disturbance." In *Fundamentals of Language,* edited by Roman Jakobson and Morris Halle, 69–96. 2d ed. Paris: Mouton, 1975.

Jameson, Frederic R. *The Political Unconscious: Narrative as a Socially Symbolic Act.* Ithaca, N. Y.: Cornell Univ. Press, 1982.

———. "The Symbolic Inference; or, Kenneth Burke and Ideological Analysis." In *The Ideologies of Theory: Essays 1971–1986.* Vol. 1: *Situations of Theory.* Theory and the History of Literature 48, edited by Wlad Godzich and Jochen Schulte-Sasse, 137–52. Minneapolis, Minn.: Univ. of Minnesota Press, 1988.

Johnson, Mark, ed. *Philosophical Perspectives on Metaphor.* Minneapolis, Minn.: Univ. of Minnesota Press, 1981.

Jonas, Hans. *The Gnostic Religion: The Message of the Alien God and the Beginnings of Christianity.* 2d ed. Boston: Beacon, 1963.

Jülicher, Adolph. *Die Gleichnisreden Jesu.* 2 vols. Tübingen: J. C. B. Mohr (Paul Siebeck), 1888–89.

Kahn, Charles H. "Stoic Logic and Stoic Logos." *Archive für Geschichte der Philosophie* 51 (1969): 158–72.

Kennedy, George. *The Art of Persuasion in Greece.* Princeton: Princeton Univ. Press, 1963.

———. *Classical Rhetoric and Its Christian and Secular Tradition from Ancient to Modern Times.* Chapel Hill, N. C.: Univ. of North Carolina Press, 1980.

Kenyon, F. G. *Books and Readers in Ancient Greece and Rome.* 2d ed. Oxford: Clarendon Press, 1951.

Kermode, Frank. *The Sense of an Ending: Studies in the Theory of Fiction.* New York: Oxford Univ. Press, 1967.

———. *The Genesis of Secrecy: On the Interpretation of Narrative.* Cambridge, Mass.: Harvard Univ. Press, 1979.

———. *The Classic: Literary Images of Permanence and Change.* Cambridge, Mass.: Harvard Univ. Press, 1983.

———. *Forms of Attention.* Chicago and London: Univ. of Chicago Press, 1985.

Klijn, A. F. J. "Jewish Christianity in Egypt." In *The Roots of Egyptian Christianity.* Studies in Antiquity and Christianity, edited by Birger A. Pearson and James E. Goehring, 161–75. Philadelphia: Fortress, 1986.

Knapp, Steven. *Personification and the Sublime: Milton to Coleridge.* Cambridge, Mass.: Harvard Univ. Press, 1985.

Kneale, Martha, and William Kneale. *The Development of Logic.* Oxford: Clarendon Press, 1962.

Koester, Helmut. *Introduction to the New Testament.* 2 vols. Philadelphia: Fortress, 1982.

Kugel, James L. *The Idea of Biblical Poetry: Parallelism and Its History.* New Haven: Yale Univ. Press, 1981.

———. "Two Introductions to Midrash." *Prooftexts* 3 (1983): 131–55.

Kurz, Gerhard. *Metapher, Allegorie, Symbol.* Göttingen: Vandenhoeck & Ruprecht, 1982.

Lamberton, Robert. *Homer the Theologian: Neoplatonist Allegorical Reading and the Growth of the Epic Tradition.* The Transformation of the Classical Heritage 9, edited by Peter Brown. Berkeley and Los Angeles: Univ. of California Press, 1986.

Lampe, G. W. H., ed. *A Patristic Greek Lexicon.* Oxford: Clarendon Press, 1961.

Layton, Bentley. "The Significance of Basilides in Ancient Christian Thought." *Representations* 28 (Fall 1989): 135–51.

Lentricchia, Frank. *After the New Criticism.* Chicago: Univ. of Chicago Press, 1980.

———. *Criticism and Social Change.* Chicago: Univ. of Chicago Press, 1983.

Lévêque, Pierre. *Aurea catena Homeri: Une étude sur l'allégorie grecque.* Paris: "Les Belles Lettres," 1959.

Lewis, C. S. *The Allegory of Love: A Study in Medieval Tradition.* 1936. Reprint. New York: Oxford Univ. Press, 1967.

Lieberman, Saul. *Hellenism in Jewish Palestine.* 2d ed. New York: Jewish Theological Seminary, 1962.

———. "Rabbinic Interpretation of Scripture." In *Essays in Greco-Roman and Related Talmudic Literature,* selected with a prolegomena by Henry A. Fischel, 289–324. The Library of Biblical Studies, edited by Harry M. Orlinsky. New York: KTAV, 1977.

Lilla, S. R. C. *Clement of Alexandria: A Study in Christian Platonism and Gnosticism.* London: Oxford Univ. Press, 1971.

Lind, L. R. "Roman Religion and Ethical Thought: Abstraction and Personification." *Classical Journal* 69 (December 1973–January 1974): 108–19.

———. "Primitivity and Roman Ideas: Survivals." *Latomus* 35 (April–June 1976): 245–68.

Lindbeck, George A. *The Nature of Doctrine: Religion and Theology in a Postliberal Age.* Philadelphia: Westminster, 1984.

———. "Barth and Textuality." *Theology Today* 43 (October 1986): 361–76.

Lloyd, A. C. "Grammar and Metaphysics in the Stoa." In *Problems in Stoicism,* edited by A. A. Long, 58–74. London: Athlone, 1971.

Loewe, Raphael. "The 'Plain' Meaning of Scripture in Early Jewish Exegesis." In *Papers of the Institute of Jewish Studies, London,* vol. 1, edited by J. G. Weiss, 140–85. Brown Classics in Judaica Series. Lanham, Md.: Univ. Press of America, 1989.

Long, A. A. "Aisthesis, Prolepsis and Linguistic Theory in Epicurus." *Bulletin of the Institute of Classical Studies* 18 (1971): 114–33.

———, ed. *Problems in Stoicism.* London: Athlone, 1971.

———. *Hellenistic Philosophy: Stoics, Epicureans, Sceptics.* 2d ed. Berkeley and Los Angeles: Univ. of California Press, 1986.

————. "Stoic Readings of Homer." Paper presented at symposium, Homer's Ancient Readers, 6–7 October 1989, Princeton University, Princeton.

Longenecker, Richard N. *The Christology of Early Jewish Christianity.* Studies in Biblical Theology, 2d ser. 17. Naperville, Ill.: Alec R. Allenson, 1970.

Louth, Andrew. "Return to Allegory." Chapter 5 in *Discerning the Mystery: An Essay on the Nature of Theology.* Oxford: Clarendon Press, 1983.

Lubac, Henri de. "'Typologie' et 'Allegorisme.'" *Recherches de science religieuse* 34 (1947): 180–226.

————. *Exégèse médiéval: Les quatre sens de l'écriture.* 4 vols. in 2. Paris: Aubier, 1959–64.

Maas, Paul. *Textual Criticism.* Translated by Barbara Flower. Oxford: Clarendon Press, 1958.

McCall, Marsh H., Jr. *Ancient Rhetorical Theories of Simile and Comparison.* Cambridge, Mass.: Harvard Univ. Press, 1969.

McConnell, Frank, ed. *The Bible and the Narrative Tradition.* New York: Oxford Univ. Press, 1986.

McGuire, Anne Marie. "Valentinus and the *Gnōstikē Hairesis:* An Investigation of Valentinus's Position in the History of Gnosticism." Ph.D. diss., Yale University, 1983.

Mack, Burton L. "Exegetical Traditions in Alexandrian Judaism: A Program for the Analysis of the Philonic Corpus." *Studia Philonica* 3 (1974–75): 71–112.

————. "Philo Judaeus and Exegetical Traditions in Alexandria." *ANRW* II.21.2 (1984): 227–71.

McKusick, James C. *Coleridge's Philosophy of Language.* New Haven: Yale Univ. Press, 1986.

MacMullen, Ramsay. *Enemies of the Roman Order: Treason, Unrest, and Alienation in the Empire.* Cambridge, Mass.: Harvard Univ. Press, 1966.

Man, Paul de. "Semiology and Rhetoric." Chapter 1 in *Allegories of Reading: Figural Language in Rousseau, Nietzsche, Rilke, and Proust.* New Haven: Yale Univ. Press, 1979.

————. "The Rhetoric of Temporality." Chapter 10 in *Blindness and Insight: Essays in the Rhetoric of Contemporary Criticism.* 2d ed., rev. Minneapolis, Minn.: Univ. of Minnesota Press, 1983.

Mansfeld, Jaap. "Philosophy in the Service of Scripture: Philo's Exegetical Strategies." In *The Question of "Eclecticism": Studies in Later Greek Philosophy,* edited by John M. Dillon and A. A. Long, 70–102. Hellenistic Culture and Society 3. Berkeley and Los Angeles: Univ. of California Press, 1988.

Marks, Herbert. "Pauline Typology and Revisionary Criticism." In *Modern Critical Views: The Bible,* edited by Harold Bloom, 305–21. New York: Chelsea House, 1987.

Marrou, H. I. *A History of Education in Antiquity.* Translated by George Lamb. 1956. Reprint. Madison, Wis.: Univ. of Wisconsin Press, 1982.

Mates, Benson. *Stoic Logic.* Berkeley and Los Angeles: Univ. of California Press, 1953.

Matter, E. Ann. *The Voice of My Beloved: The Song of Songs in Western Medieval Christianity.* Philadelphia: Univ. of Pennsylvania Press, 1990.

Mayer, Günter. *Index Philoneus*. Berlin: Walter de Gruyter, 1974.

Meecham, Henry G. *The Letter of Aristeas: A Linguistic Study with Special Reference to the Greek Bible*. Manchester: Manchester Univ. Press, 1935.

Meeks, Wayne A. "The Divine Agent and His Counterfeit in Philo and the Fourth Gospel." In *Aspects of Religious Propaganda in Judaism and Early Christianity*, edited by Elizabeth Schüssler Fiorenza, 43–67. Notre Dame, Ind.: Univ. of Notre Dame Press, 1976.

Méhat, André. *Étude sur les 'Stromates' de Clément d'Alexandrie*. Paris: Éditions du Seuil, 1966.

Ménard, Jacques-É. *L'évangile de vérité*. Nag Hammadi Studies 2. Leiden: Brill, 1972.

Mette, Hans Joachim. Sphairopoiia: *Untersuchungen zur Kosmologie des Krates von Pergamon*. Munich: Beck, 1936.

———. Parateresis: *Untersuchungen zur Sprachtheorie des Krates von Pergamon*. Halle: Max Niemeyer, 1952.

Miller, J. Hillis, ed. *Aspects of Narrative: Selected Papers from the English Institute*. New York: Columbia Univ. Press, 1971.

———. "The Critic as Host." In *Deconstruction and Criticism: Harold Bloom, Paul de Man, Jacques Derrida, Geoffrey Hartman, J. Hillis Miller*, 217–53. New York: Seabury Press, 1979.

———. "The Two Allegories." In *Allegory, Myth, and Symbol*, edited by Morton W. Bloomfield, 355–70. Harvard English Studies 9. Cambridge, Mass.: Harvard Univ. Press, 1981.

Miller, Patricia Cox. "In Praise of Nonsense." In *Classical Mediterranean Spirituality*, edited by A. H. Armstrong, 481–505. Vol. 15 of *World Spirituality: An Encyclopedic History of the Religious Quest*. New York: Crossroad, 1986.

———. " 'Words With An Alien Voice': Gnostics, Scripture, and Canon." *Journal of the American Academy of Religion* 57 (Fall 1989): 459–83.

Miner, Earl, ed. *Literary Uses of Typology from the Late Middle Ages to the Present*. Princeton: Princeton Univ. Press, 1977.

Mitchell, W. J. T., ed. *On Narrative*. Chicago: Univ. of Chicago Press, 1980–81.

———. *Iconology: Image, Text, Ideology*. Chicago: Univ. of Chicago Press, 1986.

Momigliano, Arnaldo. *Alien Wisdom: The Limits of Hellenization*. Cambridge: Cambridge Univ. Press, 1975.

Mondésert, C. *Clément d'Alexandrie: Introduction à l'étude de sa pensée religieuse à partir de l'écriture*. Paris: Aubier, 1944.

Morford, Mark. "Nero's Patronage and Participation in Literature and the Arts." *ANRW* II.32.3 (1985): 2003–31.

Mortley, Raoul. *Connaissance religieuse et herméneutique chez Clément d'Alexandrie*. Leiden: Brill, 1973.

Most, Glenn W. "Cornutus and the Stoic Allegoresis: A Preliminary Report." *ANRW* II.36.3 (1989): 2014–65.

Murrin, Michael. *The Veil of Allegory: Some Notes toward a Theory of Allegorical Rhetoric in the English Renaissance*. Chicago: Univ. of Chicago Press, 1969.

———. *The Allegorical Epic: Essays in Its Rise and Decline*. Chicago: Univ. of Chicago Press, 1980.

————. Review of *Allegory: The Dynamics of an Ancient and Medieval Technique*, by Jon Whitman. *The Journal of Religion* 69 (April 1989): 296–97.

Nikiprowetzky, V. *Le commentaire de l'écriture chez Philon d'Alexandrie: Son caractère et sa portée, observations philologiques.* Leiden: Brill, 1977.

Norris, R. A., Jr. *God and World in Early Christian Theology: A Study in Justin Martyr, Irenaeus, Tertullian, and Origen.* New York: Seabury, 1965.

Nuttall, A. D. *Two Concepts of Allegory: A Study of Shakespeare's "The Tempest" and the Logic of Allegorical Expression.* London: Routledge & Kegan Paul, 1967.

Oberman, Heiko A. *The Roots of AntiSemitism in the Age of Renaissance and Reformation.* Translated by James Porter. Philadelphia: Fortress, 1983.

Ong, Walter J. *Orality and Literacy: The Technologizing of the Word.* 1982. Reprint. New York: Methuen, 1983.

Osborn, Eric. "Clement of Alexandria: A Review of Research, 1958–1982." *Second Century* 3 (1983): 219–44.

Pearson, Birger A. "Earliest Christianity in Egypt: Some Observations." In *The Roots of Egyptian Christianity.* Studies in Antiquity and Christianity, edited by Birger A. Pearson and James E. Goehring, 132–56. Philadelphia: Fortress, 1986.

————. "The Problem of 'Jewish Gnostic' Literature." In *Nag Hammadi, Gnosticism, and Early Christianity,* edited by Charles W. Hedrick and Robert Hodgson, Jr., 15–35. Peabody, Mass.: Hendrickson, 1986.

————. *Gnosticism, Judaism, and Egyptian Christianity.* Studies in Antiquity & Christianity. Minneapolis, Minn.: Fortress, 1990.

Pépin, Jean. *Dante et la tradition de l'allégorie.* Conférence Albert-le-Grand, 1969. Montreal: Institut d'études médiévales, 1970.

————. *Mythe et allégorie: Les origines grecques et les contestations judéo-chrétiennes.* New ed. Paris: Études Augustiniennes, 1976.

Perrin, Norman. *Jesus and the Language of the Kingdom: Symbol and Metaphor in New Testament Interpretation.* Philadelphia: Fortress, 1976.

Peters, F. E. *The Harvest of Hellenism: A History of the Near East from Alexander the Great to the Triumph of Christianity.* New York: Simon and Schuster, 1970.

Pfeiffer, Rudolf. *History of Classical Scholarship: From the Beginnings to the End of the Hellenistic Age.* Oxford: Clarendon Press, 1968.

Pinborg, Jan. "Classical Antiquity: Greece." In *Current Trends in Linguistics,* vol. 13, edited by Thomas A. Sebeok, 69–126. The Hague: Mouton, 1975.

Placher, William C. "Revisionist and Postliberal Theologies and the Public Character of Theology." *The Thomist* 49 (1985): 392–416.

————. *Unapologetic Theology: A Christian Voice in a Pluralistic Conversation.* Louisville, Ky.: Westminster/John Knox, 1989.

Pohlenz, Max. *Die Stoa: Geschichte einer geistigen Bewegung.* 2 vols. Göttingen: Vandenhoeck & Ruprecht, 1948, 1949.

————. "Tò Πρέπον: Ein Beitrag zur Geschichte des griechischen Geistes." In *Kleine Schriften,* vol. 1, 100–39. Hildesheim: Georg Olms, 1965.

Pollitt, J. J. *The Ancient View of Greek Art: Criticism, History, and Terminology.* New Haven: Yale Univ. Press, 1974.

Preminger, Alex, ed. *The Princeton Encyclopedia of Poetry and Poetics.* Enl. ed. Princeton: Princeton Univ. Press, 1974.

Preus, James Samuel. *From Shadow to Promise: Old Testament Interpretation from Augustine to the Young Luther.* Cambridge, Mass.: Harvard Univ. Press, Belknap Press, 1969.

Quasten, Johannes. *Patrology.* 3 vols. 1953. Reprint. Utrecht-Antwerp: Spectrum, 1975.

Quilligan, Maureen. *The Language of Allegory: Defining the Genre.* Ithaca, N. Y.: Cornell Univ. Press, 1979.

Quispel, Gilles. "Qumran, John and Jewish Christianity." In *John and Qumran,* edited by James H. Charlesworth. London: Geoffrey Chapman, 1972.

Rad, Gerhard von. "Typologische Auslegung des Alten Testament." *Evangelische Theologie* 12 (1952): 17–33.

Richards, I. A. *The Philosophy of Rhetoric.* New York: Oxford Univ. Press, 1936.

Ricoeur, Paul. *The Rule of Metaphor: Multi-disciplinary Studies of the Creation of Meaning in Language.* Translated by Robert Czerny, with Kathleen McLaughlin and John Costello, S. J. Toronto: Univ. of Toronto Press, 1977.

———. *Essays on Biblical Hermeneutics.* Edited by Lewis S. Mudge. Philadelphia: Fortress, 1980.

———. *Time and Narrative.* 3 vols. Vols. 1 and 2 translated by Kathleen McLaughlin and David Pellauer; vol. 3 translated by Kathleen Blamey and David Pellauer. Chicago: Univ. of Chicago Press, 1983–88.

Rist, J. M. *Stoic Philosophy.* Cambridge: Cambridge Univ. Press, 1969.

———, ed. *The Stoics.* Berkeley and Los Angeles: Univ. of California Press, 1978.

Roberts, Colin H. *Manuscript, Society and Belief in Early Christian Egypt.* The Schweich Lectures of the British Academy. London: Oxford Univ. Press, 1979.

Roberts, Louis. "The Literary Form of the Stromateis." *Second Century* 1 (1981): 211–22.

Rollinson, Philip, and Patricia Matsen. *Classical Theories of Allegory and Christian Culture.* Pittsburgh: Duquesne Univ. Press, 1981.

Roncaglia, Martiniano Pellegrino. "Pantene et le didascalé d'Alexandrie: Du Judéo-christianisme au christianisme hellénistique." In *A Tribute to Arthur Vööbus: Studies in Early Christian Literature and Its Environment, Primarily in the Syrian East,* edited by Robert H. Fischer, 211–33. Chicago: The Lutheran School of Theology at Chicago, 1977.

Rorty, Richard. *Contingency, Irony, and Solidarity.* Cambridge: Cambridge Univ. Press, 1989.

Rudolph, Kurt. *Gnosis: The Nature and History of Gnosticism.* Translated by P. W. Coxon, K. H. Kuhn, and R. Mcl. Wilson. New York: Harper & Row, 1983.

Ruether, Rosemary Radford. *Faith and Fratricide.* New York: Seabury, 1974.

Russell, D. A. *Plutarch.* Classical Life and Letters, edited by Hugh Lloyd-Jones. New York: Scribners, 1973.

———. *Criticism in Antiquity.* London: Duckworth, 1981.

Sacks, Sheldon, ed. *On Metaphor.* Chicago: Univ. of Chicago Press, 1979.

Said, Edward W. *The World, the Text, and the Critic.* Cambridge, Mass.: Harvard Univ. Press, 1983.

Sanders, James. *Torah and Canon.* Philadelphia: Fortress, 1972.

Sandys, John Edwin. *A History of Classical Scholarship.* 3 vols. 1958. Reprint. New York: Hafner, 1964.

Schenke, Hans-Martin. "Das sethianische System nach Nag-Hammadi-Hand-schriften." In *Studia Coptica,* edited by Peter Nagel, 165–73. Berliner byzan-tinistischer Arbeiten 45. Berlin: Akademie, 1974.

———. "The Phenomenon and Significance of Gnostic Sethianism." In *The Re-discovery of Gnosticism,* edited by Bentley Layton. Vol. 2: *Sethian Gnosticism,* 588–616. Studies in the History of Religions 41. Leiden: Brill, 1981.

Schleiermacher, F. D. E. *Hermeneutics: The Handwritten Manuscripts.* Edited by Heinz Kimmerle and translated by James Duke and Jack Forstman. American Academy of Religion Texts and Translation Series 1. Missoula, Mont.: Scholars Press, 1977.

Schneidau, Herbert N. *Sacred Discontent: The Bible and Western Tradition.* Berkeley and Los Angeles: Univ. of California Press, 1976.

Schoedel, William R. "Gnostic Monism and the Gospel of Truth." In *The Rediscov-ery of Gnosticism,* edited by Bentley Layton. Vol. 1: *The School of Valentinus,* 379–90. Leiden: Brill, 1980.

Scholes, Robert, and Robert Kellogg. *The Nature of Narrative.* London: Oxford Univ. Press, 1965.

Searle, John R. "Literal Meaning." Chapter 5 in *Expression and Meaning: Studies in the Theory of Speech Acts.* Cambridge: Cambridge Univ. Press, 1979.

Sells, Michael. "Apophasis in Plotinus: A Critical Approach." *Harvard Theological Review* 78 (1985): 47–65.

Shibles, Warren A. *Metaphor: An Annotated Bibliography and History.* Whitewater, Wis.: The Language Press, 1971.

Shroyer, Montgomery J. "Alexandrian Jewish Literalists." *Journal of Biblical Litera-ture* 55 (1936): 261–84.

Siegfried, Carl. *Philo von Alexandria als Ausleger des Alten Testaments, an sich selbst und nach seinem geschichtlichen Einfluss betrachtet.* Jena: Harmann Dufft, 1875.

Smallwood, E. Mary. *The Jews under Roman Rule: From Pompey to Diocletian.* Leiden: Brill, 1976.

Smith, Barbara Herrnstein. *On the Margins of Discourse.* Chicago: Univ. of Chicago Press, 1978.

Smith, Charles Forster. "Personification in Thucydides." *Classical Philology* 13 (July 1918): 241–50.

Smith, Jonathan Z. "Sacred Persistence: Towards a Redescription of Canon." Chapter 3 in *Imagining Religion: From Babylon to Jonestown.* Chicago: Univ. of Chicago Press, 1982.

Smith, Macklin. *Prudentius' "Psychomachia": A Reexamination.* Princeton: Princeton Univ. Press, 1976.

Smith, Morton. *Clement of Alexandria and a Secret Gospel of Mark.* Cambridge, Mass.: Harvard Univ. Press, 1973.

Smith, Robert W. *The Art of Rhetoric in Alexandria: Its Theory and Practice in the Ancient World.* The Hague: Martinus Nijhoff, 1974.

Sörensen, Bengt Algot, ed. *Allegorie und Symbol: Texte zur Theorie des dichterischen Bildes im 18. und frühen 19. Jahrhundert.* Ars poetica: Texte und Studien zur Dichtungslehre und Dichtkunst 16. Frankfurt: Athenäum, 1972.

Soskice, Janet Martin. *Metaphor and Religious Language.* Oxford: Clarendon Press, 1985.

Standaert, Benoit. "'L'évangile de vérité': Critique et lecture." *New Testament Studies* 22 (1976): 243–75.

Stein, Edmund. *Die allegorische Exegese des Philo aus Alexandreia.* Giessen: Alfred Töpelmann, 1929.

Steiner, George. *After Babel: Aspects of Language and Translation.* New York: Oxford Univ. Press, 1975.

———. *Real Presences.* Chicago: Univ. of Chicago Press, 1989.

Steinmetz, Peter. "Allegorische Deutung und allegorische Dichtung in der alten Stoa." *Rheinische Museum* 129 (1986): 18–30.

Sternberg, Meier. *The Poetics of Biblical Narrative: Ideological Literature and the Drama of Reading.* Bloomington, Ind.: Indiana Univ. Press, 1985.

Stevens, Wallace. "Notes Toward a Supreme Fiction." In *The Palm at the End of the Mind: Selected Poems and a Play,* edited by Holly Stevens, 207–34. New York: Knopf, 1971.

Stokes, John Lemacks. "Schools of Allegorical Interpretation in Hellenistic Judaism." Ph.D. diss., Yale University, 1936.

Stroup, George W. "A Bibliographic Critique." *Theology Today* 32 (1975): 133–43.

Sullivan, J. P. *Literature and Politics in the Age of Nero.* Ithaca, N. Y.: Cornell Univ. Press, 1985.

Susemihl, Franz. *Geschichte der griechischen Litteratur in der Alexandrinerzeit.* 2 vols. Leipzig: Teubner, 1892.

Tanner, Kathryn E. "Theology and the Plain Sense." In *Scriptural Authority and Narrative Interpretation,* edited by Garrett Green, 59–78. Philadelphia: Fortress, 1987.

Tate, J. "The Beginnings of Greek Allegory." *Classical Review* 41 (1927): 214–15.

———. "Cornutus and the Poets." *Classical Quarterly* 23 (1929): 41–45.

———. "Plato and Allegorical Interpretation." *Classical Quarterly* 23 (1929): 142–54; *Classical Quarterly* 24 (1930): 1–10.

———. "On the History of Allegorism." *Classical Quarterly* 28 (1934): 105–14.

Tcherikover, V. "Jewish Apologetic Literature Reconsidered." *Eos* 48 (1956): 169–93.

———. "The Ideology of the Letter of Aristeas." *Harvard Theological Review* 51 (1958): 59–85.

———. *Hellenistic Civilization and the Jews.* Translated by S. Applebaum. 1959. Reprint. Philadelphia: Jewish Publication Society of America, 1977.

Thompson, Cynthia Louise. "Stoic Allegory of Homer: A Critical Analysis of Heraclitus' 'Homeric Allegories.'" Ph.D. diss., Yale University, 1973.

Tobin, Thomas H. *The Creation of Man: Philo and the History of Interpretation.* Washington, D.C.: The Catholic Biblical Association of America, 1983.

Todorov, Tzvetan. "On Linguistic Symbolism." *New Literary History* 6 (1974): 111–34.

———. *Theories of the Symbol.* Translated by Catherine Porter. Ithaca, N. Y.: Cornell Univ. Press, 1982.

Tracy, David. *Blessed Rage for Order: The New Pluralism in Theology.* New York: Seabury, 1978.

———. *The Analogical Imagination: Christian Theology and the Culture of Pluralism.* New York: Crossroad, 1981.

———. "Lindbeck's New Program for Theology: A Reflection." *The Thomist* 49 (1985): 460–72.

Trimpi, Wesley. *Muses of One Mind: The Literary Analysis of Experience and Its Continuity.* Princeton: Princeton Univ. Press, 1983.

Turner, E. G. *Greek Papyri: An Introduction.* Oxford: Clarendon Press, 1968.

Turner, John D. "Sethian Gnosticism: A Literary History." In *Nag Hammadi, Gnosticism, and Early Christianity,* edited by Charles W. Hedrick and Robert Hodgson, Jr., 55–87. Peabody, Mass.: Hendrickson, 1986.

Tuve, Rosemond. *Allegorical Imagery: Some Medieval Books and Their Posterity.* Princeton: Princeton Univ. Press, 1966.

Vallée, Gérard. *A Study in Anti-Gnostic Polemics: Irenaeus, Hippolytus, and Epiphanius.* Studies in Christianity and Judaism 1. N.p.: Canadian Corporation for Studies in Religion, 1981.

Van der Valk, M. *Textual Criticism of the* Odyssey. Leiden: Sijthoff, 1949.

———. *Researches on the Text and Scholia of the* Iliad. 2 vols. Leiden: Brill, 1963–64.

Van Dyke, Carolynn. *The Fiction of Truth: Structures of Meaning in Narrative and Dramatic Allegory.* Ithaca, N. Y.: Cornell Univ. Press, 1985.

Vogel-Weidemann, Ursula. "The Opposition under the Early Caesars: Some Remarks on Its Nature and Aims." *Acta Classica* 22 (1979): 91–107.

Wailes, Stephen L. *Medieval Allegories of Jesus' Parables.* UCLA Center for Medieval and Renaissance Studies Series 23. Berkeley and Los Angeles: Univ. of California Press, 1987.

Wallace, Mark, I. *The Second Naiveté: Barth, Ricoeur, and the New Yale Theology.* Studies in American Biblical Hermeneutics 6. Macon, Ga.: Mercer Univ. Press, 1990.

Walter, Nikolaus. *Der Thoraausleger Aristobulos: Untersuchungen zu seinen Fragmenten und zu pseudepigraphischen Resten der jüdisch-hellenistischen Literatur.* Berlin: Akademie-Verlag, 1964.

Wardman, Alan. *Religion and Statecraft Among the Romans.* Baltimore: Johns Hopkins Univ. Press, 1982.

Watson, Gerard. *The Stoic Theory of Knowledge.* Belfast: Queen's Univ., 1966.

Wehrli, F. *Zur Geschichte der allegorischen Deutung Homers im Altertum.* Borna-Leipzig: Noske, 1928.

White, Hayden. *Metahistory: The Historical Imagination in Nineteenth-Century Europe.* Baltimore: Johns Hopkins Univ. Press, 1973.

———. "Interpretation in History." Chapter 2 in *Tropics of Discourse: Essays in Cultural Criticism.* Baltimore: Johns Hopkins Univ. Press, 1978.

———. "The Value of Narrativity in the Representation of Reality." In *On Narrative,* edited by W. J. T. Mitchell, 1–23. Chicago: Univ. of Chicago Press, 1980–81.

Whitman, Jon. *Allegory: The Dynamics of an Ancient and Medieval Technique.* Cambridge, Mass.: Harvard Univ. Press, 1987.

Wilde, Oscar. "The Critic as Artist." In *The Artist as Critic: Critical Writings of Oscar Wilde,* edited by Richard Ellmann, 340–408. New York: Random House, 1968.

Wilkin, Robert L. *The Myth of Christian Beginnings.* Notre Dame, Ind.: Univ. of Notre Dame Press, 1980.

Williams, Jacqueline A. *Biblical Interpretation in the Gnostic Gospel of Truth from Nag Hammadi*. SBL Dissertation Series 79. Atlanta: Scholars Press, 1988.

Williams, Raymond. *Marxism and Literature*. New York: Oxford Univ. Press, 1977.

Winston, David, and John Dillon. *Two Treatises of Philo of Alexandria: A Commentary on* De Gigantibus *and* Quod Deus Sit Immutabilis. Chico, Calif.: Scholars Press, 1983.

Wolfson, Harry Austryn. *Philo: Foundations of Religious Philosophy in Judaism, Christianity, and Islam*. 2 vols. Cambridge, Mass.: Harvard Univ. Press, 1947.

———. *Faith, Trinity, Incarnation: The Philosophy of the Church Fathers*. 3d ed. Cambridge, Mass.: Harvard Univ. Press, 1970.

Woodhead, William Dudley. *Etymologizing in Greek Literature from Homer to Philo Judaeus*. Montreal: Univ. of Toronto Press, 1928.

Woollcombe, K. J. "The Biblical Origins and Patristic Development of Typology." In *Essays on Typology,* edited by G. H. W. Lampe and K. J. Woollcombe, 39–75. Naperville, Ill.: A. R. Allenson, 1957.

Zeller, Eduard. *Die Philosophie der Griechen in ihrer geschichtlichen Entwicklung* 3.1. 4th ed. Edited by Eduard Wellmann. Leipzig: O. R. Reisland, 1909.

Zetzel, James E. G. *Latin Textual Criticism in Antiquity*. Monographs in Classical Studies. Salem, N. H.: The Ayer Company, 1981.

Zuntz, Günther. *The Text of the Epistles: A Disquisition Upon the Corpus Paulinum*. The Schweich Lectures of the British Academy, 1946. London: Oxford Univ. Press, 1953.

GENERAL INDEX

Abel, 211

Abraham: in Clement, 186, 210; in *Epistle of Barnabas*, 154, 175; and Isaac, 83–84, 87, 90, 94, 96, 97, 98, 100, 101, 234; in Philo, 107, 108, 109, 217, 233; and Sarah, 102

Achilles, 45, 46, 48, 61, 68, 69, 203

An Account of the World's Creation Given by Moses (Philo), 123

Acts, Book of, 155

Adam: in Clement, 210; in Gnostic myth, 132, 135, 147; in Philo, 84–85, 87, 88–90, 91, 93, 95, 97; in Valentinus, 133, 136–49, 152–53. *See also* Fall, of Adam and Eve

Address to the Greeks (Tatian), 204

Adonai, 154, 161

Aeneid, 76

Against Heresies (Irenaeus), 187, 198

Against Heresies (Justin), 198

Agamemnon, 42, 45, 46, 48, 49, 61, 62

A-gnōsis, 146, 159. *See also* Error

Agrippa, 173

Aidoneus, 49

Alcaeus, 203

Alexander (bishop of Jerusalem), 183

Alexandrian: bishop, 171–72, 219, 220, 221, 222; Catechetical School, 219–22, 294–95n65; church, 221–22, 229; gymnasium, 115, 116, 173; Library, 75, 78, 117; Museum, 75; scriptorium, 229; social and political life, 113–16

Alexandrian textual critics (or editors, phi-lologists, grammarians): allegory and etymology opposed by, 24, 52; and Aristobulus, 80; and Christian exegesis, 229–30; and Clement, 71, 202, 229, 230, 291n45; editorial theory and prac-tice of, 66–71, 75, 268n89, 268–69n93, 269n100; and Hellenistic culture, 66, 71; and Pantaenus, 229; and Philo, 71, 102–3; and Plutarch, 65; and Ptolemaic Jewish interpretation, 74–75, 269n105, 269–70n2. *See also* Criticism, ancient lit-erary; Textual criticism

Allegorical composition, 4; ancient myth as, 32; *Gospel of Truth* as, 153, 157–70; as interpretation, 4, 127–28, 129–31; as a rhetorical strategy, 75

Allegorical interpretation

——as approached in this book, 3–4, 23, 235–38, 246n17

——as composition, 4; in Nabokov, 246n14; in Valentinus, 127–31, 133–45 (fragments), 145–70 (*Gospel of Truth*)

——functions of: apology (defensive alle-gory), 12–13, 36, 38–39, 48, 250–51n34; cultural accommodation, 7, 10, 35, 47, 50–51, 237; cultural revision, 9, 10, 16, 35, 107, 184, 235–37, 240; philosophical reflection (positive alle-gory), 12–14, 251n35; subordination of precursors, 78–79, 82, 130–31; sup-port for social practices, 74, 113–26, 185, 224–25, 227, 228–29; textualiza-tion, 10–11, 35, 75

——classical: Clement on, 184, 185, 199–
206; Justin on, 197; Philo on, 108–10,
205–6; Valentinus on, 167, 168. *See also*
Myth, pagan

Logos (or Word): and allegorical reading, in
Justin, 186–99; in Clement, 71, 128,
200, 201, 205, 206, 210, 211, 213, 224,
239; and deconstruction, 241n2; in the
Gospel of John, 131; and Middle Platonism, 184, 187–91; in Philo, 83–84,
107, 191; in Stoicism, 34, 189; and traditional view of allegory, 2; in Valentinus, 128, 149–50, 168, 279n12. *See
also* Christ; *Davar;* God, second; Jesus
of Nazareth; Son of God; Voice, divine;
Word of God

Lord, 154, 161
Loukuas-Andreus, 174
Lucan (pupil of Cornutus), 37
Lucius Verus, 187
Lurianic Kabbala, 162
Lutheran pietist tradition, 239
Lycurgus, 112
Lysimachus, 116

3 Maccabees, 114, 116, 174
Malachi, 226
Manetho, 116
Marcion, 8, 211–12, 223, 229, 230, 295n77
Marcus Aurelius, 38, 187
Mark (evangelist), 172, 219, 285n53
Meaning, 5, 7–8, 15, 235, 240; indetermi-
nate (= semantic indeterminacy or am-
biguity), 33–34, 80, 164–65, 225–26,
237, 270–71n8; in Stoicism, 28–34,
261n24, 261–62n26; and textuality, 86,
102, 106, 164, 239. *See also* Etymology;
Language

Medea, 62
Menelaus, 67
Messiah, Jesus as, 196
Metaphor, 264n46; and allegory, 5–6; in
Cornutus, 32; in Philo, 107; in Plu-
tarch, 63; Quintilian on, 92–93; in Val-
entinus, 133, 143, 145, 146, 152, 153,
157, 160, 161, 165, 284n45

Methuselah, 96
Middle Platonism, 128, 184, 187–90, 190–
99, 205, 279n12, 288n15. *See also* Plato
Midrash, 175
Mimesis: and etymology, 29–30, 31, 34,

35; and language, 34–35, 87, 88, 90; in
poetry, 62; in Valentinus, 283–84n45

Monism: in Theodotus, 179, 180; in
Valentinus, 158, 166, 170, 177, 178,
281n40, 282–83n44, 283–84n45, 294–
95n65

Monotheism, 82, 97, 176, 177, 190,
284n45

Moses
——in Clement, 186, 204, 210, 222–23,
234
——in Justin, 187, 196, 197
——in Philo: and Alexandrian Jewish political life, 116–19, 124–25; as composer of allegory, 71, 84, 130, 168; and
divine writing, 110; Hellenistic virtues
embodied by, 108, 118, 120; linguistic
techniques used by, 92, 93–98; as a living law, 110–11; pagan precursors subordinated to, 74, 109–10; and the
Septuagint, 86–87, 184
——in Ptolemaic Jewish interpretation, 75,
77, 79
——in Valentinus, 162

Mysteries, Greek, 86, 121, 205
Mysticism, 2, 167, 239
Myth
——Babylonian, 136
——Egyptian, Plutarch on, 52, 55, 58–61
——Gnostic, 132–33; Genesis interpreted
in, 135–36; interpreted by Valentinus,
127, 133, 136–53, 163–64; Plato interpreted in, 127, 138. See also *Gnōsis*;
Gnosticism
——pagan: in Chrysippus, 54, 265n65; in
Cicero, 53, 55; in Cleanthes, 53; in
Clement, 203; in Cornutus, 23, 24–38,
39, 54, 59, 129, 195, 265n65; Epicureans on, 55; in Heraclitus, 39; in
Justin, 194–95; in Philo, 107; in Plutarch, 60–61. *See also* Gods, pagan; Literature, classical
——Valentinian, 72, 128, 132, 136, 146–
47, 148, 151, 153, 168. *See also* Valentinus

Name, divine: in the *Gospel According to
Philip,* 181–82; and Jerusalem Christianity, 153–56; in Philo, 93; in Theodotus, 178–81; in Valentinus, 20, 128,

SCRIPTURE PASSAGES CITED

ANCIENT PASSAGES CITED

Compositor: Keystone Typesetting, Inc.
Text: 10/12 Baskerville
Display: Baskerville
Printer: Thomson-Shore, Inc.
Binder Thomson-Shore, Inc.